D1719010

"In Christ All Will Be Made Alive" (1 Cor 15:12-58)

European Studies in Theology, Philosophy and History of Religions

Edited by Bartosz Adamczewski

Vol. 6

Mariusz Rosik

"In Christ All Will Be Made Alive" (1 Cor 15:12-58)

The Role of Old Testament Quotations
in the Pauline Argumentation for the Resurrection

PETER LANG
EDITION

Bibliographic Information published by the Deutsche Nationalbibliothek
The Deutsche Nationalbibliothek lists this publication in the
Deutsche Nationalbibliografie; detailed bibliographic data is
available in the internet at http://dnb.d-nb.de.

This publication was financially supported
by the Pontifical Theological Faculty in Wrocław.

Cover Design: © Olaf Gloeckler, Atelier Platen, Friedberg

Library of Congress Cataloging-in-Publication Data

Rosik, Mariusz, 1968-
  In Christ all will be made alive : (1 Cor 15:12-58) the role of Old Testament
quotations in the Pauline argumentation for the resurrection / Mariusz Rosik.
  First edition
    pages cm — (European studies in theology, philosophy and history of religions ; vol. 6)
  Includes bibliographical references.
  ISBN 978-3-631-64251-1
  1. Bible. Corinthians, 1st, XV, 12-58—Criticism, interpretation, etc. 2.
Resurrection—Biblical teaching. 3. Bible. Corinthians, 1st—Relation to
the Old Testament. 4. Bible. Old Testament—Relation to Corinthians, 1st. 5.
Bible. Old Testament—Quotations in the New Testament. I. Title.
  BS2675.6.R47R67 2013
  227'.206—dc23
                                                                    2013014292

                                      ISSN 2192-1857
                                      ISBN 978-3-631-64251-1
                                © Peter Lang GmbH
                        Internationaler Verlag der Wissenschaften
                                Frankfurt am Main 2013
                                   All rights reserved.
                    Peter Lang Edition is an Imprint of Peter Lang GmbH.

             Peter Lang – Frankfurt am Main · Bern · Bruxelles · New York ·
                                Oxford · Warszawa · Wien

www.peterlang.de

Table of Contents

Introduction

The conviction about the universal resurrection from the dead constitutes an integral part of the Christian faith. The Catechism of the Catholic Church contains the following article concerning this issue: "The Christian Creed—the profession of our faith in God, the Father, the Son, and the Holy Spirit, and in God's creative, saving, and sanctifying action—culminates in the proclamation of the resurrection of the dead on the last day and in life everlasting. We firmly believe, and hence we hope that, just as Christ is truly risen from the dead and lives forever, so after death, the righteous will live forever with the risen Christ and he will raise them up on the last day. Our resurrection, like his own, will be the work of the Most Holy Trinity" (988–989). Tertullian even emphasised that we "are" Christians because we believe in the resurrection of the dead: *Fiducia christianorum resurrectio mortuorum; illam credentes, sumus* (Res. 1:1).

Chapter fifteen of the First Letter to the Corinthians is essentially dedicated to the topic of resurrection, although there is also mention of other eschatological events. First, Paul refers to the christophany that confirmed the resurrection of Christ (vv. 1–11). He then discusses the resurrection of the faithful, and the resurrection of Christ (vv. 12–58) in his argumentation. 1 Cor 15 does not constitute the Apostle's response to the direct question posed by the inhabitants of the Christian community in Corinth as was the case in other parts of the letter that directly refer to the said questions (cf. 1 Cor 7:1; 8:1; 11:2; 12:1, and 16:1). The proper motivation for the said disquisition we can find in v. 12: "Now if Christ is proclaimed as raised from the dead, how can some of you be saying that there is no resurrection of the dead?" It was this very conviction of "some" of the members of the local church in *bimaris Corinthia* that "there is no resurrection," which propels the Apostle, who established that community, to undertake this issue. In his disquisition, Paul not only outlines the foundations of hope in the resurrection, but also speaks—as mentioned earlier—of other eschatological events, which include the Parousia, overcoming the forces of evil, the destruction of death, and the triumph of Christ and the reign of God the Father. The Apostle spends a lot of time explaining the very nature of the body after the resurrection.

In his argumentation defending the resurrection of the dead, Paul, a Pharisee by education and a scholar of Gamaliel I, grandson of the famous Hillel, reaches for the Old Testament. Acquainted with Hebrew, Aramaic and Greek, the Apostle could use the Hebrew Bible as well as the Septuagint with ease.[1] Both versions of the Bible (seeing that the Septuagint also contains books that are

---

1   N. Hyldahl, "Paul and Hellenistic Judaism in Corinth," in *The New Testament and Hellenistic Judaism* (eds. P. Borgen and S. Giversen; Peabody 1997), 204.

absent from the Hebrew Bible), include fragments that constitute the grounds for hope in the future resurrection. J. Lemański discussed this in detail several years ago in his study.[2] It is worth asking which fragments of the Old Testament were used by Paul in his argumentation for the resurrection of the dead and how the Apostle actually treats them. The fact that the author of the letter, the Apostle "born of the race of Israel, of the tribe of Benjamin, a Hebrew born of Hebrew parents" (Phil 3:5), quotes the Old Testament in his writings is of no surprise. Surely, it is natural that "in his doctrinal arguments the Apostle Paul constantly refers to the Scriptures of his nation, clearly differentiating between scriptural arguments and the 'human way of thinking.' The scriptural arguments are attributed an irrefuted value. For him, the Jewish Scriptures also have an ever pertinent value in guiding the spiritual life of Christians" (*The Jewish Nation and Its Sacred Scriptures in the Christian Bible*, 5)[3].

In this study, we shall be dealing with a multi-aspect analysis of the Old Testament citations in 1 Cor 15:12–58. It should once again be noted that we are concerned with that part of the Pauline interpretation of the teaching about the resurrection, in which he concentrates on the resurrection of the faithful departed after earlier authenticating the resurrection of Christ (1 Cor 15:1–11). The research problem and objective (1), the current state of research concerning the said issue (2), and the adopted research methodology (3) shall be presented hereinbelow.

1. Research Problem and Objectives

The issue of citing the OT in 1 Cor gives rise to much interest even for purely statistical reasons. Out of approx. 16–18[4] of the OT citations in the entire epistle,

---

2   J. Lemański, *„Sprawisz, abym ożył!" (Ps 71: 20b). Źródła nadziei na zmartwychwstanie w Starym Testamencie* (RiS 532; Szczecin 2004). The author includes the following passages in this group: Gen 5:21–24; 1 Kgs 17:17–24; 2 Kgs 2:1–15; 4:8–37; 13:25; 2 Macc 7:1–42; 12:38–45; 15:12–16; Pss 16:9–11; 17:15; 22:30; 49:15–16; 71:20; 73:23–24; Prov 10:2.16; 11:30–31; 12:28; 14:32; 15:24; 23:17–18; 24:19–20; Job 19:25–27; Eccl 3:11b.16–17.21; 9:1b; Sir 1:13b; 7:17; 46:12; 48:11–13; 49:10; Wis 3:8; 4:19; 16:13–14; Hos 6:1–3; 13:14; Ezra 37:1–14; Isa 25:8; 26:19; 52:13; 3:10–11a; Dan 12:1–3. Much fewer OT passages that are at the foundation of the idea of the resurrection have been discussed by R. Martin-Achard, "Resurrection (OT)," *ABD* V: 680–684. This list is extended somewhat by G. W. E. Nickelsburg, "Resurrection (Early Judaism and Christianity)," *ABD* V: 684–691.

3   The document of the Pontificia Commissio Biblica was published in 2001.

4   The number of quotes depends on the adopted criteria defining which fragment can be acknowledged as a quote, and which as an allusion.

as many as 6 (i.e. approx. 33%) appear in 1 Cor 15:12–58[5]: such a high concentration of citations in one section only, which in size is even smaller than a chapter, should not be deemed as coincidental. It is also worth posing several questions that highlight the research problems discussed in this work:

(1) Why does Paul quote the OT when he speaks of the resurrection of the dead?
(2) Do the quotes he uses in his interpretation speak of the hope of resurrection also in the original context?
(3) What is their rhetorical role?
(4) What function do they fulfil in the text from the theological perspective?
(5) Were they derived from the LXX or the HB? Perhaps the Apostle cites the Targums or quotes from memory.
(6) Does he select the quotes, based on his own education as a Pharisee, or does he draw from the already established early Christian tradition?

The object of this study is to attempt to answer the above questions. The way this objective will be reached has been described in the presentation of the method which we use in this work. The conclusions that emerge after the application of this method constutute (at least partial) answers to the questions posed above, and are included in the final chapter of the book.

2. The Current State of Research

Let us proceed to the presentation of the current state of research on the issue, which is of interest to us, of the OT quotations in 1 Cor 15:12–58. It is worth concentrating, at first, on the very phenomenon of the Pauline texts taken from the OT. In the last decades, many titles and far more articles appeared on the theological and exegetical market. They raise issues being the object of the research, carried out in this study. Here, we will devote some time to the most significant ones; however, other issues will be brought up in the main part of this work. Each of the authors presents a slightly different approach to the previously mentioned issues of citing the OT by Paul; that is because of the specificity of the conducted analyses (most often expressed clearly or mentioned in the title of the monograph or the article). Above all, it is necessary to notice a surge of an interest in the subject matter of quoting in the literature, in the last decades. In older rhetoric or religious studies textbooks, these issues were not widely elaborated. It is enough to mention that in the classical work in this field,

---

5   D. A. de Silva, "Let the One Who Claims Honor Establish That Claim in the Lord. Honor Discourse in the Corinthian Correspondence," *BTB* 28 (1998): 63.

the textbook by C. Perelman and L. Olbrechts-Tyteca, the references to the entry "quoting," included in the index placed at the end of their work, can be found only four times![6] At present, however, the research on the theory of quoting has considerably developed. Presenting the current state of the research on the subject matter, which is of interest to us, we shall begin with the issue of quoting in general (fundamentally from a point of view of the study of literature). Next, we shall present the phenomenon of quoting the OT in Corpus Paulinum, especially taking into account 1 Cor 15:12–58.

2.1. The Issue of Citing in General

C. D. Stanley dealt with depicting the practice of quoting from the rhetorical point of view.[7] At first, he explains that referring to quotations invokes arguments "from an authority" in the disquisition. Quotations in such a function usually open or close the disquisition. The quotation, above all, performs the authoritative role when it comes from the source recognised by listeners or readers as important or sacred. Arguments from the authority usually act as the subsidy in the disquisition; they contribute to the support of the author's or the speaker's key points. However, they are not fundamental arguments. Apart from that, these arguments have persuasive force mainly when the listener or the reader has a bias in favour of the speaker or author.[8] From the rhetorical perspective, the quotations also function as a factor helping to create the agreement between the speaker and the audience. When the audience has a positive attitude towards the speaker, the phrases quoted from works valued by both sides intensify the agreement between them. On the other hand, when the audience treats the speaker with reserve, then the audience tends rather to place its confidence in the quotation. This is because the quotation reflects their common values or views. In both cases, however, the quotation appeals to the emotional sphere of the audience. Each time, the force of speaking of the quotation depends on its content, the way of expressing its thoughts and the value of the source from which it comes. In his research, based on the works of

---

6   The entire work is quite extensive because it consists of 514 pages. See index in C. Perelman and L. Olbrychts-Tyteca, *The New Rhetoric: A Treatise on Argumentation* (trans. J. Wilkinson and P. Weaver; Notre Dame 1969).

7   C. D. Stanley, *Arguing with Scripture: The Rhetoric of Quotation in Letters of Paul* (New York 2004), 12–21.

8   D. Leith and G. Myerson, *The Power of Address: Explorations in Rhetoric* (London 1989), 124.

E. White,[9] Stanley reaches the conclusion that not all quotations have the same effect on the listeners or readers. To a considerable extent, the effect depends on the author or speaker's intention, and we can define the intention on the strength of five factors:

(1) the author's or speaker's basic point;
(2) the essence of submitting;
(3) the arrangement of the conveyed ideas;
(4) the degree of the author's or speaker's intelligibility of the language;
(5) the speaker's non-verbal communication.[10]

This rhetorical theory, with reference to Paul's letters, was developed by Stanley, who has argued that quotations in Paul's letters serve as a form of arguments appealing to the authority, emotions or to a way of thinking of addressees of his letters, rather than constituting "windows to theology." Such an analysis of the OT quotations included in *Corpus Paulinum* leads to much deeper understanding of the Apostle of the Nation's reasoning; the better we are able to determine the role of the OT quotations in the way of arguing, the more accurately we can assess their significance.

This way of understanding the rhetorical role of quotations by Stanley and White stems from earlier studies which were settled in wider literary perspective. One of the first books within this field, taking by the handful from the concept of the language, was written by John Langshow Austin, and led to creation of the theory known as *"speech-act theory."*[11] According to the author, a language—whether it's said or written—not only conveys information, but also has the task of "making" something in the listener/reader and has the task of making a reply in the recipient. Consequently, speaking and writing are activities causing a change in the listener/reader.[12] Although the work of Austin does not deal directly with the role of quotations in *speech-act theory*, it still provides an incentive for other authors, who subsequently included this issue into the scope of their examinations.

In this context, Anna Wierzbicka also suggested an interesting theory. Examining the functions of direct and indirect quotations, the author reaches the

---

9   E. White, *The Context of Human Discourse: A Configurational Criticism of Rhetoric* (Columbia 1992).
10   Stanley, *Arguing*, 17; White, *Context*, 64.
11   J. L. Austin, *How to Do Things with Words* (Cambridge 1962²).
12   The author shows it in the following way: "Once we realize that what we are to study is not the sentence but the issuing of an utterance in speech situation, there can hardly be any longer a possibility of not seeing that stating is performing an act"; Austin, *How to Do*, 139.

conclusion that the aim of all the quotations is to "dramatize" the words of
previous (original) author.[13] Following this thought, one can make a claim that a
quoting person "impersonates" the author of the quoted words, playing his part
for a moment. Thus, two people, the author of the quotation and the quoting
person, are speaking with one voice. The "dramaturgy" of quoting consists in
emphasizing not only what the author of the quotation said but also in what way
he says it. It implies that people who refer to a quotation in order to back their
reasoning up with the outside argument identify themselves not only with the
content of the quotation but also with its form. M. Sternberg sheds a different
light on the issue of citing. In his studies, the researcher poses a question; what
happens with the text excluded from one literary context and included into the
new one?[14] The author starts with the justifiable premise that the quoted
fragment was originally rooted in the speaker's or the writer's subjective
experience. However, the quotation—included into the new context—has
already been interpreted by the quoting person. This decontextualization is not
meaningless in order to understand the quotation by the communication
receiver. In this case, the stress changesand that change leads to the modification
of the original meaning of the quotation. Moreover, one should not forget that if
the addressee is not familiar with the source from which the quotation was
taken, then the original context is incomprehensible to him. This remark is
valuable with reference to the research conducted in our study because a
situation of a majority of listeners or addressees of Paul's Letters originated
from paganism (as noted above). They gained knowledge of the OT later, only
through propagating Christian *kerygma* and through religious education.

Herbert Clark and Richard Gerrig present another view on citing. They, like
Anna Wierzbicka, show this phenomenon from a linguistic perspective.
According to Wierzbicka, certain animation of the discourse and its peculiar's
dramatization result in the use of direct quotations. However, when the
quotation appears in the new context, it is not possible to communicate its exact

---

13   In this context, the author says about a specific role played by the person from which
      the quotation comes: "The person who reports another words by quoting them,
      temporarily assumes the role of that other person, 'plays its part,' that is to say,
      imagines himself as the other person and for a moment behaves in accordance with this
      counter—factual assumption"; A. Wierzbicka, "The Semantics of Direct and Indirect
      Discourse," *Papers in Linguistics* 7 (1974): 272.

14   The author notices: "Quotation brings together at least two discourse-events: that in
      which things were originally expressed (said, thought, experienced) by one subject
      (speaker, writer, reflector), and that in which they are cited by another"; M. Sternberg,
      "Proteus in Quotation—Land: Mimesis and the Forms of Reported Discourse," *Poetics
      Today* 3 (1982): 107.

meaning with all the shades and scopes that it had in the original context. The quotation creates a certain kind of the solidarity between the speaker/the author and the addressee.

If the addressee is familiar with the sources, this solidarity causes him to identify himself with the opinion of the author expressed in the quotation.[15] In this perspective, quoting biblical citations in ancient times not only enhanced argumentation, but also produced the shared bond; joining the person quoting the phrase and its addressee and creating a bond based on faith and a common religious legacy. Apart from that quotation, what is equally essential, leads to the indirect meeting of the addressee with the source of the quotation, and this source with its authority enhances the position of the quoting the citations.

Gillian Lane-Mercier understands the role of quotations in another way. The researcher approaches these issues through an interdisciplinary perspective. Her analysis has linguistic, philosophical, literary and rhetorical character. The author agrees with others that fundamentally, the quotations perform the role of arguments enhancing the theses of the quoting and are arguments from the authority. However, she also pays attention to the issue unappreciated by other researchers; the quoting person, by excluding a quotation from its original context and then including it into the sequence of own disquisitions, imposes his own interpretation of the quotation upon its addressee.[16] Owing to such use of the quotations, the quoting person can achieve the rhetorical or ideological purpose established by him. The author even says that the "metaphorical death of the quoted fragment" which consists in the fact, is first taken out of its original context, and then put in new, often very different one. As a result, the quoting person puts his own interpretation on it; modifying its meaning according to the earlier made assumption.[17] A consequence of such perception of the phenomenon of quoting is a statement that a quoting person can easily manipulate the addressee.[18]

As indicated earlier, approaches towards the phenomenon of quoting and understanding its role in literary works, might be useful for deeper analysis of the role of Old Testament quotations in Paul's letters.

---

15   H. Clark and R. Gerrig, "Quotations as Demonstrations," *Language* 66 (1990): 786–788.

16   G. Lane-Mercier, "Quotation as a Discursive Strategy," *Kodikas* 14 (1991): 199–214.

17   The researcher perceives the way of dealing with quotations as "the metaphorical death of the quote, whose utterance, apparently intact, has nonetheless been decontextualized, severed from its 'origin,' and subsumed by the utterance of the quoter"; Lane-Mercier, "Quotation," 206.

18   Cf. id., "Quotation," 207.

2.2. The Issue of the OT Quotations in 1 Cor 15:12–58

After first exploring the analytical research concerning the role of the OT quotations in 1 Cor 15:12–58, one should gain an understanding of the current state of this specific issue. In recent years, at least a few monographs dealing with the old-testamentary quotations in Paul's letters (and many more articles in which authors limited themselves to some parts of *Corpus Paulinum*)[19] have become available. Researchers have different approaches: Insawn Saw, in his PhD dissertation, takes a rhetorical approach. The work is entitled *Paul's Rhetoric in 1 Corinthians 15. An Analysis Utilizing the Theories of Classical Rhetoric* (Lewiston–Queenston–Lampeter 1995). The title indicates the approach of the author to 1 Cor 15. It is an analysis of Paul's text, in which he uses typical elements of classical rhetoric. They are introduced in the second chapter of the book which refers to Aristotle, Cicero, Quintilian, Longinus and Plato's theories. Saw perceives the rhetoric *Dispositio* of the various parts of the fifteenth chapter in 1 Cor as follows:

(1) *praeparatio* (vv. 1–11):
    a. *exordium* (vv. 1–2);
    b. *narratio* (vv. 3–11);
(2) *argumentatio* (vv. 12–34):
    a. *partitio* (v. 12);
    b. *probatio* (vv. 13–34);
(3) *refutatio* (vv. 35–49);
(4) *peroratio* (vv. 50–57);
(5) *exhortatio* (v. 58).[20]

---

19   A little bit older studies in this field were carried out by: J. Blank, "Erwägungen zum Schriftverständnis des Paulus," in *Rechtfertigung. Fs. E. Käsemann* (eds. J. Friedrich, W. Pöhlmann and P. Stuhlmacher; Tübingen–Göttingen 1976), 37–56; C. Dietzfelbinger, *Paulus und das Alte Testament. Die Hermeneutik des Paulus, untersucht an seiner Bedeutung der Gestalt Abrahams* (Theol. Ex. Heute 95; München 1961); M. D. Hooker, "Beyond the Things that are Written? St Paul's Use of Scripture," *NTS* 27 (1980–1981): 295–309; J. Schmid, "Die alttestamentlichen Zitate bei Paulus und die Theoria vom sensus plenior," *BZ* 3 (1959): 161–173; P. Vielhauer, "Paulus und das Alte Testament," in *Studien zur Geschichte und Theologie der Reformation. Fs. E. Bizer* (eds. L. Abramowski and F. J. G. Goeters; Neukirchen 1969), 33–62. In the broader context, with OT and NT quotations also deals J. A. Fitzmyer, "The Use of Explicit Old Testament Quotations in Qumran Literature and in the New Testament," *NTS* 7 (1960–1961): 297–333.

20   I. Saw, *Paul's Rhetoric in 1 Corinthians 15. An Analysis Utilizing the Theories of Classical Rhetoric* (Lewiston–Queenston–Lampeter 1995), 223–226. Cf. also: M. Bünker, *Briefformular und rhetorische Disposition im 1. Korintherbrief* (Göttingen 1984).

The author has a superb command of ancient books of rhetoric and applies the methods included in them to his work on the 1 Cor 15 text. It must also be noted that an application of the rhetorical methods, which were verified by Stanley, gives an assurance of the great value and the accuracy of the study. In this context, Saw analyses the OT quotations, showing their rhetorical function. It is also necessary to notice that Saw limits himself only to Greco-Roman rhetoric, but Paul was also familiar with Hebrew rhetoric because speeches as a literary genre developed not only amongst Greek-Roman residents of the basin of the Mediterranean Sea, but also in the Semitic world.[21]

In his study titled *Polarity and Change in 1 Corinthians 15: A Study of Metaphysics, Rhetoric, and Resurrection* (HUT 42; Tübingen 2000), J.R. Asher also presents a rhetorical approach to 1 Cor 15. The author gives an in-depth analysis of Paul's style, exploring particular fragments of 1 Cor 15 according to an appointed earlier *dispositio* of the text. Based on these analyses he arrives at the conclusion that Paul's rhetoric does not have polemical, but rather pedagological character. The apostle does not refute accusations of Corinthians or fight their false beliefs but preferably preaches. In addition, he uses well known rhetorical techniques in order to convince addressees that rejection of the resurrection of the dead is absolutely inconsist due to the earlier accepted conviction about the resurrection of Christ.[22] Such view, presented by Asher indicates the didactic role of OT quotations included in 1 Cor. To put it another way, the quotations were inserted into the letter mainly to teach the Corinthians.

J.P. Heil is the author of the paper titled *The Rhetorical Role of Scripture in 1 Corinthians* (SiBL 15; Leiden–Boston 2005). The title makes it clear that Heil was mainly interested in the rhetorical function of the OT quotations in 1 Cor. His testing method was applied consistently in his monograph and it consists of several stages. First, the author outlines the old-testamentary background of the fragment quoted by Paul, adducing it in the record of the MT and the LXX.

---

21 J. S. Synowiec, *Gatunki literackie w Starym Testamencie* (Kraków 2003), 138. The author regretted that exegetes usually deal with Greek-Roman rhetoric in *Corpus Paulinum* but omit Hebrew rhetoric. Cf. also: J.-N. Aletti, "La dispositio rhétorique dans les épîtres pauliniennes," *NTS* 38 (1992): 385–401; id., "L'Argumentation de Paul et la position des Corinthiens. 1 Co 15,12–34", in *Résurrection du Christ et des chrétiens (1 Co 15)* (ed. L. De Lorenzi, SMB; Section Biblico-Oecuménique 8; Rome 1985), 63–81.

22 The author reaches to the following conclusions: "Paul's rhetoric is didactic, not polemical; his aim is to teach and correct, not revile and condemn. He wants to improve the Corinthians; he does not want to defeat them"; J. R. Asher, *Polarity and Change in 1 Corinthians 15: A Study of Metaphysics, Rhetoric, and Resurrection* (HUT 42; Tübingen 2000), 90.

Next, he carries out literary-rhetorical analysis (by his own admission) of the quotation, examining in addition, whether it is preceded by the introducing formula (*formula quotationis*). The further step of acting, undertaken by Heil, was to show the relationship between the studied quotation and the context preceding or following it. This part of the analyses consists fundamentally in the exegesis of the context. Concise conclusions can be drawn in which the author shows the role of the OT quotation, through comparing it to the disquisitions of the Apostle to the Nations.

A completely different approach to 1 Cor 15 is taken by Joost Holleman. The title of this book is *Resurrection and Parousia: A Traditio-Historical Study of Paul's Eschatology in 1 Cor 15* (NovTSup 84; Leiden–New York–Köln 1996). Joost focuses on rhetorical studies, as well as according to the title of the book—historical analyses. All analyses in this book are based on both a study of tradition and a study of history. The analyses are conducted from the eschatological perspective and the author has never lost sight of the perspective. At first, the situation of the Corinthian community was presented in which a group of followers rejected the physical resurrection of the dead. Holleman shows connections between resurrection of the dead and resurrection of Christ and between resurrection of the dead and the parousia of Christ.[23] An analysis of the OT quotations in 1 Cor 15 is a part of the historical-critical method, although the author did not omit entirely rhetorical threads.

The historical-critical method which was applied in 1 Cor 15 is also presented by M.C. de Boer in his book titled The Defeat of Death: Apocalyptic Eschatology in 1 Corinthians 15 and Romans 5 (JSNTSup 22; Sheffield 1988). This thesis has an exegetical and comparative character because the author studies two excerpts (1 Cor 15 and Rom 5) and then presents conclusions as a result of his comparative studies. The originality of the conclusions consists in the fact that the author argues (against Käsemann and Beker) that the death was definitively defeated by the resurrection of Christ. According to him, the victory over death constitutes not only futuristic hope, but also a fait accompli.[24] First,

---

23   J. Holleman, *Resurrection and Parousia: A Traditio-Historical Study of Paul's Eschatology in 1 Cor 15* (NovTSup 84; Leiden–New York–Köln 1996), 35–65.

24   The author shows his thesis in the following way: "Paul's apocalyptic eschatology is not defined, as Käsemann (like Baker) would have us believe, by the fact that Christ has defeated all powers 'except death.' The thesis of the passage is actually that Christ will defeat all the inimical powers, including death. The foundation of that soteriological promise is Christ's own resurrection from the dead, which means that 'all things,' i.e., all the powers including death, have now been subordinated under his feet"; M. C. de Boer, *The Defeat of Death: Apocalyptic Eschatology in 1 Corinthians 15 and Romans 5* (JSNTSup 22; Sheffield 1988), 139–140.

De Boer enunciates two apocalyptic currents of Judaism that existed in the 1st century after Christ. Paul refers to them in his disquisitions. The first one has a cosmological aspect: the death is seen as the dominance of the power of the evil over the life of a man; the second is tied with the pharisaical understanding of the Law (the faithfulness to the Law will only decide of the fate of a man after his death). Christ's work of salvation consists in defeating the power of the evil (Jewish apocalyptic cosmology) and in freeing from the supremacy of Law (legislative current). The author treats 1 Cor 15 as the specific treatise on resurrection.[25]

Quotations from the OT included in this paper are recognized by the author as "evidence" for defeating death as the personified power of evil ("apocalyptic eschatology" presented in 1 Cor 15:12–58 runs deep in Jewish apocalyptic cosmology).

Very important in this field (although deprived practically of rhetorical analyses) is a book written by Scott Brodeur, entitled *The Holy Spirit's Agency in the Resurrection of the Dead: An Exegetico-Theological Study of 1 Corinthians 15:44 b–49 and Romans 8:9–13* (TG 14; Rome 1996). In his book, the author devotes a lot of space for exegetical in-depth analysis of two fragments of *Corpus Paulinum*; like M.C. de Boer, he has put together the part of 15 chapter of 1 Cor with the fragment of Rom 8:9–13. Based on exegetical analysis of the both fragments, Brodeur reached conclusions of the theological nature. Both the exegesis and the theology of this work concentrate on actions of the Holy Spirit in the life of Christ and the Christians.[26] Therefore, the study neither refers directly to the resurrection, nor to the OT quotations in 1 Cor 15 (in the excerpt studied by the author there is only one quotation, taken from Gen 2:7b). Obviously Brooder reaches into the exegesis for direct context of the discussed excerpt in 1 Cor, in which there were also OT quotations inserted.

---

25 The author defines it as "a self-contained treatise on the resurrection"; de Boer, *Defeat of Death*, 93.

26 The author devotes the first part to his study to analysis of 1 Cor 15: 44b–49 (in the second part he examines Rom 8:9–13). Discerning the uniting role of the Holy Spirit is a result of these analyses: "The Holy Spirit is the eschatological link that joins earth to heaven and connects the present to the future. He unites sinners to God by welcoming them into the body of Christ, the Church; he brings God to believers by dwelling in their hearts as in a temple. In bearing the image of their Lord and Savior, Christians in fact come to participate in God's great salvific deed accomplished in Christ and actualized by the Holy Spirit who dwells in them"; S. Brodeur, *The Holy Spirit's Agency in the Resurrection of the Dead: An Exegetico-Theological Study of 1 Corinthians 15,44b–49 and Romans 8,9–13* (TG 14; Rome 1996), 162.

They will be the subject of deliberations of this study and historical-critical method is used by the author to analyze them.

The thesis of Maurizio Teani, titled *Corporeità e risurrezione. L'interpretazione di 1 Corinti 15:35–49 nel Novecento* (Aloisiana. Pubblicazioni della Pontifcia Facoltà Teologica dell'Italia Meridionale – Sezione "San Luigi" 24; Roma–Brescia 1994) looks at the matter in another way. It is clear from the book's title, that the author does not deal with the whole chapter 15 of 1 Cor, but only with a piece of it (vv. 35–49). *De facto*, it is not exactly an exegetical work but rather the work on the history of the exegesis. The author probably used all the known 19th-century commentaries on 1 Cor (especially on 1 Cor 15), and he systematized them, according to the earlier adopted criteria, and presented the results of his analyses. In this book a vast, stricter exegetical part was included. However the exegesis, is based mainly (although not only) on 19th-century commentaries.[27] It is possible to say from a point of view of our interests, of course with some simplification, that in many commentaries two centuries before, the quotations from the OT were recognized as *ornamentum* rather than *argumentum*. The role of the *ornamentum* was to intensify the disquisition.

In this regard, a few of the most prominent *positions* have recently appeared. They pertain to the issue of quoting in general, as well as discuss (directly or indirectly) the role of the OT quotations in 1 Cor 15:12–58.

3. Presentation of the Method and the Content of this Study

The method that will be used to achieve the previously set aim will consist of several stages. The first chapter is devoted to the introduction of the whole problem being the subject of the analysis. The introduction includes a general discussion devoted to the use the OT quotes in *Corpus Paulinum*, an attempt to define the notion of a citation, a discussion about a place of 1 Cor 15:12–58 in the structure of the entire letter, and a determination of the Old Testament quotes and their direct context in 1 Cor 15:12–58.

Chapters II–VII are devoted to the analysis of six citations from the OT that have been designated assuming predetermined criteria. These quotes are analyzed in their direct context. However, if this analysis could be regarded as conceivable, one must first determine the source of each quote and explore its

---

27   M. Teani, *Corporeità e risurrezione. L'interpretazione di 1 Corinti 15,35–49 nel Novecento* (Aloisiana. Pubblicazioni della Pontifcia Facoltà Teologica dell'Italia Meridionale – Sezione "San Luigi" 24: Roma–Brescia 1994), 157–287.

meaning in the original context. Thus, each of these six chapters is based on a three-step analysis: identifying the source of a quotation, considering the phrase quoted in its direct OT context, and discussing the importance of the quote in various parts of 1 Cor 15:12–58. In the analysis of Old Testament texts from which quotations have been taken, a historical-critical method of exegesis was essentially used. The same method was used in 1 Cor 15:12–58, often extending it for rhetorical analysis of individual fragments. It ought to also be noted, that generally in this study our own translation of 1 Cor 15:12–58 was used.

The conclusions of the analysis conducted in six central chapters were presented in the final chapter of this book, in which the particular paragraphs indicate the role played by the Old Testament quotations in the Pauline argumentation for the resurrection. In a very synthetic form they were also shown in the ending of the study.

I. Introductory Issues

The manner of discourse by Saul of Tarsus, the would-be Apostle of the
Nations, whose mentality had been developed on the basis of excellent standards
of the Pharisee education, is utterly steeped in the thought of the Hebrew Bible,
as H.A.A. Kennedy has shown in his influential study. The style is generally
revealed in abundant use of the Old Testament terminology.[28] H.A.A Kennedy
argues that almost all of Paul's theological concept is anchored in the pages of
the OT and grows from the soil of Jewish religiosity, or more exactly from the
Biblical Judaism, which soon after Paul's death gave rise to the Rabbinic
Judaism. The latter is mainly a work of the Pharisees gathered in Yavne in 90
C.E. These Pharisees (who renamed themselves Rabbis) were also members of
the faction to which Saul himself belonged. Through dogmatic concepts,
angelology, pneumatology, Messianic ideas, parenesis, as well as through the
language, the thought of the authors of the Hebrew Bible often comes to light in
Paul's style and imagery. Paul refers to the Old Testament thought in three
ways: by using proper quotations, deliberate or casual allusions, and the
theological subject-matter.

1. Paul's Use of the Old Testament Quotations— Introductory Issues

A detailed discussion of the role of the OT quotations in Paul's argumentation
for the resurrection in 1 Cor 15:12–58 requires a previous explanation of the
very idea of quoting and the essential reasons behind it. The Apostle of the
Nations, of Jewish birth and Pharisee education, had gained his education
mainly on the basis of the Torah, extended by the prophetic books and the
Writings. For example, he learned from the compilation of books which would
be later named Tanakh by the Jewish tradition. Since this education was based
on mostly oral acquisition and commenting of the Biblical material, there is no
doubt that Paul was excellently well acquainted with the contents of the Hebrew

---

28   H. A. A. Kennedy, *St Paul and the Mystery Religious* (London 1913), 154–160; see also
     E. E. Ellis, *Paul's Use of the Old Testament* (Grand Rapids 1991), 10–11.

Bible, as well as with the interpretation methods then in use.[29] Such acquisition of the Biblical material was often a usual form of memorization of important fragments of the Bible. Occasionally, fragments of non-Biblical literature (such as David's elegy to the death of Saul and Jonathan) were also memorized. Rabbinic schools, developing the methods of exegesis, resorted to interpretation of the Holy Scriptures through the Scriptures alone. Hillel's seven *middoth* consisted mainly in arguing on the basis of Biblical quotations. Over time, the Jewish exegesis had developed these methods into the thirteen rules of halachic interpretation of the Torah, outlined by Rabbi Ishmael ben Elisha and his successors. In any case, argumentation in the discourse on the basis on the Bible was the most common and most convincing method of arguing in religious disputes. Saul of Tarsus is no exception in this regard.

Therefore, a thesis that Paul used the OT quotations in his discussion and argumentation gives rise to no objections. However, the very idea of quotation remains problematic. Dictionaries and encyclopedias vie for defining what a quotation is, yet still no clear and universally accepted criteria of recognition of quotations have been developed. As a result, what is first to be dealt with is a distinction between an allusion and a quotation, as well as the matter of analogies and typologies. This problem is examined in the first part of the given discussion. It will present criteria that allow us to recognize a phrase or sentence as a quotation, and will also outline their essential differences. This will make it possible to distinguish quotations from allusions, typologies and analogies. The question of so-called linked quotations will also be approached.

The exegetes unanimously agree that Paul was eager to use the OT quotations, although they specify a different number of such quotations in the *Corpus Paulinum*. This number depends, of course, on the adopted criteria of a given quotation. Regardless of some fluctuations in the number of the OT quotations in Paul's writings, it is clear that such quotations play a clearly defined role in the context of particular discourses. Before we proceed to the detailed discussion of the function of the OT quotations in 1 Cor 15:12–58, a more general reflection on the role played by the OT quotations in Paul's writings should occur. The essential aspects of the function of the OT quotations in Paul's writings will be defined in the second part of this chapter. Only when we have prepared the background we will proceed to a more detailed clarification of the role of quotations in 1 Cor 15:12–58.

---

29   Knowledge of the Bible was already widespread in ancient Israel. The fact that the form of study was essentially oral is evidenced by such texts as Exod 13:8; Deut 6:7; or Ps 78:3–4. The rabbis of Jesus's and Paul's age have adopted this method of study; R. de Vaux, *Instytucje Starego Testamentu* (vols. I–II; trans. T. Brzegowy; Poznań 2004), 59.

1.1. The Old Testament Quotations in Paul's Letters— Clarification of Terms and Criteria of Classification

Linguists claim unanimously that definition of the concept of quotation is extremely difficult, and in some cases even impossible.[30] It can be even more difficult to distinguish between a quotation and an allusion: "Precise clarification of the concept of quotation as compared with allusion is extremely difficult in view of the complexity of the Old Testament texts used in the New Testament and of the very method of modification of the quoted material. In a way, a distinction may become highly arbitrary and differ from the intent of the New Testament author."[31] Already in the 4th century, the Christians knew the practice of distinguishing between quotations in the text. In codices A, B, and ℵ, marks indicating quotations can be found. Since the subject of the present study are the Old Testament quotations in 1 Cor 15:12–58, an attempt to point out the criteria distinguishing them from allusions should be made. Paul's style and vocabulary are so specific that it is often very difficult to make an attempt to draw the line between Biblical quotations and allusions in *Corpus Paulinum*.[32] Therefore, determining the definition of the term "quotation" in Paul's writings often remains somewhat arbitrary.

As for distinguishing the OT quotations in the *Corpus Paulinum*, a lot of circumstances should be taken into account and clear criteria of extraction of such quotations should be specified.[33] Complexity of this subject matter is

---

30   Formerly, a quite schematic, and therefore artificial and hardly useful, criterion of quotations was sometimes assumed. Namely, it was assumed that a sequence of several (usually three or four) words is a quotation. If there were less words in a given word sequence, the fragment was rejected and not deemed a quotation. However, sometimes two words make a quotation, while longer utterances do not. It is hard to recognize e.g. a question "What time is now?" as a quotation, and on the other hand, phrases "Alas! Poor Yorick!" or "The rest is silence" are unquestionable quotations, even if they have equal or smaller number of words in the sequence.

31   J. Klinkowski, *Zużytkowanie Starego Testamentu w Nowym. Studium egzegetyczne tekstów Ewangelii synoptycznych* (BDL 13; Legnica 2000), 23.

32   E. E. Ellis says: "The style and vocabulary of the apostle are such that it is often difficult to distinguish between quotation, allusion and language colouring from the OT. This is not only the Word of God but also his mode of thought and speech; thus it is not unnatural that he should find in it vivid phraseology to apply to a parallel situation in his own day"; Ellis, *Paul's Use of the Old Testament*, 10.

33   Biblical scholars usually extract about 93 OT quotations from Paul's letters. This number is approximately one-third of all OT quotations in the NT. These quotations come from sixteen books of the OT (including 31 from the Pentateuch, 25 from Isaiah, 19 from the Psalms). They are both single and linked quotations. This number, however, changes in various studies and sometimes reaches 107.

caused by different recensions of the Biblical text and its translations. The following layers overlap here:

(1) The first one is the layer of the original text of the Hebrew Bible. The HB text has different recensions, and each of them could have become a basis of translation into Greek or Aramaic (targumim). The exegete's task is to determine the original text by means of textual criticism, yet even determination of such text (using normal criteria) still will not prove that Paul used this very lection rather than another one (e.g. one that had been rejected by the criticism). While examining this layer, it should be kept in mind that in times of the Apostle of the Nations, the Hebrew text had not been vocalized yet.

(2) The second layer is a layer of the text translated into Greek or Aramaic from the original HB text (or from a text claimed by the textual criticism as non-authentic, though it had already functioned in Paul's times). Greek translations of the HB exist in many versions; even LXX fragments differ from each other in different codices. Moreover, the Hebrew text had been translated into Aramaic in targumim, which means that Paul could use targumim and translate them into Greek, rather than use an existing Greek translation.

(3) The third layer is the Paul's record. First, Paul's record should be determined by means of textual criticism. Next, it should be taken into account that a fragment of Paul's letter intended to be deemed an OT quotation could have been translated directly from the HB, from the LXX, or from the targumim. It could have also been made as a translation from memory. In the latter case, if Paul translated *ad hoc* a fragment intended to be qualified as a quotation, he could have done it on the basis of a memorized text of the HB or the LXX, as well as of the memorized Aramaic targumim.

These factors should be considered each time a quotation is determined to be a fragment or not. The issue is therefore very complex. Having taken it into account, the next thing to do is to examine the texts intended to be called quotations in the light of the clearly specified criteria. Such texts may have been written in different textual variants of individual books. Biblical manuscripts discovered among the Dead Sea scrolls illustrate the existence of different textual forms of many Biblical books. These textual variants are revealed in the OT quotations of the NT. Some quotations are more similar to one Greek version or another, while others are closer to the Hebrew version; yet other quotations show similarities to both or to no version at all.[34] The history of exegesis knows various criteria of recognizing a NT text fragment as an OT quotation. The forms of references between the OT and the NT are diverse. They include not only direct quotations but also allusions, narrative parallels, themes and the language itself. The most difficult to define clearly are the criteria distinguishing a direct quotation from an Old Testament allusion. Sometimes, a direction quotation may be defined as a sequence of two, three or four words, another time it can be an allusion referring to a specific OT text, and in yet another case it will be just a normal manner of expression of an author whose mind had been formed on the basis of inspired texts, because in many cases the vocabulary, expressions, phrases or specific terms constitute the manner of expression of authors with good and strong knowledge of the Bible. For this reason, some authors define a quotation as a fragment of a work in which the author refers to another source and this reference is obvious enough for every cautious reader to recognize the derived nature of the presented material.[35]

Narrative parallels are different from quotations or allusions, since NT authors would sometimes compose their narrations on the basis of the OT patterns.[36] Many OT themes occur in the NT; however, in no way do they have to imply a necessity of quoting. Besides, the language of the NT is itself largely identical with the language of the OT, because it not only stems from the same religious tradition but also has the same cultural background. Despite all these complexities, an assumption of clear criteria that determines what we have to do with a quotation is necessary to conduct the study. In the present study, we assume the following criteria to qualify a fragment under examination as a quotation[37]:

---

34 B. Lindars and A. J. Saldarini, "Cytaty ze Starego Testamentu w Nowym Testamencie," in *Encyklopedia biblijna* (ed. P. J. Achtemeier; trans. T. Mieszkowski; Warszawa 1999), 176.

35 "The term 'citation' is limited here to those places where the author's appeal to an outside source is so blatant that any attentive reader would recognize the secondary character of the materials in question"; C. D. Stanley, *Paul and the Language of Scripture: Citation Technique in the Pauline Epistles and Contemporary Literature* (SNTSMS 74; Cambridge 1992), 4.

36 E.g. Matt 1–2 and Luke 1–2 are built on patterns present in the narrations on Jacob, Moses, the exodus or birth of the patriarchs and Samuel. The history of the Passion is largely based on the pattern of Ps 22.

37 Such criteria of quotation distinguishing have also been assumed by K. Stendhal (*The School of St. Matthew and its Use of the Old Testament* [Lund 1968], 45–48). His way had been paved by H. B. Swete (*An Introduction to the Old Testament in Greek* [Cambridge 1900)]).

(1) Paul's use of a formula introducing a quotation or a literary link which could indicate that the following words, phrases, or expressions can be an excerpt from another text;
(2) a large degree of verbal concordance, and of concordance of Paul's text under examination with regard to sequence of words in the sentence, phrase or expression, with the confronted OT text, both in the HB and the LXX version (if there is no such concordance with the HB or LXX, another reliable source of quotation, such as the targumim, should be pointed out, or a possibility of quoting from the memory or of an *ad hoc* translation, made by Paul when writing or dictating of the letter, should be substantiated. In the latter case, it should be also substantiated whether the apostle translated from a Hebrew text, a Greek text, or an Aramaic Targum);
(3) intent of quoting deduced from the context of the fragment under examination which could indicate the use of the OT.[38]

Moreover, it should be emphasized that joint occurrence of all three criteria is not necessary to recognize a fragment as a quotation. Let us take a brief look on each of the criteria and ask how and to what degree they influence the decision on whether the examined fragment can be recognized as the OT quotation or is rather just an allusion or a common terminological similarity, unwitting even in the allusion form, but caused by similarity of the religious language functioning in the cultural *milieu* of Judaism and nascent Christianity.

Quotation Introducing Formulas

The Apostle of the Nations did not use the modern concept of quotation. As a result, some fragments introduced by a typical quotation formula (*formula quotationis*) only reflect the thought contained in a relevant OT text, while fragments without a quotation-introducing formula often turn out to be a *verbatim ac litteram* quotation.[39] Therefore, an introductory formula does not

---

38   S. E. Porter wonders whether the intent of quoting should be recognized by the audience (reader); in other words, he speculates if a fragment written by the author intentionally as a quotation, but not recognized as such by the reader, can be deemed a quotation; S. E. Porter, "Further Comments on the Use of the Old Testament in the New Testament," in *The Intertextuality of the Epistles. Explorations of Theory and Practice* (eds. T. L. Brodie, D. R. MacDonald and S. E. Porter; Sheffield 2006), 103–106. Such assumption seems to disregard the ignorance of readers (not necessarily their fault) and is too subjective.

39   This is the case with 1 Cor 15:32. In two instances when the apostle recalls the same quotation, for the first time it is introduced by a quotation formula, and for the other

appear before Paul's quotation of the OT. When the apostle decided to introduce a quotation by a formula, it usually has one of three forms: γέγραπται (29 times), λέγει ἡ γραφή (6 times) and λέγει (about 30 times). The latter expression has different subjects. The speaking person can be David (Rom 4:7–8, 11:9–10), Isaiah (Rom 10:16.20; 15:12), Moses (Rom 10:19), God himself (2 Cor 6:16; see Rom 9:15; 2 Cor 6:2; Rom 11:4). The subject of the verb λέγει can also be the Law (Rom 7:7; 1 Cor 14:34); sometimes it occurs without a clearly specified subject, although the context indicates that the "speaker" is God or the Scriptures (Rom 9:25; 10:21; 15:10; Gal 3:16; Eph 4:8; 5:14).[40]

In the vast majority of occurrences, Paul's introductory formulas are typical for the Jewish literature and have numerous parallels both in the OT and in non-Biblical literature. In the HB, parallels occur in Exod 24:4; 2 Chr 20:37; 36:2; Neh 6:6; 10:34; Dan 9:13. Even more literal parallels can be found in the *Damascus Document* (*CD*) as well as the rabbinic literature. The latter had developed a long time after Paul's activity. However, it can be assumed that in the 1st century C.E. such manner of quoting had been present in the Pharisee environment and subsequently made its way to rabbinic works. The examples below are just a few:

CD 7:8: כאשר אמר	2 Cor 6:16: καθὼς εἶπεν
CD 5:1: כתוב	Gal 3:13: γέγραπται
CD 7:19: כאשר כתוב	Rom 1:17: καθὼς γέγραπται
CD 5:8: ומשה אמר	Rom 10:19: Μωϋσῆς λέγει
CD 6:7-8: אשר אמר ישעיה	Rom 10:16: Ἡσαΐας γὰρ λέγει
Pes. 81b: כתוב אומר	Rom 4:3: ἡ γραφὴ λέγει
Yebam. 39a: כתוב אמר	Rom 4:3: ἡ γραφὴ λέγει
Abot 3,7: ככתוב בדויד	Rom 11:2: ἐν Ἠλίᾳ τί λέγει ἡ γραφή
Yoma 35b, 66a: משה ככתוב בתורה	1 Cor 9:9: ἐν γὰρ τῷ Μωϋσέως νόμῳ γέγραπται
Sanh. 2a: שנאמר--ואומר	Rom 15:9–10: καθὼς γέγραπται - καὶ πάλιν λέγει
Qidd. 82a: מהו אומר	Rom 10:8: ἀλλὰ τί λέγει

time the formula is omitted. The quotations are Jer 9:24 in 1 Cor 1:31 and 2 Cor 10:17, as well as Hab 2:4 in Rom 1:17 and Gal 3:11.

40   The quotation formulas indicate a "clear recognition of the authority" of the quoted fragment; B. Polok, "Autorytet pism ST w NT na przykładzie starotestamentalnych cytatów w ewangelicznych opisach męki Pańskiej," in *Izrael i Biblia Hebrajska w Nowym Testamencie* (ed. K. Ziaja; Sympozja 53; Opole 2003), 47.

The comparison above evidences a large concordance between Paul's introductory formulas and quotation introductions used in the Jewish literature. Such concordance reveals itself not only in normal references to quotations in declarative sentences but also in questions and introductions to linked quotations.[41]

So-called "links", indicating the presence of a quotation, are somewhat more difficult to distinguish than quotation-introducing formulas. In the HB, the role of such links is played by the term לֵאמֹר which is a *de facto* equivalent of quotation marks. It usually occurs as an indicator of an utterance in direct or reported speech.[42] Sometimes translators render this term by a participle of the verb "to say" (said), yet it usually seems unnecessary; such participle is a substitute for quotation marks, non-existent in Biblical Hebrew. The term לֵאמֹר is a *qal* form of the verb אמר in the *status constructus*, connected with the preposition לְ-. Exegetes are not sure whether in a case when the term לֵאמֹר occurs after the verb "to send" (a message through a messenger), it should be interpreted as a symbol introducing the content of the message, or rather translated as "send to tell" (see Num 21:21; Deut 9:23; Josh 2:1.3; 10:3.6; 2 Kgs 3:7; Amos 7:10). There are also cases when this term functions as a normal infinitive (Gen 41:15; Deut 13:13; 1 Sam 13:4; 1 Kgs 16:16; Isa 37:9), and sometimes it indicates an intent to speak (usually after movement verbs; see 1 Sam 23:19; Josh 17:4; Ezra 9:1).[43] The translator of the LXX often renders לֵאמֹר as λέγων. However, with such translation, לֵאמֹר ceases to be a link indicating the presence of a quotation and becomes a quotation formula. In other cases, the term לֵאמֹר is translated as normal ὅτι, which may be such a link indicating the presence of a quotation. Such links may also include other prepositions, particles or conjunction.

Verbal Concordance with the Quoted Text

In the vast majority of the quoted fragments, the Apostle of the Nations follows the LXX[44]; Paul adopts the HB version rather than the LXX in only a few cases,

---

41   It is worth to quote Warfield's opinion in this context: "here is probably not a single mode of alluding to or citing Scripture in the entire NT which does not find its exact parallel among the Rabbis. The New Testament so far evinces itself a thoroughly Jewish book"; Ellis, *Paul's Use of the Old Testament*, 49.

42   P. Briks, *Podręczny słownik hebrajsko-polski i aramejsko-polski Starego Testamentu* (Warszawa 1999), 37.

43   S. Wagner, אָמַר *'āmar*, *TDOT* I: 333–334.

44   T. Söding even claims that Paul only used LXX and some Judeo-Hellenistic recensions of the text but never used the HB; see the chapter *Heilige Schriften für Israel und*

while in almost forty quotations, Paul's version differs from both the HB and the LXX. The fact that the author of the letters is definitely more eager to use the Greek LXX than the HB may be attributed to the wish of the first advocates of the Gospel which was to use the translation accepted in the world of the diaspora of Hellenistic Jews.[45] LXX has been a particular *regula fidei* for the Jewish diaspora, and subsequently, for the first generations of Christians.[46] However, studies by Biblical scholars show that the Apostle of the Nations did not follow any single form of the LXX text. Sometimes, a quotation complies with the LXX-A (*Codex Alexandrinus*), another time it complies with the LXX-B (*Codex Vaticanus*), and in yet other cases, with the LXX from the *Codex Sinaiticus* (א).[47] When explaining these discrepancies, the newer studies on the origins of the LXX should be taken into account. The hypothesis of the famous *Letter of Aristeas* has been subject to much criticism. The reason was that some OT quotations by Jewish writers (e.g. by Philo), in the NT, and by early Church Fathers do not seem to follow any of the known versions of the LXX but instead follow yet another source. The studies conducted in this regard led to a hypothesis that the *Letter of Aristeas* has been written in late 2nd century B.C. as a propaganda work intended to promote the translation of the Seventy and make it the standard.[48] The development of the LXX was to be similar to the process of formation of the recorded targumim which had originally been a part of the oral tradition passed from one synagogue to another, were written down afterwards, and finally became subject to the final redaction which resulted in

---

Kirche. Die Sicht des 'Alten Testament' bei Paulus, in: T. Söding, *Das Wort vom Kreuz. Studien zur paulinischen Theologie* (WUNT 93; Tübingen 1997), 223–241. Likewise: D.-A. Koch, *Die Schrift als Zeuge des Evangeliums. Untersuchungen zur Verwendung und Verständnis der Schrift bei Paulus* (Tübingen 1986), 57.

45   H. B. Swete argues that a vast majority of the OT quotations in Paul's writings is taken from the LXX; *Introduction*, 392.

46   The most important witnesses of the text in this regard include the recensions of Hesychius, Lucian and Origen.

47   Some fragments of the text are lacking in the codices. They have often been supplemented later by medieval copyists. As far as Codex B is concerned, "initium codicis usque ad Gen. 46:28 ηρωων et Ps. 105;27—137,6 periit et ab aliquo XV. saeculi suppletum est; quae supplementa hic negleguntur, cum alium textum habeant atque B. Ceterum Vetus Testamentum integrum est; soli libri Maccabaeorum et Psalmi Salomonis ut in ceteris codicibus antiquissimis desunt"; from an introduction to the edition: *Septuaginta. Id est Vetus Testamentum graece iuxta LXX interpretes*, published by A. Rahlfs, Stuttgart 1979², XXXVI. The Codex A lacks the following fragments: 1 Kgs 2:17–14:9 and Ps 49:20–79:11; ibid.

48   P. E. Kahle explicitly claims: "'the Letter of Aristeas' has put us on a wrong truck"; id., *The Cairo Geniza* (London 1947), 175.

formation of the great targumim as literary works. This also brings to mind the "Greek targumim"[49] from which the first Greek translations of the Bible had developed and were finally unified in the Christian LXX. Such an attempt to reconstruct the process of development of the LXX was met with open criticism from many scholars who had found it to be weak (the most significant ones include lack of arguments for a later origin of the *Letter of Aristeas*, inaccurately and selectively examined fragments of Philo, as well as lack of comprehensive Greek targumic traditions).[50]

The influence of the LXX on Paul's works is not only revealed in quotations but also in its vocabulary and style: such influence is inevitable. Since the people of the diaspora had begun to read the Alexandrian translation of the HB, the Greek terminology of Judaism began to show up. Greek terms (being counterparts of Hebrew words) would, in a sense, acquire the shades of meaning of their equivalents.[51] Paul began to express his own concepts and ideas by means of Greek terminology describing the Jewish religion and beliefs of Judaism, which had already been largely stabilized. Often, in order to understand Paul's terms, phrases, or expressions better, one should take a look at their use in the Greek Bible.

Although the text of the Bible of the Seventy is essentially the base of Paul's quotations, the author occasionally differs from the LXX, slightly altering the original text, or follows the HB. The study of the epistolography of the Apostle of the Nations resulted in making several hypotheses explaining these discrepancies with the Greek translation of the OT. The most valid hypotheses explaining the changes in the original text of the LXX include:

(1) reference to a Hebrew etymology and use of another Greek word in translation of particular terms[52];
(2) use of Aramaic targumim or of their Greek translations;
(3) use of Greek translations of the HB other than the LXX[53];
(4) quoting of memorized fragments of the LXX.[54]

---

49   Ellis, *Paul's Use of the Old Testament*, 17.
50   Stendhal and Roberts openly criticized Kahle's hypothesis.
51   Ellis's opinion in this regard is worth quoting: "It was inevitable that, after the translation of the Hebrew Bible, words in the Greek version would acquire something of the value of the Hebrew words they represent"; id., *Paul's Use of the Old Testament*, 13.
52   This is the case, e.g., of Rom 9:17; 10:15; 12:19; E. Huhn, *Die Messianischen Weissagungen* (II; Tübingen 1900), 279.
53   H. Lietzmann, *An die Galater* (Tübingen 1923), 32–34.
54   The classification of the hypotheses has been cited from: Ellis, *Paul's Use of the Old Testament*, 14. "... the text difference can be partially explained by the manner of quotation of the Scripture by authors. They often quoted the texts inaccurately, from

The first and second hypothesis may be connected with Paul's use of quoting on the basis of *midrash pesher*. Some of Paul's quotations that differ from both the LXX and the HB can be explained on the basis of another textual base. Nevertheless, compliance of these quotations with targumim, Peshitta or Greek versions other than the LXX are rather occasional. In such a situation, it is also not easy to agree with the thesis that it is Paul's *ad hoc* translation of the HB or the LXX, because the nature of the changes contradicts it. For example, inclusion of the term πᾶς in Rom 10:11 (πᾶς ὁ πιστεύων ἐπ' αὐτῷ οὐ καταισχυνθήσεται) cannot be explained because there is no evident reason of such inclusion; besides, in Rom 9:33, the apostle drops this term (ὁ πιστεύων ἐπ' αὐτῷ οὐ καταισχυνθήσεται). Therefore, it should be assumed that Paul interprets the quoted texts on the basis of *midrash pesher*. It can be clearly seen in the example of 2 Cor 6:2, where a quotation from Isa 49:8 ("I heard you at the acceptable time, and in the day of salvation I helped you.") is commented by the words: "Look, now is the acceptable time; look, now is the day of salvation!" It would be most certain to assume Paul interprets the OT as *midrash pesher* in the quotations in which the MT and the LXX comply with each other but differ from Paul's use. The changes introduced by the apostle usually concern the grammatical number or person and are sometimes motivated by messianic or apocalyptic perspective.

Use of a targum (second hypothesis) can be seen e.g. in Rom 12:19. A comparison of three versions – the text of Rom 12:19, the Hebrew text and the text of a targum – clearly shows that Paul follows the latter one:

NT: "Vengeance is Mine, I will repay";
HB: "Vengeance is Mine and retribution";
Targum: "Vengeance is before Me, I will repay."[55]

A targum is a possible source of change of the verb into "worship" or "praise" (ἐξομολογήσεται) in Rom 14:11: "For it is written: As I live, says the Lord, every knee will bow to me, and every tongue will give praise to God." The targum uses the verb תקים ("praise," "confirm"), while the MT in Isa 45:23 reads שבע ("make an oath"). Paul also follows the targumic version in Eph 4:8: "Therefore it says: When he ascended on high he captured captives; he gave gifts to men."

---

their memory, adjusted the OT texts to their new context in the NT books and combined several OT texts in one entirety, creating a new fragment based on OT words and expressions. NT authors would usually modify the OT quotations in a subtle manner, on the basis of the Biblical text, oral Christian tradition, Jewish interpreting tradition and their own understanding of the Biblical history"; Lindars and Saldarini, *Cytaty ze Starego Testamentu*, 176.

55   Ellis, *Paul's Use of the Old Testament*, 140.

The MT and the LXX have the verb "take" instead of "capture," and such lection is present both in the targum and in the Peshitta; Paul had also changed the second person singular into third person.

The third hypothesis concerns quoting of Greek translations of the HB, rather than the LXX. There are three old HB translations into Greek other than the LXX. They are Aquila's, Symmachus's and Theodotion's translations. Aquila was a proselyte and studied at Rabbi Akiva's school. His translation is sometimes so literal it loses the spirit of the Greek language. However, the literality of the translation allows for the recreation of the Hebrew original where it is uncertain. Aquila's translation is polemical with both the LXX and the NT, since his way of conversion to Judaism was quite lengthy: Aquila abandoned paganism and become a Christian, and later he even embraced Judaism. Theodotion of Ephesus was also a proselyte. His translation virtually consists of corrections made to the LXX so the text could be adjusted to the teaching of the rabbis. The loosest is the translation by a Samaritan named Symmachus. The last two of the mentioned translations (Theodotion and Symmachus) are, however, are written too late to have any influence on Paul's epistles. Yet, they could influence the copyists of the *Corpus Paulinum*, who interfered (intentionally or not) with the text of the letters. A similar remark applies to Aquila's translation. The hypothesis on Paul using Greek translations other than the LXX is therefore hardly probable, unless there had been some fragmentary translations, e.g. of individual OT books, which have not survived until today.

Many authors support the fourth hypothesis.[56] Saul, being educated by Gamaliel, not only must have read the Bible in Hebrew but also translated it into Aramaic as a targum. While debating on the Law, learning the Jewish methods of exegesis, discovering the secrets of the Prophets and Scriptures, Saul used the Aramaic language. As a Jew born in the Cilician city of Tarsus (which is in the Hellenistic diaspora) he must have known the LXX. Therefore, he used Biblical quotations in at least three languages: Hebrew, Aramaic and Greek. He must have also memorized many fragments, since the study of Torah included memorization. Besides, psychological research has shown that if someone studies the Bible in more than one language, he is not deeply attached to a single form of the text.[57] In Judaism, attached to various forms of tradition, a large emphasis was put on faithful memorization of Biblical texts. According to

---

56   This is the case with Swete, Sandy, Headlam and others.

57   Ellis, *Paul's Use of the Old Testament*, 14.

B. Gerhardsson, this Judaic tradition was strictly respected[58] and it was taught at academies (בת־המדרש). The goal was to remember the words as exactly as possible (*ipsissima verba*). To achieve it, various mnemotechnical methods were employed, chiefly including loud recitation and frequent repetition phrases.[59] Many factors and manners of learning influenced the memorization of the Biblical text. R. Riesner argues that fragments of the Bible were learnt during religious service, during recitation and reading of the Holy Scripture, during discussion of various fragments, and during rabbinic lectures.[60]

Sometimes the memorized quotations do not reflect the original text exactly. The discrepancies may result from two factors: either from incorrect (inaccurate) memorization of the text or from deliberate adjustment of the quotation to a new context. The latter case is much more frequent than the former.[61] Introduction of a quotation in the new context sometimes requires the use of a declination or conjugation, or changing of the sequence of words, in order to put a sufficient emphasis on the term the author wants to stress.[62] Sometimes, inaccurate quoting from memory is also motivated by syntax of the new context.

To the four hypotheses proposed above, a fifth can be added: it is possible that during Paul's time there were some Christian anthologies of the OT texts in Greek used in the field of apologetics. It can be assumed that there was some function of the oral tradition into Christian OT Greek translations. Such texts could have been transmitted by kerygmatic, homiletic or catechetic preaching and did not have to be recorded in any work. It was the record in Paul's epistles which had established them in the scriptural tradition of Christianity.

---

58 This scholar, originating from the so-called Scandinavian school, is an author of several studies on this subject: *Memory and Manuscript. Oral Tradition and Written Transmission in Rabbinic Judaism and Early Christianity* (Uppsala 1964[2]); *Tradition and Transmission in Early Christianity* (Lund 1964); *The Origins of the Gospel Tradition* (London 1979). The Scandinavian school was initiated by H. Riesenfeld, author of the essential study *The Gospel Tradition and Its Beginnings. A Study in the Limits of "Formgeschichte"* (TU 73, Berlin 1957). His disciple was the mentioned Gerhardsson, and German scholars joined them over time.

59 R. Bartnicki, *Ewangelie synoptyczne. Geneza i interpretacja* (Warszawa 2003[3]), 231.

60 R. Riesner, *Jesus als Lehrer. Eine Untersuchung zum Ursprung der Evangelien-Überlieferung* (WUNT 2, 7; Tübingen 1981), 14.

61 J. Bonsirven virtually completely rejects the human error; Ellis, *Paul's Use of the Old Testament*, 15.

62 Introduction of such changes does not change the fact that a fragment included in a work remains a quotation; Porter, "Further Comments," 108.

Context Pointing at the Intention of Quoting

One of the criteria adopted in this study, which decide if we deal with a quote, focuses on a context indicating the intention of quoting. Even if Paul abandons the typical quotation introductory formula and the verbal sound of the text aspiring to be a quote does not fully meet the original source material, the context itself may indicate the intention of the quote. In this case, it is mainly a theme and a subject. If the problem mentioned by the apostle is vividly present in the OT, and moreover, the dispute conducted by Paul consists of similar segments as in the OT, we can assume that the fragment that is not entirely consistent with the supposed verbal source should be a quote. One must take into account the fact that Paul had to adapt quotations to the rules of grammar and style of the context. Sometimes, he left out some expressions or phrases, which he considered irrelevant for the adopted earlier purposes, and sometimes he also added explanatory words. To focus attention on the core of the problem, for example, the apostle could had shortened the quoted passage. He could have also left out parts improper for interpretation. This practice was known in Greco-Roman literature.[63]

Combined Citations

In *Corpus Paulinum* two models of combined citations can be seen. The first is presented by quotes put together (*amalgamated quotation or merged quotation*), and the other citations are linked using a conjunction, or any other term or phrase on a "chain of citations" basis (*chain quotation*). The first model is not very common in rabbinical texts. Two examples are usually given: *Sanh.* 38b and *Sabb.* 20a.[64] The second model of linked citations, called in Hebrew חרז was derived from preaching in the synagogues where the speaker quoted the first passage from the Torah, and then drew on similar quotes from the Prophets and the Scriptures. Paul had never used combined quotes under a chain scheme in a typical rabbinical manner, namely using the formulas like "Law says," "Prophets say," and "Scriptures say."

Paul does not often combine quotes on a key-word base (*Stichwort*), and it is because the cause of the combination is much deeper than just the convergence of expression. Based on the example of Rom 9–11, we can show four quotes combined by *Stichwort*:

---

63 Lindars and Saldarini, *Cytaty ze Starego Testamentu*, 179.
64 *Sanh.* 38b contains nine linked biblical passages: Gen 1:26–27; 11:7; 11:5; 35:7; 35:3; Deut 4:7; 2 Sam 7:23; Dan 7:9. *Sab.* 20a combines two parts: Ezek 15:4 and Jer 36:22.

SIGLUM	KEY-WORD	QUOTATION	TEXT
Rom 9:32–33	λίθος	Isa 8:14; 28:16	διὰ τί; ὅτι οὐκ ἐκ πίστεως ἀλλ᾽ ὡς ἐξ ἔργων· προσέκοψαν τῷ λίθῳ τοῦ προσκόμματος (Isa 8:14) , καθὼς γέγραπται· ἰδοὺ τίθημι ἐν Σιὼν λίθον προσκόμματος καὶ πέτραν σκανδάλου , καὶ ὁ πιστεύων ἐπ᾽ αὐτῷ οὐ καταισχυνθήσεται (Isa 28:16)
Rom 9:25	λαός	Hos 1:9; 2:23	ὡς καὶ ἐν τῷ Ὡσηὲ λέγει· καλέσω τὸν οὐ λαόν μου λαόν μου καὶ τὴν οὐκ ἠγαπημένην ἠγαπημένην (Hosea 1:9) καὶ ἔσται ἐν τῷ τόπῳ οὗ ἐρρέθη αὐτοῖς· οὐ λαός μου ὑμεῖς, ἐκεῖ κληθήσονται υἱοὶ θεοῦ ζῶντος (Hos 2:23)
Rom 11:8–10	ὀφθαλμοὺς	Deut 29:3; Ps 68:23–24	καθὼς γέγραπται· ἔδωκεν αὐτοῖς ὁ θεὸς πνεῦμα κατανύξεως, ὀφθαλμοὺς τοῦ μὴ βλέπειν καὶ ὦτα τοῦ μὴ ἀκούειν (Deut 29:3) , ἕως τῆς σήμερον ἡμέρας. καὶ Δαυὶδ λέγει· γενηθήτω ἡ τράπεζα αὐτῶν εἰς παγίδα καὶ εἰς θήραν καὶ εἰς σκάνδαλον καὶ εἰς ἀνταπόδομα αὐτοῖς, σκοτισθήτωσαν οἱ ὀφθαλμοὶ αὐτῶν τοῦ μὴ βλέπειν καὶ τὸν νῶτον αὐτῶν διὰ παντὸς σύγκαμψον (Ps 68:23–24).
Rom 15:9–11	ἔθνη	2 Sam 22:50; Ps 18:50; 32:43; Ps 117:1	τὰ δὲ ἔθνη ὑπὲρ ἐλέους δοξάσαι τὸν θεόν, καθὼς γέγραπται· διὰ τοῦτο ἐξομολογήσομαί σοι ἐν ἔθνεσιν καὶ τῷ ὀνόματί σου ψαλῶ (2 Sam 22:50; Ps 18:50) . καὶ πάλιν λέγει· εὐφράνθητε, ἔθνη, μετὰ τοῦ λαοῦ αὐτοῦ (Deut 32,43). καὶ πάλιν· αἰνεῖτε, πάντα τὰ ἔθνη, τὸν κύριον καὶ ἐπαινεσάτωσαν αὐτὸν πάντες οἱ λαοί (Ps 117:1).

The chain of quotations frequently arises in rabbinic literature. The connector used by the rabbis is usually the conjunction "and" or the phrase "and then," but sometimes there are longer phrases such as "and then it is said." It is arguable whether Paul combines citations in a similar way.

The Difficulties in Identifying the Sources of Quotations

Some difficulties with a classification evoke these fragments of letters in *Corpus Paulinum*, in which the author reveals his intention of citing (by applying the quotation formulas or by a clear indication in a context, that it is a quotation), however, the cited fragment does not exist in books recognized as the canonical

HB.[65] The fact is, at the time when the Apostle of the Nations used to write to young Christian communities, the Jewish canon was not yet fully established. Nevertheless, it was clear which writings the Jews used in synagogues during their services and which of them enjoyed the greatest authority. In such cases, when the intention of citation is known but the analyzed piece is not a direct quote, you should consider one of these possible solutions:

(1) Paul paraphrases some fragments from the OT or paraphrases several fragments that he connects, or repeats some versions that had already been in use in the oral tradition;

(2) Paul quoted non-canonical writings (i.e., apocryphal writings), which had already cited the OT in a sense of paraphrase; nevertheless, it does not mean that the Apostle ascribes to the writings the same authority as the OT, but only that he wants to use the OT paraphrases included in them;

(3) Pauline "canon" differs from the canon of Palestinian Judaism because the apostle builds the declamations of Jesus and early Christian prophets into it; by referring to these declamations, he uses the quotation introductory phrase, or he indicates by through context that it is a citation of authoritative statement;

(4) Pauline "canon" includes some Jewish apocryphal writings, which the apostle uses, giving them equal authority to the OT canonical writings[66]; it is also possible that there are some differences between Palestine and the Diaspora in the adopting of the writing as authoritative.[67]

The Old Testament Allusions

The allusions to the Old Testament in the *Corpus Paulinum* is another issue. Allusions refer to the knowledge of recipients of the epistles and require interpretation and supplementation *in* a single specific way; therefore, literature theorists call allusions "a partial postulating concealment."[68] An important

---

65   To such quotations belong *inter alia*: 1 Cor 2:9 (an introductory formula: γέγραπται); Eph 4:8 (an introductory formula: λέγει); Eph 5:14 (an introductory formula: λέγει); 1 Tim 5:18b (an introductory formula: γραφὴ λέγει).

66   Ellis, *Paul's Use of the Old Testament*, 33.

67   In this regard, more than a century ago H. E. Ryle argued that at least in Philo of Alexandria it is difficult to see a different canon than in Palestinian Judaism, one must be aware that the works of Philo do not represent the whole of the Diaspora; *The Canon of the Old Testament* (London 1892), 177–178.

68   S. Sierotwiński, *Słownik terminów literackich. Teoria i nauki pomocnicze literatury* (Wrocław et al. 1986⁴), 21.

statement in this regard seems to be that the author of the letters assumes the readers' knowledge of the subject matter he alludes to. Since the epistles had been basically addressed to Christians of pagan origin, it should be assumed that Paul, in his oral preaching during his stay in different communities, would explain the subject matter of the Old Testament, to which his later allusions refer, to the listeners (the would-be recipients of his letters). Assuming this was the case, i.e. that the readers of Paul's letters had at least basic knowledge to understand his allusions to the OT, a question on the criterion of distinguishing between quotations and allusions should be made. It had been mentioned previously that a quotation should be introduced by a formula or a link indicating the intent of quoting. However, in some cases, both the formula and the link have been omitted. The second criterion is a context indicating the intent of quoting. However, sometimes the context does not indicate clearly that the author had intent to quote another text. The third criterion remains: one of verbal concordance between the fragment under examination and the text which can be recognized as a source of a quotation. Here is where the joint between a quotation and an allusion takes place. Automatically, a question arises: how profound should such verbal concordance be and how far should the compatibility of both fragments be advance to call one of them a quotation and not an allusion? The matter is made difficult, as mentioned above, by use of different versions of the OT by the NT authors.

Another problem is the difference between an allusion and the paraphrase of a text. In the studies during the last few decades, a paraphrase is defined as an intentional reference to a specific fragment, even if it is made in a different form or using different words; it does not have to contain any definite number of words originating from the other work; such words may occur in a different order, their sequence can be interrupted by other words, and some words can be replaced by different words. An allusion, on the other hand, is an intentional or unintentional reference—although to a place, person or a literary work rather than a particular fragment.[69]

Many scholars argue that the form of allusion could have been influenced by rhetorical rules of exegesis, ascribed to Hillel, with which Paul was probably acquainted—even if he did not necessarily have to know them in a manner systematized in a seven-point list. It seems that in the creation of allusions, the most helpful principles were *gezerah shavah*. This consists in occurrence of relations between an NT fragment intended to be recognized as an allusion, and

---

69   Porter, "Further Comments," 108–109.

a more extensive part of OT material or a description connected with a particular character, rather than one particular OT fragment.[70]

To unravel the dilemma "quotation or allusion" in the exegesis some direct solutions were proposed. In addition to paraphrases or combined quotes[71]—the concept of "allusive quotation" was introduced."[72] The precise distinction between the quote and the allusion in Paul's writings is so difficult to catch that it is impossible to draw an upfront boundary or to give a clear criterion for the distinction. It is not enough to reach for these texts in which a quotation introductory formula appears to recognize the analyzed fragment as a real citation. Additionally, one should not consist only in literary proximity based essentially on the sequence of words.

Sometimes, changes of the OT texts in the *Corpus Paulinum* may be intentional, other times they may be due to inaccuracies in remembering them by the apostle, and in yet other cases, they can be quite casual. The person who

---

70   I. Rapoport, "Zasady żydowskiej egzegezy tekstu do czasów końcowej redakcji Talmudu," in M. Rosik and I. Rapoport, *Wprowadzenie do literatury i egzegezy żydowskiej okresu biblijnego i rabinicznego* (Bibliotheca Biblica; Wrocław 2009), 183–184. Other rules are: *qal wahomer* (conclusion drawn from a smaller to larger premises), *binyan av mi-katuv yehad* (construction of a conclusion of principle from one fragment), *binyan av mi-shenei ketuvim* (constructiing a conclusion based two fragments) and *kelal u-pherat i perat u-khelal* (a conclusion is drawn assuming the general principle in the text concerning a specific example); S. Mędala, *Wprowadzenie do literatury międzytestamentalnej* (Biblioteka Zwojów. Tło Nowego Testamentu 1; Kraków 1994), 354–355. Cf. also: M. Hadas-Lebel, *Hillel. Maestro della Legge al tempo di Gesù* (trans. P. Lanfranchi; Casale Monferrato 2002), 57–59.

71   E. E. Ellis, "Biblical Interpretation in the New Testament Church," in *Mikra. Text, Translation, Reading and Hebrew Bible in Ancient Judaism and Early Christianity* (Philadelphia 1988), 692.

72   Regarding to the current state of research on the influence of the OT in the NT, it is said not only about (direct and indirect) quotations, but also about allusive quotations (conscious or unconscious), allusions (conscious or unconscious), paraphrases, typologies, reminiscences, echo and influences (direct or indirect) as well as even traditions; S. E. Porter, "The Use of the Old Testament in the New Testament: A Brief Comment on Method and Terminology," in *Early Christian Interpretation of the Scriptures in Israel: Investigations and Proposals* (eds. C. A. Evans and J. A. Sanders; JSNTSup 14; Sheffield 1997), 80. Terms as „OT echo", „allusion" or „paraphrase" became deeply rooted in exegesis through the work by R. B. Hays, *Echos of Scripture in the Letters of Paul* (New Haven 1981). C. D. Stanley distinguishes, apart from the direct and indirect quotations, so-called "free indirect quotes"; C. D. Stanley, *Arguing with Scripture: The Rhetoric of Quotation in Letters of Paul* (New York 2004), 4; S. E. Porter instead identifies the indirect quotations with paraphrases; Porter, "Further Comments," 103.

knows the Hebrew Bible perfectly (and such a person was certainly Paul) may use certain phrases rooted in the biblical text, without realizing this fact. The "allusive quote" is *de facto* a transition from between the appropriate quote and the allusion. Not referring, in this study, to this concept let us adopt the criteria that can help to define (if it is possible) what the allusion is:

(1) occurrence of verbal connection between the text examined in the NT and the OT; if this connection is not strong enough to consider it as a citation (in the light of the criteria outlined earlier) then it can be determined as an allusion;

(2) occurrence of semantic dependence between the NT and the OT, in terms of fragments in which the content of OT and NT is clearly convergent; although it is difficult to determine from which version of the OT the fragment of the NT was taken;

(3) occurrence of a relation between a fragment, aspiring to be regarded as an allusion, and a more extensive part of the OT text associated with a description of a particular character, rather than one specific fragment of the OT.[73]

The Problem of Paul's Allegories and Typologies

Allegories sometimes occur in the rabbinic literature. Two probably best known allegories are the allegorical interpretation of the dream of the chief cup-bearer of the Pharaoh's court and the interpretation of the Song of Songs. The content of the dream is presented in Gen 40:9–11: "In my dream, there was a vine in front of me. On the vine there were three branches. As it budded, its blossoms opened and its clusters ripened into grapes. Now Pharaoh's cup was in my hand, so I took the grapes, squeezed them into his cup, and put the cup in Pharaoh's hand." In the allegorical interpretation of the rabbis, the vine is Israel, while its three branches are Moses, Aaron and Miriam. The Song of Songs had been often commented as an allegory of Go—the Bridegroom, and Israel—the Bride.

However, Paul's allegorical exegesis seems to have more in common with Philo's Alexandrian school than with the allegorical method used by the rabbis. Certain important theological themes had become a subject of allegorical exegesis by both Philo and Paul. These include the creation, the deeds of the Patriarchs, and the exodus. However, during a more profound analysis, it turns out that the interpretational similarities are formal rather than real. Paul regards these themes as a part of the history of redemption, culminating in Christ; Philo lacks this historical perspective.

---

73   J. Klinkowski, *Zużytkowanie Starego Testamentu w Nowym*, 37–38.

The distinction between a typology and an allegory has already been defined by J. Gehard in 1762. He wrote: "Typus consistit in factorum collatione. Allegoria occupatur non tam in factis, quam in ipsis concionibus, e quibus doctrinam utilem et reconditam depromit."[74]

A typology is based on a comparison of facts, while an allegory is based on an extraction of meaning from the gathered facts. Therefore, "an allegory is determined by use of two or more cognate figurative phrases with regard to specific elements of a fact or an event. It is important that texts which are not actually allegorical should not be treated as if they were allegorical."[75]

Paul seems to be a master of typologies. In Gal 4:29, he shows the relationship between Jews and Christians on the basis of a parallel, utilizing the relation between Isaac and Ishmael: "But just as at that time the one born by natural descent, persecuted the one born according to the Spirit, so it is now." On the basis of typology, Paul also argues in Rom 4 and Gal 3 that the faith preceded the Law; in this context he presents his understanding of the Law.[76] Also evident in Paul's writings is the typology showing Christ in reference to Isaiah's Suffering Servant of God (in Rom 15:3, he puts the words from Ps 69:9 into mouth of Christ addressing the Father). In 1 Cor 15, which is the subject of our examination in the further part of the study, a typology appears between Christ and Adam. Making use of typologies, the Apostle of the Nations sometimes utilizes relevant quotations from the OT. However, this is not always the case; there are also typologies without direct quotations.

1.2. The Phenomenon of Quoting the Old Testament in the Corpus Paulinum

The role of Old Testament quotations in the *Corpus Paulinum* cannot be effectively demonstrated if the essential reference of the Apostle of the Nations to the Bible in general is ignored. In Paul's theological beliefs, the Hebrew Bible is a holy and inspired text, and God's speech addressed to man is a redemption dialogue. The Holy Scripture has a prophetic nature because it has been given by

---

74 This passage is quoted in: L. Goppelt, *Typos. Die typologische Deutung des Alten Testaments im Neuen* (Gütersloh 1939), 8.

75 A. J. Bjørndalen, "Alegoria," in *Słownik hermeneutyki biblijnej* (eds. R. J. Coggins and J. L. Houlden; Polish ed. W. Chrostowski; trans. B. Widła; Warszawa 2005), 9.

76 The apostle proves that Abraham was justified by faith, before the circumcising; A. Tyrrell Hanson, "Cytaty ze Starego Testamentu w Nowym Testamencie," in *Słownik wiedzy biblijnej* (eds. B. M. Metzger and M. D. Coogan; Polish ed. W. Chrostowski; trans. P. Pachciarek; Warszawa 1996), 95.

God (διὰ τῶν προφητῶν αὐτοῦ; Rom 1:2), it contains divine prophecies (τὰ λόγια τοῦ θεοῦ; Rom 3:1–2) and has been written for our instruction (εἰς τὴν ἡμετέραν διδασκαλίαν ἐγράφη; Rom 15:4). Substantiating the divine inspiration of "every scripture," Paul uses the term θεόπνευστος (2 Tim 3:16). All theological concepts of the author to the communities established and visited by Paul are anchored in the OT.

Therefore, when speaking about the phenomenon of Paul's quoting of the OT, it should be, above all, kept in mind that the Apostle regards the Bible as the word of God himself. This word, however, could be interpreted incorrectly; hence the theme of tension between the "spirit" and the "letter" of the Law appears in Paul's deliberations. When discussing the phenomenon of quoting in Paul's writings, a question on the source of quotations should also be made: is it the HB, the LXX, or rather targumim or Paul's own translation? One should mention the main theological themes in which the OT quotations occur most frequently. The change of context of the quoted fragment, natural in the phenomenon of quoting, is impossible to be ignored; this includes the literary, historical and theological context. This change is connected with another one: the change of the recipient of the quoted fragment; the OT was not addressed to the Israelites anymore, but to the recipients of Paul's epistles. Even a rough presentation of all these questions will contribute to a better understanding of the phenomenon of the quoted OT in the *Corpus Paulinum*.

The OT as the Word of God

The books gathered in the collection of the Torah, the Prophets and the Writings were Holy Scriptures of the Jews. The apocryphal *Fourth Book of Ezra* explains these books are holy because they have been given directly by God. It was Ezra who, at God's request, was to dictate all ninety-four books to five scribes; twenty-four books were to be intended for all, the rest only for the chosen. "And when the forty days were ended, the Most High spoke to me, saying, 'Make public the twenty-four books that you wrote first and let the worthy and the unworthy read them; but keep the seventy that were written last, in order to give them to the wise among your people. For in them is the spring of understanding, the fountain of wisdom, and the river of knowledge'" (*4 Ezra* 14:45–47).[77] Flavius Josephus wrote on the sacred nature of the holy scriptures and, consequently, on their importance to Israelite religiosity: "we have not an

---

77 J. A. Soggin, *Introduzione all'Antico Testamento. Dalle origini alla chiusura del Canone alessandrino. Con appendici sulle iscrizioni palestinesi della prima metà del I millennio a.C. e sui reperti manoscritti dei primi secoli dopo l'esilio* (Brescia 1987⁴), 45.

innumerable multitude of books among us, disagreeing from and contradicting one another, but only twenty-two books, which contain the records of all the past times; which are justly believed to be divine, and of them five belong to Moses, which contain his laws and the traditions of the origin of mankind till his death... [Later] the prophets, who were after Moses, wrote down what was done in their times in thirteen books; the remaining four books contain hymns to God, and precepts for the conduct of human life" (*Ap* 1:8).

Such is the approach of the Apostle of the Nations to the Old Testament. Referring to the Holy Scriptures, Paul sometimes uses the terms "Law" (νόμος; e.g. 1 Cor 14:21), "Writings" (γράμματα; e.g. 2 Tim 3:15) or "the Law and the Prophets" (ὁ νόμος καὶ οἱ προφῆται; e.g. Rom 3:21); however, the most frequent term in his writings is γραφή, also translated as "the Writings." The quotation-introducing formulas alone speak volumes about Paul's approach to the Bible.[78] Paul, quoting the Bible, considers it to be the word of God, and not only in these texts, which cites the speech of God as an indirect speech (Rom 9:12, cf. Gen 25:23; Rom 9:15, cf. Exod 33:29; Rom 25, cf. Hos 2:25 and 3,1; Rom 11:4, cf. 1 Kgs 1:18) but also in those in which the words of God are conveyed by intermediaries (1 Cor 9:9, cf. Deut 25:4; Rom 15:3–9, cf. Ps 68:10 and 17:50).[79]

Phrases such as "Scripture says," "says Isaiah," "Moses says," are for the apostle—as indeed for any Jew of that time[80]—synonymous with the phrase

---

78   "The Scripture is adduced as a final authority and one divinely planned whole whose significance is bound up inseparably with the New Covenant Community of Christians"; Ellis, *Paul's Use of the Old Testament*, 25.

79   M. Nobile, "Le citazioni veterotestamentarie di Paulo," in *Atti del VII Simposio di Tarso su S. Paulo Apostolo* (ed. L. Padovese; Turchia: la Chiesa e la sua storia XVI; Roma 2002), 23.

80   The greatest respect and authority among the Jewish scriptures enjoyed the Torah, whose authorship was attributed to Moses. Moreover, the prophetic works and other books of the Hebrew Bible (the Scriptures) were regarded as sacred, and as such they served for teaching. Sanders notes: "Gli ebrei in generale credevano che i loro testi sacri fossero realmente Sacra Scrittura: Dio aveva dato loro la Legge tramite Mosè, e ad essa dovevano obbedire. I Profeti e gli altri libri (gli 'Scritti') erano anch'essi destinati alla guida e all'istruzione"; E. P. Sanders, *Il giudaismo. Fede e prassi (63 a.C.–66 d.C.)* (trans. P. Capelli and L. Santini; Brescia 1999), 64; W. Chrostowski, "Żydowskie tradycje interpretacyjne pomocą w zrozumieniu Biblii," *CT* 66 (1996): 1, 43. "The Scripture was not only Law, not only the warrant behind the orthopraxy which helped to keep Jewish identity alive, both in Palestine and, not least, in the Diaspora. It also provided the material for defense against religious foes, for reflection on human conditions, for strengthening Jewish self-confidence, for comfort under social or existential pressure"; L. Hartman, "'Guiding the Knowing Vessel of your Heart': On

"God says."[81] In two fragments of Paul, the Holy Scripture itself is being impersonated: "for the Scripture says to Pharaoh: I raised you up for this very purpose, that I might display my power in you and that my name might be proclaimed in all the earth" (Rom 9:17) and "The Scripture foresaw that God would justify the Gentiles by faith, and announced the gospel in advance to Abraham: 'All nations will be blessed in you'" (Gal 3:8). The fact is that even the statements of people recorded in the pages of the HB, Paul treats as the words of God. The evidence of this approach is the introduction of such a phrase as, "the Lord says" to the quotations in which the expression does not exist. What is more, they are utterances of people, not God himself. In Rom 12:19 Paul cites a quotation from Lev 19:18 (cf. Deut 32:35): A similar case occurs in 1 Cor 14:21, where Paul introduces the quote from Isa 28:11! In the Law it is written: It is mine to avenge; I will repay—the Lord says—but: "If your enemy is hungry, feed him." In the original text there is no expression "The Lord says." A similar case occurs in 1 Cor 14:21, where Paul introduces the quote from Isa 28:11: "In the Law it is written: very well then, with foreign lips and strange tongues God will speak to his people— says the Lord." Again, the phrase "says the Lord," should be attributed to the editorial work of the author. The same procedure, Paul finally applies in 2 Cor 6:17, where there is a quotation from Isa 52.11: "Therefore, come out from them and be separate, says the Lord. Touch no unclean thing, and I will receive you." Through the inclusion, "says the Lord" (λέγει κύριος) the apostle recognizes not only the authority of Scripture, but he indirectly teaches the recipients of his letters.

The Opposition: Letter–Spirit

Two opposites, "letter" and "spirit" (γράμμα - πνεύμα) express Paul's approach to the Scriptures as well as the opposition "letter" and "Law" (γράμμα - νόμος), to which the apostle refers many times. The term γράμμα does not stand in Paul par excellence for the alphabetic characters, but must be understood in a legalistic sense; γράμμα becomes for Paul, who was educated in Pharisaic School, the byword for the precept of the Law (νόμος). Both νόμος, and γραφή means for the Apostle of the Nations the revealed will of God. But we should not understand the law (νόμος) only as a legalistic system, which is devoid of the

---

Bible Usage and Jewish Identity in Alexandrian Judaism," in *The New Testament and Hellenistic Judaism* (eds. P. Borgen and S. Giversen; Peabody 1997), 19; see also: A. J. Heschel, "Mitologia Żydów," in *Judaizm* (ed. M. Dziwisz; trans. K. Stark; Kraków 1990), 135.

81   Ellis, *Paul's Use of the Old Testament*, 23.

Spirit (πνεῦμα) and becomes a mere "letter" (γράμμα). Let is look at a few statements of the Apostle, who returns to the opposition "letter" and "spirit" and sometimes "letter" and "Law":

> Rom 2:27: "The one who is not circumcised physically and yet obeys the law will condemn you who, even though you have the written code and circumcision, are a lawbreaker";

> Rom 2:29: "and circumcision is circumcision of heart, by the Spirit, not by the written code";

> Rom 7:6: "But now, by dying to what once bound us, we have been released from the law so that we serve in the new way of the Spirit, and not in the old way of the written code";

> 2 Cor 3:6: "He has made us competent as ministers of a new covenant—not of the letter but of the Spirit; for the letter kills, but the Spirit gives life";

> 2 Cor 3:7–8a: "if the ministry that brought death, which was engraved in letters on stone, came with glory, so that the Israelites could not look steadily at the face of Moses because of its glory, fading though it was, will not the ministry of the Spirit be even more glorious."

The Law becomes just a simple letter if it is understood in a legalistic sense and interpreted without the enlightenment of the Holy Spirit. This can be said not only with regard to the Law, but also with regard to the entire Scriptures. Observation of the Law has almost become an end in itself, but does not lead to the discovery and experience of God's grace. Due to an incorrect interpretation, the word of God can become ineffective (compare Matt 5:6). Proper understanding of the Scripture is impossible without the Holy Spirit (1 Cor 2:2; 2 Cor 3:14). Because of this state of affairs, it is understandable that Paul reaches in his epistolary activity for numerous citations from the OT. He interprets them while enlightened by the Holy Spirit and he does not treat the quotations as merely the "letter" of law.

The Source of the OT Quotations in Corpus Paulinum

As a Jew from the Pharisee provenance, Paul was educated based on the Gamaliel formation school, in which he studied the scriptures in their original language, namely, Hebrew. He probably mainly spoke Aramaic in daily life but was well familiar with the synagogal paraphrases of the Hebrew Scriptures, which were referred to as targums.

The issue of the source of the OT quotations in the writings of Paul does not have to be given extensive consideration here because it was presented in the part of the work that was dedicated to the congruence of the quotations with the original text. Paul, in the majority of cases, follows the LXX,[82] contrary to the MT.[83] There are only a few instances where the Apostle accepts the HB text contrary to LXX, while in almost forty quotations, Paul's version differs from both the HB and the LXX. The extensive use of the LXX is understandable; the Apostle wanted to use the translation that was approved at the time in the Hellenistic Diaspora of the Jews.[84] It should also be noted that even in places where the LXX is congruent with the MT in terms of words; a translation is always an interpretation. This is because every translation of the Bible text involves its transfer into a new cultural circle.[85] Paul fundamentally follows the LXX, not only in terms of quotations, but also in his Old Testament references which reflect the language of the LXX (Rom 4:4.5.13.19; 7:8.10.11; 8:32; 1 Cor 10:6.9.10; 2 Cor 3:3.7–11.13.16.18; 4:4.6; and Gal 4:22–23.24).[86] The fact that the Apostle to the Nations uses the Greek text of the Bible does not mean, as it has already been mentioned, that this concerns only one version of the LXX. The Pauline quotations seem to be taken from different reviews of the LXX and sometimes are similar to other Greek translations. It should also not be excluded—which has already been mentioned previously—that quotations can come from targums or were recalled from memory.

The Recipients of the OT Quotations in Corpus Paulinum

Contemporary studies on the phenomenon of citations give more appreciation to the role of the recipients.[87] The Pauline letters prove that the Apostle to the

---

82   Söding, *Das Wort vom Kreuz*, 223; Koch, *Die Schrift als Zeuge des Evangeliums*, 57.

83   The most vivid examples of quotations from the LXX, against MT, is Gal 3:17 (Ex 14:40); 1 Cor 10 (Num 25:9); 1 Cor 2.16 (Isa 40:13). Michel O. has already noticed that; *Paulus und seine Bibel* (Darmstadt 1972²), 68.

84   Swete, *Introduction*, 392.

85   C. Dohmen and G. Stemberger, *Hermeneutyka Biblii Żydowskiej i Starego Testamentu* (trans. M. Szczepaniak; Myśl Teologiczna; Kraków 2008), 73–74; Chrostowski, "Żydowskie tradycje interpretacyjne," 46.

86   C. D. Stanley stresses the impact of the LXX into the Letters of Paul: "Paul's manner of expression was also heavily molded by the vocabulary, diction, idioms, and thought-forms of the Greek translation of the Jewish Scriptures"; Stanley, *Arguing with Scripture*, 52.

87   We should mention about studies presented in the introduction as a result of the analysis of such scholars as: G. Lane-Mercier, D. Leith, G. Myerson, S. E. Porter, C. D. Stanley, A. Wierzbicka, H. Clark, R. Gerrig, and J. L. Austin.

Nations sees direct quotations of the OT, as well as all other forms of reference to the Bible, as effective instruments for convincing the recipients of his correspondence of the views and teachings he preached. This means adopting the assumption that the recipients of the Pauline letters not only accept the authority of the OT but are also familiar with it to such an extent that they can appreciate the strength of the argumentation of the fragments that were recalled thereby. Paul seems to assume that the addressees of his correspondence are capable of recalling the original context of the texts he invokes. This familiarity may come from Paul's teachings in given communities, from the teachings of teachers other than Paul, or from private studies of given members of the community.[88] But can this premise of Paul be accepted without any reservations? Were the recipients of his letters indeed familiar with the OT and were they well founded in this knowledge to the extent that they could, with full comprehension (or at least such that was in line with the intentions of the Apostle to the Nations), appreciate the value of the cited quotations? Unfortunately, there is no external evidence that would provide conclusive answers to these questions. All that remains, therefore, is to take into account the internal evidence present in *Corpus Paulinum* in order to verify these assumptions.[89]

It is usually accepted without a shadow of a doubt that the recipients of Paul's letters accept the authority of the Bible as a source of the truth because they are guided by the conviction of the Divine source of the Holy Scriptures. At least this is the image that is shaped by Paul in his writings that not only refers to the OT as an authoritative text but also requires the same from the recipients of his letters. Apart from that, Paul's opponents also refer to the OT. In this perspective, it is clear that the Biblical arguments were, at the times of the Apostle to the Nations, effective instruments in the art of convincing. However,

---

88 C. D. Stanley claims: "Paul's firs-century addressees must have been reasonably familiar with the text of the Jewish Scriptures, whether from Paul's earlier teaching or their own study, since Paul would not have made impossible demands upon his audience"; Stanley, *Arguing with Scripture*, 38. Even further in this discussion goes on R. B. Hays, who distinguishes between the first recipients of Paul's letters and later recipients, so Christians, who read NT that includes those letters; Hays, *Echos of Scripture*, 29.

89 Research in this matter, confined to the Romans were led by R. Wagner, who came to the conclusion that: "there is no way to be certain that the theoretical construct of the ideal hearer actually represents any of the first real empirical hearers of the letter"; R. Wagner, *Heralds of the Good News: Isaiah and Paul 'in Concert' in the Letter to the Romans* (NovTSup 101; Leiden 2002), 35. The author concludes that Paul assumed that the Romans would read his letter, holding it in one hand, and in the other one, the LXX; ibid., 39.

following this line of thought further, it should be stated that if the opponents of Paul used Biblical argumentation and their teaching was rejected by the followers of Paul, who also referred to the Bible, it means that scriptural arguments were not definitive. Among the Christians of pagan descent it was probably the case that prior to accepting faith in Christ they had very little awareness of the Bible. Earlier, they could have had a similar esteem for the writings of Homer.[90] Nevertheless, it goes without doubt that the OT became a normative book in many areas of life of the arising Church. Its authority must have been accepted even among Christians of pagan descent, although probably to a somewhat smaller degree and with a smaller awareness than among Christians from Judaic communities.[91]

But can this premise of Paul be accepted without any reservations? Were the recipients of his letters indeed familiar with the OT and were they well founded in this knowledge to the extent that they could, with full comprehension (or at least such that was in line with the intentions of the Apostle to the Nations), appreciate the value of the cited quotations? Unfortunately, there is no external evidence that would provide conclusive answers to these questions. All that remains, therefore, is to take into account the internal evidence present in *Corpus Paulinum* in order to verify these assumptions.[92] Secondly, the LXX in the form that we know today was disseminated after the codes were found (towards the end of the first century after Christ). Earlier, only scrolls and collections of given books were available, which themselves were often incomplete. To this day, we cannot specify exactly when given scrolls were put together to form books.[93] Apart from this, books were incredibly expensive; many affluent Jews or Christians could only afford to buy one scroll of the Scriptures.[94] The probability, therefore, that every one of the recipients of Paul's letters had direct access to all the books comprising the LXX (or at least those cited by Paul) is incredibly small. The same concerns Paul himself. Researchers have shown that the Apostle did not possess one single collection of the OT books on the basis of which he would cite because their comparative analysis

---

90   An interesting comparative study on the recognition of Homer by the Hellenistic world
      and authority of the Bible by the Christian communities presented C. D. Stanley, "Paul
      and Homer: Greco-Roman Citation Practice in the First-Century CE," *NT* 32 (1990):
      48–56.

91   Stanley, *Arguing with Scripture*, 40.

92   A. Millard, *Reading and Writing in the Time of Jesus* (Biblical Seminar 69; Sheffield
      2000), 164–165.

93   Stanley, *Paul and the Language of Scripture*, 41–51.

94   W. Harris, *Ancient Literacy* (Cambridge 1989), 193.

has shown that they come from different types of text.[95] There is a probability, however, that the leaders of local communes had all the books of the LXX or the HB in their possession and could lend them to the Apostle when he was writing his letters; this possibility, however, has in no way been proven in Paul's correspondence. It is equally feasible that Paul, similarly to many ancient writers, would make a note of the most significant fragments of the Bible and learn them by heart.[96]

The existence of the phenomenon of quoting the OT in *Corpus Paulinum* also indirectly assumes that the recipients of Paul's letters devoted themselves to Bible studies, and not only while reading his correspondence. The time they spent reading would be their only chance of gaining a deeper insight into the nature and characteristics of the sources from which the quotes were derived. Paul himself also assumed that his readers were familiar with the context of the OT (Rom 4:9–22; 9:10–13; 11:1–4; Gal 3:6–9; 4:21–31). To what extent that knowledge was, is difficult to say. Additionally, the small amount of Bible scrolls that ordinary Christians had access to should be taken into consideration, as well as the widespread illiteracy at the time. It is presently accepted that in the first century after Christ, only 10–20 percent of the population was familiar with the art of writing, and even less with the art of reading. Research has revealed that even some scribes could not read despite being involved in copying Sacred Scriptures and copying given letters, the meaning of which they were often unfamiliar with.[97] Thus, in Paul's communities only a small amount of Christians could study the Holy Scriptures independently.[98] These findings are of great significance for studies on the phenomenon of citing the OT in the

---

95   Koch, *Die Schrift als Zeuge des Evangeliums*, 48–57. Besides, the apostle often struggled with financial problems and lost their belongings in the shipwrecks.

96   This type of note-taking method has been authenticated case of Socrates, Aristotle, Cicero, Pliny the Elder, Seneca, Plutarch; H. Y. Gamble, *Books and Readers in the Early Church: A History of Early Christian Texts* (New Haven 1995), 50–53.

97   Harris, *Ancient Literacy*, 328–330. Gamble expresses his opinion in these words: "not only the writing of Christian literature, but also the ability to read, criticize and interpret it belonged to a small number of Christians in the first several centuries, ordinarily not more than about 10 percent in any given setting, and perhaps fewer in the many small and provincial congregations that were characteristic of early Christianity"; Gamble, *Books and Readers in the Early Church*, 5–6. The degree of the illiteracy was greater in the population of women than amongst men; S. G. Cole, "Could Greek Women Read and Write?," in *Reflections of Women in Antiquity* (ed. H. P. Foley; New York 1981), 219–245.

98   P. J. J. Botha, "The Verbal Art of Pauline Letters: Rhetoric, Performance and Practice," in *Rhetoric and the New Testament: Essays from 1992 Heidelberg Conference* (eds. S. E. Porter and T. H. Olbricht; JSNTSup 90; Sheffield 1993), 409–428.

letters of Paul. The recipients of these letters were to a greater extent Christians of pagan descent and therefore unfamiliar with the OT prior to their baptism; but even among the few that entered the Church and were of Jewish descent, only a very small number of them were able to read and interpret the HB or LXX. Knowledge of the Bible was, therefore, acquired largely through verbal teaching. At this point, it is worth noticing the significance of ancient mnemotechniques. However, even with the extensive use of such techniques it is difficult to assume that pagans, prior to their acceptance of Christian faith, would memorize fragments of Jewish sacred texts.

With this state of things, it is only natural that if Paul does not explicitly state in his letters that a given fragment is a quote (e.g. by an introductory remark or by providing the source text), the recipients of the letters (which were usually publicly read out loud) were not only incapable of recognizing the quotation, but also could not identify its source or appreciate the value of the given argumentation. It was probably easier for them to catch allusions, typologies or allegories based on the books of the OT. Educated Christians of Jewish descent were probably the most skilled in detecting quotations from the OT in Paul's correspondence.[99] Therefore, did Paul really expect that his recipients would be capable of recognizing cited fragments and interpreting them properly? The response to this question is based largely on presumptions. It is assumed that at least in certain communities, the Holy Scriptures were studied cyclically so that the Christians of pagan descent would in this way become familiarized with the history of salvation. It is also assumed that Paul did not expect everyone to immediately grasp and understand the cited fragments. He himself had no problem with this because of his Scripture-based education; it was easy for him to think in categories of the Bible, to reach for Biblical images, metaphors and allusions. This was something very evident and natural to him but he was aware that this was not the case for Christians of pagan descent. This is why it is also presumed that the Apostle directed his letters to the educated elite of given communities so that they could then convey their content to the remaining members of the local churches. It is also thought that despite the fact that the majority of Christians would be incapable of identifying the OT quotations easily in Paul's correspondence; the Apostle used them with careful consideration in order to educate the faithful about the authority of the Bible. All these assumptions are, to a large extent, probable but still remain insufficiently documented.

---

99 Stanley, *Arguing with Scripture*, 47–48. The author adds: "In any event, the idea that Paul expected his Gentile audiences to recognize and appreciate his many allusions and other unmarked references to the Jewish Scriptures appears to be mistaken"; ibid., 48.

Seeing that the OT citations in 1 Cor 15:12–58 are the objects of consideration in this work, it is pertinent to ask about the capacity of the inhabitants of the community of Corinth. This will help us grasp and understand the said quotes. The answer, once again, can only be found based on internal findings, mainly from 1–2 Corinthians and from the Acts, because there is no external evidence that would reveal the condition of the religious and "theological" awareness of the education of the Christians living at the time. There are three persons at the foundations of the community of Corinth: Paul, Priscilla and Aquila. All three met in Corinth in approximately 51: "After this Paul left Athens and went to Corinth, where he met a Jew called Aquila whose family came from Pontus. He and his wife Priscilla had recently left Italy because an edict of Claudius had expelled all the Jews from Rome." It is not known whether the couple were already Christians at the time or whether they were converted after their encounter with Paul.[100] For the purpose of our deliberations, what is important is that Judeo-Christians are at the start of the community in Corinth and they certainly knew the OT. Thesis why it was easier for them to grasp Old Testament citations entailed in Paul's texts. This not only concerns Aquila (it is not known whether his wife Priscilla was Jewish). Paul quickly began preaching the Gospel in Corinth—as was his custom—from the synagogue. However, he soon came into conflict with the Jewish community: "When they [Jews] turned against him and started to insult him, he took his cloak and shook it out in front of them: 'Your blood be on your own heads; from now on I will go to the gentiles with a clear conscience'" (Acts 18:6). That was also when Paul moved out of the house of Priscilla and Aquila where he stayed when in Corinth, and transferred to a man named Justus, of pagan descent. He belonged to the group of "God fearing men," sympathized with Judaism and became a believer of monotheism. His house stood near the synagogue. Luke mentions that Paul in his synagogal teaching proved to the Jews that Jesus is the Messiah (Acts 18:5). His teaching reached the president of the synagogue, Crispus, who accepted the Christian faith with his entire household. He was baptized by Paul himself (1 Cor 1:14).

Although Luke does not fully present the content of Paul's teaching about the Messianic mission of Jesus, it seems that its fundamental outline can be traced by parallel texts, assuming that the Apostle used a similar method of argumentation. An example of such a disquisition is the preaching in Antioch in Pisidia (Acts 13:16–47). What is of significance to us are the OT quotes in the preaching (Exod 6:6; 12:51; Deut 7:1; 1 Sam 13:14; 16:12; Ps 89:21; Isa 44:28;

---

100   K. Romaniuk favors the second possibility; id., *Uczniowie i współpracownicy Pawła* (Warszawa 1993), 10–11.

Ps 2:7; Isa 55:3; Ps 16:10; 1 Kgs 2:10; Hagg 1:5; Isa 49:6). The great abundance of cited texts in this relatively short lapse of preaching shows that Paul used Biblical arguments extensively in his argumentation. The Apostle preached the Good News for eighteen months while he stayed in the home of Crispus. It is completely justified to accept the premise that during these eighteen months the Apostle to the Nations had to refer to the Sacred Texts of his nation on many occasions. It is not known, however, how often he made such references and what their nature was. It is also justified to acknowledge that Paul, in his later correspondence with the Corinthians, could have referred to his own teaching preached during his physical presence in the community.

This is what constituted the very beginnings of the Corinthian church. What is already known is that several Jews who were well familiar with the HB stood at the foundation of the community. Taking the topic further, it can be assumed that Christians of pagan descent also quickly became familiar with the Sacred Scriptures of Judaism although the scale, depth and breadth of this knowledge are not known. This assumption is based on the tension that started to appear between the Christian community and the Jewish community in Corinth.[101] It is understandable that tension between the two sides of a dispute must give rise to the desire to become familiar with the reasons of the other side, hence—at least to a minimal extent—the familiarization of Christians of pagan descent with the Jewish writings. Also, it was Christians of pagan descent that formed the basic core of the community in Corinth (1 Cor 6:11; 8:7; 12:2).

Not much else is known about the possibility of Corinthian Christians studying Jewish writings from the correspondence between Paul and the members of this community. As mentioned above, Paul's reference to the OT assumed that at least some of the Christians in Corinth were somewhat familiar with the OT and/or constituted part of Paul's rhetoric. It is known that the Apostle sent at least four letters to Corinth: the first (non-canonical) letter to the Christians; then 1 Cor, namely, the first canonical letter; then the so-called "letter of tears"; and finally 2 Cor. Seeing that the object of these analyses are fragments of 1 Cor, the only letter that Paul sent to Corinth earlier was his first

---

101 The intensification of these tensions was caused by the fact that the Jews brought an action at law, which they aimed against Christians, when a newly appointed consul of Achaia, Gallo appeared in Corinth. Followers of Christ were accused of introducing a new religion without the permission of the state authorities. Proconsul recognized the whole problem as a conflict within the Jews: "If the point was about a crime or some bad act, I would attend to a matter of you, the Jews, properly, but when the dispute is about words and meanings, and about your own law; consider it yourselves! I do not want to be a judge in these matters" (Acts 18:14–15). Therefore, he sent off the Jews delegation with nothing.

non-canonical letter. The reason for writing this letter was the immoral behavior of Corinthians. The fragment in 1 Cor 5:9 testifies to this: "In my letter, I wrote to you that you should have nothing to do with people living immoral lives."

The letter must have been written after Paul's departure from Corinth, most probably in Ephesus.[102] Nothing else is known about the content of the letter which is why it cannot be groundlessly assumed that the Apostle included some sort of significant teaching in terms of its value or the OT content for the Christian churches.

A somewhat different topic in the light of certain fragments in 1 Cor is the issue of familiarity of certain passages and episodes from the OT among the inhabitants of the community in Corinth. It seems completely logical to adopt the thesis that if the Apostle refers to some sort of episode or passage in 1 Cor from the OT, he assumes at least a partial familiarity with the text by his readers. This assumption is based on Luke's statement about the eighteen-month teaching of Paul during his stay in the city. These reflections accept such an assumption unless analyses of given fragments will reveal something contrary. An example of this is 1 Cor 10:1–10. In this passage, the Apostle refers to several episodes connected with the departure of the Israelites from Egypt and assumes that his readers are familiar with these episodes. Here, he refers to the passage through the Red Sea, the cloud above the wandering Israelites, the spiritual food and drink (drawing water from the rock and the mysterious manna) and the "pillar" accompanying the travellers; he spoke of those that died on the desert, he mentions the golden calf, the debauchery of the Moabite women, the serpent elevated on the desert, and the rebellion of Corah. This is the very reason why he does not need to explain these episodes.[103] Careful reading of 1 Cor also reveals a certain number of other fragments in which Paul seems to accept *a priori* some degree of familiarity with the OT by his readers. In several fragments, the Apostle refers to the story of origins described in Genesis, assuming that the Corinthians were to some extent familiar with it: God created everything that exists (1 Cor 8:6; 11:12); the first man, Adam, was created from the dust (1 Cor 15:21–22). The Apostle assumes also that the readers of his correspondence are familiar with certain commandments of the

---

102　M. Rosik, *Pierwszy List do Koryntian. Wstęp, przekład z oryginału, komentarz* (NKB 7; Częstochowa 2009), 44–45.

103　C. D. Stanley argues: "Paul simply assumes that the Corinthians are familiar with stories to which He refers; if they had never heard of the exodus story, his brief allusions would have made no sense"; Stanley, *Arguing with Scripture*, 76. The same is true for 2 Cor 11:3, where Paul refers to the story of Eve, who was deceived. If the Corinthians had never heard of Eve, they could have not properly understood Paul's argument.

Torah; this mainly concerns the legal regulations concerning the celebrations of the Passover (making offerings of a Paschal Lamb, removing all leaven from houses, eating unleavened bread), the prohibition of marrying the wife of one's father (1 Cor 5:1), and about women's behaviour at assemblies (1 Cor 14:34). Paul seems to think that the Corinthians are also familiar with some ideas that are rooted in the Bible, such as the "Lord's Day," circumcision and observing the commandments (1 Cor 7:18), the consumption of food from the altar by the priests (1 Cor 8:13) and certain moral principles.

The OT Citations in Fundamental Topics of Pauline Theology

In the letters of Paul, fragments that have been acknowledged as authentic citations from the OT can be found in Romans, 1–2 Corinthians and Galatians and in Deutero-Pauline letters in Ephesians and 1–2 Timothy.[104] They are spread out with uneven intensity and sometimes appear in great abundance in relatively small passages (e.g. Gal 3). In 1 Corinthians there are approximately 17 citations, in 2 Corinthians there are 11 at the most, whereas in the relatively short Galatians—there are as many as 10 quotations. Paul most readily refers to Isaiah (approximately 28 times), a little less frequently to the Psalms (approximately 20 times), Deuteronomy (15 times), Genesis (15 times) and the Minor Prophets (8 times). Paul quotes passages derived from Exodus, Numbers, Proverbs, 1 Kings, and Job the least.[105]

The theology of Paul's letters is incredibly rich and discusses almost all of the dimensions of Christian teaching. J. Gnilka lists the following domains mentioned by Paul that can be found: Christology, theology of the apostolate, anthropology, soteriology, ecclesiology, sacramentology, and pneumatology.[106] However, J. Dunn presents the theological topics of Paul's letters in a somewhat different manner. His discussion refers to the following topics: God and humanity, the Gospel of Jesus Christ, the beginnings of salvation, the process of salvation, the Church, and the life of believers.[107] The work that was published in 2008 in Poland concerning the theological aspects in the letters of Paul includes the image of God the Father, Christology, pneumatology, ecclesiology, anthropology, eschatology, and ethical

---

104 M. Silva claims that in Paul's letters acknowledged as the authentic ones there are 107 quotes from the OT; M. Silva, "Old Testament in Paul," in *Dictionary of Paul and His Letters. A Compendium of Contemporary Biblical Scholarship* (eds. G. F. Hawthorne and R. P. Martin; Dovners Grove–Leicester 1993), 631.

105 H. Hübner, "New Testament, OT Quotation in," *ABD* IV: 1097–1098.

106 J. Gnilka, *Teologia Nowego Testamentu* (trans. W. Szymona; Kraków 2002), 13–168.

107 The issues were taken from the titles of particular chapters of the book by J. D. G. Dunn, *The Theology of Paul the Apostle* (London–New York 2005[4]).

issues.[108] One can list a great many different approaches to the theology of Paul. However, this is not the purpose of the present discussion. The point is to single out those topics from different areas of theology in which the Apostle to the Nations reaches for arguments derived from the Old Testament. The following passages are among the most significant:

(1) *The election of Israel and the participation of pagans in the Kingdom of God.* Paul fundamentally accentuates that salvation has its beginning in the Chosen Nation by God, that it was to that very Nation that God entrusted the "Words of God" (Rom 3:2) and "Christ in the body" (Rom 9:4–5). Seeing that in the OT the motive of pagans entering the sphere of action of the kingdom of God belongs fundamentally to Gen and Is, Paul most readily quotes Gen 12:1–3 and Isa 65:1, as well as Deut 32:43 and Hos 2:25.

(2) *The justification by faith as a manifestation of the righteousness of God.* In discussing this topic, Paul reaches for Gen 15:6 and Gen 12:3. He bases his disquisition on the statement that Abraham was justified by faith at a time when he was still uncircumcised (Rom 4:3; Gal 3:6). Circumcision is perceived by the Apostle to the Nations as one of the "deeds of the Law," and the entire disquisition leads to the conclusion that justification does not come from fulfilling the "deeds of the Law," but from faith in Jesus Christ, Son of God. In this context, he returns several times to the statement quoted by Paul of Hab 2:4, about "the upright will live through faithfulness." The passage from Hab explicitly mentions "faithfulness," but what is important is faithfulness to God, not the "upright." This is also how this statement is explained by LXX: ὁ δὲ δίκαιος ἐκ πίστεώς μου ζήσεται. Paul, nevertheless, interprets faithfulness as an attitude of the "upright," according to the interpretational tradition that he was familiar with (thus: Aquila, Symmachus, Theodotion, *1QpHab* 7:17–8,3; Targum, *midrQoh* 3:9). In discussing the issue of justification by faith, Paul refers also to Is 28:16 and Job 3:5 (quoted after LXX). In this context, the typology of Sarah and Hagar was also extensively developed (Gal 4:21–31; cf. Isa 54:1 and Gen 21). In this eleven-verse fragment alone (Gal 3:6–16), Paul reaches for as many as seven quotations of the OT.

(3) *The departure of the Israelites out of slavery in Egypt.* The Apostle frequently returns to the motive of the Exodus, interpreting the fact of Christianity as a new Exodus (Rom 8:14–39; Gal 4–6). The departure of

---

108 *Teologia Nowego Testamentu*, III, *Listy Pawłowe, Katolickie, List do Hebrajczyków* (ed. M. Rosik; Bibliotheca Biblica; Wrocław 2008).

the Israelites, the wandering through the desert, the conclusion of the covenant on Sinai, the murmuring of the Israelites in the wilderness, the miracles of God performed throughout the forty-year stay on the desert or finally the settling in Canaan resound in Paul's thoughts as images, figures or allegories of the work of Jesus and Christian life.[109]

(4) *Elements of Deuteronomic tradition.* The Apostle assumes from Deuteronomy the theology of history in which he perceives the fulfilment of the eternal salvific plan of God. This plan was to lead to maturity in the fulfilment of the covenant by the Chosen Nation, and with time of all the other nations. This type of way of thinking is present throughout Paul's letters and returns both in direct quotations, allusions and in other forms of reference.[110]

Re-Contextualisation of the OT Quotations in Corpus Paulinum

It is completely comprehensible that the fragment used as a citation appears in a context that is different to the original context. Taking a fragment out of its original context (literary, theological and historic) and putting it in a new context may give rise (and usually does) to a shift in the emphasis in the very meaning of the quotation and its way of understanding by the recipient. In other words, the same fragment read in two different letters, and subsequently, in two different contexts, may take on a somewhat different meaning in both instances. From the point of view of contemporary methodology, the axiom is accepted that the original context and the secondary context should at least partially be identical. If, for example, a sentence comes from the sapiential reflections on life after death, it seems natural to include it as a quotation referring precisely to life after death and not in thoughts about fasting practices or laws of sacrifice. However, contemporary methodology of logical deduction does not necessarily have to explain the practice of quoting used in ancient times: this is also the case with Paul. On numerous occasions, the Apostle to the Nations, includes a citation of the OT in a context which is related to the original context. There are instances, however, and it is not that uncommon, that the re-contextualisation is so far reaching that the new context has little in common with the original context. The changes in themathic can be observed in Rom 2:24 (Isa 52:5);

---

109 Entire monograph was devoted to this subject by S. C. Keesmaat (*Paul's use of the Exodus Tradition in Romans and Galatians* [Oxford 1994]). See also: S. C. Keesmaat, "Exodus and the intertextual transformation of tradition in Romans 8,14–30," *JSNT* 54 (1994): 29–56.

110 J. M. Scott, "Paul's use of Deuteronomic Tradition," *JBL* 112 (1993): 645–665.

9:25–26 (Hos 2:23;1:10); 10:5–8 (Deut 30:12–14); 10:18 (Ps 18:5); 1 Cor 14:21 (Isa 28:11–12); 2 Cor 4:14 (Ps 116:10); Gal 3:10 (Deut 27:26).[111] Contextual changes are shown in the table below:

Corpus Paulinum	Paul's context	The OT	Original context
Rom 2:24: As it is written: **God's name is blasphemed among the Gentiles** because of you.	The need to justify the Jews.	Isa 52:5b: … For my people have been taken away for nothing, and those who rule them mock, declares the Lord. And all day long **my name is constantly blasphemed.**	Justification for slavery as a punishment for unfaithfulness.
Rom 9:25–26: As he says in Hosea: **I will call them my people who are not my people**; and I will call her my loved one who is not my loved one, and, "It will happen that in the very place where it was said to them, **You are not my people,** they will be called sons of the living God."	Israel and the justification by faith.	Hos 2:23, 1:9: I will plant her for myself in the land; I will show my love to the one I called Not my loved one. I will say to those called Not my people, **You are my people**; and they will say, You are my God. …; Then the Lord said, "Call him Lo-Ammi, for **you are not my people,** and I am not your God."	God and the unfaithfulness of the chosen people.
Rom 10:6–8: But the righteousness that is by faith says: "Do not say in your heart, '**Who will ascend into heaven?'**" (that is, to bring Christ down) "or 'Who will descend into the deep?'" (that is, to bring Christ up from the dead). But what does it say? "**The word is near you; it is in your mouth and in your heart**," that is, the word of faith we are proclaiming.	Righteousness that is by faith and righteousness that is by Law.	Deut 30:12–14: It is not up in heaven, so that you have to ask, "**Who will ascend into heaven to get it and proclaim it to us** so we may obey it?" Nor is it beyond the sea, so that you have to ask, "Who will cross the sea to get it and proclaim it to us so we may obey it?" No, the word is very near you; it is in your mouth and in your heart so you may obey it.	The value of the Law for the Israelites wandering to the Promised Land from Egypt.

---

111 C. Stanley says that in these cases, Paul completely departs from the original context: "The point is not that Paul wholly neglects the original context in these cases, but rather that he quotes verses in such a way that their relation to the source text would have been difficult, if not impossible, for a knowledgeable reader to figure out"; Stanley, *Arguing with Scripture*, 56.

Rom 10:18: But I ask: Did they not hear? Of course they did: **"Their voice has gone out into all the earth, their words to the ends of the world."**	Rejection of justification by faith by the Jews.	Ps 19:5a: **... their voice goes out into all the earth, their words to the ends of the world.**	The glory of God in the nature and in the Law.
1 Cor 14:21: **Through men of strange tongues and through the lips of foreigners I will speak to this people, but even then they will not listen to me,** says the Lord.	Rules for the use of charismata.	Isa 28:11–12: Very well then, **with foreign lips and strange tongues God will speak to this people,** to whom he said, "This is the resting place, let the weary rest"; and, "This is the place of repose"—**but they would not listen.**	Oration against the priests and false prophets.
2 Cor 4:13: It is written: "**I believed; therefore I have spoken.**" With that same spirit of faith we also believe and therefore speak, ...	Hardships and sufferings of the apostolic ministry.	Ps 116:10: **I believed; therefore I said,** "I am greatly afflicted."	Thanksgiving of a person who was saved from death.
Gal 3:10: All who rely on observing the law are under a curse, for it is written: **"Cursed is everyone who does not continue to do everything written in the Book of the Law."**	Justification by faith but the law as the source of the curse and promise.	Deut 27:26a: **Cursed is the man who does not uphold the words of this law by carrying them out....**	Blessings and curses in connection with imposing the Law on Israelites.

Indeed, the change in context is so far reaching that the authors do not hesitate in calling the phenomenon of the OT citations of Paul as a "radical rereading" of the OT text.[112] It is, therefore, understandable that those readers of Paul's letters that knew the OT (whether as Christians of Jewish descent that were familiar with the Sacred Scriptures of Judaism, or as Christians of pagan descent who, after their conversion, started studying the Holy Scriptures), could have difficulties in accepting Paul's method of argumentation with such use of quotations. If the Apostle were to assume that his readers knew the original context of the cited fragments well, he would, at times, have risked complete rejection of his method of argumentation. If, however, he decided to quote the

---

112 Wagner, *Heralds of the Good News*, 25. The author also uses other terms referring to Paul's study of OT. It is "shocking" (ibid., 82), "biased" (ibid., 185, 212), "astonishing" (ibid., 205) or even "cheeky" (ibid., 211).

topic of the context differently, this means that he probably used these quotations as a rhetorical argument rather than a substantive one. Despite being aware that few will be capable of grasping the full significance of the text, he also knew that in order to achieve rhetorical purposes, a full understanding of the cited fragment was not necessary.[113] It is for this very reason that Paul often commented the citations he included by interpreting them, thus, giving the reader of his letters the direction that the Apostle himself chose to take. In rare instances, his commentaries to given excerpts of the OT become somewhat more extensive in form (Rom 4:1–22; 9:6–13; Gal 3:6–18; 4:21–31; 1 Cor 10:1–10). Paul also uses citations from the OT when he implements rabbinical methods of exegesis (e.g. Rom 9–11; Gal 3). In order to support his own opinion, he uses fragments of the Torah, the Prophets, or Letters (e.g. Rom 11:8–10; 15:9–12). In such cases, the citations have an authenticating value of Paul's teaching, although rabbinical methods of quoting are also sometimes connected with a radical change of context.

2. 1 Cor 15:12–58—Place in the Structure of the Letter and Its Inner Structure

Some of the direct subjects of our analysis are the Old Testament quotes which were used in 1 Cor 15:12–58. The statement, that the fragment consists of a literary unit with clearly defined borders, is of great significance. These boundaries determine both the content and the literary criteria. 1 Cor 15:12–58 is a fragment of an ancient letter, and these were built based on an almost universally accepted scheme. It is therefore necessary to show first the place of our passage in 1 Cor and then show its role in its structure. For this purpose, it will be essential to test the nearest context; a separate part of a whole, to justify its isolation from a whole text. To determine a boundary line of the fragment, we will use the content criteria, which have been already mentioned (thematic or substantive criteria) and literary criteria (forms, tenses, persons, terminology, syntax, inflection, etc.). After determining the boundaries of units in 1 Cor 15:12–58, its inner structure will be decided. This will be done based on the use of the same criteria.

---

113   P. van der Horst, "Sortes: Sacred Books as Instant Oracles in Late Antiquity," in *The Use of Sacred Books in the Ancient World* (eds. L. V. Rutgers et al.; Leuven 1998), 143–173.

2.1. The Place of 1 Cor 15:12–58 in the Structure of the Letter

If you are trying to explain the basic structure of 1 Cor, you must understand the place of 1 Cor 15:12–58 in its structure and the content, and you should also realize that Paul's letters belong to a specific literary genre. The ancient epistolography had determined the layout of the composition of a letter. A successful letter should have consisted of an introductory paragraph, a main body and an appropriate ending. Introduction usually included an indication of the sender and the recipient, the address, salutation and an expression of thanks. Greetings were also placed at the end of the letter. The content of the main body depended on the reason for writing. In the case of 1 Cor, Paul applies himself to the ancient letter-writing scheme. His introduction includes address, salutation and thanksgiving (1:1–9); the ending of his letter is extensive and consists of greetings and farewells (16:19–24).

The basic structure of 1 Cor contains nine compositional themes. The author raises the most important issues through these themes, and for examples he answers the questions of recipients, admonishes them, and gives them necessary explanations and instructions. These nine themes include: divisions in the Church (1:10–2:16), status and the task of Paul and Apollo (3:1–4:21), immorality of the Corinthians (5:1–6:20), marriage and the issue of virginity (7:1–40), the issue of participation in pagan religious feasts (8:1–11:1), liturgical meetings (11:2–34), charismatic gifts (12:1–14:40), the issue of the resurrection of Christ and his followers (15:1–58) and final issues (16:1–18). After entering these themes in the ancient form of the letter, the following elements may be noticed:

(1) Introduction (1:1–9);
(2) Main body:
    1. divisions in the Church (1:10–2:16);
    2. status and the tasks of Paul and Apollo (3:1–4:21);
    3. immorality of the Corinthians (5:1–6:20);
    4. marriage and the issue of virginity (7:1–40);
    5. the issue of participation in pagan religious feasts (8:1–11:1);
    6. liturgical meetings (11:2–34);
    7. charismatic gifts (12:1–14:40);
    8. the issue of the resurrection of Christ and his followers (15:1–58);
    9. final issues (16:1–18);
(3) Ending (16:19–24).

Following the thematic motifs of the epistle after the introduction (including as mentioned before, an indication of the sender and the recipients (1:1–2), salutation and thanksgiving (1:3–9)), the place where the Apostle put the section concerning resurrection (15:12–58) should be analyzed. Thus, we will determine the context of the entire section from which we will examine the function of the OT quotations. Nevertheless, determining very precisely the limits between particular sections and their parts in these portions of the letter, which are quite significantly distant from 15:12–58, is not the most important thing in our study. For example, the question whether the section on liturgical gatherings begins in 11:1 or in 11:2 has no impact on the interpretation of the section 15:12–58, and therefore the most common scheme of 1 Cor will be shown below. However, more emphasis will be put on the substantiation of the textual limits of 15:12–58, including the content-related and literary criteria.

Paul begins with a description and criticism of the existential situation of the Corinthian community tainted with divisions and dissent. The clearly distinguished factions stress their views instead of accepting power from Christ who is Himself power and wisdom of God. This power and wisdom, as shown in the cross, is the essential message of the good news (1:10–2:16). The apostle begins this section with his appeal to unity, and then characterizes the divisions in the Corinthian community and shows their pointlessness, and finally to give thanks to God (1:10–17). The mention of preaching the gospel allows the author of the epistle to switch to the theme of apostolate. Paul does this using a particle γάρ of an adversative nature. First, he describes the essential message of the cross, which he in turn applies to the situation of the Corinthians, stating that for believers, Christ is the real power and wisdom of God (1:18–31). This is Christ—the crucified Christ, he preached in Corinth, and he preached Him not by human wisdom but by demonstration of spirit and power (2:1–5). Such activity is preaching of God's wisdom, hidden from people who reject the message of redemption. Those who are led by the Holy Spirit (2:6–16) can reveal it. Afterwards, Paul substantiates the use of the title of apostle with regard to himself, demonstrating the authenticity of his mission. Each of the preachers of the good news has a different task appointed by God (3:1–4:21). Paul begins this reasoning by stating the immaturity of the Corinthians and the characterization of his apostolic work (3:1–17), and goes on to practical instructions; differentiating between the wisdom of this world and freedom of Christians (3:18–23).

Another motif taken up by Paul concerns the servants to Christ. Each apostle is solely responsible before God for his work (4:1–13). The entire section ends with admonitions by Paul who sees himself as the father of the Corinthian community and announces his arrival to the community in such a role (4:14–21).

Another large part of the epistle is made up by admonitions that Paul addresses to the Christian inhabitants of Corinth. He essentially concentrates on three issues: incest, seeking justice before pagan courts and sexual immorality (5:1–6:20). Condemning incest, Paul first shows its outrageousness, uses a metaphor of yeast leavening the whole dough, and addresses further admonitions; in this context, a catalogue of vices appears (5:1–13). The practice of settling of legal disputes between Christians before pagan courts is reprehensible as well; in the context of this condemnation, another catalogue of vices appears (6:1–11). Sexual immorality has also been condemned, and the apostle ends the discussion of this issue with an appeal to avoid fornication (6:12–20). The question of sexual immorality gives an impulse to go on to the questions of marriage and of virginity for Christ.

The apostle discusses the role of each status in the Christian community (married couples, virgins and widows; 7:1–40). He first focuses on the state of marriage in the form of direct expressions addressed respectively to married persons, unmarried persons and widows, married nonbelievers, and finally, to people in mixed marriages (7:1–16). In the next part, Paul sets forth two principles: to follow the Lord's indication and to remain in the current marital status. The first one is applied to the circumcised and the uncircumcised, the second one—to slaves and the free (7:17–24). Finally, he goes on to discuss the question of virginity, which the apostle encourages, substantiating his standpoint by alluding to a "shortness" of time and being free from concern about the things of the world (7:25–40).

Directly after discussing the issues of marriage and virginity, Paul takes up another topic: the participation in sacrificial feasts. There are two kinds of feasts: pagan and Christian. First, the apostle gives his instructions regarding consumption of food sacrificed to idols and participation in pagan feasts (8:1–11:1); next he points out the errors which had arisen in the liturgical gatherings (11:2–34). With regard to consumption of food sacrificed to idols, one should be led by righteous conscience, love and freedom which cannot be devoid of concern about the brothers (8:1–13). Subsequently, Paul takes up a personal motif: he speaks about the rights to which he is entitled as an apostle. He states that he intentionally resigns from his right to be supported by the community, because he wants to be "all things for all people" (9:1–27). The next motif is a warning against idolatry. The apostle points out Israel's experience in this regard and warns the Corinthians against similar behaviour (10:1–13). In the next part of his reasoning, Paul speaks about the risk of idolatry in Corinth: first, he utters a general warning against idolatry, and subsequently he contrasts the pagan feasts with sharing of Body and Blood of Christ (10:14–22). The last fragment concerning pagan feasts includes a reference to righteous conscience and the principle of freedom in terms of eating food sold in the marketplace which could have been sacrificed to idols. The entire section ends with general final encouragements (10:23–11:1).

Having discussed the pagan feasts, the apostle takes up the subject of Christian feasts. Christian feasts, as Paul claims, should distinguish themselves with their prayerful character. It is in meetings of such nature that the gifts of the Holy Spirit are revealed (including the spectacular charismata) and are vividly present in the Corinthian community. The author of the epistle devotes the following issue to these charismata (12:1–14:40): the Christian meetings are a manifestation of unity in diversity. The principle of unity is that the Holy Spirit enables people to make use of various services and functions, as well as use the charismatic gifts in the community (12:1–11). In this context, Paul utilizes the metaphor of the Church as the Body of Christ, which allows him to demonstrate the principle of unity in diversity (12:12–31). One of the most beautiful and poetic fragments of the entire letter is the hymn to love—consisting of a prologue, two parallel stanzas, and an epilogue (13:1–13). Further, mu has been devoted to the gift of tongues, as well as other supernatural manifestations of the Holy Spirit (14:1–33a). The apostle references the example of other communities, pointing out what the appropriate attitude of those serving with charismata should be (14:33–40).

Paul goes on to the issues concerning resurrection after he indicates the principles of the charismata. These issues are directly connected with the subject of our study (15:1–58). The essential claim of the apostle, which has already been set forth in the beginning of his reasoning, is that the resurrection of the Christians is based on the resurrection of Christ. Rejection of the faith in Christ's resurrection makes the faith futile. Since 1 Cor 15 includes the research material of our study, we should look more carefully at the internal structure of this chapter. The essential subject matter of this chapter is the truth about Christ's resurrection. Already, the first reading of the text suggests that Paul discusses two issues: the truth about Christ's resurrection and the resurrection of those who believe in Him. Each of these issues is shown in a different aspect. While the author connects the truth of Christ's resurrection with substantiation of his own apostolic mission, the truth of the resurrection of Christians is developed towards the substantiation of the very fact of resurrection, and is therefore connected with the issue of the nature of body after it is raised from the dead. Paul begins his reasoning to confirm Christ's resurrection with the gospel he had himself preached, and in which the Corinthians persevere.[114] Referencing the motif of preaching the good news, Paul uses the technical

---

114   See 1 Cor 12:3; 2 Cor 8:1; Gal 1:11.

terms: εὐαγγελίζω and κηρύσσω. This preaching concerns the truth about Christ's resurrection and about christophanies. Pointing out the latter, Paul, in a peculiar catalogue of revelations of the Resurrected, uses the term ὤφθη in the form of *indicativus aoristi*, which suggests a single perfective action. It has been around this verb that the reasoning leading to the substantiation of Paul's apostolic activity has been built. Christ's death and resurrection had been done "according to the Scriptures" (κατὰ τὰς γραφάς), and after these events, a sequence of christophanies took place. The entire construction of verses 3–7 is an early Christian kerygmatic formula, adopted by Paul from the material of the tradition and modified to be included in the context of his discussion.[115] Christ had successively revealed himself to Cephas, the Twelve, more than five hundred brothers at once, James and all the apostles. The list ends with Paul, who describes himself as a "miscarriage" (ἐκτρῶμα) since he was the last one to whom the Resurrected had appeared.[116]

With regard to Christ's action towards him, Paul uses the same verb as other people to whom Christ had appeared; it is the form ὤφθη. However, although Paul shows himself in the sequence of christophanies, the nature of his seeing of the Resurrected was *de facto* different from with the apostles or five hundred brothers. A christophany is a revelation of resurrected Christ to His disciples in such sense that He reveals Himself in his physical body. The disciples may talk to Him, touch Him, have a meal with Him or receive instructions and admonitions. Descriptions of christophanies have been included, above all, in the Gospels (Mark 16:9–20; Matt 28:9–10; 16–20; Luke 24:1–12.13–49; John 20:1–18; 20:19–21:19). Therefore, christophanies in the strict meaning of this word would have taken place for forty days from the resurrection to the ascension.[117] However, some exegetes are inclined to speak about a christophany near Damascus for the very reason that Paul mentions his own

---

115 H. W. Hollander and G. E. van Der Hout, "The Apostle Paul Calling Himself an Abortion: 1 Cor 15,8 within the Context of 1 Cor 15,8–10," *NT* 38 (1996): 224–236; P. R. Jones, "1 Cor 15:8: Paul the Last Apostle," *TynBul* 36 (1985): 5–34; E. J. Jezierska, "Chrystologia," in *Teologia Nowego Testamentu*, III, *Listy Pawłowe, Katolickie i List do Hebrajczyków* (ed. M. Rosik; Bibliotheca Biblica; Wrocław 2008), 76.

116 J. Munck, "Paulus tanquam abortivus, 1 Cor 15:8," in *NT Essays: Studies in Memory of T.W. Manson* (ed. A. J. B. Higgins; Manchester 1959), 180–183. See also: G. W. E. Nickelsburg, "An ektrōma, Though Appointed from the Womb: Paul's Apostolic Self-Description in 1 Cor 15 and Gal 1," *HTR* 79 (1986): 198–205. However, many scholars prefer to speak about "an infant delivered by Caesarean section" rather than a "miscarriage."

117 X. Léon-Dufour, "Chrystofanie," in *Słownik teologii biblijnej* (ed. X. Léon-Dufour; trans. K. Romaniuk; Poznań–Warszawa 1973), 128.

name as a witness of a christophany.[118] Others are inclined to qualify it as a mystical vision (J. Gnilka,[119] X. Léon-Dufour, though he shows Paul's effort to qualify the vision as a christophany,[120] and J. M. Everts[121]). Paul's effort to qualify the vision as a christophany is reflected in the verbs he uses: as early as in 1 Cor 9:1, the verb ἑόρακα is used, which has also been utilized in John 21:7 and Luke 24:16.31. In 1 Cor 15:8, Paul uses the aforementioned verb ὤφθη, which is also characteristic of the confession of faith in resurrection (Luke 24:34; Acts 9:17; 13:31; 26:16). Christophanies used to be connected with recognition of the Resurrected as historical Jesus; Paul had never met historical Jesus. Nevertheless, christophanies were also connected with communicating a mission or instruction, and this is the way the apostle shows the event at the gates of Damascus: his apostolic mission is clearly anchored in this event. For this reason, many authors regard the event near Damascus, reported by Luke in Acts 9:1–9, as a description based on the model of narrations on vocation (K. Stendhal,[122] J. Gnilka,[123] C. Dietzfelbinger,[124] G. Pani[125] or R. Orłowski[126]). Galatians 1:1–17 confirms that Paul himself regards the event near Damascus as a vocation. The sender of the epistle introduces himself as "an apostle not from men, nor by human agency, but by Jesus Christ" (Gal 1:1). After the Damascene experience, Paul already considers himself an apostle: "nor did I go up to Jerusalem to see those who were apostles before me, but right away I departed to Arabia and then returned to Damascus" (Gal 1:17).[127] Throughout Paul's

---

118 H. Windisch, "Die Christophanie vor Damascus und ihre religionsgeschichtliche Parallelen," *ZNW* 31 (1932): 1–23.

119 Léon-Dufour, *Chrystofanie*, 128.

120 J. M. Everts, "Conversion and Call of Paul," in *Dictionary of Paul and His Letters. A Compendium of Contemporary Biblical Scholarship* (eds. G. F. Hawthorne and R. P. Martin; Dovners Grove–Leicester 1993), 156.

121 A. Paciorek, "Wydarzenie pod Damaszkiem w świetle nowotestamentowych wypowiedzi," in *Mów, Panie, bo sługa Twój słucha. Księga pamiątkowa dla Księdza Profesora Ryszarda Rubinkiewicza SDB w 60. rocznicę urodzin* (ed. W. Chrostowski; Warszawa 1999), 167.

122 K. Stendhal, *Paul Among News and Gentiles* (Philadelphia 1976).

123 J. Gnilka, *Paweł z Tarsu. Apostoł i świadek* (trans. W. Szymona; Kraków 2001), 51–62.

124 C. Dietzfelbinger, *Die Berufung des Paulus als Ursprung seiner Teologie* (WMANT 58; Neukirchen 1985).

125 G. Pani, "Vocazione di Paulo o conversione? La documentazione della lettera ai Galati e ai Romani," in *Il simposio di Tarso su S. Paulo Apostolo* (Roma 1993), 50–51.

126 R. Orłowski, *Łukaszowy przekaz o powołaniu Pawła. Studium literacko-teologiczne* (Bibliotheca Biblica; Wrocław 2008); Gnilka, *Paweł z Tarsu*, 53.

127 Paul is convinced that God, who revealed Himself to him, had already chosen and called him in his mother's womb (Gal 1:15). This is a clear reference to the scenes of prophetic vocations

reasoning, one can notice his emphasis on righteously calling himself an apostle by using an old Christian kerygmatic formula. He did this by stating the fact that Christ's resurrection had been done according to the Scriptures, and by recalling christophany. Where does Paul's reasoning end? Here is where the literary criteria come to aid. C. H. Albert notices that verses 1–2 and verse 11 constitute inclusions, by virtue of the use of verbs "to preach" (εὐαγγελίζω, κηρύσσω) and "to believe" (πιστεύω).[128]

Verse 12 is a beginning of a new motif, which, from the literary point of view, is emphasized by Paul using the strong phrase, "now if" (εἰ δέ).[129] The term δέ is clearly adversative here. The same verse announces a new subject of Paul's discussion; the apostle starts to argue in favour of resurrection of the believers, to counter the opinions of those who reject this belief. The author of the epistle continues the subject matter of the resurrection of believers until the end of the fifteenth chapter, highlighting its different aspects. The reasoning of the apostle can be rendered by the following logical sequence: a substantiation that rejection of the resurrection of believers leads to rejection of Christ's resurrection, and *vice versa*; an analogy between Adam and Christ; submission of everything to Christ and God; Paul's admonitions supported by his personal experience; the nature of bodies after the resurrection; the second analogy between Adam and Christ; end times; an eschatological hymn and final admonitions. Although this is a large accumulation of motifs, all of them revolve around the issue of resurrection, which the apostle looks at from various viewpoints and highlights from many aspects. In these ways, he answers the doubts of the recipients of the letter. Transitions between the motifs are based on

---

(Jer 1:5; Isa 49:1–6; Ezek 2:1). Jerome noticed a clear similarity between the event at Damascus and Jeremiah's vocation: "Et Jeremias antequam formaretur in utero et conciperetur in vulva matris suae, notus Deo sanctificatusque perhibetur" (*Ad Galatas*, PL 26, 349–350); Paciorek, "Wydarzenie pod Damaszkiem," 164.

128 C. H. Talbert, *Reading Corinthians: A Literary-Theological Commentary on 1 and 2 Corinthians* (New York 1992), 121; J. B. Lightfoot, *Notes on the Epistles of St. Paul* (Peabody 19994), 141. See also: J. Murphy-O'Connor, *"Tradition and Redaction in 1 Cor 15:3–7," CBQ* 43 (1981): 582–589; A. Gieniusz, "Najstarszy przekaz o zmartwychwstaniu: 1 Kor 15,1–11," *ZHTZ* 3 (1997): 73–81; V. Hasler, "Credo und Auferstehung in Korinth. Erwägungen zu 1 Kor 15," *TZ* 40 (1984): 12–41; R. M. Price, "Apocryphal Apparitions: 1 Cor 15:3–11 as a Post-Pauline Interpolation," *JHC* 2 (1995): 69–99; W. Radi, "Der Sinn von gnōrizō in 1 Kor 15:1," *BZ* 28 (1984): 243–245; W. Schenk, "Textlinguistische Aspekte der Strukturanalyse, dargestellt am Beispiel von 1 Kor xv. 1–11," *NTS* 23 (1977): 469–477; P. Von der Osten-Sacken, "Die Apologie des paulinischen Apostolatu in 1 Kor 15:1–11," *ZNW* 64 (1973): 245–262.

129 H. Binder, "Zum geschichtlichen Hintergrund von 1 Cor 15,12," *TZ* 46 (1990): 193; K. Usami, "How Are the Dead Rised? (1 Cor 15:35–38)," *Bib* 57 (1976): 473.

a logical line of reasoning. However, 16:1 sees a completely new subject matter, not connected with resurrection: Paul gives instructions regarding a collection for the Church in Jerusalem. The change of topic is signalized by the expression περὶ δέ ("with regard to"). It is an introduction to the discussion of the current matters of the Church. These include not only the collection for poor Christians in Jerusalem (16:1–4) but also Paul's mission plans (16:5–8), the visit of Timothy and Apollo to Corinth (16:9–12) and general encouragements to the believers (16:13–18).

Having given this information, the sender of the letter goes on to final greetings (16:19–21) and the farewell (16:22–24). Eventually, the place of 1 Cor 15:12–58 in the general scheme of the epistle is situated after pointing out the gospel of Christ's resurrection and christophanies (15:1–11), and before the final issues and conclusion of the letter (16:1–24). This scheme can be rendered as follows:

(1)   Greeting and thanksgiving prayer (1:1–9)
      1. Greeting (1:1–3)
      2. Thanksgiving prayer (1:4–9)

(2)   Divisions in the community and preaching of the gospel (1:10–2:16)
      1. Divisions in Corinth (1:10–17)
      2. Christ as God's power and wisdom (1:18–31)
      3. Paul's preaching of the crucified Christ in Corinth (2:1–5)
      4. Revelation through the Holy Spirit (2:6–16)

(3)   Statute and task of Paul and Apollo (3:1–4:21)
      1. Spiritual immaturity of the Corinthians (3:1–17)
      2. Practical instructions (3:18–23)
      3. Servants to Christ (4:1–13)
      4. Paul as the "father" of the community (4:14–21)

(4)   Immorality of the Corinthians (5:1–6:20)
      1. The sin of incest (5:1–13)
      2. Christian lawsuits before pagan courts (6:1–11)
      3. Sexual immorality (6:12–20)

(5)   The question of marriage and virginity (7:1–40)
      1. The question of marriage (7:1–16)
      2. Social status (7:17–24)
      3. The question of virginity (7:25–40)

(6)   Participation in pagan sacrificial feasts (8:1–11:1)
      1. Conscience, love and freedom (8:1–13)
      2. Rights and life of the apostle in freedom and love (9:1–27)
      3. Idolatry in Israel (10:1–13)

4. The risk of idolatry in Corinth (10:14–22)
5. Conscience, freedom and glory of God (10:23–11:1)

(7)   Liturgical gatherings (11:2–34)
       1. Women and men in a liturgical gathering (11:2–16)
       2. Lord's Supper in Corinth (11:17–34)

(8)   Gifts of the Holy Spirit (12:1–14, 40)
       1. Unity in diversity (12:1–11)
       2. The Church as the Body of Christ (12:12–31)
       3. The hymn to love (13:1–13)
       4. Meaning and principles of use of the charismata (14:1–33a)
       5. The example of other communities (14:33b–40)

(9)   The question of resurrection (15:1–58)
       1. The gospel of resurrection, preached by Paul (15:1–11)
       2. Resurrection of the dead (15:12–58)

(10)   Final issues (16:1–18)
       1. The issue of the collection for the Christians in Jerusalem (16:1–4)
       2. The journey plans of the apostle (16:5–8)
       3. The issue of the visit of Timothy and Apollo to Corinth (16:9–12)
       4. Encouragements to the believers (16:13–18)

(11)   Ending (16:19–24)
       1. Greetings (16:19–21)
       2. Farewell (16:22–24).[130]

As the scheme above shows, the fragment under consideration (1 Cor 15:12–58) has been put by Paul in the final part of the letter. It is preceded by a pericope in which the apostle testifies to the fact of Christ's resurrection, evoking the list of christophanies and bearing witness that he has himself seen the resurrected Lord (15:1–11). This pericope contains the oldest instance of the Christian creed (15:3–7). After 1 Cor 15:12–58, Paul puts only the final issues in the content of the epistle, in which he discusses the matter of collection of money for Christians in Jerusalem, mentions his journey plans, as well as the arrival of Timothy and Apollo to Corinth, and gives final encouragements to the recipients (16:1–18). Such position of 1 Cor 15:12–58 in the structure of the entire letter shows that this fragment is quite strictly connected with the preceding context (through the subject matter of resurrection), whereas there is no strict connection with the final issues constituting the following context.

---

130   Cf. H. D. Betz and M. M. Mitchell, "Corinthians, First Epistle to the," *ABD* I: 1143–1145.

2.2. The Structure of 1 Cor 15:12–58

Since we have substantiated above, on the basis of the literary and content-related criteria, that the section on resurrection begins in 15:12 and ends in 15:58, now we should distinguish the smaller units within it.[131] While performing this distinction, we will also follow the literary and content-related criteria. It has been mentioned above that Paul begins the entire fragment (15:12–58) with a strong phrase "now if" (εἰ δέ). In Paul's writings, the use of δέ in the adversative character often indicates a beginning of a new literary unit.

The apostle rejects the opinions of those who deny the resurrection, but he means the resurrection of Christ first, and then those who believe in Him. The logic of his argumentation is as follows: if Christ has not been raised, then the dead have also not been raised.[132] However, Christ has been raised from the dead, contrary to Adam, by whom the death came. In Christ, they are all raised, just as earlier in Adam they had all been subjected to the death. Resurrection will be one of the events of the last times in which Christ and God will reign over everything. The rejection of the resurrection makes it so the practice of baptism for the dead is senseless (its significance is still under the exegetes' dispute), and it is no use exposing our life to danger, which the apostle does, confessing faith in the resurrection. Therefore, Paul initially shows the consequences of the negation of the resurrection of Christ, then compiles the resurrection of Christ and the faithful, and finally, he reveals the consequences of rejecting the resurrection of all the dead. From a literary point of view, the phrase, which indicates the rejection of the resurrection and which was mentioned in this fragment as many as eight times, marks a fundamental line of the argument:

(1) "... how can some of you say that there is no resurrection of the dead?" (v. 12);

(2) "If there is no resurrection of the dead, then not even Christ has been raised" (v.13);

(3) "And if Christ has not been raised ..." (v. 14);

(4) "If in fact the dead are not raised" (v. 15);

(5) "For if the dead are not raised, then Christ has not been raised either" (v. 16);

(6) "And if Christ has not been raised ..." (v. 17);

---

131 Lightfoot, *Notes on the Epistles*, 141; M. Bachmann, "Zur Gedankenführung in 1. Kor. 15,12ff," *TZ* 34 (1978): 265–276; M. Bachmann, "Rezeption von 1. Kor 15 (V.12ff.) unter logischem und unter philologischem Aspekt," *LB* 51 (1982): 79–81.

132 A. M. Cenci, *La nostra risurrezione è una certezza! Prima e Seconda Lettera di san Paulo ai Corinzi* (Milano 1999), 76.

(7) "If the dead are not raised at all ..." (v. 29);

(8) "If the dead are not raised" (v. 32).

The phrase that negates the resurrection (of Christ or the dead) dominates from v. 32, to v. 12, and later to the end of the unit (that is to v. 58), but does not appear any further. It marks out, thus, the first wholeness of the unit in 1 Cor 15:12–58.[133] After v. 32, the first literary criterion which indicates the beginning of a new unit, is the use of ἀλλά in v. 35.[134] The meaning of the term ἀλλά is adversarial and of even greater intensity than de. in v. 12. On this basis, it can be assumed that 1 Cor 15:12–34 constitutes a separate periscope in which Paul argues for the resurrection of Christ, and the dead.[135]

After beginning a new periscope in v. 35, the apostle sets its basic theme by asking, "How are the dead raised? With what kind of body will they come?" (v. 35). Then he begins his argument on the nature of the resurrected body. First, Paul takes the images from the natural world, to show the transformation that takes place in the body in the resurrection. Afterwards, as in the previous periscope—the apostle reaches for an analogy, Adam–Christ, but now the first man is a type, not antitype of Christ. After such a depiction of the relationship, Adam–Christ and its reference to the believers, the apostle returns to the basic theme of the transformation of the body after resurrection. From the point of view based on literary criteria, and after determining the subject of the argumentation in v. 35, numerous oppositions can be seen. That is to say, you can notice the oppositions of the following terms:

(1)   come to life–die (v. 36);

(2)   heavenly–earthly (v. 40): two times;

(3)   perishable–imperishable (v. 42);

(4)   dishonour–glory (v. 43);

(5)   weakness–power (v. 43);

(6)   natural–spiritual (v. 44): two times;

(7)   the first–the last (v. 45);

(8)   spiritual–natural (v. 46);

---

133   In contrast to T. G. Bucher, who points that the unit ends in v. 20; "Die logische Argumentation in 1 Korinther 15,12–20," *Bib* 55 (1974): 465–486.

134   In contrast to: R. J. Sider, "St. Paul's Understanding of the Nature and Significance of the Resurrection in I Corinthians XV:1–19," *NovT* 19 (1977): 132–143. The author notices the limits of the unit in vv. 1–19.

135   S. Grasso, *Prima Lettera ai Corinzi* (Nuovo Testamento – Commento esegetico e spirituale; Roma 2002), 164–165; "Les v. 12–34 forment une unité littéraire aisément reconnaissable, grâce à une série d'indicesconvergents, syntaxiques, stylistiques, lexicographiques et sémantiques"; Aletti, "L'Argumentation de Paul," 63–64.

(9)   of the earth–from heaven (v. 47);
(10)   earthly–of heaven (v. 48);
(11)   earthly man–man from heaven (v. 48);
(12)   earthly man–man from heaven (v. 49);
(13)   perishable–imperishable (v. 50);
(14)   perishable–perishable (v. 53);
(15)   mortal–immortal (v. 53).

In addition to the "sharp," oppositions, that is direct, in Paul's argumentation, also "less sharp" ones are indirect or inaccurate oppositions. They seem to be as follows:

(1)   men's flesh–flesh of animals (v. 39);
(2)   men's flesh–flesh of birds and fish (v. 39);
(3)   splendour of the sun–splendour of the moon and the stars (v. 41);
(4)   a living being–spirit (v. 45);
(5)   the first–the second (v. 47).

The accumulation of so many oppositions revolves around a single theme which is the transformation of our bodies after the resurrection. This is joined with the analogy: Adam– Christ (which also constitutes a kind of antithesis of the two characters)[136] and leads to the assumption that they are all contained in one periscope. It is known from the above analysis that this begins in v. 35. Additionally, in v. 54, there are also two oppositions (perishable– imperishable, mortal–immortal). Nonetheless, they are the literal repetitions of the oppositions included in v. 53 and constitute a part of the introduction to the combined quote derived from both Isa 28:8a and Hos 13:14b. In fact, the oppositions finish alongside v. 54, but those in v. 54 are repetitions of the oppositions from v. 53, and they form wholeness with the introduction to a quotation, which in turns initiates a new subject in Pauline argumentation. It is therefore necessary to assume, that v. 53 is the last verse in the periscope relating to the transformation of bodies after the resurrection. Thus, the passage from 1 Cor 1:35–53 should be considered as a separate section of 1 Cor 15:12–58.

Owing to the fact that the oppositions in v. 54 are included in the same sentence, which is an introduction to a quotation, they cannot be separated from that sentence, and consequently, cannot be considered to remain a part of the previous argument which is also marked by oppositions (i.e. vv. 35–53). Because the oppositions included in v. 54 are the same as those in v. 53, and

---

136 C. K. Barrett, "The Significance of the Adam-Christ Typology for the Resurrection of the Dead: 1 Co 15,20–22.45–49," in *Résurrection du Christ et des chrétiens (1 Co 15)* (ed. L. De Lorenzi; SMB. Section Biblico-Oecuménique 8; Rome 1985), 99–100.

were comprised in the introduction to a combined quotation, we must conclude that by repeating the oppositions the apostle builds a bridge between the two threads: the theme of transformation of bodies in the resurrection and the issue, which is foreshadowed by OT citations. These oppositions should be considered as a connector used by Paul rather than a continuation of previous threads. Hence, the conclusions were drawn that new periscope starts in v. 54. This thesis is reinforced by the fact that v. 54, which starts with the phrase ὅταν δέ, and δέ, is adversative in its character. In the studies carried out above, it was shown that the new unit also starts in 16:1, by using περὶ δέ. Thus the fragment of 1 Cor 15:54–58 should be considered as a separate periscope. The content, which is introduced by quotations from Isa 25:8a and Hos 13:14b, consists of an eschatological hymn, that is addressed directly by God (v. 57) and the recipients as well (v. 58).

To summarize this part of our considerations, we note that in section 1 Cor 15:12–58 we can distinguish three smaller integrities, which are separate periscopes within one unit:

(1)   resurrection of the dead alike the resurrection of Christ (vv. 12–34);
(2)   resurrection of the body (vv. 35–53);
(3)   eschatological hymn and exhortation (vv. 54–58).[137]

3. Defining of the Old Testament Quotations in 1 Cor 15:12–58 in Their Immediate Context

After determining the text borders for particular unit in 1 Cor 15:12–58 and stating its internal structure, we will proceed to the determination of the direct subject of our analysis. The best way would be to extract sentences, expressions or phrases from the given fragment which should be regarded as the Old Testament quote. What is more, it would be useful to indicate their immediate (direct) context. It is understood that in order to determine the significance of a quote in the entire fragment, you would first have to define its role in the immediate context. It seems that our study has clearly shown that the fragment which constitutes 1 Cor 15:12–58 consists of three parts. Each of them deals successively with the resurrection of the dead in imitation of Christ (vv. 12–34), resurrection of the body (vv. 35–53); and eschatological issues put within the framework of hymn and linked with exhortation (vv. 54–58). To begin, it is necessary to determine, the OT quotations in each of these parts. We shall analyse sentences, phrases and expressions that "aspire" to be called quotes by a

---

137   de Boer, *Defeat of Death*, 94–95.

predetermined set of criteria. In this way, all the quotes taken from the OT will be separated in particular segments which form the structure of 1 Cor 15:12–58. Then, when the exact location of these quotations has been known, our main aim will be to determine the direct context of each of them. In the following chapters of the given paper, we will examine the meaning of each quote in its immediate context, and finally; we will identify its role and contribution to the development of theological thought.

3.1. Defining the Old Testament Quotations in 1 Cor 15:12–58

We have already mentioned above that for the purposes of analysis conducted in this paper, we have to accept, somewhat arbitrarily, certain criteria which will let us separate 1 Cor 15:12–58 from some expressions, phrases, or full sentences, which can be defined as quotes from the OT. Three factors were taken into account:

(1) The presence of the introductory formula of a quotation or other links for the literary purpose which could indicate that the following phrases or sentences are a quote;

(2) The level of verbal concordance of the Pauline text with the OT text;

(3) Intentionality of the referencing to the OT, which can be seen most clearly by examining the context of this fragment aspiring to be recognized as a quotation.

At this point, you need to make some reservations about the second criterion. The examination of verbal closeness of Pauline text with the OT text does not mean the determination of an accurate source of the possible quote. The results of the reflections mentioned above indicate that could be several sources of Pauline quotations from the OT: the Hebrew Bible, the Septuagint, targums, Christian anthologies of quotations (passed on by written or oral tradition), and passages memorized by Paul or translated *ad hoc*. The attempts to determine the precise sources for each of the quotations will be made in subsequent parts of this work, where the various texts will be analysed in detail. Now, however, we will indicate whether the compliance of the Pauline text, with the OT text (derived from any of the above-mentioned sources, although always the compliance with the HB and the LXX will be analysed in the first place) is sufficient in order to consider the given fragment as a citation.

Of course, the presence of *formula quotationis* and the verbal compliance of Pauline text with the OT text is evidence of the intent of quoting. Nevertheless, you should keep in mind that the expected quote does not always occur after introduction of a quotation's formula. Even in the context of the field of our study (1 Cor 15:12–58), the phrase "according to the Scriptures" appears twice (κατὰ τὰς γραφάς; 1 Cor 15:3–4), but is not followed by a citation. The existence of the first criterion (the presence of the *formula quotationis* or other literary links replacing it) is not enough to consider some fragment as a quote. The more important one seems to be the second criterion: the compliance of Pauline text with the given fragment of a text included in the OT. The third criterion, namely the intention of citing (which emerges from the context) should be considered as supplementary because it is impossible to consider a fragment as a quote on the basis of only one criterion. Again, in this case, the most important thing is verbal compliance of Pauline text with the OT text. It seems that the following passages of 1 Cor 15:12–58 should be analysed in terms of the above set of criteria because—as the analyses which these issues will be subjected to in a further part of the study will show—these fragments are characterized by the greatest degree of verbal compliance with the OT texts:

(1) "until he has put all his enemies under his feet" (v. 25b);
(2) "has put everything under his feet" (v. 27a);
(3) "Let us eat and drink, for tomorrow we die" (v. 32b);
(4) "The first man Adam became a living being" (v. 45b);
(5) "Death has been swallowed up in victory" (v. 54b);
(6) "Where, O death, is your victory? Where, O death, is your sting" (v. 55).

The Presence of Formula Quotationis

The first criterion indicating the presence of the presumed quote is the appearance of the *formula quotationis* or other links indicating the intention of the citation. The quotations formula occurs twice in 1 Cor 15:12–58. These are: v. 45a ("So it is written"; οὕτως καὶ γέγραπται) and in v. 54b ("then the saying that is written will come true"; τότε γενήσεται ὁ λόγος ὁ γεγραμμένος). After the first formula there is a sentence "the first man Adam became a living being" (in v. 45b), which aspires to be recognised as a quotation from Gen 2:7: "the Lord God formed the man from the dust of the ground and breathed into his nostrils the breath of life, and the man became a living being." In regards to the second criterion, the degree of the verbal closeness between 1 Cor 15:45b and Gen 2:7 concerns the sequence of four (in HB) or five (in LXX) words: "become" – "man" – ("Adam") – "being" – "living." The issue of a personal name ("Adam") will be described in a more detailed way in the part of this study devoted to analyses of a quote. However, now it is satisfactory to note that even if the name, which can be regarded as Paul's inclusion interrupting the quote is true, there is a sequence of four consecutive words that are identical to 1 Cor 15:45b and Gen 2:7. In this case, it is unnecessary to refer to the context because Paul's intention to refer to the OT can be seen in the introductory formula itself.

In conclusion, it should be noted that *formula quotationis* is located in v. 45a, and reveals the author's intent to recall the source text (the first and third criterion). Nevertheless, it may still be said that verbal agreement between v. 45b and Gen 2:7 concerns four or five words. In the clause, the level of verbal accordance is not too high, but the presence of the *formula quotationis* decides that the phrase "The first man Adam became a living being," included in 1 Cor 15:45b, can be considered as a quote.

The *formula quotationis* occurs in v. 54a for the second time. It reads, "Then the saying that is written will come true." This formula takes the form of the singular, although it is followed by a combined quotation. Therefore, it would seem that Paul, by conscious use of the editorial procedure, wanted to combine the two quotes and present them as a part of the Bible.[138] After the phrase, there are the following words: "Death has been swallowed up in victory" (v. 54b). It is possible that this fragment is a quote from Isa 25:8a that reads: "he will swallow up death forever." In the Greek text (both in the LXX, and in other Greek translations) at least three words exactly agree with Paul's words: κατεπόθη - ὁ - θάνατος. The same is true in comparison with the text of HB. Profound concordance may be indicated in Theodotion's translation, but this translation came into being later than the letter of Paul. It is not our aim to decide, in this part of our study, what is the source of this quote, but it should be stressed that verbal compliance is noticeable here. Again, although the degree of the afore mentioned verbal compliance is not too close (three words, including an article in the LXX and HB and five words in Theodotion's translation: κατεπόθη - ὁ - θάνατος - εἰς - νῖκος), the fact remains that if this compliance is accompanied by the presence of the *formula quotationis*, it indicates the existence of a quote. We may therefore, determine the phrase "Death has been swallowed up in victory" as a quotation from Isa 25:8a. Nevertheless, that is not all. The context of Paul's utterance suggests that the introductory phrase may also involve following sentences written in the form of rhetorical questions: "Where, O death, is your victory? Where, O death, is your sting?" (v. 55). In this case, the degree of verbal concordance with the source of a quotation, identified as Hos

---

138 "The introduction to the combined scriptural quotation in 1 Cor 15:54b–55, 'Then will come to be the word that is written,' prepares the audience to hear a 'word' or 'saying' (λόγος) written in the past with a scriptural authority that remains valid for the present time of the audience"; J. P. Heil, *The Rhetorical Role of Scripture in 1 Corinthians* (SiBL 15; Leiden–Boston 2005), 251.

13:14b, is much closer. The fragment of Hos 13:14b in translation from the HB reads: "Where, O death, are your plagues? Where, O grave, is your destruction?". The verbal concordance with HB refers to the five words: קָטָבְךָ אֱהִי מָוֶת דְּבָרֶיךָ אֱהִי (but in the terms קָטָבְךָ and דְּבָרֶיךָ with regard to a concordance of the possessive pronoun "your," not the entire word). Seven words are consistent with the text from LXX, they are as follows: ποῦ - σου - θάνατε - ποῦ - τὸ - κέντρον - σου. Thus, a fairly large degree of verbal concordance (especially in LXX) and the presence of the *formula quotationis* allow to qualify both rhetorical questions: "Where, O death, is your victory? Where, O death, is your sting?" as a quote coming from Hos 13:14b.

We are convinced that three quotations from the OT, were included in 1 Cor 15:12–58 in light of the first criterion (or rather its part): "The first man Adam became a living being" (v. 45b), "Death has been swallowed up in victory" (v. 54b) and "Where, O death, is your victory? Where, O death, is your sting" (v. 55).[139] It appears that v. 55 and v. 54b were joined together in the text of Pauline letter, and as a result, they form an uninterrupted argument which should be recognized as a combined citation, preceded by the introductory formula words as follows: "then the saying that is written will come true: Death has been swallowed up in victory. Where, O death, is your victory? Where, O death, is your sting?" (vv. 54b–55).

The Presence of Combined Quotations Indicating the Intent of Quoting

It was mentioned above that the first criterion to determine the presence of a quote from the OT is the presence of the *formula quotationis* or some other link that would indicate the intent of citation. The *formula quotationis* appears twice in Paul's letter. The verbal concordance of the letter with the OT text extracted three passages from the group out of six which should be considered a quotation. Some space should be now given to examine the three other criteria, remaining in the area of the first one, by asking whether apart from the *formula quotationis*, there is not another link that would indicate the presence of a quote. The first text from the other three verses would turn out a quote because it reads

---

139 The results of these studies coincide with the results presented by R. B. Terry; however, the author states (in a presented by himself table) that before a citation in v. 55, there is not the *formula quotationis*. Except for the fact that in vv. 54–55 which are a combination of two citations and the *formula quotationis*, the citation in v. 54b includes at the same time v. 55. However, in spite of the omission, in the table, the *formula quotationis* in v. 55, he notices: "It is possible to view the introduction to 15:54 as introducing both passages [that is in v. 54b and v. 55]"; R. B. Terry, *A Discourse Analysis of First Corinthians* (Linguistics 120; Arlington 1955), and in Linguistics 156.

in a full line: "For he must reign until he has put all his enemies under his feet" (v. 25). A quote from Ps 110[109]:1b (translation from HB: "until I make your enemies a footstool for your feet") may turn out the second part of the verse: "until I make your enemies a footstool for your feet." The only link that exists between the Pauline text and the fragment which may be a quote is the particle "until." Paul wrote it as ἄχρι. Some linguists refer to it as "a conjunction of an adverbial of time sentences" that is found with a relative pronoun.[140] The term ἄχρι may be a translation from Hebrew עַד, and also a synonym of ἕως[141] or the expression ἕως ἄν, which term can be found out in Ps 110[109],1b in the LXX. Therefore you cannot recognize the term ἕως as a link added by Paul, which would introduce a quotation. Instead, it should be assumed that it is a part of a possible citation. In 1 Cor 15:25 that is, there is no link that might herald a quote. A similar situation occurs in v. 27a: "has put everything under his feet." In the full, preceding and following context, the sentence has been placed in the following way: "has put everything under his feet." Now when it says that "everything" has been put under him, it is clear that this does not include God himself, who put everything under Christ. When he has done this, then the Son himself will be made subject to him who put everything under him" (vv. 26–28). Although it is known that in the original text, we deal with capital letters or minuscule punctuation, this division on the sentences of the cited fragment should be considered as the most appropriate. In addition, if you adopt such a distinguishment of sentences, then it becomes clear that the fragment which intends to be considered as a quote, is not preceded by any link. This indicates an intention of quoting because this fragment is a separate sentence. Thus, the criterion says replacing the formula quotations in this case is useless and the sentence, "has put everything under His feet" tested with the use of this criterion, may not be regarded as a quote. Nevertheless, the words immediately following it are an indication that this sentence can be a quote: "Now when it says that ..." (v. 27b). Such a statement may suggest the presence of a citation.

The third fragment should be examined on the strength of the criterion indicating the presence of a link replacing the introductory phrase, too. This link

---

140 R. Popowski, *Wielki słownik grecko-polski Nowego Testamentu. Wydanie z pełną lokalizacją greckich haseł, kluczem polsko-greckim oraz indeksem form czasownikowych* (Warszawa 1955), 88. The author also points out other places in NT where this word is used in the same syntactic function: Luke 21:24; Acts 7;18; 27;33; Rom 11:25; 1 Cor 11:26; Gal 3:19; Heb 3:13; Rev 2:25. Cf. J. H. Thayer, *Thayer's Geek-English Lexicon of the New Testament. Coded with Strong's Exhaustive Concordance of the Bible* (Peabody 1996⁴), 91.

141 Popowski, *Wielki słownik grecko-polski Nowego Testamentu*, 253; Thayer, *Thayer's Greek-English Lexicon*, 268–269.

could show the occurrence of the alleged quote in v. 32b: "Let us eat and drink, for tomorrow we die." This formulation is a subordinate sentence of the following sentence: "If the dead are not raised, let us eat and drink, for tomorrow we die." Before the sentence which could be considered a citation, there is not a link replacing the *formula quotationis*; based on the presence of this link the sentence cannot yet be regarded as a quotation. It should be analysed taking into account other criteria.

Assuming the part of our analysis mentioned above is true, you can clearly indicate that none of the three fragments aspiring to be considered a quotation from the OT (v. 25b; v. 27 and v. 32b) can be considered a quote, especially after they are found to lack a link replacing the introductory phrase. To determine whether these fragments are quotations or not, they should also be examined in terms of other criteria suggested above.

Verbal Concordance of Pauline Text with the OT Fragments

Let us pass on to the second criterion to analyse the other three texts, which we have not yet determined to be quotations (v. 25b, v. 27a and v. 32b). V. 25b reads: "until he has put all his enemies under his feet" (ἄχρι οὗ θῇ πάντας τοὺς ἐχθροὺς ὑπὸ τοὺς πόδας αὐτοῦ). From the LXX (Ps 110[109]:1b) this verse has the following joint words (sometimes occurring in a different form, but derived from the same root): θῇ - τοὺς - ἐχθροὺς - πόδας. They are therefore, exactly four words. The phrase used by Paul ὑπὸ τοὺς πόδας shows a strong phonetic similarity to the expression ὑποπόδιον from LXX. The verbal concordance with the HB is even larger and includes the following words: until – put – enemies – under – feet. In addition to verbal concordance of four (from LXX) or five (from HB) words, the intention of the citation is also indicated by the context of this passage. Starting from v. 21 1 Cor 15, Paul makes an analogy between Adam and Christ (Adam–Christ), opposing "the first man" to Christ. When Paul refers to the first human being, who appears in the pages of the OT, it seems logical to assume that quotations from the OT may appear in this context. The fragment "until he has put all his enemies under his feet," written in 1 Cor 15:25b should be thus recognized as a quote from the OT. In favour of it speaks both the verbal concordance of Pauline text with the OT (exactly with Ps 110[109]:1b) and its context.

Another part of 1 Cor 15, which should be examined to determine whether it is a quotation from the OT, is v. 27a: "For all that he threw at his feet." Its verbal concordance with Ps 8:7b should be examined. The LXX translation of the verse has the following common words (sometimes in a slightly different form): πάντα - ὑπέταξεν - τοὺς - πόδας - αὐτοῦ. The Pauline text accords with the Hebrew version in all words except one particle γάρ. The verbal concordance with the OT from the statistic's standpoint relates to five words in case of the LXX and six words in case of the HB. The particle itself is enough to say that we deal with a quote from the OT. The intention of citation can also be inferred from the context; it is still an analogy: Adam–Christ. To ensure that v. 27a is not preceded by formula quotation, or there is no other connector replacing the formula (as shown above), this passage should be considered a quotation. This confirms the use of the second criterion, and strengthens the third criterion which was adopted earlier.

Another fragment to be analyzed for verbal concordance with the OT is the call "let us eat and drink, for tomorrow we die" (v. 32b), which should be confronted with Isa 22:13. In this case, a check of verbal concordance with just one source—either LXX or the HB—would be enough. It turns out that in confrontation with the LXX, all six words of Paul's fragment exactly correspond with the LXX text: φάγωμεν καὶ πίωμεν αὔριον γὰρ ἀποθνῄσκομεν. The case is similar with the HB. Although there are five words in the HB fragment, the conjunction "and" is connected with the verb "to drink," constituting a single word: וְנִשְׁתֶּה. Due to a large degree of verbal concordance with the OT, Paul's fragment should be recognized as a quotation. The direct context (the third criterion) does not necessarily indicate the intent of quoting, but a slightly further context allows for such possibility, since Paul begins the Adam–Christ analogy in v. 21 and resumes it in v. 45.

There is no doubt that 1 Cor 15:12–58 includes at least one more fragment which could be recognized as a quotation. It is the sentence: "Bad company corrupts good morals" (v. 33b). It is not preceded by any quotation introducing formula. As for the presence of a link substituting the introductory formula, the case is the same as with v. 27. In the full preceding and following context, this sentence is as follows: "Do not be deceived! Bad company corrupts good morals. Sober up as you should, and stop sinning" (vv. 33–34a). Here we have a well-performed distinction of sentences from both majuscule and minuscule codices. A fragment intended to be recognized as a quotation is a separate sentence without a link substituting the introductory formula. Therefore, the criterion of occurrence of a link instead of an introductory formula is still not enough to recognize this fragment as a quotation. Moreover, there is no verbal concordance whatsoever, even to a negligible degree, with any OT text. On the other hand, such concordance occurs to the highest degree with a fragment of a work by Menander, a Greek author of comedies. This fragment (v. 33b) should be regarded as a quotation but not one from the OT, and thus excluded from the scope of our study.

Menander (342–293/292) was an Athenian. He received his education from Theophrastus at the Lyceum but was also Epicurus's comrade-in-arms.[142] He was an unusually prolific author; his comedies include more than one hundred titles, although not all of them were staged during his life. His works are mostly known from quotations in other works. About one thousand quotations from Menander have been preserved. He wrote in the Attic dialect, using iambic trimeter as the dialogue verse. He was considered an excellent observer of social traits of the society of his times, therefore it is no wonder that he had coined the expression that "bad company corrupts good morals" (*Thais*, 218).[143] It should be mentioned that the same sentence in a slightly altered form is found in Euripides (*Fr.* 1013), Diodorus Siculus (*Bib. hist.* 16:54,4) and Philo (*Deter.* 38).

Two more quotations occur in 1 Cor 15:12–58: one of them is indirect, the other hypothetical. They will not be the subject of our discussion either, since their source is not the OT text. The first so-called indirect quotation is found in v. 12b: "how can some of you say there is no resurrection of the dead?" (... πῶς λέγουσιν ἐν ὑμῖν τινες ὅτι ἀνάστασις νεκρῶν οὐκ ἔστιν). Here, Paul paraphrases what he knows about the erroneous teaching propagated in the Corinthian community. This indirect quotation is introduced by a formula "[they] say ... that" (λέγουσιν ... ὅτι). However, since its source is not the OT, this quotation is not an object of interest of the present analyses. The second quotation, the so-called hypothetical, has been written in v. 35: "But someone will say, 'How are the dead raised? With what kind of body will they come?'" (Ἀλλὰ ἐρεῖ τις· πῶς ἐγείρονται οἱ νεκροί ποίῳ δὲ σώματι ἔρχονται). This fragment also quotes hypothetical words which might have been uttered by the inhabitants of Corinth contemplating the issue of resurrection of the dead.[144] However, in this case the OT is not the source of quotation either, so it cannot be a subject of our analyses.

---

142 M. Borowska, "Meander i komedia nowa," in *Literatura Grecji starożytnej*, I, *Epika – liryka – dramat* (ed. H. Podbielski; Źródła i Monografie 255; Lublin 2005), 901.

143 J. Łanowski, „Menandros," in *Słownik pisarzy antycznych* (ed. A. Świderkówna; Warszawa 1982), 312–315.

144 Paul repeatedly refers to a hypothetical question, thus introducing a hypothetical quotes: "The second largest class of quotations are those that represent hypothetical speech. The hypothetical speakers range from a host at a party (10:28) to a person speaking under the influence of the spirit (12:3) to body parts such as the foot (12:15), ear (12:16), eye (12:21), and head (12:21) to a stranger entering the assembly (14:25) to an opponent of Paul's (15:35)"; Terry, *Discourse Analysis*, 157.

A Collation of the Old Testament Quotations in 1 Cor 15:12–58

To sum up the analyses conducted in the present part of this study, it should be stated that six fragments of 1 Cor 15:12–58, intended to be recognized as the OT quotations, have been examined. They were, consequently, the following sentences, phrases or expressions: "until he has put all his enemies under his feet" (v. 25b); "he has put everything in subjection under his feet" (v. 27a); "let us eat and drink, for tomorrow we die" (v. 32b); "The first man, Adam, became a living person" (v. 45b); "Death has been swallowed up in victory" (v. 54b); and "Where, O death, is your victory? Where, O death, is your sting?" (v. 55). These fragments have been analyzed for three criteria which may indicate the intent of quoting: the presence of a quotation introducing formula or another link of literary nature, which could indicate that the following phrases, expressions or sentences constitute a quotation; the extent of verbal closeness of Paul's text to the OT text; and the intentional nature of the OT reference, which can be noticed most clearly when examining the context of the fragment intended to be considered a quotation. All of the analyzed fragments have met the criteria necessary to be recognized as quotations. Apart from this, 1 Cor 15:12–28 includes one more sentence constituting a quotation (v. 33b). However, it has been quoted from a play by Greek comedy author Menander rather than from the OT. 1 Cor 15:12–58 also includes a so-called indirect quotation (v. 12b) and a hypothetical quotation (v. 35), yet neither of them is derived from the OT. Thus finally, the subject of our work and further analyses have been narrowed down to the following fragments of 1 Cor 15:12–58, which have been recognized as OT quotations:

1 Cor 15	Wording of a quotation	The OT
v. 25b	ἄχρι οὗ θῇ πάντας τοὺς ἐχθροὺς ὑπὸ τοὺς πόδας αὐτοῦ	Ps 110[109]:1b
v. 27a	πάντα γὰρ ὑπέταξεν ὑπὸ τοὺς πόδας αὐτοῦ	Ps 8:7b
v. 32b	φάγωμεν καὶ πίωμεν, αὔριον γὰρ ἀποθνῄσκομεν	Isa 22:13b
v. 45b	ἐγένετο ὁ πρῶτος ἄνθρωπος Ἀδὰμ εἰς ψυχὴν ζῶσαν	Gen 2:7b
v. 54b	κατεπόθη ὁ θάνατος εἰς νῖκος	Isa 25:8a
v. 55	ποῦ σου, θάνατε, τὸ νῖκος; ποῦ σου, θάνατε, τὸ κέντρον;	Hos 13:14b

Three of the quotations above (v. 45b, v. 54b and v. 55) are preceded by an introductory formula which only occurs twice (v. 45a and v. 54a) in 1 Cor 15:12–58. This is due to the fact that the quotations in v. 45b and in v. 55 constitute a *de facto* linked quotation in which Paul put Isa 25:8a and Hos

13:14b together. The statistic above allows for one more important observation. The author of 1 Corinthians references Isaiah twice, Psalms twice, and both Genesis and Hosea—once. Therefore, a quotation from Torah occurs once, a quotation from the Writings—twice, and from the prophetic books—three times.

3.2. Determination of the Closest Context of the Old Testament Quotations in 1 Cor 15:12–58

Having indicated which fragments of 1 Cor 15:12–58 are the OT quotations referenced by Paul in his argumentation in favor of resurrection, one should situate them in the closest context of the part of the epistle under discussion. Linguists have developed a sound rule of interpretation saying that a text can only be properly interpreted when taking its literary context into account.[145] The direct context influences the understanding of the analyzed fragment, allowing for the notice of certain nuances of particular words, phrases or entire sentences which could escape the notice of an exegete or even be interpreted improperly if the text is stripped of its direct literary context.

In the previous analyses, we have shown the position of 1 Cor 15 in the structure of the entire letter and distinguished individual literary units included in 1 Cor 15:12–58. We have shown that essentially, two main parts can be distinguished in 1 Cor 15; first, they considering the good news of Christ's resurrection, as evidenced by christophanies (vv. 1–11),[146] and the other—the resurrection of the believers (vv. 12–58). It should be kept in mind that in vv. 12–58, the following literary units can be distinguished:

1. Resurrection of the dead after the example of Christ (vv. 2–34);
2. Resurrection of bodies (vv. 35–53);
3. Eschatological hymn and admonition (vv. 54–58).

The OT quotations are found in each of these units and are distributed as follows: the first one includes three quotations: Ps 110[109]:1b, Ps 8:7b, and Isa

---

145 Some would express it as follows: "A text without a context is a pretext."

146 A. Jankowski regards this fragment as the earliest account of Christ's resurrection; *Kerygmat w Kościele apostolskim. Nowotestamentowa teologia głoszenia słowa Bożego* (Częstochowa 1989), 110. See H. Langkammer, *Obraz Jezusa Chrystusa w świetle Nowego Testamentu. Przyczynek do chrystologii analogicznej Nowego Testamentu* (Rzeszów 2009), 356–357; R. H. Fuller, „Resurrection," in *Harper's Bible Dictionary* (ed. P. J. Achtemeier; New York 1985), 864–865; H. Witczyk, "Narodziny wiary w cielesne zmartwychwstanie Jezusa z Nazaretu," *VV* 15 (1009): 215–216; J. G. Dunn, *Christianity in Making*, I, *Jesus Remembered* (Grand Rapids–Cambridge 2003), 842–844.

22:13b. Ps 8:7b includes a quotation from Gen 2:7b; and Isa 22:13b includes two quotations: one from Isa 25:8a and the other from Hos 13:14b. On the basis of literary and content-related criteria, we will now proceed to determine the internal structure of each of those units, which will allow us to determine the limits of the direct context of each quotation.

Resurrection of the Dead After the Example of Christ (vv. 12–34)

The entire unit of 1 Cor 15:12–34 is predominated by the subject matter of resurrection of the dead, which is done after the example of Christ's resurrection. First, let us deal with the issues of vocabulary to observe what terms predominate in each part of Paul's argumentation, and then (on their basis) we will proceed to a more detailed discussion of the themes used by the apostle in his reflections presented to the Corinthians. We will also refer to particular grammatical forms that will allow for the designation of the elements of internal structure of the entire fragment (regarding terminology).

Paul discusses this subject matter using specific terminology. The verb ἐγείρειν occurs 18 times in the unit out of 20 occurrences in 1 Cor. The formula "resurrection of the dead" (ἀνάστασις νεκρῶν) is present three times in the unit (v. 12, v. 13 and v. 21). The occurrence of the verb ὑποτάσσω is extremely important from the viewpoint of the analysis of quotations. This verb appears 6 times in only two verses (vv. 27–28). In v. 14, a noun κήρυγμα also occurs, and the section also contains the verb κηρύσσω with the same root (v. 11 and v. 12). In v. 22, the proper name of Adam appears, who has already been referenced earlier by Paul (in v. 21) who called him the "man" (ἄνθρωπος).[147] The terminology of reign is clearly outlined from v. 24, by use of words "to reign" (βασιλεύειν), "to hand over" (ὑποτάσσω), and "kingdom" (βασιλεία). In v. 29, the term "to baptize" (βαπτίζω) occurs for the first time in the unit. The theme of baptism (for the dead) is referenced in vv. 29–30. Since v. 31, a change of the grammatical person occurs: Paul begins a personal motif, speaking in the first person singular. Since v. 35, the term "body" (σῶμα), predominating in the unit until v. 44 (also in v. 35, vv. 37–40, v. 44), begins to occur. Since v. 44b, the proper name of Adam and the noun "man" (ἄνθρωπος) return again and the motif of the Adam–Christ analogy is continued until v. 49. From v. 50 onwards, Paul decides again to use a personal statement in grammatical first person singular. The motif of the kingdom of God appears (v. 50), shown by Paul in the final terms, which are expressed in the terminology by oppositions: "mortal"–"immortal" and "perishable"–"imperishable" (v. 53).

---

147 Cenci, *La nostra risurrezione è una certezza!*, 79.

Let us now proceed to the subject matter of the argumentation. As mentioned before (and suggested by the terminology), its subject is the resurrection of the dead, which is done after the example of Christ's resurrection. Paul develops this theme modulating individual motifs. The apostle begins the entire unit with a rhetorical question (v. 12) in which he contrasts two opinions with one another: the first one expresses the opinion of those who preach Christ's resurrection, while the other is advocated by those Corinthians who claim there is no resurrection.[148] In the following verses (vv. 13–16), Paul argues that these two opinions cannot be reconciled with each other, and when rejecting Christ's resurrection, the resurrection of the dead should be rejected as well. Continuing this motif, he shows the consequences of denying Christ's resurrection: uselessness of faith, remaining in sins and a pitiful state in which those Christians who deny Christ's resurrection remain (vv. 17–19). From v. 20, Paul radically changes the tone of the previous argumentation. He begins this phrase with the emphatic form of the pronoun νυνί, to announce Christ's resurrection in a solemn voice and an apocalyptical tone.[149] In his discussions, the author covers the history of redemption in a very wide spectrum using the Adam–Christ analogy (vv. 21–23). From v. 24, the subject of the reign of Christ appears, strongly emphasized by the terminology shown above. Paul ends this part of his argumentation with an equally solemn apocalyptic claim that the history of redemption finally heads to a situation when "God may be all in all" (v. 28).

From v. 29, a completely new subject appears, namely, the practice of baptism for the dead. From the rhetorical viewpoint, the apostle continues this motif asking three rhetorical questions (vv. 29–30). Another motif, this time of personal nature, includes Paul's reflections on the suffering he experienced while preaching the gospel (vv. 31–32a). It would make no sense whatsoever, if there was no resurrection (v. 32b). This reflection changes into a parenethic appeal to the recipients of the letter to not be deceived (v. 33), sober up and stop sinning (v. 34).

Both the terminology and individual motifs developed by Paul within the discussed theme of resurrection of the dead after the example of Christ's resurrection allow to distinguish three parts in the unit, constituting its concentric structure based on the scheme A– B–A':

---

148 C. H. Talbert, *Reading Corinthians: A Literary-Theological Commentary on 1 and 2 Corinthians* (New York 1992, 123.

149 C. Zimmer, "Das argumentum resurrectionis in 1 Kor 15:12–20," *LB* 65 (1991): 27. An answer to Zimmer's views has been expressed by M. Bachmann, "Zum 'argumentum resurrectionis' von 1 Kor. 15,12ff nach Christoph Zimmer, Augustin und Paulus," *LB* 67 (1992): 29–39. See also: T. G. Bucher, "Überlegung zur Logik im Zusammenhang mit 1 Kor 15,12–20," *LB* 53 (1983): 70–98.

A: The consequences of denial of Christ's resurrection (vv. 12–19);
B: Christ's resurrection and ours (vv. 20–28);
A': The consequences of denial of resurrection of the believers (vv. 29–34).

The OT quotations are situated in the second (B) and third (A') part of the designated structure. The second part includes two quotations (from Ps 110[109]:1b and Ps 8:7b), while the third one contains a quotation from Isa 22:13b. The second part contains two smaller, clearly distinct units. The first is marked by the Adam–Christ typology (vv. 20–22), while the other is connected with eschatological events (vv. 23–28).[150] Such division is indicated by both the terminology indicated above and a change in motifs of the argumentation: having shown the Adam–Christ typology, the Apostle of the Nations presents to the Corinthians a vision of what will happen when the "end" (τέλος; v. 24) comes. Both quotations from Psalms occur in the second part of this part of the unit, i.e. in vv. 23–28.

In the last part of the structure of 1 Cor 15:12–34 as designated above, two clearly outlined parts can be distinguished on the basis of literary and thematic criteria. The first one is designated by a double occurrence of the verb "to baptize" (βαπτίζω) in v. 29 and by the rhetoric of the fragment, since it is made of three rhetorical questions (vv. 29–30). The practice of baptism for the dead is only mentioned at this place of the NT, therefore such mention is a completely unusual motif in the entire NT theology. From v. 31, a change of tone occurs: Paul proceeds to solemn allegations that he "dies" (suffers for Christ) everyday and this would make no sense if he did not believe in resurrection. Such assertions alter, in a completely logical and natural way, into an admonition to the Corinthians that they should not be deceived by erroneous views of people who deny the resurrection (vv. 33–34). Thus, in the fragment of 1 Cor 15:29–34, two parts can be distinguished; one of them concerns the practice of baptism for the dead (vv. 29–30), the other is Paul's admonition to the Corinthians supported by his personal experience of suffering (vv. 31–34). It is the second part that contains a quotation from Isa 22:13b.

To sum up the conducted analyses, we see that the OT quotations in the fragment of 1 Cor 15:12–34 occur in smaller segments of a unit. One tells about the eschatological events (vv. 23–28), while the other is an admonition to the Corinthians, supported by Paul's personal experience of suffering (vv. 31–34). They will be the essential subject of the further examination of the role of the OT quotations in this part of Paul's letter.

---

150   J. Czerski, *Pierwszy List do Koryntian* (Bibliotheca Biblica; Wrocław 2009), 681–682.

The Resurrection of Bodies (vv. 35–53)

The second unit of 1 Cor 15:12–58 consists of vv. 35–53, in which Paul writes on the resurrection of bodies and their nature after the resurrection. Literary and content-related criteria allow us to distinguish smaller parts within a unit, designating its internal structure. Let us first look at the literary criteria, including the issues of terminology. The essential terms occurring in the entire unit are condensed in the introductory questions: "How are the dead raised? With what kind of body will they come?" (v. 35). They are mostly the terms: ἐγείρω, οἱ νεκροί, σῶμα. The latter term, "body," appears 9 times in vv. 35–44. In the first part of the argumentation, the apostle uses the terminology anchored in the world of nature. There are such nouns as "seed," "animal," "fish," "bird," "sun," "moon," "star," as well as verbs: "sow," "come to life," "die." From v. 42, the apostle bases his argumentation on oppositions, which should be considered one of his rhetorical methods. Here, adjectives and participles are opposed to each other: "perishable"–"imperishable," "in dishonor"–"in glory," "in weakness"–"in power," "natural"–"spiritual." This last pair of opposing terms (v. 44b) introduces the next part of the argumentation, in which the apostle returns to the Adam–Christ typology. Paul continues the opposition of two areas, whereas the pairs of opposing concepts are different. This time, he contrasts the terms: "of the earth"–"of heaven" and "natural"–"spiritual." Paul shows "The first Adam" as "of the earth" (χοϊκός; and literally: "made of dust"; vv. 47, 48 [2 times], 49). This corresponds to "the last Adam," shown as "of heaven" (ἐπουράνιος; vv. 48 [2 times], 49; ἐξ οὐρανοῦ; v. 47). From the viewpoint of literary criteria, it should be also noticed that in v. 50, the first person singular appears again, which often marks the beginning of the next segment of the textual structure in Paul's writings. This is also the case this time. V. 50 introduces a narration on the events of the eschatological times connected with the theme of the "kingdom of God" (βασιλεία θεοῦ). The phrase "kingdom of God" is used only once in the entire unit (v. 50), although it is what gives the tone to the last part of the argumentation, including a solemn declaration of the apostle beginning with the words: "Listen, I will tell you a mystery" (ἰδοὺ μυστήριον ὑμῖν λέγω; v. 51a). After this prophetic declaration, the apostle resumes the opposition of "perishable" and "imperishable" as well as "mortal" and "immortal" (vv. 52–53).[151]

　　From the viewpoint of content, the apostle's argumentation regarding the nature of bodies after the resurrection is conducted with a systematical change in accents. At first, Paul asks questions connected with the nature of these bodies (v. 35). Then he uses a series of comparisons taken from the world of plants and

---

151　A. C. Perriman, "Paul and the Parousia: 1 Corinthians 15.50–57 and 2 Corinthians 5.1–5," NTS 35 (1989): 514.

animals (vv. 36–41). In this context, four *hapax legomena* occur in 1 Cor: "bare," "seed," "animal," and "bird." After the comparisons are presented in such a way, Paul uses another series of comparisons: this time, these are four antitheses showing the difference between a natural and spiritual body (vv. 4–44a). All these devices (rhetorical questions, natural comparisons, antitheses) are intended to show the difference between the body before and after the resurrection, and simultaneously, they constitute an introduction to the main opposition of the argumentation: the opposition between the first man (Adam) and the last man (Christ). Having introduced the subject of the "kingdom of God," the author focuses for a moment on some eschatological events, the narration which is preceded by a prophetic formula (v. 51). In these events, Paul includes: the fact that not everyone will die; a change of everyone; the sound of a trumpet, and the rising from the dead (vv. 51–52). The conclusion of the entire argumentation is an indication of the necessity to change the perishable into the imperishable and the mortal into the immortal (v. 53).

Taking into account the literary and content-related issues indicated above, the internal structure of the unit of 1 Cor 15:35–53 can be designated. It is mainly determined by changes in terminology rouse of different literary devices such as rhetorical questions, contrasts, antitheses, typology, solemn prophetic declaration, and a change of grammatical person. The entire fragment of 1 Cor 15:35–53 can be divided into an introduction with questions (v. 35) and three parts of a concentric structure—like in the previous fragment (1 Cor 15:12–34)—based on the scheme A–B–A'. This concentric scheme is as follows:

A: Change of bodies in nature and of bodies after the resurrection
     (vv. 36–44a);
B: Typology: Adam–Christ (vv. 44b–49);
A': Change of bodies after the resurrection and the eschatological events
     (vv. 50–53).

A quotation from Gen 2:7b, written in v. 45b, is situated in the second part of this designated structure, i.e. in the section where the apostle makes a typology between Adam and Christ (vv. 44b–49). This part is the direct context of the quotation which will be the subject of our detailed analyses.

Eschatological Hymn and Admonition (vv. 54–58)

The third section of the unit of 1 Cor 15:12–58 includes only five verses (vv. 54–58) consisting of an eschatological hymn (vv. 54–57) ending with a prayer appeal directed to God through Jesus Christ (v. 57) and an admonition to the recipients of the epistle (v. 58). To determine the internal structure of this fragment, we should use the literary (especially terminology) and content-related criteria again. R. Fabris calls the terminology of these few verses "specialist."[152] This is because there are five terms here that are non-existent in 1 Cor outside this fragment: "mortal" (θνητόν), "immortality" (ἀθανασία), "victory" (νῖκος), "sting" (κέντρον), and the verb "to put on" (ἐνδύσασθαι). All of these terms (some of them repeated twice) have been included in vv. 54–57. However, v. 57 includes a direct address to God in a thanksgiving prayer; this change of tone allows to distinguish v. 57 out of the entire eschatological hymn.

From the rhetorical viewpoint, in v. 54 the apostle resumes the opposition written in the form of an antithesis between the mortal and the immortal and between the perishable and the imperishable. In v. 54b–55, there is a quotation introducing formula (strictly speaking, it is a linked quotation from Isa 25:8a and Hos 13:14b) and OT fragments quoted by Paul. The last quotation has been provided with an explanation: "The sting of death is sin, and the power of sin is the law" (v. 56). After a prayer appeal (v. 57), the apostle gives the Corinthians an admonition in the form of encouragement to be firm and engage in the "work of the Lord" (v. 58). A direct apostrophe to the recipients has the form "dear brothers," and a change in discourse has been indicated by the use of the conjunction ὥστε (v. 58a).

The terminology indicated above, and changes in the character of the argumentation (antitheses, introduction of quotations, the OT quotations, explanation of the quotation from Hos 13:14b, a prayer apostrophe to God in the form of a thanksgiving call directed "through our Lord Jesus Christ," as well as an admonition written in the form of a direct apostrophe to the recipients), allow us to determine the structure of the fragment of 1 Cor 15:54–58 as follows:

A: Antitheses supported by the OT quotations (vv. 54–56):
    a. "perishable"–"imperishable" and "mortal"–"immortal" (v. 54aα);
    b. Quotation introducing formula (v. 54aβ);
    c. Quotations from Isa 25:8a and Hos 13:14b (vv. 54b–55);
    d. An explanation of quotations (v. 56).
B: An apostrophe to God in a thanksgiving prayer (v. 57);
C: An apostrophe to the recipients (v. 58).

In such a designated structure of 1 Cor 15:54–58, the quotations from Isa 25:8a and Hos 13:14b are situated in its first segment, i.e. in vv. 54–56, where Paul continues the antitheses "perishable"–"imperishable" and "mortal"–"immortal" (introduced in vv. 52–53). Therefore, this part of vv. 54–58 is the direct context of the quotation and it will be the subject of more detailed analyses.

---

152 R. Fabris, *Prima Lettera ai Corinzi. Nuova versione, introduzione e commento* (I Libri Biblici. Nuovo Testamento 7; Torino 1999), 196.

Fragments Constituting the Closest Context of the OT Quotations in 1 Cor 15:12–58

To determine the direct context of the OT quotations in 1 Cor 15:12–58, we have previously determined the internal structure of the three essential parts of this unit: resurrection of the dead after the example of Christ (vv. 12–34); the resurrection of bodies (vv. 35–53); and eschatological hymn and admonition (vv. 54–58). The first and second parts have been built on the basis of a concentric model. In the first, three elements of the structure have been designated: consequences of denial of Christ's resurrection (vv. 12–19); Christ's and our resurrection (vv. 20–28); and consequences of denial of the resurrection of believers (vv. 29–34).[153] Out of vv. 20–28, we can select a smaller segment concerning the eschatological events (vv. 23–28), while in vv. 29–34, a segment constituting Paul's admonition to the Corinthians and connected with his personal experience (vv. 31–34) can be distinguished. Similarly, three segments of the structure are distinct in the second part: a change of bodies in nature and bodies after the resurrection (vv. 36–44a); an Adam–Christ typology (vv. 44b–49); and a change of bodies after the resurrection and eschatological events (vv. 50–53). The third part also contains three segments, although they do not constitute any concentric structure: antitheses supported by OT quotations (vv. 54–56); an apostrophe to God in a thanksgiving prayer (v. 57); and an apostrophe to the recipients (v. 58). Since, as shown above, the Old Testament quotations in 1 Cor 15:12–58 occur in v. 25b, v. 27a, v. 32b, v. 45b, v. 54b, v. 55, the fragments constituting their direct context should be analyzed in order to determine their function in this part of the epistle. These are the following four fragments: eschatological events (vv. 23–28); an admonition to the Corinthians, supported by the apostle's personal experience of suffering (vv. 31–34); an Adam–Christ typology (vv. 44b–49), and antitheses "mortality"–"immortality" and "perishability"–"imperishability," supported by quotations.

To sum up, in 1 Cor 15:12–58 there are six citations from the OT which are included in four fragments, forming their immediate context:

1 Cor 15	Wording of a quotation	Immediate context
v. 25b	ἄχρι οὗ θῇ πάντας τοὺς ἐχθροὺς ὑπὸ τοὺς πόδας αὐτοῦ	vv. 23–28
v. 27a	πάντα γὰρ ὑπέταξεν ὑπὸ τοὺς πόδας αὐτοῦ	vv. 23–28
v. 32b	φάγωμεν καὶ πίωμεν, αὔριον γὰρ ἀποθνήσκομεν	vv. 31–34

---

153 J. Lambrecht, "Paul's Christological Use of Scripture in 1 Cor. 15.20–28," *NTS* 28 (1982): 502–503.

v. 45b	ἐγένετο ὁ πρῶτος ἄνθρωπος Ἀδὰμ εἰς ψυχὴν ζῶσαν	vv. 44b–49
v. 54b	κατεπόθη ὁ θάνατος εἰς νῖκος	vv. 44b–49
v. 55	ποῦ σου, θάνατε, τὸ νῖκος; ποῦ σου, θάνατε, τὸ κέντρον;	vv. 54–56

II. Quotation from Ps 110[109]:1b in 1 Cor 15:25b

1 Cor 15:25b: ἄχρι οὗ θῇ πάντας τοὺς ἐχθροὺς ὑπὸ τοὺς πόδας αὐτοῦ

Ps 110[109]:1b (LXX): ἕως ἂν θῶ τοὺς ἐχθρούς σου ὑποπόδιον τῶν ποδῶν σου

Ps 110[109]:1b (HB): עַד־אָשִׁית אֹיְבֶיךָ הֲדֹם לְרַגְלֶיךָ

1. Source of the Quotation

In order to determine the source from which Paul took the quotation in 1 Cor 15:25b, it is necessary to indicate the differences between the LXX and the HB. A literal translation of the text from Hebrew, gives us the following sentence: "until I make your enemies a footstool for your feet." It can therefore be assumed that the text of the LXX is a literal translation from the HB, without any modification of the Hebrew text. In relation to both the LXX and the HB, Paul makes two changes: he adds the term πάντας and changes a grammatical person of the subject of a sentence from the second to the third one. The first change is probably made for the sake of rhetoric: the apostle wants to emphasize the power of God, who ultimately defeats "all" the enemies. The second change was necessary to build the quoted passage into the new context (in a grammatically correct way) in which the apostle uses the grammatical third person singular. Paul, also conveyed, a bit differently, the initial phase of the quote: the expression ἕως ἄν, referring in Psalm 110:1b[154] to God, was changed to ἄχρι οὗ, referring to Christ. Taking into account the fact that Paul usually takes quotes from the LXX, there is no sufficient evidence in this case, opting for the HB to the detriment of the LXX.[155]

---

154 From that moment, for practical reasons, we will only use sigillum of Ps 110.1b, not the extension of Ps 110[109],1b.

155 M. C. de Boer suggested that Paul may take the quotation not directly from The Bible, but from early Christian tradition; de Boer, *Defeat of Death*, 118; id., "Paul's Use of a Resurrection Tradition in 1 Cor 15,20–28," in *The Corinthian Correspondence* (ed. R. Bieringer; BETL 125; Louvain 1996), 648. This thesis, however, was rejected by most exegetes as not sufficiently supported by strong arguments.

2. The Meaning in the Original Context

The quotation ἄχρι οὗ θῇ πάντας τοὺς ἐχθροὺς ὑπὸ τοὺς πόδας αὐτοῦ comes from Ps 110:1b. The original text reads: עַד־אָשִׁית אֹיְבֶיךָ הֲדֹם לְרַגְלֶיךָ. This quote is a fragment of a sentence, which was written as follows:

> "Sit at my right hand,
> until I make your enemies
> a footstool for your feet."

That sentence was preceded by an introductory formula: "The Lord says to my Lord." The whole psalm belongs to a collection of royal psalms,[156] which in their content refer to the ritual of coronation.[157] They follow this division: 2, 21, 45, 72, 89, 101 and just Ps 110. Some authors also add the following psalms to this list: 20, 132 and 144. The vast majority of exegetes agree that Ps 110 refers to a real historical king.[158] There is no agreement; however, between exegetes if this psalm is messianic.[159] There is no doubt, that the song was interpreted by Christ and by the authors of the NT as relating to a Messiah promising deliverance. Nevertheless, it is reasonable to ask whether such was also an intent of the author of the psalm. Exegetical analysis presented in this study will not only allow us to determine the role of v. 1b in its immediate context, but will also give an answer to the question about the possible messianic character of the psalm.

---

156 H. W. Bateman IV, "Psalm 110:1 and the New Testament," *BSac* 149 (1992): 438; C. Westermann, *Praise and Lament in the Psalms* (Grand Rapids 1984), 245; T. Brzegowy, *Psalmy i inne Pisma* (Academica 10; Tarnów 1997), 138.

157 Until recently, the thesis has been maintained that this psalm celebrates the reign of David over the twelve tribes of Israel, his enthronement in Jerusalem and the establishment of the sidekick priesthood; H. H. Rowley, "Melchizedek and Zadok," in *Festschrift für Alfred Bertholet zum 80. Geburstag* (eds. W. Baumgartner et al.; Tübingen 1950), 461–472.

158 J. A. Fitzmyer, "Melchizedek in the MT, LXX and the NT," *Bib* 81 (2000): 63.

159 About the fact that the NT psalm was read by inspired writers as messianic, bespeak: Matt 22:44; 26:64; Mark 12:36; 14:62; 16:19; Luke 20:42–44; 22:69; Acts 2:34–35; Rom 8:34; 1 Cor 15:25; Eph 1:20; Col 3:1; Heb 1:3.13; 5:6; 7:17.21; 8:1; 10:12–13; 12:2. More about the messianic use Ps 110 in NT see: D. M. Hay, *Glory At the Right Hand. Psalm 110 in Early Christianity* (SBL Monograph 18; Nashville 1973). See also: S. Rinaudo, *I Salmi. Preghiera di Cristo e della Chiesa. Quinta edizione completamente rifusa secondo l'uso e l'interpretazione della liturgia rinnovata dal Vaticano II* (Torino 1999), 599; T. Callan, "Psalm 110:1 and the Origin of the Expectation That Jesus Will Come Again," *BQ* 44 (1982), 622–636.

2.1. Ideological Undertow and Literary Structure of Ps 110:1–7

There is no doubt that Ps 110 belongs to the royal psalms, probably combined with enthronement ritual[160]; nevertheless on the grounds of the Psalms themselves, we cannot fully recreate the various stages of the ritual. In this psalm, the term "king" is not used at all, but an attribute of kingship is mentioned—a sceptre. This psalm also describes the reign over enemies and this topic fits well with the theme of kingship. It reflects this part of the ritual of enthronement, in which the new ruler wished to overcome all his enemies. It is also possible that the mention of Melchizedek, who was a priest and a king (Gen 14:17–20), belonged to the firm elements of the enthronement.[161] One is inclined to argue that the psalm stems from the time of the Babylonian exile[162] and that it expresses the hope of the Israelites, humiliated by the occupation and high taxes, for the coming of the descendant of David who will defeat all the gentiles. However, it seems that the psalm was written in the days of the king because that is when the rule of priestly nature of royal power was compulsory. The denomination indicates this: "You are a priest forever, in the order of Melchizedek" (v. 4b). After the Babylonian captivity, it was impossible to combine the dignity of royal and priestly authority. Zech 4:1–14 clearly distinguishes the prince from the high priest. God explained to Zechariah the meaning of the symbol of two olive twigs, which the Prophet saw in a supernatural vision: "These are the two who are anointed to serve the Lord of all the earth" (Zech 4:14). In a historical context, they pointed to Joshua and Zerubbabel as the representatives of the priestly and secular authority; this concept of the separation of those two authorities was quickly rooted in Israel. At least three fragments from Ezekiel demonstrate this clearly by highlighting the fact that the prophet forbids a king to exercise the priests' functions: "Son of man, this is the place of my throne and the place for the soles of my feet. This is where I will live among the Israelites forever. The house of Israel will never again defile my holy name—neither they nor their kings—by their prostitution and the lifeless idols of their kings at their high places. When they placed their threshold next to my threshold and their doorposts beside my doorposts, with only a wall between them, and me they defiled my holy name by their detestable practices. Therefore, I destroyed them in my anger. Now let them put away from

---

160 M. Hengel, "'Setze dich zu meinen Rechten!' Die Inthronisation Christi zur Rechten Gottes und Psalm 110,1," in *Le Trône de Dieu* (ed. M. Philonenko; WUNT 69; Tübingen 1993), 108–112.

161 R. Krawczyk, *Nadzieje mesjańskie w Psalmach* (Warszawa 2007), 157–158.

162 To them belong for example M. Manatti and E. de Solms (*Les Psaumes* [Paris 1966], 53).

me their prostitution and the lifeless idols of their kings, and I will live among them forever" (Ezek 43:7–9); "the prince is to enter from the outside through the portico of the gateway and stand by the gatepost. The priests are to sacrifice his burnt offering and his fellowship offerings. He is to worship at the threshold of the gateway and then go out, but the gate will not be shut until evening" (Ezek 46:2); "and the prince must not take any of the inheritance of the people, driving them off their property. He is to give his sons their inheritance out of his own property, so that none of my people will be separated from his property" (Ezek 46:18). The psalm was written in a royal period but it is difficult to determine exactly when it took place. Most of the exegetes refer to David, Solomon, or Amun, because there are some reasons that the psalm was written in full bloom of royal authority (vv. 1–2, 5–6) and then during the period of its decadence (vv. 3–4 can be interpreted as a concern about a descendant of David, who would bring the nation to a victory during the trial and humiliation).[163]

Application of the relevant content and literary criteria allows us to determine the structure of the psalm which is based on two oracles and a fixed schedule: promise and the announcement of a victory. After the initial information: "Of David. A psalm," the first promise (making his enemies a footstool for the king's feet) is introduced by the formula "The Lord says to my Lord." A formula of similar theological charge can be found in v. 4: "The Lord has sworn and will not change his mind." It introduces the promise of eternal priesthood for the king, in the order of Melchizedek. After the first and the second formulas introducing promises and after the promises themselves (putting the enemies under the feet of the king and the eternal priesthood), the elements of the structure of the work appear. They are the announcements of a victory: in vv. 2–3—the announcement of the victory over enemies and powerful rule in triumph, in vv. 5–7—the announcement of the victory over the pagan kings, combined with the motive of the court. The structure of the text can be presented in the following way:

A: Promise (v. 1);
    B. Announcement of a victory (vv. 2–3);
A': Promise (v. 4);
    B': Announcement of a victory (vv. 5–7).[164]

---

163   Difficulties with determining the time when the psalm was written are the causes of an inability to point accurately its author; K. Kaznowski, "Autor Ps 110," *RTK* 7 (1960): 51–70.

164   Scheme after: W. A. Van Gemeren, "Psalms," in *The Expositor's Bible Commentary with the New International Version of the Holy Bible*, V, *Psalms – Song of Songs* (ed. F. E. Gaebelein; Grand Rapids 1991), 697. Exegetes also propose other divisions of the

2.2. Exegetical Analysis of Ps 110:1–7

V. 1 With the help of one of the prophetic formulas (יְהוָה נְאֻם; "Oracle of God"; Lat. *oraculum*) the Psalmist proclaims God's promise to David and his dynasty. The phrase "oracle of Lord" belongs to the language of the prophets, which was usually placed in their writings in the middle or at the end of a statement. The promise applies to the covenant between the Lord and one of the rulers from the royal line of David's dynasty. To show the relationship lord–vassal, which should prevail between the king and his people, the MT uses the phrase אֲדֹנִי ("my Lord"), but not אֲדוֹנָי, which usually points to God. Similar use of this phrase can be found in 1 Sam 22:12; 26:18; and 1 Chr 1:13; 18:7.

The king's power comes from God himself, hence the king from the generation of David is a theocratic ruler. He exercises authority over God's people but he is under the authority of God and participates in His power, which the formula: "at my right hand" expresses. This formula may indicate the location of the King's throne during the coronation next to the Ark of the Covenant, the symbol of God's presence. It seems that the king had his own appointed place in the temple, next to the column, probably on the right side of the Ark. This fact may indicated in the passage from 2 Kgs 23:3: "The king stood by the pillar and renewed the covenant in the presence of the Lord—to follow the Lord and keep his commands, regulations and decrees with all his heart and all his soul, thus confirming the words of the covenant written in this

---

text. A. Tronina says of two parts: vv. 1–4 (the prophet refers to the king on behalf of Yahweh) and vv. 5–7 (prayer for the King); A. Tronina, *Teologia Psalmów. Wprowadzenie do lektury Psałterza* (Lublin 1995), 189. In this psalm J. S. Synowiec also sees two parts: vv. 1–3 (oracle of Yahweh) and vv. 4–7 (oath of Yahweh); J. S. Synowiec, *Wprowadzenie do Księgi Psalmów* (Kraków 1996), 280–281. However, S. Łach proposes another division: verse I (vv. 1–2), verse II (v. 3), verse III (v. 4), verse IV (vv. 5–7); S. Łach, *Księga Psalmów. Wstęp – przekład z oryginału – komentarz – ekskursy* (PŚST VII/2; Poznań 1990), 469. T. Brzegowy sees three parts in the psalm, in accordance with the chiastic structure A–B–A': A; Royal investiture (vv. 1–3), B; Investiture of priests (v. 4), A': Commentary on the royal investiture (vv. 5–7); T. Brzegowy, *Psałterz i Księga Lamentacji* (Academica 65; Tarnów 2007), 183. The same author also suggests, however, another division: I. The royal investiture (vv. 1–3); II. Investiture of priests (vv. 4–6); Liturgical final section (v. 7) but T. Tułodziecki sees in the text two enthronement acts: A. Act relating to the royal dignity (vv. 1b–3) preceded by the formula: "The Lord says to my Lord"; B. Act relating to the dignity of the priesthood (vv. 4b–6) preceded by the formula: "The Lord has sworn and will not change his mind"; T. Tułodziecki, "Psalm 110 jako przykład teologii kapłaństwa w Psałterzu," *VV* 12 (2007): 35; see P. Auffret, "Note sur la structure littéraire du Psaume cx," *Sem* 32 (1982): 83–88.

book. Then all the people pledged themselves to the covenant."[165] Several texts from OT work for establishing and strengthening the theocratic nature of the authority in Israel: "Of all my sons—and the Lord has given me many—he has chosen my son Solomon to sit on the throne of the kingdom of the Lord over Israel" (1 Chr 28:5); "So Solomon sat on the throne of the Lord as king in place of his father David. He prospered and all Israel obeyed him. All the officers and mighty men, as well as all of King David's sons, pledged their submission to King Solomon. The Lord highly exalted Solomon in the sight of all Israel and bestowed on him royal splendor such as no king over Israel ever had before" (1 Chr 29:23–25); "Praise be to the Lord your God, who has delighted in you and placed you on his throne as king to rule for the Lord your God. Because of the love of your God for Israel and his desire to uphold them forever, he has made you king over them, to maintain justice and righteousness" (2 Chr 9:8); "You are my King and my God, who decrees victories for Jacob" (Ps 44:4); "Your throne, O God, will last for ever and ever; a scepter of justice will be the scepter of your kingdom" (Ps 45:7).

The promise given by God, to the royal ruler of the tribe of David comprises two aspects: a place at the right hand of God and victory over enemies. The place at the right side of the king was considered the most honorable in the ancient monarchy of Israel: "When Bathsheba went to King Solomon to speak to him for Adonijah, the king stood up to meet her, bowed down to her, and sat down on his throne. He had a throne brought for the king's mother, and she sat down at his right hand" (1 Kgs 2:19). Of course, the most important place there was the central place which only king had the right to reside. The second important place was the place at the right, and the third most important place was at the left side of the king. A similar topos "right" existed throughout the ancient Near East, from Egypt to Mesopotamia. Sumerian hymn in honor of one of the goddesses says: "seated on the royal throne, shines like daylight. The king, like the sun, shines radiantly by her side."[166] The same applies to the Greek tradition. The text by Callimachus, entitled Hymn to Apollo (No. 29), refers to the fact that its main character is seated at the right hand of Zeus the supreme god of the Pantheon.[167]

The second part of the promise includes putting the king's enemies as a footstool under his feet. This is part of v. 1, which was quoted by Paul in 1 Cor 15:25b. This is the ancient Middle East metaphor, which indicates the absolute control and complete domination of a king over his enemies. In order to indicate

---

165 Brzegowy, *Psalmy*, 139.
166 Synowiec, *Wprowadzenie do Księgi Psalmów*, 282.
167 M. Treves, "The date of Psalm XXIV," *VT* 10 (1960): 430.

clearly such a meaning of this metaphor it would be useful to cite a few passages: "When they had brought these kings to Joshua, he summoned all the men of Israel and said to the army commanders who had come with him, 'Come here and put your feet on the necks of these kings.' So they came forward and placed their feet on their necks" (Josh 10:24); "You know that because of the wars waged against my father David from all sides, he could not build a temple for the Name of the Lord his God until the Lord put his enemies under his feet" (1 Kgs 5:3); and "This is what your Sovereign Lord says, your God, who defends his people: 'See, I have taken out of your hand the cup that made you stagger; from that cup, the goblet of my wrath, you will never drink again. I will put it into the hands of your tormentors, who said to you 'Fall prostrate that we may walk over you.' And you made your back like the ground, like a street to be walked over'" (Isa 51:22–23).[168] Furthermore, pharaohs' vassals used to call themselves footrests of their kings (such as the Canaanite princes in the fourteenth-century B.C.), whilst the pharaohs sat on the throne placed on the right side of the deity. For example, hymn of victory devoted to Thutmose III (1490–1436), cites the words of the god Amun-Re to Pharaoh: "I make your opponents fall under your sandals."[169]

It should be stressed that the Hebrew particle "until" (עַד) in the wording "until I make your enemies a footstool for your feet" opens a forward-looking perspective.[170] Enemies have not been subjected to the king yet; he has not ruled over them yet. So this is a promise of victory, which will come into existence in the future. This fact leads to the messianic and eschatological interpretation of the text.

Vv. 2–3 The promise of victory over its enemies is related to the handing over of the king's sceptre from Zion. The mention of Zion clearly implies that the hero of the psalm is the king of Jerusalem. Zion, first meant the south-eastern hill, behind which the oldest part of Jerusalem stretched, but over time this name was extended to the whole city (2 Sam 5:7; Isa 2:3; 60:14; Jer 31:6). The following words from 1 Sam 2:10 are similar in meaning: "those who oppose the Lord will be shattered." He will thunder against them from heaven; the Lord will judge the ends of the earth. "He will give strength to his king and exalt the horn of his anointed." Handing over a sceptre usually means handing over the rule over enemies.[171] The scepter is a typical attribute of the king, as evidenced by the

---

168   See also Ps 45:6; 47:4; 60:10; 89:11; 108:10; Isa 51:23.

169   Synowiec, *Wprowadzenie do Księgi Psalmów*, 283.

170   *BDB:* 723–724.

171   Brzegowy, *Psalmy*, 141.

following texts: "The scepter will not depart from Judah, nor the ruler's staff from between his feet, until he comes to whom it belongs and the obedience of the nations is his" (Gen 49:10); "You will rule them with an iron scepter; you will dash them to pieces like pottery" (Ps 2:9); "Your throne, O God, will last for ever and ever; a scepter of justice will be the scepter of your kingdom" (Ps 45:7). To highlight the power of the king the author uses two procedures: he adds that the royal scepter is "mighty," and he puts the whole phrase "Your mighty scepter" in an emphatic position—at the beginning of a sentence. The scepter of the Upper and Lower Egypt was put into the hands of Pharaoh on the day of his coronation. A similar custom existed in Mesopotamia. The author of the psalm probably alludes to this custom, which was also present in Israel.

Because of the ambiguity of the Hebrew particles which was used here, an order directed to the king can be understood in two ways. It may be understood according to the text: "rule in the midst of your enemies!" or "rule over your enemies!". The first version makes it possible that the king will reign over his people, surrounded by other nations hostile towards him, but despite the belligerent environment, he will be able to exercise his power. The second version points to the reign of the king not only over his own people, but also over the hostile nations. This second version appears to be more likely for two reasons: firstly, the particle has been as well used in the sense of "rule over" (Ps 72:8), and secondly, the context itself points to victory of the king over his enemies (v. 5).

V. 3 creates special textual difficulties (as it belongs to *crux exegetarum*).[172] The literal translation seems to be confusing, and it differs from the context: "Your troops will be willing on your day of battle. Arrayed in holy majesty, from the womb of the dawn you will receive the dew of your youth."

In Hebrew Codes, there are many versions of this literal translation of MT. They do not conform to each other; hence, it is extremely difficult to reconstruct their original text. One can search for its meaning, though. In this case, the LXX is helpful: μετὰ σοῦ ἡ ἀρχὴ ἐν ἡμέρᾳ τῆς δυνάμεώς σου ἐν ταῖς λαμπρότησιν τῶν ἁγίων ἐκ γαστρὸς πρὸ ἑωσφόρου ἐξεγέννησά σε ("Your troops will be willing on your day of battle. Arrayed in holy majesty, from the womb of the dawn you will receive the dew of your youth"). In this version, the text of v. 3 appears as a natural continuation of the content of vv. 1–2. As a result, content-related arguments suggest that the king is entitled to be God's son because he was begotten by God himself. If we consistently adopted the LXX's different wording of the term יַלְדֻתֶיךָ ("your youth"), rather than in the MT, and read the

---

term as "I have begotten you," then we could understand the phrase "before dawn" (מֵרֶחֶם מִשְׁחָר) as "before foundation of the world." The content of v. 3 read off in such a way (after LXX) does not indicate the messianic nature of the psalm yet. The phrase "I have begotten you" concerns in this context, adoption of the king, in accordance with Ps 2:7b: "You are my Son; today I have become your Father." In the same way we may interpret the oracle of Nathan included in (2 Sam 7:14): "I will be his father, and he will be my son." The fact of being begotten is synonymous, to some extent, to adoption, which takes place at the same time as the enthronement. Therefore, the begetting can be understood in the figurative sense of this word. Considering the proposals of exegetes and taking into an account the ancient translations (mainly from the LXX), and the context itself, suggested in v. 3; we are inclined to suggest the following wording of this verse:

> "Your people is willing
> on the day of your power
> on the sacred hills.
> From the womb of the dawn
> like the dew I have begotten you."

Concerning the "dawn," it must be assumed that the initial מ was formatted as a result of its doubling. Whereas in the phrase which can mean "in the sacred array," "in the holy light" or "in the edifice of a temple" (after the LXX), there is probably a confusion of the consonant ר with ד. As they are very similar in spelling, the letters can be easily confused. There is nothing to keep us from adopting the phrase: "in the holy mountains."[173] Besides, the LXX, Vulgate, Targum and Symmachus precisely read out this expression in this way. If were are to interpret this phrase in its immediate context, it should be acknowledged that it was Mount Zion. David placed the Ark of the Covenant there and in this place a temple was founded later.[174]

Returning to the initial phrase included in v. 3, the formulation עַמְּךָ נְדָבֹת creates considerable difficulties. The term נְדָבֹת literally means "voluntary sacrifice," but in this case the problem is probably about so-called "plural of intensification."[175] The meaning of the first part of v. 3 is probably the following: the people willingly fight, which will turn out to be successful. One can find a similar meaning in the Song of Deborah: "When the princes in Israel take the lead, when the people willingly offer themselves—praise the Lord!"

---

173 J. Coppens, *Le mesianisme royal. Ses origines. Son développement. Son accomplissement* (Paris 1968), 58.

174 Brzegowy, *Psalmy*, 143.

175 H.-J. Kraus, *Psalmen* (Biblischer Kommentar. Altes Testament, II: Neukirchen 1960), 753.

(Judg 5:2) and "My heart is with Israel's princes, with the willing volunteers among the people. Praise the Lord!" (Judg 5:9). If we assumed that the content of this part of v. 3 refers rather to "your people" (MT), then the person of the king (LXX); subsequently, the comparison aiming at emphasizing the fact that God's people willingly fight would even go on further: the sentence "from the womb of the dawn you will receive the dew" means that the number of warriors abounds like the dew in the morning.[176] The basis for such an interpretation of this part of the verse comes from 2 Sam 17:12: "Then we will attack him wherever he may be found, and we will fall on him as dew settles on the ground. Neither he nor any of his men will be left alive." The statement of Hushai addressed to Absalom, clearly gives the military features to allegory, which is plentiful in dew and covers the ground in the morning. It seems, therefore, empowered to see also such a connotation in v. 3. Besides, a little confusing wording about the birth from the womb of the dawn can be explained by the belief of the Israelites, that the life-giving dew is a creation of celestial bodies: "May God give you of heaven's dew and of earth's richness—an abundance of grain and new wine" (Gen 27:28; see Isa 45:8).

V. 4 The first sentence of v. 4 refers to the oath given by God: "God will not withdraw it" ("will not regret it"). An oath is an act in which a man refers to God, to confirm the accuracy and value of the given words (see Gen 21:22–32; Judg 21:7; 1 Sam 20:3). When God gives the oath, it will never be cancelled. God himself is the guarantor of the words of the oath (Gen 22:16; Amos 6:8; Isa 45:23; Jer 51:14).

The current verse describes the issue of the existence of the royal power in ancient Israel which was exercised by priests. The sacerdotal code clearly separates three functions. They are as follows: the prophetic, the priestly and the royal function. However, HB mentions that on the day of bringing the ark to Jerusalem, David was dressed in sacerdotal robes: "David, wearing a linen ephod, danced before the Lord with all his might" (2 Sam 6:14). In addition, he also made sacrifices and performed activities intended for priests: "They brought the ark of the Lord and set it in its place inside the tent that David had pitched for it, and David sacrificed burnt offerings and fellowship offerings before the Lord. After he had finished sacrificing the burnt offerings and fellowship offerings, he blessed the people in the name of the Lord Almighty" (2 Sam 6:17–18). David—as it is clear from the last mention—also gave the people the priestly blessing. This also included Solomon (1 Kgs 8:14.55.62–64), whose

---

176 A. Weiser, *Die Psalmen* (II; Göttingen [7]1966), 477.

authority extended over even the high priest: "So Solomon removed Abiathar from the priesthood of the Lord, fulfilling the word the Lord had spoken at Shiloh about the house of Eli ... replaced Abiathar with Zadok the priest" (1 Kgs 2:27.35). Priestly functions were also exercised by Jeroboam (1 Kgs 12:33). The sons of David are also called Priests (2 Sam 8:18).[177] It should be noted, however, that all the texts that contain passages about the kings' exercise of priestly functions come from the period before the Babylonian captivity.

The law clearly states that to serve God, the tribe of Levi was appointed by God himself to exercise the priestly functions: "At that time the Lord set apart the tribe of Levi to carry the ark of the covenant of the Lord, to stand before the Lord to minister and to pronounce blessings in his name, as they still do today" (Deut 10:8). When King Uzziah tries to take the place of priests, the latter expressly is opposed to it, recalling the command of the Lord (2 Chr 26:18). Both the priest and the king were subjected to the anointing ritual. During the monarchy, not all priests, however, were probably anointed. This ceremony was the foundation of a specific dignity of the king and his unique relationship with Yahweh. He became a consecrated person. This fact gave him the prerogative to exercise; in exceptional situations, strictly sacerdotal functions, though no king was a priest in the strict sense. The anointment of the king took place during the enthronement. Quite similar customs were deeply rooted among other nations of the Ancient Near East. For example, the Hittites anointed the ruler to succeed the throne with fragrant oil. In Egypt, the pharaoh himself anointed many of his subordinate officials (for anointing pharaohs themselves; you do not have the appropriate proof). In Syria and Canaan, the anointing must have taken place in order to inherit the throne legally. Presumably, this practice was also well known in Damascus. The OT mentions the anointing of David (1 Sam 16:3.12; 2 Sam 2:4.7; 5:3.17; 12:7; Ps 89:20; 1 Chr 11:3; 14:8), Saul (1 Sam 9:16; 10:1; 15:1.17), Solomon (1 Kgs 1:34.39.35; 5:15; 1 Chr 29:22), Joash (2 Kgs 11:12; 2 Chr 23:11) and Josiah (2 Kgs 23:30). The ritual of anointing was as follows: first, a horn was filled with oil (1 Sam 16:13; 1 Kgs 1:39). It could have also been a holder (1 Sam 10:1; 2 Kgs 9:3.6). Then an authorized person poured its contents on the head of the chosen one. The OT is familiar with the ritual of the anointing of the priesthood as well. The Priestly Code P certifies that (Exod 28:41; 30:30; 40:15; Lev 7:36; Num 3:3).[178] The nations that bordered by Israel had the custom according to which priestly functions were often performed by

177   C. E. Armerding, "Were David's Sons Really Priests?," in *Current Issues in Biblical and Patristic Interpretation* (ed. G. F. Hawthrorne; Grand Rapids 1975), 75–86.

178   M. Rosik, "Biblijne namaszczenie na króla, kapłana i proroka jako konsekracja. 'Namaścił ciebie olejkiem radości' (Ps 45 [44] 8)," *ŻK* 6 (38) 2002: 42–53.

the king himself. A similar situation was in Mesopotamia and Egypt. Such a king-priest was just mentioned in v. 4 Melchizedek: "Then Melchizedek king of Salem brought out bread and wine. He was priest of God Most High, and he blessed Abram, saying, 'Blessed be Abram by God Most High, Creator of heaven and earth'" (Gen 14:18–19).

The hero of the psalm combines royal and priestly dignity. His priesthood is not, however, a result of the fact that he comes from Levi's family, but instead that he is entitled to it by Yahweh. No other text of the OT gives, in this sense, the king the sacerdotal status.[179] Indeed, we have biblical evidence that comes from the era after the exile. It denotes a combination of spiritual and secular authority (Hagg 1:1; 2:2; Zech 4:14; 6:9–15) but it is not sufficient for one to speak for the existence of such a connection. The evidence only says that Joshua, the son of Jozadak, sat on his throne, but the hypothesis that Joshua was enthroned king of Israel seems to be unlikely.[180] Another proposal connecting the kingship and priesthood authority in Israel relates to the Hellenistic period, during the reign of the Seleucid Empire and. the dynasty of Zadok. In the year 160 B.C., Jonathan, the brother of Judah Maccabee, was awarded with the title of an etnarchy and a high priest. From this point on, the attributes of priestly power go on the Zadokites and Hasmonean (cf. 1 Macc 10:20–21). Twenty years later, Maccabaeus received the power of the high priest under the law of its succession by his successors. 1 Macc 14:41 says: "And the Jews and their priests decided that Simon should be their leader and high priest for ever." There is a great similarity in terminology between this fragment and the presented verse. Thus, some exegetes assume that Ps 110 is a work written in connection with the enthronement and delegation of the priestly power to Jonathan and Simon. What also speaks in favour of this hypothesis is the structure of the psalm; the beginning (first letter) of individual lines form an acrostic of the name Simon, which translates as "Simon is terrible" or "Simon scary."[181] Although, at first glance, this hypothesis seems to be appealing and convincing, it does not stand a literary criticism. Behind it is the fact that the terminology used in Ps 110 is more similar to the Ugaritic language and phraseology than the Greek one.[182]

Another proposition for identifying the priest and king from Ps 110 refers to David. His robes, being priestly robes, have been mentioned before, as well as the priest-like roles he fulfilled, especially those connected with transferring the

---

179 T. Brzegowy, *Miasto Boże w Psalmach* (Kraków 1989), 127.
180 Such a hypothesis is proposed by S. Schreiner, "Psalm CX und die Investitur des Hohenpriesters," *VT* 27 (1977): 219–220.
181 Tułodziecki, *Psalm 110*, 38; M. Treves, "Two Acrostic Psalms," *VT* 15 (1965): 86.
182 Extensive argumentation on this issue cites Tułodziecki, *Psalm 110*, 40–41. See also: H. G. Jefferson, "Is Psalm 110 Canaanite?," *JBL* 73 (1954): 153.

Ark from the house of Obed-Edom to Jerusalem. However, the very circumstance that David fulfilled the roles which customarily belonged to a priest, does not prove that he was a priest according to the particular meaning of this word. Therefore, many exegetes invoke the topography argument, claiming that Salem, where Melchizedek was a king, can be identified with Jerusalem, the city of David. The basis for these divagations is a remark from the Book of Genesis: "Then Melchizedek, king of Salem, brought bread and wine; he was a priest of God Most High, and he blessed Abram saying: 'Blessed be Abram by God Most High, maker of heaven and earth! And blessed be God Most High who has delivered your enemies into your hands!' And Abram gave him a tenth part of everything" (Gen 14:18–20). Whereas, the former exegesis identified Salem with Jerusalem,[183] nowadays, in the light of current research, such identification can no longer be maintained. The name of Salem does not indicate Jerusalem anywhere.[184] The oldest name of Jerusalem comes from the Egyptian inscription made about twenty centuries before Christ. It says "Urusalim," so it has little to do with the name of Salem. The tablets from Tel Amarna provide a similar case (14th century B.C.), as well as the letter of pharaoh Ramses II (13th century B.C.). Jerusalem was also referred to as Jebus by the tribe of Benjamin. Moreover, since none of these names has any connection to Salem, the homeland of Melchizedek has now been moved to Shiloh, Shechem or Nob.[185] The hypothesis about the priesthood of David based only on the topography remark referring to Melchizedek cannot be maintained. If a priestly function can be attributed to David, it is rather due to his role in the cult, his appointments of staff, and safeguarding the cleanliness of liturgical procedures.[186]

Others suggest that the priestly prophesy of Ps 110 refers to the priest Zadok, who worked among the entourage of David (2 Sam 15:24–29; 17:15; 19:12). These Bible researchers usually provide two reasons as their arguments for such identification: first, the name of Zadok is etymologically connected with the name of Melchizedek, and secondly, the genealogy of Zadok seems to have no beginning and end. The name of Melchizedek consists of two Hebrew words, whose translation means "king" and "just," and "righteous." It is primarily a proper name, but it can also be translated as a sentence "Milku is just/righteous" or "Zedek is a king." The second option is more probable because the OT confirms the existence of a king with this name (Josh 10:1.3). The correspondence found in Tel Amarna contains letters exchanged between

183   Fitzmyer, *Melchizedek*, 65.
184   Text of Ps 76:3 ("Salom is indeed his tent; he has made Zion his dwelling place") is too late to form a convincing argument on this issue.
185   J. G. Gammie, "Loci of Melchizedek Tradition," *JBL* 90 (1971): 385–396.
186   Tułodziecki, *Psalm 110*, 45.

the pharaoh and Adoni-Zedek.[187] However, the name Zedek itself is not a typical Hebrew name, but was confirmed in Egypt, Ugarit, and among the Amorites and Canaanites. It is beyond doubt that Melchizedek or Adoni-Zedek were pagan rulers (the latter is presented in the Bible as the king of Jerusalem Jebusites; Josh 10:1.3 and 2 Sam 5:6–10). It is therefore possible that Zadok also has the Jebusite ancestors in his genealogy. He made a quick career at the court of David, because he perfectly knew the weak points of the city defence (2 Sam 15:24–29). Considering this interpretation, Ps 110 seems aetiology of David priesthood.[188] As far as the genealogy of Zadok is concerned, the relevant information is contained in 2 Sam 8:16–18 and 1 Cor 5:27–34; 6:35–38. However, the detailed research showed that this is secondary information, created for the purpose of genealogical establishment of such an important figure as the priest at the court of David.[189] However, even if one accepts that Ps 110 mentions Zadok whose genealogy was not known (as the one of Melchizedek), it is very difficult to accept that the words "You are the priest forever, in the order of Melchizedek" are addressed to him, because Melchizedek was at the same time a king and priest. These two combined offices constitute the genuine sense of this biblical figure. Therefore, it is difficult to accept the opinion suggesting that the author of Ps 110 wanted to change the archetype of a king established from time immemorial—priest Melchizedek, in view of the political and religious transformations at the beginning of the Israeli monarchy (2 Sam 5–6).[190]

The aformentioned analyses have not led to indicating the historical figure who would be the hero of Ps 110. However, it does not mean that such a figure has not existed. In addition, although we cannot establish him within a specific historical environment or indicate his name, it does not exclude the analyses, which could show the theological implications of such a figure. This is where the perspective of the messianic interpretation of Ps 110 opens.

The office of a priest-king shall be unlimited in time, where it shall last "forever." However, it must be assumed that it does not refer to the idea of

---

187   L. R. Fisher, "Abraham and his Priest-King," *JBL* 81 (1962): 265–266.

188   Tułodziecki, *Psalm 110*, 49.

189   A. Cody, *A History of the Old Testament Priesthood* (Rome 1969), 89. "Melchizedek is mentioned in the Hebrew Old Testament only in Gen 14:18–20 and Ps 110,4. The details about this (originally Canaanite) priest-king in these passages were further read and understood in the Hellenistic and Roman periods of Jewish, and later Christian, history. This is seen in the translation or interpretation of the passages in the Septuagint, the writings of Flavius Josephus, the Epistle to the Hebrews, and in the Peshitta, where a process of allegorization was at work"; Fitzmyer, *Melchizedek*, 69.

190   Tułodziecki, *Psalm 110*, 51.

eternity, but permanence. Such expression of this idea can be found, for example, in the Book of Exod 21,6 and Lev 25,46, where the servant is supposed to work for his Lord "forever," that is, until death.[191] Besides, the clear idea of immortality appeared in the OT only in the Wis 3:1–10 and 5:15. Therefore, it would be an anachronism to detect it in the discussed psalm. The king shall therefore maintain his office until he dies. At the same time, it is an honour shrouded with mystery, as in the case of the priest and king Melchizedek. A question then arises: what is the similarity between the hero of Ps 110 and Melchizedek? The main role of the priest is to offer sacrifices (Exod 28–29; Lev 21). The procedure of offering sacrifice marks the priestly status: "Priests Levites, the whole tribe of Levi, will have no share or inheritance as the rest of the children of Israel have, but they shall live on the burnt offerings in the honour of Yahweh and on what is consecrated to him. The Levite shall have no share in the inheritance received by his brother because Yahweh is his inheritance as he has promised" (Deut 18:1–2). Although in the case of Ps 110 offering sacrifices is not mentioned, it is clear that this was the role of Melchizedek. According to the Gen 14:18–20, the sacrifice offered by Melchizedek during the meeting with Abram was bread and wine. It is the sacrifice mentioned in Num 15:2b–5: "When you have entered the land I give to you, when you make a fragrant offering to Yahweh, either as a burnt offering or in payment of a vow, or as a voluntary gift, or on the occasion of one of your solemn feasts, whoever takes from his herds and flocks for a fragrant offering to Yahweh shall bring also, as a gift to Yahweh, a grain offering of two pounds of fine flour mixed with two pints of oil. He shall also make a wine offering, two pints for each lamb, in addition to the burnt offering or sacrifice."[192] This type of offering was to be added to the sacrifice of a lamb, goat or bull (Num 15:1–16). In case of the sacrifice offered by Melchizedek no blood offering of any animal is mentioned, so the meaning of this sacrifice cannot be explained on the basis of the OT alone.[193]

---

191   When Bathsheba wishes David "May my lord King David live forever!" (1 Kgs 1:31) she does not mean eternity, but long life; A. Vanhoye, *Struttura e teologia nell'Epistola agli Ebrei* (Roma 1996³), 135; D. Dziadosz, *Gli oracoli divini in 1 Sam 8 – 2 Re 25. Redazione e teologia nella storia deuteronomistica dei re* (Romae 2002), 60–61.

192   Two pounds of fine flour is about four litres. This is the amount of flour which was supposed to be mixed with about two and a half litres of oil.

193   The Christian tradition adopted the opinion that historically, it might only refer to celebrating the victory of Abram, but the author of the Epistle to Hebrews shows this sacrifice in a completely different theological dimension: "All know that he belonged to the tribe of Judah that is not mentioned by Moses when he speaks of the priesthood. All this however, becomes clear if the priest after the likeness of Melchizedek has in fact

Vv. 5–7 When the king goes to war, the Lord supports him by standing "on his right." Therefore, there is a change in position. In v. 1, the king stands on the right of the Lord, whereas, in v. 5 the places are exchanged: the Lord as a supporter is standing on the right side of the king. Some exegetes explain this discrepancy by clarifying that v. 1 describes the scene of enthroning, whereas, v. 5 describes the scene of fighting, so these are two different situations. However, it is enough to state that the expression "on the right" does not have to signify a specific place, but a close bond between Yahweh and the king.

The motif of God the helper, who remains on the right of the *orant* often recurs in Psalms: "I keep the Lord always before me, for with him at my right hand, I will never be shaken" (Ps 16:8); "To the Lord I will give my thanks, I will praise him in the great assembly, he stands at the right hand of the needy, to save them from those who condemn them" (Ps 109:30–31); "The Lord is at your right hand to crush the kings on his day of wrath" (Ps 109:5). It is thanks to the help of the Lord that the kings will be conquered. This will happen on the day of wrath, the God who established the king ridicules the pagan nations in his anger: "the one enthroned in heaven laughs, the Lord looks at them in derision. Then in anger he speaks to them, terrifying them in the fury of his wrath 'Behold the king I have installed in Zion, upon my holy hill'" (Ps 2:4–6). Therefore, the Psalmist calls those who have the Lord on their side happy, whereas, those against whom he turns in his wrath are condemned: "Serve the Lord with fear and fall at his feet, lest he be angry and you perish when his anger suddenly flares. Blessed are all who take refuge in him" (Ps 2:12). Sometimes the Psalmist simply wishes his enemies to be reached by the wrath of the Lord: "Your hand, oh Lord, will reach your enemies, and lay hold of all your foes" (Ps 21:9). Similarly as in v. 5, Isaiah also connects the wrath of the Lord with the specific day: "See how the day of Yahweh comes, it is a cruel day coming with wrath and fierce anger. It will make the earth desolate, it will destroy sinners within it" (Isa 13:9). The only ones who will be spared on "the day of wrath" are

---

received his mission, not on the basis of any human law, but by the power of an immortal life. Because Scripture says: You are a priest forever in the priestly order of Melchizedek ... But Jesus remains forever and the priesthood shall not be taken from him. Consequently, he is able to save for all time those who approach God through him. He always lives to intercede on their behalf. It was fitting that our High Priest be holy, undefiled, set apart from sinners and exalted above the heavens; a priest who does not first need to offer sacrifice for himself before offering for the sins of the people, as high priests do. He offered himself in sacrifice once and for all" (Heb 7,14–17.24–27). Thus the prophecy about the Suffering Servant of Yahweh has been fulfilled (Isa 53:7), whose death was preceded by the sacrifice of bread and wine offered in the Cenacle (Matt 26:26; Mark 14:22–25; Luke 22:19–20; 1 Cor 11:23–27).

"the poor of the land": "Seek Yahweh, all you poor of the land who fulfil his commands, do justice and are meek, and perhaps you will find refuge on the day Yahweh comes to judge" (Song 2:3).

V. 6 directly indicates that "the day of His wrath" is the same as the day of judgment: "He will judge the nations, heaping up corpses, smashing heads on the wide plain." It is the eschatological judgment over the world foretold by the prophets. It is enough to invoke several prophesies: "This is why the heavens tremble and the earth shakes its foundation, at the wrath of Yahweh Sabbaoth on the day of his burning anger" (Isa 13:13); "What a dreadful day—the day of Yahweh that draws near and comes as ruin from the Almighty" (Joel 1:15); "In raging fury I will take vengeance upon the nations that have not obeyed me" (Mic 5:14); "The great day of the Lord is near, it already comes, its sound is so frightening that even the valiant cries out in terror. It is a day of wrath, anguish and distress; a day of destruction and devastation, of gloom and darkness; it is a day of dark clouds and fog when the trumpet sounds the call for battle, and the enemy attacks the fortress and the high fortified towers. I will bring misfortune on these people and they will grope along like the blind. Their blood will be poured out like dust and their remains will lie like dung. Neither their gold nor their silver will rescue them when the anger of God burns against them. The land of Judah will be burnt in the fire of his zeal when he destroys even the traces of all who dwell in that land" (Song 1:14–18).

It is on the day of his wrath that the Lord will "judge the nations." The judgement over the nations on the day of the Lord's wrath is prophesied by the Psalmist several times: "You shall rule them [the nations] with an iron sceptre and shatter them as a potter's vase" (Ps 2:9); "Let the nations gather around you, and you take your seat high above them. Proclaim, oh Lord, my righteousness, you see that I am blameless" (Ps 7:8–9); "But the Lord reigns forever, having set up his throne for judgement. He will judge the nations with justice and govern the peoples in righteousness" (Ps 9:8–9; compare with Ps 76:9). The image of the heaps of corpses signifies the severity of the judgement, it is also emphasised by the remark about "the wide plain." This remark suggests the motif of limitless land, as if they were "limits of the earth" (cf. Ps 2:8).

A grammatical difficulty appears in v. 7; the subject of the sentence can be both "the king" and "the Lord." Some exegetes solve it by explaining that the king wins victory thanks to the actions of the Lord; it is God who fights. If v. 3 refers to the king (which is more probable, because adopting "the Lord" as the subject would entail serious anthropomorphisms which are not necessary in this case), the gesture of lifting his head is a triumphal one: "But you are my shield, oh Lord, my glory, you lift up my head" (Ps 3:4); "Then my head will be lifted up over the enemies round about me" (Ps 27:6a). The motif of drinking water from the stream indicates restoring the power to fight. However, it can be a reference to the fighting of Gideon's army: "Yahweh said to Gideon: 'There are still too many people. Take them down to the water and I myself will test them for you. If I say: This one shall go with you, he will go. And if I say: Not this one, he shall not go.' So Gideon brought them down to the water and Yahweh told him: 'Those who lap the water like a dog, you shall place on one side. And those who kneel down to drink, you shall place on the other side'" (Judg 7:4–5).[194] The source of the king's power is the water from the stream. The logic of reasoning is the following: the king will lift his head (which is the gesture of a winner), because he will drink water from the stream. This context provides an analogy to the common customs in Ras Samra, where the king went to the holy stream during coronation to drink water. Some exegetes interpret 1 Kgs 1:38–39 according to this meaning, when it is mentioned that the priest Zadok and Prophet Nathan took Solomon to the stream of Gihon. Such understanding of v. 7 matches the OT symbolisms of water which is the source of life (cf. Ps 65:10–11; Ezek 47:2; Isa 33:20–21; 35:6).

2.3. Contribution of v. 1b to Ps 110:1–7

Based on this exegetical analysis of Ps 110:1–7, it would seem that this is a royal psalm, associated with the enthronement. It is difficult to definitively identify the king's name, but he was certainly a historical figure. The king is asked to take the place at the right hand of God, and thus to participate in the divine dominion over the earth. This king is also a priest, who will have held the office "for ever," that is—as shown above—by the end of his days. This is a fundamental dimension of the interpretation of the text.[195] This interpretation is also open to the messianic prospect,[196] although Messianic interpretation is

---

194   Van Gemeren, *Psalms*, 700. The supporters of adopting the messianic interpretation of the psalm see it as a reference to Isa 35,6. Cf. also to: R. J. Tournay, "Les relectures du Psaume 110 (109) et l'allusion à Gédéon," *RB* 105 (1998): 321–331.

195   J. Becker, "Zur Deutung von Ps 110,7," in *In Freude an der Weisung des Herrn: Beiträge zur Theologie der Psalmen* (eds. H. Gross, E. Haag and F.-L. Hossfeld; SBB 13; Stuttgart 1987²), 31.

196   In the second and third centuries A.D. rabbis strongly rejected assumed previously by Judaism the messianic interpretation of the Psalm and they claimed that the hero of the text was Abraham, Hezekiah, or David. This change took place based on the controversy with the Christians, who read out the psalm from the messianic perspective. Later, a lot of rabbis have returned to the messianic interpretation. See J. Coppens, *La*

neither basic nor original in this case.[197] From the time of Nathan's prophecy (2 Sam 7:14a) every ruler in Israel had to embody the ideal of the ruler—Anointed of God. Only in this psalm, the king is also called a priest, and just in this psalm, his position is located at the right hand of Yahweh. However, Jesus himself (Matt 22:41–46; 26:63–64; Mark 12:35–37; Luke 20:41–44; 22:70), followed by the authors of the NT, understood the psalm by Messianic theories. The author of Hebrews confirms that the first oracle of the psalm is said by God the Father to His Son, Jesus Christ (Heb 1:2–4.13; and the entire Chapter 7). Some NT texts refer to Ps 110 in respect of ascension into heaven (Mark 16:19; Acts 2:33–36). Paul sees the glorification of the Son of God on the right hand of the Father as the source of Christian hope (Eph 1:18–23; Rom 8:34; Col 3:1).[198]

V. 1b refers to the position of enemies of the king as a footstool for his feet. In the Temple of Jerusalem, there was the Ark of the Covenant, which was a stool of Yahweh (cf. 1 Sam 4:4; Ezek 43:7). The combination of the image of the ark under the "feet" and the image of enemies of Yahweh under the feet of the King emphasize the dignity of royalty. No matter whether the invitation to the king, "Sit at my right hand" is to be taken literally (as the enthronement, so the moment of coming to power) or figuratively (as a representation of the closeness of the king to Yahweh), the idea included in it is clear: the king participates in the power of Yahweh. And such is the essential meaning of v. 1b, and at the same time its contribution to the theological content of Ps 110.

3. The Meaning in 1 Cor 15:23–28

To determine the exact purpose of the quotation from Ps 110:1b in v. 25b first, we have to examine the immediate context of this quotation which is found in vv. 23–28.[199] Our analysis will be conducted from an exegetical and theological angle. First, we will extract those contents from vv. 23–28, which will facilitate the understanding of the meaning of the quotation in v. 25b. In v. 22 Paul mentions that "all will be made alive" (πάντες ζῳοποιηθήσονται; v. 22). At the

---

portée messianique du Psaume 110 (Analecta Lovaniensia biblica et orientalia 3 [1956]), 5–23; G. R. Driver, "Psalm 110: Its Form, Meaning and Purpose," in Studies in the Bible Presented to M.H. Segal (eds. J. M. Grintz and J. Liver; Publications of the Israel Society for Biblical Research 17; Jerusalem 1964), 17–31.

197 This form of messianism, some biblical scholars refer to as "indirect royal messianism"; "mesjanizmu królewskiego pośredniego"; Krawczyk, Nadzieje mesjańskie, 171; Tronina, Teologia Psalmów, 194.

198 Rinaudo, I Salmi, 600–606.

199 J. P. Heil begins from testing the context of v. 24 because he sees chiasm in vv. 24–28; id., Rhetorical Role of Scripture, 213.

beginning of v. 23 there is a description of the order in which this vivification will take place: "But each in his own turn: Christ, the firstfruits; then, when he comes, those who belong to him."[200] The first statement included in this verse is ordering in its character; the apostle argues that the vivification of the dead will not be chaotic or disorderly, but everyone will be made alive ἐν τῷ ἰδίῳ τάγματι. The term τάγμα is used in military terminology, indicating the order of the troops in the rank.[201] "Own turn" means the logical order: reaching for natural figurativeness, used by Paul, "firstfruits" will be animated at first (v. 20), and then the rest of the harvest.[202] This order also indicates the chronological order: Christ has already been resurrected from the dead (past tense *perfectum*; 15:4.12.14.16.17.20) while those who belong to Him will be resurrected in the future (future tense *futurum*; 15:22.49.51.52.54). Paul clearly illustrates this order by using the following words: ἀπαρχὴ Χριστός, ἔπειτα οἱ τοῦ Χριστοῦ. It also reflects the sequence of events in history of salvation.[203] The noun ἀπαρχή shows both that Christ was resurrected as the first representative of all those who will attain the resurrection.[204]

The term ἀπαρχή, referring to Christ, seems to be very important in this context. The Apostle refers indirectly to the order of God, addressed to the Israelites, which have to be completed during the celebration of the Passover:

---

200 To see the connection between the second coming of Christ and the resurrection of the faithful go to: E. J. Jezierska, "Święty Paweł o zmartwychwstaniu wiernych w Dniu Pańskim," in *Miłość wytrwa do końca. Księga Pamiątkowa dla Ks. Profesora Stanisława Pisarka w 50. rocznicę święceń kapłańskich* (ed. W. Chrostowski; Warszawa 2004), 150–162.

201 Thayer, *Thayer's Geek-English Lexicon of the New Testament*, 613; R. Jamieson, A. R. Fausset and D. Brown, *A Commentary on the Old and New Testaments*, III (Peabody 1997), 328; Mare, *1 Corinthians*, 285. Some exegetes argue that the order of the resurrection will depend on the "dignity of resurrected from the dead"; K. Romaniuk, A. Jankowski and L. Stachowiak, *Komentarz praktyczny do Nowego Testamentu*, II (Poznań–Kraków 1999), 162; M. Henry, *Commentary on the Whole Bible Complete and Unabridged in One Volume* (Peabody 1997[7]), 2273; Talbert, *Reading Corinthians*, 124.

202 "The relation between Christ's resurrection and ours is fixed by the biblical relation of the firstfruits to the full harvest"; M. Goulder, "The Pauline Epistles," in *The Literary Guide to the Bible* (eds. R. Alter and F. Kermode; London 1989), 486.

203 Saw, *Paul's Rhetoric*, 235.

204 J. Holleman says: "Jesus is the first one of those who will be raised; his resurrection will be followed by that of the rest. In the latter idea the emphasis is on the aspect of Jesus being the 'representative' of those who will be raised: Christians will share in the resurrection of their representative. Both aspects, i.e., Jesus' role as the first one and as representative, are embraced by the word firstfruits"; id., *Resurrection and Parousia*, 49. See also: Hasler, "Credo und Auferstehung in Korinth," 27; Barrett, "Significance of the Adam-Christ Typology," 102–103.

"When you enter the land I am going to give you, and you reap its harvest, bring to the priest a sheaf of the first grain you harvest. He is to wave the sheaf before the Lord so it will be accepted on your behalf; the priest is to wave it on the day after the Sabbath. On the day you wave the sheaf, you must sacrifice as a burnt offering to the Lord, a lamb a year old without defect" (Lev 23:10–12). In 1 Cor, Paul says that Christ is the Passover of the Christians (5:7). Through Paul's reference, a specific parallel between Christ and the sheaf, which the priest is to wave, is created. As far as the sheaf symbolized the first fruits of the new harvest, Christ represents a new kind of people freed from the yoke of death and experiencing resurrection.[205] Since Christ is ἀπαρχή, from among those who died, others will also rise again after Him.

The term ἔπειτα in a very clear and rigorous way defines the sequence. First and then, however, can be read more emphatically as "and then."[206] In any case, it designates chronological order: first, the resurrection of Christ, followed by the resurrection of the faithful.[207] The expression "those who belong to Christ" (οἱ τοῦ Χριστοῦ) emphasizes soteriological character of vivification in Christ (see v. 22b: "in Christ everyone will be raised").[208] Paul mentioned earlier that the Corinthians belong to Christ: "all are yours, and you are of Christ, and Christ is of God" (3:22b–23). The belonging is synonymous with having the Spirit of Christ: "You, however, are controlled not by the sinful nature but by the Spirit, if the Spirit of God lives in you. And if anyone does not have the Spirit of Christ, he does not belong to Christ" (Rom 8:9).

This vivification will take place during the "coming" of Christ: ἐν τῇ παρουσίᾳ αὐτοῦ. Although the noun παρουσία from the view of lexicographic point can mean presence (cf. 2 Cor 10:10, Phil 2:1), in the eschatological context it means "coming."[209] It may relate to the coming of high-ranking figure in the social ladder (the king of the province), but in the NT as a theological term, it refers to the final coming of the One who is to come (Rev 1:4). So the

---

205 Barrett, "Significance of the Adam-Christ Typology," 103.

206 A. C. Thiselton, *The First Epistle to the Corinthians. A Commentary to the Greek Text* (The New International Greek Testament Commentary; Grand Rapids–Cambridge 2000), 1229; Thayer, *Thayer's Greek-English Lexicon*, 230.

207 Holleman, *Resurrection and Parousia*, 52.

208 Belonging to Christ is based on faith; A. Johnson, "Firstfruits and Death's Defect: Metaphor in Paul's Rhetorical Strategy in 1 Cor 15:20–28," *WW* 16 (1996): 458.

209 J. Roloff, "Parusie," in *Das Grosse Lexikon zur Bibel. Altes und Neues Testament* (eds. K. Koch et al.; Wien 2004), 387; R. H. Hiers, "Parousia," in *Harper's Bible Dictionary* (ed. P. J. Achtemeier; New York 1985), 751–752, and a phrase "Parusie," in H. Vorgrimler, *Neues Theologisches Wörterbuch* (Freiburg–Basel–Wien 2000²), 479–480.

resurrection of the dead will be the second coming of Christ that is the parousia.[210]

Paul's teaching about the Second Coming is essentially contained in three epistolary parts (1 Thess 4:13–18; 2 Thess 2:1–12; 2 Tim 3:1–9).[211] Heretofore in 1 Thess 4:13–18 the apostle argues that it is not necessary to worry about the fate of dead Thessalonians, and that they will rise from the dead during the second coming of Christ. The basis of faith in the resurrection of the dead during the Second Coming is the fact of Christ's resurrection.[212] At this point of his argument, the apostle confines himself to the perspective of the resurrection of the believers in Christ; they will be resurrected. There is still no question of the fate of those who do not believe in Christ. For Paul, the Second Coming is the ultimate victory over the forces of evil: Christ, renders vain the wicked, who will appear on earth in the last days (2 Thess 2:8). The apostle supplements the doctrine on parousia with a reflection addressed to Timothy, in which he promises universal exemption as an event preceding the re-appearance of Christ on earth (2 Tim 3:1–9).[213]

Apocalyptic drama has a clearly defined end: "Then the end will come, when he hands over the kingdom to God the Father after he has destroyed all dominion, authority and power" (v. 24). The commentators wonders if the term "end" (τέλος) can also mean a resurrection of those who do not belong to Christ.[214] The context, however, shows no interest in those who did not accept the Christian faith. Besides, the Jewish beliefs about the resurrection only mention the resurrection of the righteous.[215] The evidence of these beliefs is an apocryphal fragment: "Then all who have fallen asleep in hope of Him shall rise again. And it shall come to pass at that time that the treasuries will be opened in which is preserved the number of the souls of the righteous, and they shall come forth, and a multitude of souls shall be seen together in one assemblage of one thought, and the first shall rejoice and the last shall not be grieved. For they

---

210   Holleman, *Resurrection and Parousia*, 45–47; C. Rowland, "Parousia," *ABD* V: 167.

211   Jamieson, Fausset and Brown, *Commentary*, 328; J. Murphy-O'Connor, "The First Letter to the Corinthians," in *The New Jerome Biblical Commentary* (eds. R. E. Brown, J. A. Fitzmyer and R. E. Murphy; London 1993), 812.

212   A. Jankowski, *Eschatologia Nowego Testamentu* (Myśl Teologiczna; Kraków 2007), 72.

213   S. J. Stasiak, *Eschatologia w Listach Pasterskich. Specyfika terminów rzeczownikowych* (Legnica 1999), 97.

214   A. Lindemann presents different opinion: "Paulus und die korintische Eschatologie. Zur These von einer 'Entwicklung' im paulinischen Denken," *NTS* 37 (1991): 383. Otherwise J. Weiss, *Der erster Korintherbrief* (KEK; Göttingen 1977), 357–358.

215   H.-A. Wickle, *Das Problem eines messianischen Zwischenreichs bei Paulus* (Zürich 1967), 270–271.

know that the time has come of which it is said, that it is the consummation of the times. But the souls of the wicked, when they behold all these things, shall then waste away the more. For they shall know that their torment has come and their perdition has arrived" (*2 Bar.* 30:1–5).[216] We must therefore take the view that Paul mentions only of the resurrection of Christians. The term, τέλος should be adopted in this context not only as an indication of the fact of the resurrection, but more holistically, as a "fulfilment" or "crowning."[217] This is not a technical term which always points to the end of the world and its history.[218] It can refer to the end of anything, but there are parallels in which the use of the term points to the end of human history (1 Cor 15:24; 1 Pet 4:7; Matt 10:22; 24:6). In *Sibylline Oracles* the term acts in such a capacity as well: "I will give a clear sign for you to know, when everything ends on the earth" (*Sib.* 3:796–797). Similar meaning has a fragment from *4 Ezra*: "But he will deliver in mercy the remnant of my people, those who have been saved throughout my borders, and he will make them joyful until the end comes, the day of judgment, of which I spoke to you at the beginning" (12:34).

From the point of view of textual criticism, the beginning of v. 24 poses some difficulties. They are caused by the verb "hands over." Some versions (ℵ, A, D, P⁴⁶) contain the verb παραδίδω, so the verb used in the present tense in *coniunctivus* form, while others (B, G) prefer the term παραδίδοι in the form of the aorist.[219] However, regardless of which of the facts will be accepted as original, the verb combined with a term ὅταν lets you think of the indefinite time. The existing context indicates that the time of the Kingdom of God will continue until the fulfillment of two conditions; until Christ gives power to his Father, and until he destroys every authority and power. The statement about transferring the Kingdom to the Father means that the Kingdom exists between the two comings of Christ onto the earth. The first coming culminated in the passion, death and resurrection, and the second will fulfill in a parousia. In the history of interpretation of v. 24, there was a conviction (shared earlier by believers in millennial Kingdom) that at first, earthly reign of Christ will appear (after the Second Coming), and it will last until the moment when Christ

---

216 See also: 2 Macc 7:9.14.23.29.36; 12:43–44; *Pss. Sol.* 3, 16; 14, 2; *Ant.* 18, 14; *Bell.* 2, 163; *2 Bar.* 50: 1–51, 6; R. N. Longenecker, *Studies in Paul, Exegetical and Theological* (New Testament Monographs; Sheffield 2004), 194–200.

217 D. H. Stern, *Komentarz żydowski do Nowego Testamentu* (trans. A. Czwojdrak; Warszawa 2004), 688; Thayer, *Thayer's Greek-English Lexicon*, 619–620.

218 Holleman, *Resurrection and Parousia*, 60.

219 Adoption of the aorist means that it will be a single act, not a long process; W. F. Orr and J. A. Walther, *I Corinthians. A New Translation, Introduction with a Study of the Life of Paul, Notes, and Commentary* (The Anchor Bible 32; New York et al. 1976), 333.

delivers this Kingdom to the Father. Then the Kingdom of heaven will come (Eusebius, *Hist. ecc.* 7, 24:4–6).[220] Following this reasoning, many authors have adopted the idea of an earthly reign of Christ.[221] Is it acceptable? To answer this question, first it must be noted that v. 24 writes perfectly in the theme of the Kingdom of God. Terms such as βασιλεία, ὑποτάσσω or καταργέω or belong to the terminology of "reign."[222] The verb καταργέω occurs in v. 24 and v. 26, while the verb ὑποτάσσω occurs five times in just two lines: two times in v. 27 and three times in v. 28. Christ will hand over the kingdom to "God the Father" (τῷ θεῷ καὶ πατρί). The emphasis on the fatherhood of God belongs to the apocalyptic language, as the imperial propaganda of the emperor himself was depicted not only as a "divine" (Lat. *divi*), but also as the "father of the fatherland" (Lat. *pater patriae*).[223] Here, an allusion to Daniel can also be made: "He was given authority, glory and sovereign power; all peoples, nations and men of every language worshiped him. His dominion is an everlasting dominion that will not pass away, and his kingdom is one that will never be destroyed" (Dan 7:14). The prophet refers to the transferring the whole Kingdom to the Son

---

220 C. E. Hill, "Paul's Understanding of Christ's Kingdom in 1 Corinthians 15:20–28," *NovT* 30 (1988) 4: 297.

221 Among them are for example: W. L. M. de Wette (*Kurze Erklärung der Briefe an die Korinther* [Kurgefasstes exegetisches Handbuch zum Neuen Testament II/2; Leipzig 1841], 132–133), P. W. Schmiedel (*Der Briefe an die Thessalonicher und die Korinther* [Hand-Kommentar zum Neuen Testament, II/1; Freiburg 1891], 161), H. J. Holtzmann (*Lehrbuch der neutestamentlichen Theologie* [eds. A. Jürlicher and W. Bauer; II; Tübingen 1911], 227–228), W. Bousset (*Die Religion des Judentums im neutestamentlichen Zeitalter* [Berlin 1906], 331) or A. Schweitzer (*The Mysticism of Paul the Apostle* [London 1956], 90–100). Many of these exegetes see in v. 25 reference to Rev 20. The text mentions about the thousand-year reign of Christ. The sequence of events described by Paul is indeed similar to the ones reported by Rev: defeating enemies of God, and their ultimate destruction, victory over death and Hades; W. Wallis, "The Problem of an Intermediate Kingdom in 1 Corinthians 5.20–28," *JETS* 18 (1975): 229–242. The final analysis of the term in the immediate context leads to the conclusion that it may only mean here the "end/fulfillment"; Wickle, *Das Problem*, 148–149.

222 R. Deville and P. Grelot, "Królestwo," in *Słownik teologii biblijnej* (ed. X. Léon-Dufour; trans. K. Romaniuk; Poznań–Warszawa 1973), 403–406; E. Schweizer, "1 Korinther 15,20–28 als Zeugnis paulinischer Eschatologie und ihrer Verwandtschaft mit der Verkündigung Jesu," in *Jesus und Paulus* (eds. E. E. Ellis and E. Grässer; Göttingen 1975), 301–314.

223 E. M. Lassen, "The Use of the Father Image in Imperial Propaganda and 1 Cor 4:14–21," *TynBul* 42 (1991): 133; B. Witherington III, *Conflict and Community in Corinth: A Socio-Rhetorical Commentary on 1 and 2 Corinthians* (Grand Rapids 1995), 304–305.

of Man. Paul, however, points out that the Son of man is the One, who will return the Kingdom to the Father.[224]

The terms "rule and authority, and power" (ἀρχὴ καὶ ἐξουσία καὶ δύναμις) are the forces that oppose God's reign.[225] In this respect, it is enough to mention, several other fragments by Paul: "For I am convinced that neither death nor life, neither angels nor demons, neither the present nor the future, nor any powers, neither height nor depth, nor anything else in all creation, will be able to separate us from the love of God that is in Christ Jesus our Lord" (Rom 8:38–39); "[... God] raised Him [Christ] from the death and seated him at his right hand in the heavenly realms, far above all rule and authority, power and dominion, and every title that can be given, not only in the present age but also in the one to come" (Eph 1:21–22); "For our struggle is not against flesh and blood, but against the rulers, against the authorities, against the powers of this dark world and against the spiritual forces of evil in the heavenly realms" (Eph 6:12); "And having disarmed the powers and authorities, he made a public spectacle of them, triumphing over them" (Col 2:15; cf. Col 1:16; 2:10). In the history of exegesis, there was a long debate how to extract the true meaning of

---

224 Romaniuk, Jankowski and Stachowiak, *Komentarz*, 162.

225 Extensive studies on these terms and their meaning in Paul's letters were carried: C.E. Arnold, *Powers of Darkness: Principalities and Powers in Paul's Letters* (Dovers Grove 1992); H. Berkhof, *Christ and the Powers* (Scottdale 1977); G. B. Caird, *Principalities and Powers* (Oxford 1956); J. Y. Lee, "Interpreting the Powers in Pauline Thought," *NT* 12 (1970): 54–69; G. H. C. Macgregor, "Principalities and Powers: The Cosmic Background of Paul's Thought," *NTS* 1 (1954–55): 17–28; P. T. O'Brien, "Principalities and Powers: Opponents of the Church," in *Biblical Interpretation and the Church* (ed. D. A. Carson; Nashville 1984), 110–150; H. Schlier, *Principalities and Powers in the New Testament* (Freiburg 1961); Mare, *1 Corinthians*, 285; Henry, *Commentary*, 2273. H. Langkammer called powers, dominions and the authorities "the representatives of the magnates of space"; H. Langkammer, *Komentarz teologiczno-pastoralny wszystkich listów św. Pawła Apostoła z okazji Roku świętego Pawła*, I, *Wielkie listy św. Pawła* (BDL 37; Legnica 2009), 246. "In themselves, these terms are neutral, but used in conjunction with one another in a metaphysical sense, they clearly refer to evil spirits or powers"; S. M. Lewis, *"So That God May Be All in All": The Apocalyptic Message of 1 Corinthians 15,12–34* (TG 42; Rome 1998), 56; H. Lietzmann, *An die Korinther I/II* (Tübingen 1949), 81; G. Münderlein, *Die Überwindung der Mächte. Studien zu theologischen Vorstellung des apokalyptischen Judentums und bei Paulus* (Zürich 1971), 107–109; L. L. Belleville, "Enemy, Enmity, Hatred," in *Dictionary of Paul and His Letters. A Compendium of Contemporary Biblical Scholarship* (eds. G. F. Hawthorne and R. P. Martin: Dovners Grove–Leicester 1993), 236.

the terms "Rulers," "Authorities," and "Powers" in Paul's meaning.[226] Certainly, these terms are not used as common names (like Beelzebub and Belial), but they show some classified groups. The interpretation to the texts in which Paul uses these names leads to the conclusion of their ambiguous nature. In practice, this means that the relative importance of each of these names generally has to be inferred from the context. In most cases they appear in the plural, and are arranged side by side (at least two or three). These forces, unlike the demons, do not live in a man or idols, and do not reside in underworlds but their domains are rather "the heaven and the earth" and "this time."

The term "sovereignty" (ἀρχή) begins with the prefix ἀρχ-, which in classical Greek, usually indicates the position of a socially high-ranking person endowed with authority or responsibility. Such was the use of the prefix in the Jewish tradition of the Diaspora, as a translation from Theodotion says about ἀρχαί in the case of earthly monarchs:

> "Then the sovereignty, power
> and greatness of the kingdoms under the whole heaven
> will be handed over to the saints, the people of the Most High" (Dan 7:27a).

For this reason, many exegetes see the relationship of Paul's argument within the prophecy of Daniel. As the vision of Daniel presents the defeat of four kingdoms, Paul also interprets this vision on a base of *pesher*, and speaks about four opponents (Power, Sovereignty, Authority and death).[227] Probably, the equivalent of the Greek ἀρχαί there is also in the Ethiopian apocrypha, which refers to the spiritual powers which were harnessed to serve God: "And He will summon all the host of the heavens, and all the holy ones above, and the host of God, the Cherubic, Seraphin and Ophannin, and all the angels of power, and all the angels of principalities, and the Elect One, and the other powers on the earth (and) over the water. On that day shall raise one voice, and bless and glorify and exalt in the spirit of faith, and in the spirit of wisdom, and in the spirit of

---

226 Bultmann, pointing to the authorities and powers, spoke about the mythical projection of human weaknesses, Cullmann saw in them both non-material and political powers; Berkhof developed the idea of the latter, seeing in the realities not only socio-political structures but also the spiritual dimension of the society. While the research carried by W. Wink led him to the conclusion that Paul referred to "inner and outer aspects of any given manifestation of power"; W. Wink, *Naming the Powers* (Philadelphia 1984), 5. The author adds: "powers are both heavenly and earthly, divine and human, spiritual and political, invisible and structural"; ibid., 100. However, it is also worth citing early Christian interpretations. And so, for Chrysostom "authorities" are "the authorities of evil" (*1 Cor. Hom.* 39,6), for Origen they are "spiritual powers" (*Princ.* 3,3-1-3), for Cyril of Alexandria they are just the evil spirits (*Fragm. Ad 1 Cor* 3,305).

227 Lewis, *"So That God May Be All in All"*, 57.

patience, and in the spirit of mercy, and in the spirit of judgment and of peace, and in the spirit of goodness" (*1 En.* 61:10–11a).[228] In *Corpus Paulinum*, this term occurs several times: in addition to the current verse it also can be found in Rom 8:38; Eph 1:21; 3:10; 6:12; and Col 1:16; 2:10.15. The second of the terms that Paul uses to describe opponents who Chris will vanquish is ἐξουσίαι. This term can also be found in Eph 1:21, 2:2, 3:10, 6:12, and Col 116; 2:10.15. In the NT, it often means the authority given to the officials. In precisely this sense, ἐξουσίαι is used by Paul in Rom 13:1–3. However, in the apocryphal tradition, the term refers to the heavenly powers. An example in this regard may be a part of the vision of Levi, which describes the seven heavens: "And above them are the holy ones. And in the highest of all dwelleth the Great Glory, far above all holiness. In the heaven next to it are the archangels, who minister and make propitiation to the Lord for all the sins of ignorance of the righteous; Offering to the Lord a sweet smelling savour, a reasonable and a bloodless offering. ... And in the heaven next to this are thrones and dominions [ἐξουσίαι] in which always they offer praise to God" (*Test. Lev.* 3:6–8). The "Thrones and Dominions" in the vision of Levi occupy the highest heaven, and with thrones they are located in close proximity to God (cf. *1 En.* 61:10). In this case, therefore, they are servants, not enemies of God. Finally, Paul speaks of "powers" (δύναμεις) as the enemies of Christ. According to Dan 8:10 (LXX), the "powers of heaven" together with the stars have been dropped to the earth. Philo of Alexandria often uses the term δύναμεις to determine the angels (*Migr. Abr. 181*). The author of the *Book of Jubilees* also says about the "power of heaven": "And the angel of the presence who went before the camp of Israel took the tables of the divisions of the years from the time of the creation of the law and of the testimony of the weeks of the jubilees, according to the individual years, according to all the number of the jubilees [according, to the individual years], from the day of the [new] creation when the heavens and the earth shall be renewed and all their creation according to the powers of the heaven" (*Jub.* 1:29). In addition, the LXX title יְהוָה צְבָאוֹת is often interpreted as "the Most High."

To sum up, it may be said that the references to the biblical and extra-biblical Jewish literature suggests that the rulers, authorities, and powers can mean not only the forces hostile to God but also angels and spiritual powers that are in the service of God. Focusing only on one shade of the meaning of these terms, Paul in v. 24 uses them to name enemies of Christ.

---

228 R. G. Reid, "Principalities and Powers," in *Dictionary of Paul and His Letters. A Compendium of Contemporary Biblical Scholarship* (eds. G. F. Hawthorne and R. P. Martin; Dovners Grove–Leicester 1993), 748. Trans. R. Rubinkiewicz in: *Apokryfy Starego Testamentu* (ed. R. Rubinkiewicz; Warszawa 1999), 162.

Such a limitation to understanding what powers, rulers and authorities are, is justified in Paul's contemporary Qumran literature. Before Paul's day, Palestinian Judaism became a real problem. A presence of the Roman armies on the territory promised by God to Abraham was the cause of it. It was not only a social and political problem, but also theological one. As a result, an idea of war against the forces of evil as one of the solutions to the problem was developed in the first-century B.C. The idea was presented by members of the Qumran community in the *Rule of War*. Starting from Dan 11:40–12:3, and expanding the picture outlined there, the inhabitants of Qumran presented a scenario of war between the sons of light. The sons of lights were accompanied by the angelic forces while the sons of darkness were aided by Belial and the powers of evil (1QM 1:1–14). In the writings from Qumran, the evil forces are represented by pagan nations such as Edom, Moab, Philistia and Ashur. Since Paul, after he had a supernatural vision with Christ in Damascus, became a Christian, and eventually became the protagonist of the good news among the pagan nations, could no longer see the gentiles as enemies of God. Thus, the transposition of the importance of forces hostile to God from the pagan nations to the forces of evil is understandable.[229]

The final victory of Christ will therefore be preceded by a struggle with the forces of evil. This motif is also present in the Jewish apocalyptic literature. It is worth quoting in this context, only one fragment: "Blood shall drip from wood, and the stone shall utter its voice; the peoples shall be troubled, and the stars shall fall. … and the sea of Sodom shall cast up fish; and one whom the many do not know shall make his voice heard by night, and all shall hear his voice. There shall be chaos also in many places and fire shall often break out, and the wild beasts shall roam beyond their haunts" (*4 Ezra* 5:5–8).[230] The author continues this apocryphal image using the following words: "At that time friends shall make war on friends like enemies, and the earth and those who inhabit it shall be terrified, and the springs of the fountains shall stand still, so that for three hours they shall not flow" (*4 Ezra* 6:24).[231] This vision includes many artistic images

---

229 "The immediate context of 1 Corinthians 15:24 leaves no doubt about whether Paul ever spoke of the powers as being evil, for there they are listed among the eschatological enemies (1 Cor 15:25–26; cf. Eph 6:12), including death"; Reid, "Principalities and Powers," 751.

230 C. S. Keener, *1–2 Corinthians* (The New Cambridge Bible Commentary; Cambridge et al. 2005), 127.

231 *Apokryfy Starego Testamentu*, 382. This book contains seven visions, one of which concerns the fate of the dead and the end of the world, and signs of the times preceding it as well. According to the author of the apocrypha, Messianic kingdom is expected to last four hundred years. See.: M. E. Stone, "Apocalyptic Literature," in *Compendium*

drawn from the natural world. Paul, however, omits this dimension in his scenario, focusing mainly on the spiritual fight. The scenario of final events outlined by Paul in vv. 23–24 is presented as follows:

(1) resurrection of Christ;
(2) the resurrection of believers at Christ's Second Coming;
(3) coming of the end:
  a. transferring the power to God and the Father;
  b. overcoming all the rulers, authority and power.[232]

The necessity of the reign of Christ over the rulers, authorities and powers is indicated in this case by a typical Greek verb declaring an urgent need or duty: δεῖ γὰρ αὐτὸν βασιλεύειν (v. 25). The term δεῖ clearly denotes the apocalyptic context of the statement that nothing can thwart God's plans which are already being fulfilled.[233] The last verb in this statement (βασιλεύειν) confirms the terminology of domination used in this section.[234] It is also interesting to look at vv. 25–26 through the history of the chosen people. Many authors emphasize that Paul presents the history of the Messiah through the prism of his nation's own history, in which he stands a few steps including the struggle (entering the promised land), victory, coming of a monarchy, the construction of the temple, and the celebration. Similar steps can be distinguished in the Messianic work of Christ: the struggle and victory over the forces of evil (Col 2:15; cf. Col 1:12–14)—kingship of God (vv. 25–26; Phil 2:9; Col 3:1; Eph 1:20–22; 1 Tim 3:16)—a construction of the new temple (1 Cor 3:16–17; 2 Cor 6:16; Eph 2:19–

---

rerum iudaicarum ad Novum Testamentum, II, *Jewish Writings of Second Temple Period. Apocrypha, Pseudoepigrapha, Qumran Sectarian Writings, Philo, Josephus* (ed. M. E. Stone, Assen–Philadelphia 1984), 412–417.

232 G. D. Fee, *The First Epistle to the Corinthians* (NICNT; Grand Rapids 1987), 752. Cf. B. J. Malina and J. J. Pilch, *Social-Science Commentary on the Letters of Paul* (Minneapolis 2006), 125; M. L. Soards, "First Corinthians," in *Mercer Commentary on the Bible* (eds. W. E. Mills and R. F. Wilson; Macon 1995), 1187; Henry, *Commentary*, 2273–2274; J. Lambrecht, "Pierwszy List do Koryntian," in *Międzynarodowy komentarz do Pisma Świętego. Komentarz katolicki i ekumeniczny na XXI wiek* (eds. W. R. Farmer et al.; Polish eds. W. Chrostowski, T. Mieszkowski and P. Pachciarek; trans. B. Widła; Warszawa 2001), 1483.

233 H. Conzelmann, *1 Corinthians: A Commentary* (Hermeneia; Philadelphia 1975), 272; "The term δεῖ is either an apocalyptic term referring to God's fixed and detailed timetable or points to God's plan as it is manifested in Scripture"; Lambrecht, "Paul's Christological Use of Scripture," 506.

234 "From the resurrection onward Christ is reigning and the purpose of this kingship is the subjection of all enemies. This is the main part of Paul's thesis (vv. 23–24) which he proves by means of Scripture: it is contained in God's plan"; Lambrecht, "Paul's Christological Use of Scripture," 507.

22)—and the adulation (Phil 2:10–11).[235] There are also authors that, in the motif of the reign of Christ, see an indirect reference to the messianic period between the contemporary times and the future.[236] However, there are no arguments that would confirm such an idea concerning this fragment from the letter.[237]

In v. 25 there is a quote from Ps 110:1 which is particularly interesting for this analysis: "he must reign until he has put all his enemies under his feet." The other quotation from this psalm can be found only two verses further but this time it comes from Ps 8:7 (for He "has put everything under his feet"). The term "must," as mentioned above, is an apocalyptic and often, according to Paul's point of view, points to the necessity of the fulfillment of the Scriptures.[238] One cannot exclude the possibility that Paul took over the compilation of both citations from an earlier tradition which had already been stabilized in the teaching of the Church.[239] At this point, however, our preliminary attention must be paid to the first one (עַד־אָשִׁית אֹיְבֶיךָ הֲדֹם לְרַגְלֶיךָ) considering its importance in the most immediate context. We should later stop on a possible compilation of both. In the previous line (v. 24), the apostle spoke about defeating Domain, Authority and Power. Now they are directly qualified as "all enemies" (πάντας τοὺς ἐχθρούς) of Christ. This qualification is done through the incorporation of a quotation from Ps 110:1b in the context of references to the enemies of Christ. A list of such enemies also includes death: "The last enemy to be destroyed is death" (ἔσχατος ἐχθρὸς καταργεῖται ὁ θάνατος; v. 26).[240] As rulers, authorities, and powers are interpreted personally, going after the same line, the death can also be seen as having personal traits.[241] Paul wants the Corinthians to realize three things:

---

235 Reid, "Principalities and Powers," 751; Malina and Pilch, *Social-Science Commentary*, 125–126.

236 C. S. Keener, *Komentarz historyczno-kulturowy do Nowego Testamentu* (eds. K. Bardski and W. Chrostowski; trans. Z. Kościsk; Warszawa 2000), 372.

237 "According to Paul, there will not be the messianic kingdom on the earth between parousia and the last judgment. The Second Coming and the judgment coincide with each other"; Lambrecht, "Pierwszy List do Koryntian," 1483.

238 Lambrecht, "Paul's Christological Use of Scripture," 506.

239 Hill, "Paul's Understanding of Christ's Kingdom," 313. Psalm 110 is the most often quoted text in NT from the OT; Fee, *First Epistle to the Corinthians*, 755.

240 Paul sees the death as an enemy, in contrary to some of the Greek philosophers, such as Epictetus (*Diatr.* 1:27,7); Keener, *1–2 Corinthians*, 127; Romaniuk, Jankowski and Stachowiak, *Komentarz*, 162.

241 Murphy-O'Connor, "The First Letter to the Corinthians," 812.

(1) death should be seen by the recipients of the letter in the same way as they perceive the Dominion, the Authority and the Power;

(2) death is the same enemy of the Corinthians, as the powers of darkness;

(3) the reign of Christ will destroy death, like all the other forces of evil.[242]

In the OT, you can often find some mentions of the personified death. Here are just a few of them: "Like sheep they are destined for the grave, and death will feed on them. The upright will rule over them in the morning; their forms will decay in the grave, far from their princely mansions. But God will redeem my life from the grave; he will surely take me to himself" (Ps 49:14–15); "Death has climbed in through our windows and has entered our fortresses; it has cut off the children from the streets and the young men from the public squares" (Jer 9:21); "indeed, wine betrays him; he is arrogant and never at rest. Because he is as greedy as the grave and like death is never satisfied, he gathers to himself all the nations and takes captive all the peoples" (Hab 2:5). Although death will be overcome in the future, it is understandable that Paul speaks about the process that has begun with the death and resurrection of Christ. It is important to note that the adjective ἔσχατος is on the emphatic position in the sentence. As a result, it emphasizes the two following facts: that death is an enemy, and that it will be destroyed as the last one. Some exegetes see in this emphasis, Paul's response to the "obsession with the present time," which could have touched some of the Corinthians.[243]

There are a lot of discussions among exegetes regarding the subject of the phrase "until he has put" (ἄχρι οὗ θῇ). The subject of the phrase is Christ, which provides only grammatical reasons. This is because this phrase is preceded by the statement, "for he must reign," referring to Christ. For Christ also indicates the end of v. 24: "after he has destroyed all dominion, authority and power." For the fact that God may be the subject of the phrase means that it is God who is the subject of the psalm from which Paul draws the quote. It is God who subordinates everything under the feet of Christ. In addition, in v. 28, God is the one who submitted everything to Christ. However, it seems that there are insufficient reasons for which we should waive a grammar. Therefore, Christ ought to be regarded as the subject of this part of a sentence.[244]

---

242   Lewis, *"So That God May Be All in All"*, 58; "Verse 26 with its thesis that death is an inimical cosmological power to be destroyed by the reigning Christ in itself represents the crucial modification of the christological traditions known to the Corinthians deniers"; de Boer, *Defeat of Death*, 121.

243   So: C. Wolff, *Der erste Brief des Paulus an die Korinther* (THKNT 7; Leipzig 1996), 388.

244   This view is also G. D. Fee: "Almost certainly we must go with the grammar here and see Christ as the subject"; *First Epistle to the Corinthians*, 756; Lambrecht, "Pierwszy List do Koryntian," 1483.

Paul interprets Ps 110:1b in the same way as it was understood by the first Christian communities, by using this text in order to express faith in the messianic mission of Jesus. Matthew, who noted the words of Jesus, also has this opinion: "How is it then that David, speaking by the Spirit, calls him 'Lord'? For he says, 'The Lord said to my Lord: Sit at my right hand until I put your enemies under your feet.' If then David calls him 'Lord,' how can he be his son?" (cf. Matt 22:43b–45). A quote from Ps 110 appears in the speech of Peter, in which he justifies the Resurrection of Christ: "God has raised this Jesus to life, and we are all witnesses of the fact. Exalted to the right hand of God, he has received from the Father the promised Holy Spirit and has poured out what you now see and hear. For David did not ascend to heaven, and yet he said, 'The Lord said to my Lord: Sit at my right hand until I make your enemies a footstool for your feet.'" (Acts 2:32–35). As shown above, Paul quotes Ps 110:1b after the LXX, not the HB. Nevertheless, the Hebrew text reflects a bit more hostility than the Greek translation (which will rule on the day of parousia between the returning Messiah and His enemies) because it evokes the image of the footstool—referring to the old customs established in the ancient Near East. Archaeologists have shown that the footrests of former royal thrones often depicted images of the fiercest enemies of the king. Judaic thought included in the Apocrypha also presents the Messiah in his royal splendour, drawing his image as a figure sitting on a throne: "And the Elect One shall in those days sit on My throne, And his mouth shall pour forth all the secrets of wisdom and counsel: For the Lord of Spirits hath given (them) to him and hath glorified him" (*1 En.* 51:3). A similar vision appears in *Psalms of Solomon*:

> "And he shall be a righteous king, taught of God, over them,
> And there shall be no unrighteousness in his days in their midst,
> For all shall be holy and their king the anointed of the Lord"
> (*Pss. Sol.* 17:32).

In Jewish literature from the early Christian period, allusions to Ps 110 are numerous.[245] *Testament of Levi* speaks of the priestly and kingly exaltation: "And I saw seven men in white raiment saying unto me: Arise, put on the robe of the priesthood, and the crown of righteousness, and the breastplate of understanding, and the garment of truth, and the late of faith, and the turban of the head, and the ephod of prophecy. And they severally carried these things and put them on me, and said unto me: 'From henceforth become a priest of the Lord, …'. The fourth put round me a girdle like unto purple. The fifth gave me a

---

245 Hay, *Glory At the Right Hand*, 9–20. The author claims that in the NT, there are 33 citations and allusions to Ps 110:1–4. In other Christians writings produced before the mid-second century, there are seven of them. See also: T. Callan, "Psalm 110:1," 625.

branch of rich olive. The sixth placed a crown on my head. The seventh placed on my head a diadem of priesthood" *(Test. Lev.* 8). Apocrypha speaks directly of the priestly dignity; however, a wreath on his head and a purple colour girdle may also suggest the royal dignity. Additionally, the consecration of the priest is depicted in *The Book of Jubilees*: "and Levi dreamed that they had ordained and made him the priest of the Most High God, him and his sons for ever; and he awoke from his sleep and blessed the Lord" *(Jub.* 31:1). Until the third century B.C., the Jews related Ps 110 to various characters from the OT (Abraham, David, Hezekiah). During this period, the messianic interpretation of Ps 110 came into being.

The subsequent verse (v. 27) contains the next quotation from the OT. Therefore, a broader discussion of the poem and its links with the immediate context will be carried in the succeeding chapter, which will be directly devoted to this subject. Here, however, we should stop at the functions of v. 27. This approach will allow us to understand in a deeper way the importance of the quotation included in v. 25b. Verse 27 in the literal translation is as follows: "For he has put everything under his feet." Now when it says that "everything" has been put under him, it is clear that this does not include God himself, who put everything under Christ. Pauline discourse in v. 27 begins with a quote from Ps 8:7b and is followed by an explanation. The quote itself will be the subject of detailed analysis in the next chapter of this work. Here, however, we will stop at its content so far as it influences the interpretation of the quotation from Ps 110:1b, which is the subject of the analysis carried out in this chapter. In some manuscripts (P⁴⁶, B, 33, Vulg.) the term ὅτι before πάντα, is missed while others (A, B, F, G, syr) retain it. The issue of textual criticism seems to be very complicated in this place. However, the presence of the term or its lack does not substantially affect the meaning of the sentence."[246].

The formulation "He has put everything under his feet" makes it clear that Paul's writings are interpreted from the point of view of Christology.[247] We can see this not only in v. 25, but also a fragment from Ephesians: "And God placed all things under his feet and appointed him to be head over everything for the church, which is his body, the fullness of him who fills everything in every way"

---

246 Thiselton, *First Epistle to the Corinthians*, 1234.

247 "Paul and others evidently fund in Ps. 8.6b [in a different numbering—7b—my footnote] an appriopriate description of Jesus' exaltation (most clearly in 1 Cor. 15:27)"; Dunn, *Theology of Paul*, 210; F. W. Maier, "Ps 110:1 (LXX 109,1) im Zusammenhang von 1 Kor 15:24–26," *BZ* 20 (1932): 139–156; Fee, *First Epistle to the Corinthians*, 755; Conzelmann, *1 Corinthians: A Commentary*, 272–273; Lietzmann, *An die Korinther I/II*, 81; J. Hering, *The First Epistle of St Paul to the Corinthians* (London 1962), 168; E. B. Allo, *Saint Paul. Première Épître aux Corinthiens* (Paris 1956), 408.

(1:22–23; cf. Eph 3:21).[248] Because "everything" has been put under Christ (πάντα), His reign is cosmic and universal.[249] The purpose of apocalyptic events is to achieve full reign of God: "When he has done this, then the Son himself will be made subject to him who put everything under him, so that God may be all in all" (v. 28). In this perspective, Christ is seen as an intermediary to achieve the goal of subordinating everything to God. God himself is both the source and purpose.[250] "Apocalyptic drama" described in vv. 23–28 reaches its climax here: Christ who "has indeed been raised from the dead, the firstfruits of those who have fallen asleep" (v. 20), receives dominion over "everything" and then he passes the control to his Father. In this way, the state described in Ps 8:5–6 is reached: "You made him a little lower than the heavenly beings and crowned him with glory and honor. You made him ruler over the works of your hands; you put everything under his feet." The statement "all in all" (πάντα ἐν πᾶσιν) means in Paul—everything that God created and over which his dominion extends (cf. Col 3:11; Eph 4:5–6).[251] This phrase also appears in Paul in Colossians: "Here there is no Greek or Jew, circumcised or uncircumcised, barbarian, Scythian, slave or free, but Christ is all, and is in all" (Col 3:11; cf. Rom 11:36; Col 1:16–17; Eph 1:23). This idea is developed in different ways in 1 Cor and so Paul emphasizes God's dominion (1:26–28.30; 2:1.5.11–12.14; 3:6–7.9.23)[252]; everything— including the salvation of the Corinthians—comes from God (1:30; 8:6; 11:30); all head for God (8:6, 15:28), Christ himself comes from God (1:30, 11:3), and from God also the Spirit comes (2:10–14; 3:16; 6:11;

---

248 See: "and put everything under his feet. In putting everything under him, God left nothing that is not subject to him. Yet at present we do not see everything subject to him" (Heb 2:8).

249 "Everything" understood in the context of 1 Cor 15:54–58 means death, sin and the Law; Thiselton, *First Epistle to the Corinthians*, 1239; Fabris, *Prima Lettera ai Corinzi*, 205.

250 "Thus God remains the source and goal; Christ remains the means through which the goal which God purposes comes to be brought about"; Thiselton, *First Epistle to the Corinthians*, 1236; Mare, *1 Corinthians*, 286; Romaniuk, Jankowski and Stachowiak, *Komentarz*, 162.

251 Lewis, *"So That God May Be All in All"*, 66–67. C. K. Barrett argues that this phrase should be interpreted „soteriologically, not metaphysically, and that it is a matter of God's sole and unchallenged reign"; *A Commentary on the First Epistle to the Corinthians* (London 1971), 361; see: Allo, *Saint Paul*, 409; Conzelmann, *1 Corinthians: A Commentary*, 275.

252 Stern, *Komentarz*, 688; Soards, "First Corinthians," 1187.

7:40; 12:3).[253] Certainly, the phrase "all in all" is not a reference to Stoicism, which would mean that all beings will be engulfed by the original fire.[254]

To sum up, to determine the importance of the quotation from Ps 110:1b in v. 25b it should be noted that it comes from a royal psalm, and that the apostle uses it to show the reign of Christ, under whose feet all his enemies were put.[255] The author of the psalm makes the subject of the work of God, "your enemies," while Paul—"all enemies." In the psalm, the author promises that God will make the defeated enemies "a footstool for your feet." Paul instead speaks of the total subordination of all hostile forces to God.[256] Outlining this final scenario, Paul asserts that the enemies of God are dominion, authority as well as the (personified)[257] death itself. These powers have already been defeated by Christ and will eventually fail at the resurrection of believers in Christ.[258] Ultimately, Christ who conquered death will be subject to God, and He will be "all in all." The quotation takes both a Christocentric and eschatological dimension. It results from the messianic interpretation of Ps 110.

---

253 N. Richardson, *Paul's Language about God* (JSNTSup 99; Sheffield 1994), 114–115. The phrase "that God may be, all in all" became the subject of much controversy in the first centuries of Christendom. Origen argued for a temporal duration of the earth, which God is the source and purpose (*Princ.* 3,5,6). Chrysops argued that the fact that God will be "all in all" in no way diminishes the exaltation of Christ, referred to Phil 2:9. (*1 Cor. Hom.* 39:8–9). Augustine accents this fact with even greater emphasis, on the grounds that the surrender of the kingdom to the Father through Christ does not mean that Christ would lose his power (*Trin.* 1:8,16).

254 Keener, *Komentarz*, 372.

255 Mare, *1 Corinthians*, 285.

256 Heil, *Rhetorical Role of Scripture*, 208. A broader list of differences between the text of Paul and the text of Ps 110:1 presents L. Kreitzer; *Jesus and God in Paul's Eschatology* (JSNTSup 19; Sheffield 1987), 149.

257 Lambrecht, "Pierwszy List do Koryntian," 1483.

258 "Paul is going to argue that the resurrection of Christ, which the Corinthians accept, is so inextricably linked with the resurrection of the believer that to deny one is to deny the other"; Lewis, *"So That God May Be All in All"*, 73.

III. Quotation from Ps 8:7b in 1 Cor 15:27a

1 Cor 15:27a: πάντα γὰρ ὑπέταξεν ὑπὸ τοὺς πόδας αὐτοῦ

Ps 8:7b (LXX): πάντα ὑπέταξας ὑποκάτω τῶν ποδῶν αὐτοῦ

Ps 8:7b (HB): כֹּל שַׁתָּה תַחַת־רַגְלָיו

1. Source of the Quotation

It should be noted first that the LXX translation is broadly consistent with the HB. If we assume that Paul follows the LXX, it must be noted that he makes some changes: he changes the second person singular of the verb (ὑπέταξας) into the third person (ὑπέταξεν) and he replaces the wording ὑποκάτω τῶν ποδῶν αὐτοῦ from the LXX, with a different formulation with a similar meaning: ὑπὸ τοὺς πόδας αὐτοῦ. This change of ὑποκάτω to ὑπό is typical in Paul, because the term ὑποκάτω does not appear in his writings, while the term ὑπό is there often.[259] In relation to the text of the LXX and the HB, the apostle adds the particle γάρ. Pauline text agrees, however, with the grammatical person of the verb from the HB (third-person singular). The fact that in 1 Cor 15:27 there is a third person, not the second, is not caused by the fact that Paul necessarily had to reach for the HB. Rather, the reason is that he had to integrate this quote into a context in which the third person was logically essential. The person changing may also be motivated by the intention of the assimilation of the phrase to v. 25b. So, taking into account the fact that the introduced particle interferes with both the texts (the LXX and HB) and that the change of a grammatical person of the verb does not have to be justified in proceeding the HB, but the necessity of integrating the relevant quote in the context of Paul's argument; we are inclined to assume that the source of the citation is LXX.[260]

---

259 Heil, *Rhetorical Role of Scripture*, 209; Stanley, *Paul and the Language of Scripture*, 207.

260 So it: Terry, *Discourse Analysis*, 159, and Ellis, *Paul's Use of the Old Testament*, 152.

2. The Meaning in the Original Context

The quotation πάντα γὰρ ὑπέταξεν ὑπὸ τοὺς πόδας αὐτοῦ comes from Ps 8:7b, where the original version is written as follows: כֹּל שַׁתָּה תַחַת־רַגְלָיו. It is a phrase, which, as a whole reads:

> "You made him ruler over the works of your hands;
> you put everything under his feet:
> all flocks and herds,
> and the beasts of the field,
> the birds of the air, and the fish of the sea,
> all that swim the paths of the seas." (vv. 7–9)

Psalm 8 is a sapiential hymn, which praises the Creator, and express admiration for him and at the same time shows the unique position of a man in the whole work of creation.[261] Ideologically, the psalmist builds his hymn on the basis of a rule of a "triangle" whose sides are God, a man and God's creation. The main protagonist is God. The man is the measure portrayed in relation to God and to the rest of his creation.[262] The author directs the reader's thought or reciting person of the psalm not so much on the perfection and magnificence of the universe created by God, but rather on the power of the Creator, which is visible in His works. Although, the man knows his limitations (because he is mortal and sinful), he expresses his delight over the fact that God remembers him, and takes care of him.

2.1. Ideological Base and the Literary Structure in Ps 8:2–10

The Psalm begins and ends with the same acclamation of praise for God and his "majestic" name: "O Lord, our Lord, how majestic is your name in all the earth!" (v. 2a and v. 10). This inclusion takes the grammatical form of the plural, while the whole body of the psalm is written in the singular. Such changes of a grammatical person are not uncommon, especially in Hebrew poetry. Since the song is designed for public performance, probably liturgical, it can consist of parts intended for the soloist and the congregation. Initial and final acclamation, through the use of particle מָה ("how"),[263] adds a tone of admiration, and a sound of the reflective tone to this work.

---

261 Brzegowy, *Psalmy* 77.
262 G. Ravasi, *Psalmy*, I, *Wprowadzenie i Psalmy 1–19* (trans. P. Mikulska; Kraków 2007), 203.
263 *BDB*, 552.

The inclusion is one of the main structural elements of the entire work. In v. 2a it replaces the call, which is a classical element of the national anthem, and it takes the form of an antiphonal exclamation. The inclusion involves two smaller parts, like the verses of the song. They, in a progressive but opposite way, develop the thoughts of the author. With this opposition, they create the form of chiasm. Thus, in vv. 2b–5 the stability and unchangeability of the universe were contrasted to human changeability, while in vv. 6–9 the intelligence and humane dignity have been opposed to any other beings over which man is to take the control. In the first scene, the omnipotence of God was emphasized, in the second one—the power and dignity of humans.[264] The basic structure of the work is thus as follows:

Antiphon of inclusion: the acclamation to God's name (v. 2a);
    Scene one: the omnipotence of God and a man (vv. 2b–5);
    Scene two: the power of a man and God (vv. 6–9);
Antiphon of inclusion: the acclamation to God's name (v. 10).[265]

An admiration to "our Lord" is expressed in the work. His personage is seen in the perspective of the "whole earth."[266] The particle מָה composes a formal part of the division of the psalm; it comes not only to a structural decision, which sets the internal shape of the work, but also the differences in content, giving the dynamic for the text. The same particle, which in v. 2a and in v. 10 takes the character of exclamation expressing admiration, connects the wonderment with the question of the position of a man in the work of a creation in v. 5. The psalmist just drives to it. Contemplation of the creation leads to the delight of the position of a man, and the place assigned to him by God in the hierarchy of beings. The question "what is a man?" is the key to make out the meaning of the psalm. This question has, at the same time, a reflective tone and a sense of admiration. A man is a being that poses this question to him. Simultaneously, he knows and does not know the answer. This answer delights him, and at the same time leads to further reflection, and consequently—to additional questions. He asks about his place in the universe made by the God, and at the same time he asks about the work of creation itself. He thinks over what there is and what has been created and what God in his greatness and wisdom has called into existence. What is more, a man is aware that in his reflection, he will never come to an end. A man discovers, however, that he is in a completely unique and privileged position in the midst of all creations. This position is not earned

---

264 Lach, *Księga Psalmów*, 126.
265 Ravasi, *Psalmy*, 205. Quite a similar structure presents Brzegowy; *Psalmy* , 78.
266 This phrase brings to mind Isaiah's universality: "the whole earth is full of his glory" (Isa 6:3).

by his own efforts, but in a completely free manner given by the Creator to him. The verb "made him" clearly indicates to this fact (תְּחַסְּרֵהוּ; v. 6). In this question, the psalmist represents every human being. He speaks not only on behalf of the Israelite, as a member of the chosen by God people, but also on behalf of all the inhabitants of the earth.

The particle used two times מָה once to God (v. 2a and v. 10) and once to man (v. 5) establishes a double relationship on the line God-man. The relationship concerns the name and a function. As for the name, God is presented as He revealed himself to Moses. (JHWH; יְהוָה), while a man is shown in the relation of sonship to God ("son of man"; בֶּן־אָדָם). As for the function, God is shown as our Lord (אָדוֹן) which indicates to the dynamic control over the creation. God turns out to be the Lord not only of the creation but also of history. Man is shown, however, as מֹשֵׁל ("head," "leader," "ruler") always subordinated to the Lord (אָדוֹן).[267] The name of God opens and closes the psalm, and it is He, not man, who is the main focus of the psalm. This is an anthem for honoring God, not for man's honor: the Psalmist worships God through man.[268] The terms "man" and "son of man" in v. 5 are devoid of articles, which indicates that the psalmist had in mind every person as an individual.[269] Man, taken from the earth, remains closer to God than the animals. His position is thus determined by the elevation, not through lowliness. In the background of the psalm a description of the creation taken from Gen 1[270] resounds continually. In this description, the psalmist also finds a specific answer to his question "what is man?" Man is the image of God; he was created in His own image (Gen 1:26–27). It is possible that the author does not want to bring the question up directly but in this way he wants to underline its importance.

---

267   L. Alonso Schökel, *Trenta salmi: poesia e preghiera* (trans. A. Ranon; Bologna 1982), 5–67.

268   In this context L. Alonso Schökel cites the phrase of Hengstenberger: "Die Grösse Gottes in der Grösse des Menschen"; id., *Trenta salmi*, 68.

269   "L'autore non si interroga sull'umanità presa collettivamente, ma su ciascuno dei suoi membri. Tutti e ciascuno partecipano di questa condizione, tutti e ciascuno suscitano la domanda sconcertata. Per ora nessuno si appropria di questa designazione per antonomasia"; Alonso Schökel, *Trenta salmi*, 68.

270   The direct impact of the story about the creation is not certain, but it can be assumed based on the use of similar terminology by the Psalmist: "heaven," "earth," "moon," "star," "reign," "man," "host," "fish," "see." Even less certain is the influence of Gen 2– 3 on the author of the psalm, but allusions to the parade of creatures and man's fall are almost certain.

2.2. Exegetical Analysis of Ps 8:2–10

V. 2a and v. 10 As mentioned above, v. 2a and v. 10 are identical and they constitute the inclusion opening and closing the psalm, which is also a carrier element of its structure. It is an exclamation of wonder full of praising of God's name that is "majestic" "in all the earth." God is called "our Lord." In the biblical language of the OT, the title was referred to the king. Nathan asked Bathsheba: "Have you not heard that Adonijah, the son of Haggith, has become king without our lord David's knowing it?" (1 Kgs 1:11; see 1 Kgs 1:43.47). In Ps 97:5 God, exalted as the King, is called the Lord of all the earth. So this title is referred to God as the King over Israel and the whole world.[271]

A term for the earth (אֶרֶץ) shows both the territorial dimension, as well as the ethnic one; the name of God is "majestic" on the planet and among all the people inhabiting it. Although God's Shekinah has set as a dwelling the holy city of Jerusalem, and in it the temple; His name is known and admired throughout the world. The Jews were convinced of the special presence of God in the temple. Concentric circles more and more restrictively limited the access to internal parts of the sanctuary, to the extent that only one high priest could come to the Holy of Holies once a year. This peculiar geography of holiness included sequentially: Holy of Holies, Holy Place, the priestly courtyard, the Jews courtyard, the women's courtyard, the courtyard of the Gentiles, the city closed with walls and finally, the entire Holy Land given to Abraham and his descendants.[272] Despite this belief, the exclamation "in all the earth" makes a reference to a trait of universalism. It was also present in some books of the prophets. Although God chose the nation of Israel for his own and put it in the promised land, however, he is God, the Creator and a ruler of the whole inhabited earth, and he also extends his authority throughout the universe.

In the Bible, the term "majestic" (אַדִּיר) in relation to persons is restricted almost exclusively to God.[273] The words relate solely to God: "You are resplendent with light, more majestic (אַדִּיר) than mountains rich with game" (Ps 76:5) and (אַדִּיר) on "high is mighty" (Ps 93:4). This term indicates His power and glory, but in its background, the idea of majesty should also always be seen. Thus some analysts, instead of the translation "majestic," prefer to praise God's name as "mighty" or "in majesty." The author of the psalms reaches for God's personal name, written in Tetragrammaton. Yahweh's name in a full or abbreviated form occurs in the Bible over 6,800 times. This self-revelation of

---

271 Brzegowy, *Psalterz*, 98.

272 The inhabitants of Qumran believed that salvation can be achieved only in the promised land, not in the Diaspora.

273 Apart from God, the HB applies it only to the king and princes (Ps 136:18; Judg 5:13).

the name of God (Exod 3:14) is etymologically derived from the verb meaning "to be." It points to the idea of absolute being and the presence of the deity, but in this case, first of all, to God —the Creator. On the one hand, the name reveals a little of the essence of the deity, on the other hand, it makes that it still remains a mystery. To the name Yahweh, the psalmist added the second name: Lord (אָדוֹן).[274] This name determines the relationship of God to the creation. God is not only the Creator, but the Lord of everything that exists. He is the Lord of history and time, nations and individuals, and finally; he is the Lord over the other gods and over the whole universe.[275]

Vv. 2b–5 After the inclusion in a character of an acclamation, there is the main body of the psalm beginning with a fragment, which may constitute *crux interpretuum* or—as wishes Beaucamp—a "textually desperate fragment."[276] The sentence is problematic אֲשֶׁר תְּנָה הוֹדְךָ עַל־הַשָּׁמָיִם, because it is highly difficult in terms of grammar, as a result of the incorrectness of the formula אֲשֶׁר תְּנָה. From a grammatical point of view, we have the relative pronoun "that" joined to the imperative of the verb "give," recorded in the form of qal, in the masculine singular. *He paragogicum* was attached to the verb. Translated literally, we get a phrase which has no logical sense, "that place!" So how do we find our way of this problem? Exegetes usually offer one of five solutions. The first involves either the removal of the pronoun "that" as unnecessary and the awkward addition of a copyist or a change of imperative mood into indicative one. In the first case v. 2b would constitute an entirely new sentence, which in conjunction with the acclamation would sound: "O Lord, our Lord, how majestic is your name throughout the earth. Place your majesty above the heavens." In the second case (preferred in the Greek version by Symmachus and the *Psalter Iuxta Hebraeos* by Jerome), we get as follows: "O Lord, our Lord, how majestic is your name in all the earth! Place your majesty above the heavens." The second solution proposes instead of the verb נתן, read the verb

---

274 See an entry "Name" in Ryken, Wilhoit and Longman III, *Słownik symboliki biblijnej*, 255–256 and: N. Stone, *Names of God* (Chicago 1994), 18–29.

275 Stone, *Names of God*, 45–50.

276 Quotation after: Ravasi, *Psalmy*, 214. It has already been dealt by P. Sfair ("De genuina lectione Ps 8,2," *Bib* 23 [1942]: 318–322), T. Z. Vriezen ("Ps 8,2–3," *NTT* 3 [1948–49]: 11–15), J. J. Stamm ("Eine Bemerkung zum Anfang des achten Psalms," *TZ* 13 [1957]: 470–478), H. R. Moeller ("Biblical Research and O.T. Translation," *Bible Translator* 13 [1962]: 16–22), A. Tanger ("Psalm 8,1–2. Studies in Texts," *Theology* 69 [1966]: 492–496), J.A. Soggin ("Textkritische Untersuchungen von Ps. VIII, vv. 2–3 und 6," *VT* 21 [1971]: 565–571).

תנה —"repeat," "sing," "recite"[277]—in its emphatic imperative mood. The verb תנה is used in only two ancient biblical texts in this context. The first is as "the voice of the singers at the watering places" (Judg 5:11). They recite (תנה) as the righteous acts of the Lord and the righteous acts of his warriors in Israel. "From this comes the Israelite custom that each year the young women of Israel go out for four days to commemorate (תנה) the daughter of Jephthah the Gileadite" (Judg 11:39b–40). The verb also appears in Hos 8:9–10, but his text is unclear, and it would be difficult with reference to v. 2b, to draw conclusions based on it. In v. 2b the verb would have to be used in a form of *piel* ("Your name sings his majesty ...") or in the form of *pual* ("Your majesty is proclaimed/is sung ..."). This latest version has been taken over by the LXX and after it, the Vulg. With the adoption of this solution, the text of v. 2b would sound: "Sing / praise His majesty above the heavens." The third solution is also based on the adoption of the verb תנה, but in the first-person singular. In this case, the pronoun "that" should be regarded as the gloss and the verse would sound: "I will sing / will proclaim His majesty above the heavens." Solution four is based on the reconstruction of different words אֲשֶׁר תְּנָהם; they should be read as אשרח־נה, "I could sing." The text of v. 2b would read then: "May I have sang your majesty above the heavens." However, it is difficult to demonstrate such far-reaching changes in the text. Finally, the fifth solution proposes a combination of the words אֲשֶׁר תְּנָהם in אשרתננה, imperative mood from *nun energicum* of the verb שרת, which means "to serve" or "worship." This solution seems to be most appropriate because it does not interfere with the consonantal text. It was also confirmed by the Punic language. With its adoption, the text of the v. 2b sounds as follows: "I adore your majesty above the heavens."[278] The next verse (v. 3) begins with the phrase, which literally sounds: "From the mouth of infants you have established strength ...". This text does not seem to be understood, so some exegetes connect v. 2b with v. 3. In this way they form this verse: "From the lips of children and infants you have ordained praise." This translation seems to be more persuasive, but it makes that the next sentence in v. 3 should be started from the verb "put." This translation is justified because the basic meaning of the verb סיד is "to lay foundation." It is enough to cite a few biblical texts to support that view. In 1 Kings this verb refers to the foundations of a house: "At the king's command they removed from the quarry large blocks of quality stone to provide a foundation (סיד) of dressed stone for the temple" (5:17). Elsewhere, it concerns the foundations of the city: "Cursed before the Lord is the man who

---

277 H. Donner, "Ugaritismen in der Psalmenforschung," *ZAW* 79 (1967): 322–350; *BDB*: 1071–1072.

278 Ravasi, *Psalmy*, 21–216.

undertakes to rebuild this city, Jericho: 'At the cost of his firstborn son will he lay its (סיד) foundations; at the cost of his youngest will he set up its gates.'" (Josh 6:26b). Isaiah tells of the foundations of Zion: "The Lord has established (סיד) Zion, and in her his afflicted people will find refuge" (Isa 14:32b); he also mentions of foundations of the earth: "My own hand laid (סיד) the foundations of the earth, and my right hand spread out the heavens; when I summon them, they all stand up together" (Isa 48:13). In our case, the subject of the verb is a term עז which in its basic meaning indicates physical strength. The term takes this meaning in Ps 30:8 and in Ps 68:36 it indicates a political-military strength: "You are awesome, O God, in your sanctuary; the God of Israel gives power and strength to his people. Praise be to God!". In Ps 29:11 it is more about the inner strength of humans: "The Lord gives strength (עז) to his people; the Lord blesses his people with peace." There is similar meaning in Ps 81:2, but with a direct reference to God: "Sing for joy to God our strength (עז); shout aloud to the God of Jacob!" In derivative forms, however, the term means "fortress," "tower" or "shelter." Therefore, it seems more reasonable to adopt such meaning of the term in our psalm. In other words, we should not, as some exegetes still want, talk about "praise."[279] We ought to see here a reference to the creative action of God described in Gen 1. God lays the foundations of the bastion of the heavens (Ps 8:3)—that is he creates firmament (Gen 1:6):

Gen 1:6–8	Ps 8:3
"And God said, 'Let there be an expanse between the waters to separate water from water.' So God made the expanse and separated the water under the expanse from the water above it. And it was so. God called the expanse 'sky.' And there was evening, and there was morning—the second day."	"When I consider your heavens, the work of your fingers, the moon and the stars, which you have set in place."

Based on Gen 1:6–8, the Jews imagined the existence of the metallic bowl, which separated the water under the expanse from the water above the firmament. God lived above the firmament in an inaccessible fortress: "Who is like the Lord our God, the One who sits enthroned on high, who stoops down to look on the heavens and the earth?" (Ps 113:5–6). This "cosmic map" can be also seen in other texts of the OT (see Jer 5:22; Ps 74:13; 104:9; 148:6; Job 7:12; 24:12; 38:11; Prov 8:27; Isa 51:9–10).[280]

---

279   This term meaning "praise" was used in the LXX, and (after LXX) in Matt 21:16.
280   Ravasi, *Psalmy*, 220.

This bastion of the heavens has been established by God "because of"[281] three groups opposed to God, "opponents," "foes" and "enemies (the latter term carries connotations of revenge, so it can be equally well be translated as "avengers").[282] Verse (v. 3) is marked by the opposition: children–the opponents, babies–the foes/enemies (avengers). In the history of exegesis different suggestions of identifying "opponents," "foes" or "enemies" were accepted.[283] Some exegetes used to point at Leviathan ("It was you who crushed the heads of Leviathan and gave him as food to the creatures of the desert"; Ps 74:14), others Rahab ("You crushed Rahab like one of the slain; with your strong arm you scattered your enemies"; Ps 89:11), and others giants ("The Nephilim were on the earth in those days—and also afterward—when the sons of God went to the daughters of men and had children by them. They were the heroes of old, men of renown"; Gen 6:4). Alternatively, *rephaim* and *nephilim* were known in later apocalyptic tradition as "hostile forces of primordial chaos, which the Lord curbs."[284] However, it seems that you cannot go so far beyond the immediate context of the psalm. "Enemies," "opponents" and "avengers" are simply those who do not accept the submission to God and perhaps even those who would like to be equalized with the "heavenly beings" (v. 6). The term אֱלֹהִים indicates either supernatural beings ("beings of heaven") or (perhaps more likely) the God himself (Elohim). In the early stages of the religion in Israel, "heavenly beings" were considered divine beings, but over time they began to be identified with angels. Angels are superhuman beings, who in the hierarchy of beings created by God, were placed higher than man, as a result they enjoy greater closeness to God than a man. For this very reason the psalmist confesses: "Among the gods (אֱלֹהִים) there is none like you, O Lord; no deeds can compare with yours" (Ps 86:8). All אֱלֹהִים worship God the Creator: "All who worship images are put to shame, those who boast in idols—worship him, all you gods! (אֱלֹהִים)" (Ps 97:7). After all, Yahweh is called "the God of gods" (Ps 136:2). God separates himself from his "enemies," "foes" and

---

281 The term לְמַעַן can take on causal or intentional meaning. In our case, the context indicates that the first meaning is preferable.

282 The idea of revenge points to the perversity of "avengers." Revenge is a privilege reserved for God: "It is mine to avenge; I will repay. In due time their foot will slip; their day of disaster is near and their doom rushes upon them" (Deut 32:35).

283 A large part of answers was collected by S. Łach several years ago, in his appendix to his commentary on the Book of Psalms entitled "Who are the enemies in the Psalms?"; Łach, *Księga Psalmów*, 606–617.

284 Brzegowy, *Psalmy*, 79.

"avengers" with the firmament, which he founded: "I would like to sing your glory above the heavens" (v. 2b).[285]

The opposite of rebellion against God is singing him glory. The psalmist makes this "[babbling] from the lips of children and infants" (v. 3). The point is not that infants and children sing praises to God and say words of prayers of praise, but rather, that in their spontaneity, children discover the created world, and that they are full of delight over it—and thanks to that, they express their admiration for the Creator. Discovering different things, they call them; they also give those names—like Adam (Gen 2:19–20). Taking a children's attitude toward discovered beauty makes a man free from the spirit of revenge and hostility. That is why, indirectly, the psalmist to the enemies and the avengers has opposed the children and infants.[286] Similar opposition between defiance and rebellion against God, on the one hand, and on the other hand, worshiping Him, was recorded in other places of the ancient wisdom tradition of Israel. To support this point of view, we should quote the statement of Sirach:

> "What race is worthy of honor? The human race.
> What race is worthy of honor? Those who fear the Lord.
> What race is unworthy of honor? The human race.
> What race is unworthy of honor? Those who transgress the commandments"
> (Sir 10:19).

This thread can be continued: although the psalmist is an adult, he feels like a child and cannot express his admiration for the Creator, and the dignity man was gifted. This situation is analogous to that which Jeremiah experienced: "Ah, Sovereign Lord, I said, I do not know how to speak; I am only a child" (Jer 1:6). There are certain similarities with the confession of a thinker as well: "For wisdom opened the mouth of the dumb, and made the tongues of infants eloquent" (Wis 10:21).

A specific introduction to the basic question of the psalmist ("what is man?"), is a mention about celestial bodies (the moon, the stars) and the heaven that is the work of God's fingers (v. 4). The celestial bodies stretched in the sky awoke in the ancient people a sense of the majesty of the Creator; they introduced the climate of mystery and majesty of God. Considering the size of the cosmos, man turned out to be something small and inconspicuous. Despite

---

285 It seems that more appropriate translation is in the first-person singular. Firstly, because such translation clearly marks a caesura of inclusion (v. 2a and v. 10), and secondly, because the structure of אֲשֶׁר תְּנָה is grammatically incorrect and justifies the translation, both in the first and third person singular.

286 Alonso Schökel, *Trenta salmi*, 70–71.

this, however, he enjoyed an unparalleled position among other creatures, which was given to him by the Creator himself.

The question included in v. 5 ("what is man that you are mindful of him, the son of man that you care for him?")[287] creates the structural center of the psalm, introducing a double relation of man to God as the Creator and the other works of creation (among them—to "heavenly beings"). A man asks a question, and he is a question for himself. This is a question full of surprise because he understands that he does not know himself. What is more, he is the only animal that is aware of his question. The question arises from the contemplation of creation, because a man has mostly the knowledge of things that are outside of him, and after that he reflects on himself.[288]

While the psalm praises God in His work of creation, revealing a unique position of man, the man himself is seen in the perspective of the decline in sin.[289] This is what the term אֱנוֹשׁ indicates. The same echo resounds in the confession: "As for Man (אֱנוֹשׁ), his days are like Grass" (Ps 103:15) and "Who are you that you fear mortal men (אֱנוֹשׁ), the sons of men, who are but grass?" (Isa 51:12). The reflection of the question "what is man?" and its possible answer lies in the plane of this two-level consideration: on the one hand, a man is a wonderful creation of God, endowed with glory and honour, and made a little lower than God—but on the other hand; he is sinful, marked by the fall and breaks his relationship with the Creator. For this reason, a man *in genere* is presented in this psalm in several images. They show the type of his relationship with the Creator, other people and the creation. The reader will find here the image of a "child" and a "baby" but also "the opponent," "the enemy," "the avenger" (v. 3) and the one who was made a little lower than "heavenly beings" (v. 6). Finally, "all" has been subordinated to the man (v. 7): "all flocks and herds, and the beasts of the field, the birds of the air, and the fish of the sea, all that swim the paths of the seas" (vv. 8–9).

To define the relation of God to man, the psalmist uses two important verbs "be mindful of" and "care for." Both point to a personal relationship. God remembers and cares about the man, not because he has a special dignity, but opposite: a man enjoys with glory and dignity, just because God remembers and cares about him. In the question itself: "what is man that you are mindful of him, the son of man that you care for him?" is already included a partial answer: the

---

287 This verse is repeated in its entirety in Ps 144:3.

288 L. Alonso Schökel, „*Contemplatelo e sarete raggianti". Salmi ed esercizi* (Bibbia e preghiera 27; Roma 1996), 28.

289 Members of a sect from the Dead Sea claimed that a great heavenly future waits for a sinful man. Only then he will be fully endowed with glory (1QS IV:7–8; 1QH XIII,17–18; CD III,19–20).

man is a being, whom God remembers takes cares of. The biblical idea of remembrance differs significantly from that which now exists in the Western mentality. For the Israelite, "mindfulness" (זכר) is almost synonymous with the verb "believe." When the Israelite "is mindful of" the works of God, it means that he deeply believes in God's intervention in the history of the world, especially in the history of his nation. The celebration of Israeli holidays is based precisely on this sense of the idea of mindfulness/remembering. The Jews not only had past events in mind moving in time to the moments and places from the past, but rather the events that show God's intervention and "move" in time to the present. Just in this sense, often a call to remember appears in Psalms: "I will remember the deeds of the Lord; yes, I will remember your miracles of long ago" (Ps 77:11), and again, "In the night I remember your name" (Ps 119:55). God—as faithful to his covenant—always "remembers" about the man as well: "He remembers his covenant forever" (Ps 105:8). So when the psalmist says that God is mindful of man, he expresses his admiration to God and His loving attitude towards us.

God not only remembers man, but also "takes care" (פקד) of him. The verb essentially means "visit," "look after," or "show concern." God also "visits" the earth: "You drench its furrows and level its ridges; you soften it with showers and bless its crops. You crown the year with your bounty, and your carts overflow with abundance" (Ps 65:10–11); He also frequents the vineyard of Israel: "Return to us, O God Almighty! Look down from heaven and see! Watch over this vine, the root your right hand has planted, the son you have raised up for yourself" (Ps 80:15–16). Moreover, salvation has its origin in the visitation of God: "Remember me, O Lord, when you show favor to your people, come to my aid when you save them, that I may enjoy the prosperity of your chosen ones, that I may share in the joy of your nation and join your inheritance in giving praise" (Ps 106:4–5). The idea of visitation by God in the OT is thus bound up with the idea of constant concern of God for man, his development and salvation. The psalmist is amazed that God remembers and cares about people. This is what makes the human being unique.[290]

---

[290] This truth is expressed in beautiful words in the work *De beatitudine* by Gregory of Nyssa. Interestingly, he makes in it a clear allusion to 1 Cor 15, because he writes about the same kind of transformation of the believer into the body of Christ that Paul explains to the Corinthians: "Man escapes from his own nature, becoming an immortal from a mortal that he is, and from one who has a price on his head to a priceless one, and from a temporal creature to an eternal one, being man becoming wholly god ..." (PG 44, 1280).

Vv. 6–9 In this part of the psalm there is v. 7 whose passage is a quotation inserted in 1 Cor 15:25b. For this reason, this section is of our particular interest because this part above all (but also the whole psalm) will let us determine the meaning of the v. 7b in the original context. Let us start with the analysis of vv. 6–7. Four further acts of God, expressed by four different verbs, describe God's care: "make a little less," "crown," "give" and "submit/put under." They all point to the fact that God gives the man participation in his glory,[291] and simultaneously participation in power over all creations. The idea is also akin to Sirach: "The government of the earth is in the hands of the Lord, and over it he will raise up the right man for the time. The success of a man is in the hands of the Lord, and he confers his honor upon the person of the scribe" (Sir 10:4–5). Man has his glory, but God gave his glory to him; he has dominion over the creatures, but it is involvement in the power of God. He constantly raises a question of his identity "Who is man?". The fact that people ask themselves the question—as we noted above—is recognition of their limitations and incomplete knowledge. Deeper answers should be sought by the contemplation of works of creation and bringing glory to God through the example of children and infants.

First, the psalmist declares human dignity using the phrase: "You made him a little lower than אֱלֹהִים." The last word, as has already been mentioned above, was interpreted in two ways in the history of exegesis: some have seen in אֱלֹהִים celestial beings, most often the angels (according to LXX, Vulg., Targum, Peshitta, Ibn Ezra, Rashi, Kimchi) others, however, God himself. In the OT the idea of celestial court exists, where there are present "mighty ones." The psalmist calls: "Ascribe to the Lord, O mighty ones, ascribe to the Lord glory and strength!" (Ps 29:1). Before God's throne with God's sons, one could also find Satan himself: "One day the angels came to present themselves before the Lord, and Satan also came with them" (Job 1:6; cf. 38:7). The second interpretation which sees in אֱלֹהִים God himself found confirmation in Aquilla, Symmachus, Theodotion and Jerome. These translations reflect thoughts from Gen 1:26 that man was created in the image and likeness of God.

Man was also "crowned with glory and honor" (v. 6b) by God. Through this award, man reflects in himself the image of God and the king because the phrase "glory and honor" (כָּבוֹד וְהָדָר) is referenced in the pages of OT tradition, both to God and to the king. The psalmist calls for praise to God: "Ascribe to the Lord, O mighty ones, ascribe to the Lord glory and strength (כָּבוֹד וְהָדָר)!" (Ps 29:1) and "Ascribe to the Lord, O families of nations, ascribe to the Lord glory and strength (כָּבוֹד וְהָדָר)!" (Ps 96:7). Similar sounds the call: "Praise the Lord, O my soul. O Lord my God, you are very great; you are clothed with splendor

---

291   L. Alonso Schökel says that God sets man "viceroy" of the earth; id., *Trenta salmi*, 74.

and majesty (כָּבוֹד וְהָדָר)" (Ps 104:1). The psalmist combines both qualities with the dynamism of works of God: "Glorious and majestic (כָּבוֹד וְהָדָר)—are his deeds" (Ps 111:3). With respect to the king, both these qualities become a symbol of the king's sword: "Gird your sword upon your side, O mighty one; clothe yourself with splendor and majesty (כָּבוֹד וְהָדָר)!" (Ps 45:4). Man is elevated, thus by the creative work of God to the rank of "royal" in relation to creation, that was subordinated to him.[292] This dignity is a participation in God's power over all creation, because the same attributes which by nature belong to God, man has been granted in an act of grace. Royal imagery also reinforces the verb "to crown" whose root is the same as the noun "crown." The expressions and phrases used by the psalmist come from the treasury of the language and thoughts of the ancient Orient and, in accordance with their application, they were addressed to the ruler during his coronation. He was a representative of the deity; and he even was God. According to his function, the unique splendor of his glory raised him above the mass of people, and all fell at his feet because of his power of majesty. The king, the image and representative of God on earth, is not an individual or exception that feels himself exalted above all other men and reigns over them with contempt. The man who is a king is every man, powerful or miserable, rich or poor, male or female, adult or child. Every person is entitled to dignity, which this divine king demanded only for yourself and which he, because of that, distorts and falsifies.[293]

Man's dominion extends over the entire horizon of the created world: "You made him ruler over the works of your hands; you put everything under his feet" (v. 7). Confiding dominion over the "works of God's hands" to man gives voice

---

292 The consciousness of human dignity is increasing among the children of Israel in the Hellenistic period, probably not without the influence of Greek thought. Job complains to his friends about the actions of God: "He has stripped me of my honor and removed the crown from my head" (Job 19:9). Allowing on sufferings falling on Job, God deprived him of "honor" (כָּבוֹד), which covered him like a robe. Then God took the crown from his head and deprived him of the position of "the elderly" who sat in the Israeli Council: "Job laments God's treating him like an enemy. He takes this tactic in order to shock his friends into realizing that God himself is the cause of his plight, not some wrong that he has done"; J. E. Hartley, *The Book of Job* (NICOT; Grand Rapids 1988), 285. Similar belief was expressed in the prayers of the psalmist who renounces: "O Lord my God, if I have done this and there is guilt on my hands, if I have done evil to him who is at peace with me or without cause have robbed my foe, then let my enemy pursue and overtake me; let him trample my life to the ground and make me sleep in the dust" (Ps 7:4–6). In this psalm the relation between a sin, and the loss of dignity is emphasized. This relation was already outlined in the story of the fall of the first parents.

293 G. Ebeling, *Sui Salmi* (Brescia 1973), 59–60; Ravasi, *Psalmy*, 225–226.

to confidence of God. A man becomes like a victorious king, under whose feet is everything. Putting the feet on something was for the ancient Israelites a symbolic gesture of domination: "When they had brought these kings to Joshua, he summoned all the men of Israel and said to the army commanders who had come with him, 'Come here and put your feet on the necks of these kings.' So they came forward and placed their feet on their necks" (Josh 10:24). With this gesture, David showed his victory over Goliath: "David ran and stood over him. He took hold of the Philistine's sword and drew it from the scabbard. After he killed him, he cut off his head with the sword. When the Philistines saw that their hero was dead, they turned and ran" (1 Sam 17:51). The object of the reign can be the pagan people: "He subdued nations under us, peoples under our feet" (Ps 47:4). It can also be the enemies: "Sit at my right hand until I make your enemies a footstool for your feet" (Ps 110:1). Saul's confession sounds similar: "You know that because of the wars waged against my father David from all sides, he could not build a temple for the Name of the Lord his God until the Lord put his enemies under his feet" (1 Kgs 5:3). As for this psalm, however, the point is not the reign over the enemies, but over creation defined as works of God's hands. The psalmist considers the position of man in relation to animals as, for instance, "all" (כֹּל) have been subjected to him. The author makes their double division; firstly, on the animals tame and wild, secondly on those living on land, in the air and in water. He devotes the most space to the latter, presumably because the force of the sea creatures was the least explored. Consequently, the knowledge about them was limited and so the sea was regarded as hostile and unapproachable to man. "All" has been subject to man because God has honored him by endowing him with the "glory and honor" (כָּבוֹד וְהָדָר; v. 6). In this way, the words spoken by God in a universal Noahic covenant are fulfilled: "The fear and dread of you will fall upon all the beasts of the earth and all the birds of the air, upon every creature that moves along the ground, and upon all the fish of the sea; they are given into your hands" (Gen 9:2). The idea of man's dominion over the world of animals is presented in the Bible in many scenes. The animals praise God by their existence itself: "Praise the Lord from the earth, you great sea creatures and all ocean depths, lightning and hail, snow and clouds, stormy winds that do his bidding, you mountains and all hills, fruit trees and all cedars, wild animals and all cattle, small creatures and flying birds" (Ps 148:7–10).

Expressing the fundamental ideas of creation and domination, the psalmist refers to images of the body metaphorically. The idea of creation by God is reflected by the author with reference to the works of "hands" (v. 7), and before he even mentioned of God's "fingers" (v. 4); the idea of subjecting the creation to man is expressed by the metaphor "feet" (v. 7). Some researchers have expressed surprise that even the flying birds and sea creatures are portrayed as being "under" human feet, but this is typical with regards to the imagery of the biblical language.

2.3. Contribution of v. 7b to Ps 8:2–10

Verse 7b shows the central position of man in the whole world created by God. The statement saying that all were put under the feet of man shows man's extraordinary dignity amid the created world. In the ancient world of Israel, putting a leg on someone or something was a symbol of dominance. Man's dominion over the animal world, was described by the psalmist as "all flocks and herds, and the beasts of the field, the birds of the air, and the fish of the sea, all that swim the paths of the seas" (vv. 8–9). On the one hand, he shows the need of relationship between woman and man, impossible to achieve in other ways. On the other hand, he justifies eating animal meat. An inspired author already reveals the supremacy of man over the animal world in the description of the creation: "Now the Lord God had formed out of the ground all the beasts of the field and all the birds of the air. He brought them to the man to see what he would name them; and whatever the man called each living creature, that was its name. So the man gave names to all the livestock, the birds of the air and all the beasts of the field. But for Adam no suitable helper was found" (Gen 2:19–20). In this animal parade, supremacy was underlined by the motif of giving a name. The fact of knowing or giving the name was synonymous with a specific predominance of a person giving the name over the one who receives it.

The power of God extends over man. The psalmist then determines the position of man in a double relationship between the Creator and the created work. With God's choice, man dominates over creation. He was granted with the throne and received a share in the reign of God over creation. God held him responsible and at the same time honored His reign. The Lord—God and Creator of the universe—is over him. For this reason, man is both ruling and subjected. He is endowed with dignity and sinful at the same time. Summing up, v. 7b contributes an idea of man's dominion over creation to the entire psalm, revealing his unusual position in relation to God and to his works of creation.[294]

---

294 The tradition of the Church, based on Matt 21:14–16, refers this psalm to Christ. Echoes of this psalm can also be found in Rom 5:14, Col 1:15, Eph 1:22–23 and in 1 Cor 15:27; Rinaudo, *I Salmi*, 96–97.

3. The Meaning in 1 Cor 15:23–28

The detailed exegetical and theological analysis of vv. 23–28 was carried out in the previous chapter. In that chapter, an emphasis has been placed on the meaning of the quotation from Ps 110:1b in v. 25b. In the same fragment in 1 Cor 15:23–28, there is also a second quote that is the subject of our discussion in this chapter. Therefore, it will be useful to benefit from the results of exegetical analysis that we carried out in previously. Particular verses will be discussed in terms of the influence of their content on the understanding of a quotation from Ps 8:7b in v. 27a. In this analysis will be emphasized those elements which affect the significance of this quote in its Pauline context. In v. 27 the apostle shows how God is present in the whole process, which began with the resurrection of Christ, and leads through the parousia, the resurrection of believers in Christ and consequently, to overcoming dominion, authority, power and death. In the end, everything will be submitted to Christ, and the reign will be handed over to God the Father.[295]

The fragment of 1 Cor 15:23–28 is part of a larger body, which includes vv. 12–34, where Paul tells about the resurrection of the faithful people following Christ's example (about the resurrection of Christ Paul writes in vv. 1–11). In vv. 23–24. The apostle presents to the Corinthians a picture of apocalyptic events, among which he determines four stages:

(1) resurrection of Christ;
(2) resurrection of those who belong to Christ;
(3) handing over the kingdom to God the Father;
(4) destroying "dominion, authority and power."[296]

Determining the sequence of these events, the apostle first points to: "But each in his own turn: Christ, the firstfruits; then, when he comes, those who belong to him" ("Ἕκαστος δὲ ἐν τῷ ἰδίῳ τάγματι· ἀπαρχὴ Χριστός, ἔπειτα οἱ τοῦ Χριστοῦ ἐν τῇ παρουσίᾳ αὐτοῦ; v. 23). These stages do not include of course all the apocalyptic events. The apostle was familiar with Jewish beliefs about the coming of the end of time. Therefore, when he propagated the coming of Christ from Christian perspective, for example, he did not mention of the resurrection to condemnation, and he did not say directly about the parousia or the Judgement Day.

---

295 Fee, *First Epistle to the Corinthians*, 757.
296 Johnson, "Firstfruits and Death's Defect," 458; see Malina and Pilch, *Social-Science Commentary*, 125; Soards, *First Corinthians*, 1187; Henry, *Commentary*, 2273–2274; Langkammer, *Komentarz*, 247; Romaniuk, Jankowski and Stachowiak, *Komentarz*, 162.

The first stage of the scheme of the final events outlined by Paul has already taken place because Christ rose from the dead. The apostle justified the resurrection recalling the kerigmatic formula and relying on christophany (vv. 3–7). What is more, he explains that all this took place, "according to the Scriptures" (κατὰ τὰς γραφάς; v. 3 and v. 4). In kerigmatic formula, the content of the gospel of the resurrection of Christ is based on the use of four verbs: "died," "was buried," "was raised," and "appeared to." In not only the parallel texts in Acts, but also in the Aramaic name of Peter, Cephas refer to the fact that Paul used the phrase that had already been deep-rooted in the Christian prediction. The general formulation of the executioner τὰς γραφάς is not intended to reference any particular fragment of the Bible.[297] The apostle makes it clear that Christ's resurrection is the work of God—a form of passive verb ἐγήγερται (15:3)[298] points to it. In an even more emphatic way, God's action in the resurrection of Christ is emphasized in v. 15. In this verse, there is a direct statement that God raised Christ. We can therefore draw a line between God and Christ. God is the subject of an action and his work is directed to Christ. Therefore, we should call our attention to the quote that is the subject of our analysis in this chapter: "has put everything under his feet" (v. 27a). Since the phrase, "put everything under his feet" in Paul's writings is interpreted histologically,[299] it must be assumed that this time God is the one who put everything under Christ.[300] God is still the subject of an action and his work is directed to Christ. Thus, there is full correlation between the actions of God and Christ: God raises Christ from the dead and subordinates everything to him, and when everything is subjected to him, then he shall hand over the reign to God himself. The risen Christ "appeared to Peter, and then to the Twelve" (15:5). Both the name of Cephas, and the mention of the "Twelve" are unusual for Paul, so again the argument arises that the apostle took the formula from the tradition. At the end of the list of people to whom Christ appeared (Cephas, the Twelve, more than five hundred brothers, James,[301] apostles) Paul places himself. Paul is

---

297 Most often as the Bible background of this phrase the fourth song of the servant of Yahweh is referred (Isa 53:5–6.11–12).

298 J. N. Vorster, "Resurrection Faith in 1 Cor 15," *Neot* 3 (1989): 287–307; G. Wagner, "If Christians Refuse to Act, Then Christ Is Not Risen. Once More, 1 Cor 15," *IBS* 6 (1984): 27–39.

299 Dunn, *Theology of Paul*, 210.

300 Jamieson, Fausset and Brown, *Commentary*, 329.

301 In the Gospel stories about chrystophanies there is no mention of the fact that Christ appeared to James, or more than five hundred brethren at once *Gos. Heb.*, in St. Jerome (*Vir. ill.* 2) and in *Gos. Thom.* 12; P. J. Kearney, "He Appeared to 500 Brothers (1 Cor 15:6)," *NT* 22 (1980): 264–284.

also a witness of the resurrection of Christ, but as "abnormally born" (ἔκτρωμα; 15:8). It is not the purpose of our discussion to analyze the meaning of the term in reference to Paul; it is enough to quote his own statement, that this term indicates that he is the least of the apostles: "for I am the least of the apostles and do not even deserve to be called an apostle" (15:9). The fact, however, that Paul saw the risen Christ proves that the first out of the four stages outlined by him has already taken place.

The second stage is the resurrection of those who "when he comes, ... belong to him" (οἱ τοῦ Χριστοῦ ἐν τῇ παρουσίᾳ αὐτοῦ; v. 23b). The faith essentially determines the belonging to Christ (cf. 3:22). This is a common Pauline theme. The apostle, telling of belonging to Christ, refers not only to the necessity of faith, but also the necessity of acceptance of the Holy Spirit: "You, however, are controlled not by the sinful nature but by the Spirit, if the Spirit of God lives in you. And if anyone does not have the Spirit of Christ, he does not belong to Christ" (Rom 8:9). The idea of the resurrection of the faithful to God was known in the apocryphal literature. *4 Ezra* mentions: "your sons that sleep, because I will bring them out of the hiding places of the earth ... I come, and proclaim mercy to them; because my springs run over, and my grace will not fail" (7:32–33).[302] There are more similar references in the apocryphal literature. Let us mention: *1 En.* 62:15–16: "And the righteous and elect shall have risen from the earth, And ceased to be of downcast countenance. And they shall have been clothed with garments of glory, And these shall be the garments of life from the Lord of Spirits. And your garments shall not grow old, Nor your glory pass away before the Lord of Spirits."[303]

It is true that Paul says here only of the resurrection of those who belong to Christ, but sometimes the Jewish tradition argues for the universality of the resurrection (2 Macc 7:9.14.23.29.36; 12:43–44; *Pss. Sol.* 3:6, 14:2). The author of *2 Bar.* also demonstrates the universality of the resurrection:

> Hear, Baruch, this word, and write in the remembrance of your heart all that you shall learn. For the earth shall then assuredly restore the dead [Which it now receives, in order to preserve them]. It shall make no change in their form, But as it has received, so shall it restore them, And as I delivered them unto it, so also shall it raise them. For then it will be necessary to show the living that the dead have come to life again, and that those who had departed have returned (again). And it shall come to pass, when they have severally recognized those whom they now know,

---

302 That statement is only in a Syrian and Armenian version: Fabris, *Prima Lettera ai Corinzi*, 204.

303 Broadly, the theme of resurrection in *1 Enoch* discusses M. Parchem, "Zmartwychwstanie, odpłata po śmierci i życie wieczne w literaturze międzytestamentalnej," *VV* 15 (2009): 101–114.

then judgment shall grow strong, and those things which before were spoken of shall come. And it shall come to pass, when that appointed day has gone by, that then shall the aspect of those who are condemned be afterwards changed, and the glory of those who are justified. (*2 Bar.* 50:1–51,6; compare with 30:1–5).

Flavius Josephus, quoting the views of the Pharisees, announces: "They also believe that souls have an immortal rigor in them, and that under the earth there will be rewards or punishments, according as they have lived virtuously or viciously in this life; and the latter are to be detained in an everlasting prison, but that the former shall have power to revive and live again" (*Ant.* 18:14).[304] There are, however, such references in the Jewish apocryphal literature, according to which only the righteous shall obtain the resurrection: "Let the righteous man arise from slumber; let him arise, and proceed in the path of righteousness, Mercy shall be showed to the righteous man; upon him shall be conferred integrity and power for ever. In goodness and in righteousness shall he exist, and shall walk in everlasting light" (*1 En.* 92:3–4). The fact that in this argumentation Paul has in mind only the resurrection of the righteous does not mean that he rejects the resurrection of all people.[305]

The apostle argues that those who belong to Christ will find the resurrection at the time of his coming during the parousia. It is the parousia that will begin the reign of Christ, who shall finally wholly hand over his kingdom to the Father: "Then the end will come, when he hands over the kingdom to God the Father after he has destroyed all dominion, authority and power" (εἶτα τὸ τέλος, ὅταν παραδιδῷ τὴν βασιλείαν τῷ θεῷ καὶ πατρί, ὅταν καταργήσῃ πᾶσαν ἀρχὴν καὶ πᾶσαν ἐξουσίαν καὶ δύναμιν; v. 24).[306] Paul's letter based on the term δεῖ (v. 25) reminds readers that the same Christ, who shall hand over the kingdom to God the Father, when he defeats all his enemies, will have continue to "reign" as Christ, who was resurrected from the dead (v. 20a). It is in accordance with a promise included in Ps 110:1.

304 M. Wróbel, "Faryzeusze i saduceusze wobec zmartwychwstania," *VV* 15 (2009): 147.

305 W. V. Crockett, "Ultimate Restoration of all Mankind: 1 Cor. 15:22," in *Studia Biblica 1978. Sixth International Congress on Biblical Studies* (ed. E. A. Livingstone; III, JSNTSup. 3; Sheffield 1980), 83–87. From the fact that Paul says only about the resurrection of the believers, V. Hasler concludes that the resurrection of Christ is not the beginning of the eschatological events; Hasler, "Credo und Auferstehung in Korinth," 25–26. "Paul n'est pas intéressé ici par la résurrection général de tus les morts, mais des croyants et surtout de ceux qui sont déjà morts"; Aletti, "L'Argumentation de Paul," 74.

306 A. Lindemann, "Parusie Christi und Herrschaft Gottes. Exegese von Kor 15:23–28," *WuD* 19 (1987), 87; Lambrecht, "Paul's Christological Use of Scripture," 502; J. Kozyra, "Aspekty teologiczne paruzji Chrystusa w 1 Kor 15," *SSHT* 10 (1997): 14–44; Aletti, "L'Argumentation de Paul," 75.

The third stage is characterized by Christ's handing over the reign "to God the Father" (τῷ θεῷ καὶ πατρί). The apostle calls this stage "the end," though the term τέλος here should be translated rather as the "fulfilment."[307] Some biblical scholars have suggested that this term can be translated as "the rest" and may point to all non-Christians.[308] A parallelism between the v. 22 and vv. 23–24 could constitute an argument for such a postulate. The words "for as in Adam all die" included in v. 22 could correspond with the phrase "those who belong to Christ" from v. 23. While the phrase "in Christ all will be made alive" from v. 22 should be assigned to εἶτα τὸ τέλος, so "then the end will come/[then the rest]" from v. 24. In this way, Paul would say that during the resurrection, not only Christians will come but also non-believers. However, it seems that such parallelism does not exist. It is true that in Adam "all" (so Christians and non-Christians) die. In this case, nevertheless, Paul mentions only about believers, as the context clearly indicates.[309] Community with Adam leads to death; communion with Christ leads to the resurrection.[310] Due to a sin, all people are joined with Adam and that is why they all die. Christians, however, are united with Christ and therefore, they all will be made alive. It would be preposterous, from the point of view of Paul's argument, to claim that non-believers have the same relationship with Christ, as the believers in Him. What is more, it would be difficult to assume that they will be resurrected from the dead alike the believers.[311]

The subject (understood, after v. 24) of the verb "hand over" is Christ: he is the one who hands over his reign to God the Father.[312] Paul incorporates the

---

307   This term appears translated in such a way in Luke 22:37 and Rom 10:4. H. Lietzmann believes that the term τέλος can be explained as "[all] the rest," which would suggest a very different interpretation of the poem. Thus, we should take into an account the order of the events during the Resurrection, which would also include the non-believers (Christ—those who belong to Christ—[all] the rest); *An die Korinther I/II* (Tübingen 1949), 81–82. However, there are no sufficient arguments in the text in favor of keeping this thesis. The term appears 37 times in the NT, but it never means directly "the rest"; Lewis, *"So That God May Be All in All"*, 52; Aletti, "L'Argumentation de Paul," 75.

308   For a detailed critique of this opinion, see: Hill, "Paul's Understanding of Christ's Kingdom," 308–310.

309   The thesis that Paul also speaks of the unbelievers who will win the resurrection, was also convincingly rejected by H.-A. Wickle, *Das Problem eines messianischen Zwischenreichs bei Paulus* (Zürich 1967), 85–92.

310   Hill, "Paul's Understanding of Christ's Kingdom," 305.

311   Holleman, *Resurrection and Parousia*, 53.

312   Detailed interpretation of the handing over the kingdom to the Father by Christ, in the Fathers of the Church discusses E. Schendel, *Herrschaft und Unterwerfung Christi: 1.*

thought in the context of Judaism; however, already put to Christian interpolation. The Jews believed in the arriving of the messianic kingdom at the close of the age. After fighting a battle against the forces of evil, the Messiah and his allies will win. Only then the messianic kingdom will come. Having recognized the Messiah, in Christ, the apostle depicts to the Corinthians the vision of submission of the messianic kingdom to the Father. What it is and what the subjection consists of, has already previously mentioned. Finally, the fourth stage of the last things described in Paul's vision lies in overcoming "all dominion, authority and power."[313] This issue has also been discussed in the previous chapter.

In vv. 25–27 Paul reaches for quotes from the Psalms two times. The first of these citations (ἄχρι οὗ θῇ πάντας τοὺς ἐχθροὺς ὑπὸ τοὺς πόδας αὐτοῦ; v. 25b; cf. Ps 110:1b) has already been analyzed extensively in a current context, now we are going to have a closer look at the second of them (πάντα γὰρ ὑπέταξεν ὑπὸ τοὺς πόδας αὐτοῦ; v. 27a; cf. Ps 8:7b). Both of these quotes serve to illustrate the truth that, "the last enemy to be destroyed is death" (ἔσχατος ἐχθρὸς καταργεῖται ὁ θάνατος; v.26). Chiastic structure of vv. 24-28 is evidence of this. Chiasmus is the figure of speech in which two or more clauses are related to each other through a reversal of structures in order to make a larger point; that is, the clauses display inverted parallelism. Citations from Ps 110:1 and Ps 8:7b are found in structure of elements, which are equivalent to each other (C and C'):

A: ὅταν ... (v. 24a);
B: ὅταν ... (v. 24b);
C: γὰρ ... (v. 25);
D: ἔσχατος ἐχθρὸς καταργεῖται ὁ θάνατος (v. 26);
C': γὰρ ... (v. 27a);
B': ὅταν δὲ ... (v. 27b);
A': ὅταν δὲ ... (v. 28).[314]

Korinther 15,24–28 in Exegese und Theologie der Väter bis zum Ausgang des 4 Jahrhunderts (BGBE 12; Tübingen 1971).

313 S. M. Lewis, *"So That God May Be All in All": The Apocalyptic Message of 1 Corinthians 15,12–34* (TG 42; Rome 1998), 66.

314 Hill, "Paul's Understanding of Christ's Kingdom," 300–301. Slightly different structure presents W. Wallis, but also in him v. 26 is located in the centre chiasm; "The Problem of an Intermediate Kingdom," 242. See also: R. Morissette, "La citation du Psaume VIII, 7b dans I Corinthians XV, 27a," *ScEs* 24 (1972): 314–342. The author proposes a less complicated chiastic structure, based on the scheme A–B–A' (ibid., 315–324):
A: advancing thesis (v. 24);
B: scriptural developing of the thesis (vv. 25–27);
A': resumption of the thesis (v. 28).

It is likely that the combination of quotes from Ps 110:1 and Ps 8:7b were adopted by Paul from an early apologetic Christian tradition. The tradition referred to those passages of the Psalms, which recognized the Messiah in Christ. The combination of these citations can be found not only in vv. 25–27, but also in their relatively close context, that is in Heb 1:13–2:9 and in Eph 1:20–22.[315] This configuration confirms the messianic and Christological interpretation of Ps 8 and Ps 110 in the early Christian communities. The author of Hebrews shows the superiority of Christ, firstly, above every other creature, and then proves that He is the head of the messianic kingdom:

> To which of the angels did God ever say, "Sit at my right hand until I make your enemies a footstool for your feet"? (Ps 110:1). … someone has testified: "What is man that you are mindful of him, the son of man that you care for him; You made him a little lower than the angels; you crowned him with glory and honor and put everything under his feet" (Ps 8:5–8). In putting everything under him, God left nothing that is not subject to him. Yet at present we do not see everything subject to him. But we see Jesus, who was made a little lower than the angels, now crowned with glory and honor because he suffered death, so that by the grace of God he might taste death for everyone. (Heb 1:13–2:9)

he argumentation of the Hebrews' author proceeds on the following line: mankind, because of the falling into sins, departed from God's plan and did not implement plans of the Creator. Mankind failed everything made by Christ. In other words, everything was subject to him, and therefore, he is the ruler of the messianic kingdom.[316] A similar line of argumentation can be found in the Christological hymn recorded in Eph 1:20–23:

> which he [God] exerted in Christ when he raised him [Christ] from the dead and seated him at his right hand (Ps 110:1b) in the heavenly realms, far above all rule and authority, power and dominion, and every title that can be given, not only in the present age but also in the one to come. And God placed all things under his feet (Ps 8:7b), and appointed him to be head over everything for the church, which is his body, the fullness of him who fills everything in every way.

As mentioned above, a quote from Ps 8:7b in v. 27a comes from the LXX, but it should be noted that Paul has applied some changes: the second person singular of the verb, (πάντα ὑπέταξας) he turned into the third person (πάντα γὰρ ὑπέταξεν) and replaced the wording from the LXX with a different formulation of the same meaning, ὑπὸ τοὺς πόδας αὐτοῦ. The first change is caused by the need to integrate the quotation into the context in which there is a third person

---

315 Murphy-O'Connor, "The First Letter to the Corinthians," 813; J. M. García, Acontecimientos después la venida *gloriosa* (1 Cor 15:23–28), *EstBib* 58 (2000): 527–559.

316 Thiselton, *First Epistle to the Corinthians*, 1235.

singular. The second change probably was motivated by the intention to make the phrase similar to v. 25b. Paul takes a quote from Psalms preaching about the greatness of the Creator and human dignity. In the fragment, "you put everything under his feet" the psalmist refers to every human being, endowed by the Creator with great dignity. Equally, he gives the quote (and thus the whole Psalm) Christological interpretation. The apostle exemplifies this phrase, applying it to one man—Jesus Christ. Paul then himself explains how to understand the quoted words of the psalm.

In Paul's use of the quote ("Now when it says that 'everything' has been put under him, it is clear that this does not include God himself, who put everything under Christ") some manuscripts (P[46], B, 33, Vulg.) omit the term ὅτι. It does not change the meaning of the text, since the emphasis falls on the term πάντα: if death has not been subjected to Christ, we could not say that "everything" (πάντα) has been subordinated to Him.[317]

A combination of quotations from Ps 8.7b and Ps 110:1b was made in accordance with the Jewish principle of interpretation of the Bible, called *gezerah shavah*.[318] The rule lies in explaining one fragment of the text by another one, in which there is the identical word like in the first phrase. In other words, we can say that the *gezerah shavah* attaches to the word in the one passage the entire sequence of ideas which it bears in the other. In this case, it is about the term "feet." Both fragments also connect the notion of kingship. The principle of *gezerah shavah* is attributed to Hillel, but in the Jewish exegetical tradition, it had been already known before.[319] In this case, its application is used, *inter alia*, to emphasize the subordination of everything to Christ (as Ps 8:7b presents), and the power of Christ (expressed in Ps 110:1b). What is more, these facts are parallel.[320]

The last verse of the present part shows the reference of Christ to God and God to Christ: "When he has done this, then the Son himself will be made subject to him who put everything under him, so that God may be all in all" (ὅταν δὲ ὑποταγῇ αὐτῷ τὰ πάντα, τότε [καὶ] αὐτὸς ὁ υἱὸς ὑποταγήσεται τῷ ὑποτάξαντι αὐτῷ τὰ πάντα, ἵνα ᾖ ὁ θεὸς [τὰ] πάντα ἐν πᾶσιν; v. 28). This relationship is still shown in the terminology of subjection: similarly, as a Son

---

317   Mare, *1 Corinthians*, 286.

318   Keener, *1–2 Corinthians*, 127.

319   Similar words in different contexts are helpful in explaining both contexts; Rapoport, "Zasady żydowskiej egzegezy," 13; Hadas-Lebel, *Hillel*, 58.

320   Both of these events C. E. Hill describes as "contemporaneous and coextensive"; id., "Paul's Understanding of Christ's Kingdom," 310.

surrendered the kingdom to God, now the Son will also be subjected to God.[321]
The ultimate objective of apocalyptic events is to achieve a full reign of God.
Paul's Christology is thoroughly theocentric.[322] Paul connects in this verse, what
so far has been said in the entire fragment. Namely, he interprets a quote from
Ps 8:7b, and he refers to the opinion from v. 24 ("when he hands over the
kingdom to God the Father"). The phrase "put everything under him" (v. 28) is
tantamount to saying, "he has destroyed all dominion, authority and power" (v.
24b), and also death. The second part of v. 28 ("then the Son himself will be
made subject to him who put everything under him") is in turn equivalent to the
other part of v. 24 ("he hands over the kingdom to God the Father"). The apostle
calls Christ the "Son" not only once, but twice in this verse. Jewish writings,
speaking of the Messiah call him "Son of Man" (*1 En.* 46:1–6, 48:2–7; 62:5–
9.14, 63.11, 69:26–29, 70:1; 71:17) or "Son of God" (*1 En.* 105:2; *4 Ezra* 7:28–
29; 13:32.37.52).[323] Passages from *Pss. Sol.* 17:5.23 and *4 Ezra* 12:32 also
confirmed David's origin of the Messiah. That is not without significance,
because the fact that Paul refers to the Psalms of David, situates his thoughts on
the line of the OT tradition.

Throughout Paul's reasoning about submitting everything firstly to Christ
and then to God, one can find a way of argumentation akin to this used in
rabbinical writing. For example, *Pirke of Rabbi Eliezer* states: "Ten kings
reigned over the world from the beginning to the end. The first one was a
Saint—let his name be blessed! Who reigned over the heaven and the earth.
Then the thought came to him to establish the kings over the earth. The second
was Nimrod ... the third was King Joseph, ... the fourth Solomon ... the fifth
King was Ahab ... the sixth was king Nebuchadnezzar ... the seventh king was
Cyrus ... the eighth was Alexander Macedon ... The ninth will be the Messiah,
who will reign in the future, from one to the other end of the earth. With the
tenth king, the rule returns to the owner and the one who was the first king, and
will also be the last one" (*Pirke of Rabbi Eliezer* 11). The parallel between
Paul's way of portraying the passage of the kingdom by Christ (the Messiah) to
God, and the story of Eliezer is striking. In both cases, the Messiah will be the

---

321 About a motif of subjecting Christ to God, wrote Augustine: *nam secundum id quo
     Verbum Dei est, tam sine fine quam sine initio et sine intermissione est regnum [...];
     secundum id autem quod Verbum caro factum est, coepit regnare* (*Trin.* 1,8,10);
     Jamieson, Fausset and Brown, *Commentary*, 329.

322 Fabris, *Prima Lettera ai Corinzi*, 205.

323 We must be aware; however, that *4 Ezra* was written several decades after the writing
     of one Corinthians, although it is conceivable that this book is a record of a much earlier
     tradition; Hill, "Paul's Understanding of Christ's Kingdom," 311–312.

penultimate ruler over the earth and the heavens. Finally, the king of the universe will be God himself.[324]

Therefore, we may conclude that Paul uses the quotation from Ps 8 to show the extraordinary dignity of human beings in the midst of other beings. He uses the quote directly in reference to Christ, whom everything has been subjected to. As the new Adam, Jesus has the right to a universal rule, who after humiliation in the poor man's life was exalted as the King of the universe.[325] An important motif here seems to be the subjection of everything "under feet" which can already be found in the previous quotation, recorded in v. 25b. It comes from a royal psalm (Ps 110) which Paul reads in a Messianic key. The apostle also proclaimed the triumph of the Messiah, using a quote from Ps 110:1b. The theme of subjecting everything "under feet" is again present in Ps 8:7b. Hence this quote was referenced to the Messiah as well, who will be a winner over all dominion, authority and power, and ultimately over death itself. Christ will achieve a triumph over death, as the victorious king over his enemies. Both quotations from the psalms express it in the image of a foot put on the enemy. However, the quotation from Ps 8:7b emphasizes motif of the universal reign of Christ rather than just a theme of exercising power over opponents who were defeated.

---

324 It is difficult to determine whether this story was already known at the time of Paul. It is true that Eliezer Ben Hydramnios lived through the years 40–120 A.D. He was nearly contemporary with Paul, and he belonged to the second generation of Tannates. However, a book entitled *Pirke of Rabbi Eliezer* is a pseudoepigraphic midrash that was probably created in the 8th century. This work has numerous references to the apocryphal literature of the Second Temple Era; it is difficult to find convincing arguments for the fact that the quoted fragment about the ten kings goes back to that period; R. Żebrowski, "Pirke(j) de-Rabi Eliezer," in *Polski słownik judaistyczny. Dzieje, kultura, religia, ludzie* (eds. Z. Borzymińska and R. Żebrowski; II; Warszawa 2003), 321–322; Z. Borzymińska, "Eliezer ben Hyrkanos," in ibid., 383; Usami, "How Are the Dead Rised?," 475; R. Morissette, "La citation du Psaume VIII, 7b dans I Corinthians XV, 27a," *ScEs* 24 (1972): 215.

325 Brzegowy, *Psalmy*, 81.

IV. Quotation from Isa 22:13b in 1 Cor 15:32b

1 Cor 15:32b: φάγωμεν καὶ πίωμεν, αὔριον γὰρ ἀποθνήσκομεν

Isa 22:13b (LXX): φάγωμεν καὶ πίωμεν αὔριον γὰρ ἀποθνήσκομεν

Isa 22:13b (HB): אָכוֹל וְשָׁתוֹ כִּי מָחָר נָמוּת

1. Source of the Quotation

As shown below, the phrase "Let us eat and drink, 'you say,' for tomorrow we die!" (Isa 22:13b) may come from a work entitled *The Song of a Harper* by Imhotep, a high official at the court of Pharaoh, living in the XXVI century B.C. However, it seems unlikely that Paul read excerpts from the work in ancient Egyptian language. There is no evidence to suggest that the apostle of the nations knew the language. It is equally unlikely that Paul met the quote in Greek literature. That is, the hypothesis is based only on conjecture and speculation and does not have any scriptural proof.[326] And because Paul was a Jew, educated as a Pharisee belonging to Gamaliel's students, it is obvious that he knew the HB perfectly. Therefore you do not need to resort to breakneck efforts to recreate the road, on which part of the Egyptian work appeared in the pages of the letter sent to the people of Corinth, but just take the simplest solution and also the most likely; Paul took this quote from the OT. It thus remains to be decided whether he took it from the HB, or perhaps from the LXX. It is noticeable; however, that Paul's version perfectly agrees with the LXX, and the latter is also a very accurate translation from the Hebrew text.[327] There is nothing in the way to accept that Paul followed the LXX.

---

326 In Strabon, there is a mention: "eat, drink and indulge" (*Geogr.* 4:5,9), but the likelihood that Paul makes here an allusion to the reference, not quotes Isa 22:13b is small; B. W. Winter, *After Paul Left Corinth. The Influence of Secular Ethics and Social Change* (Grand Rapids 200), 79.

327 R. B. Terry, who claims that the texts of the LXX, the HB and the NT are exactly coherent with each other, agrees with this opinion; id., *Discourse Analysis*, 159. Another view presents E. E. Ellis: according to whom the Pauline text is consistent with the LXX, but against HB. The author, however, does not justify his opinion; "Paul's Use of the Old Testament," 152.

2. The Meaning in the Original Context

Part of Isa 22:13b in the original text reads as follows: ‎.אָכוֹל וְשָׁתוֹ כִּי מָחָר נָמוּת
In translation, you can express it by encouragement: "Let us eat and drink, for
tomorrow we die!" Its specificity is the fact that it is a quote in itself, which was
used by the prophet Isaiah. We assume that Paul, quoting the passage in 1 Cor
15:32b, took it just from Isaiah not from the original source. At least, three
reasons speak for it. Firstly, the apostle of nations far more likely reaches for
biblical quotations than extra-Biblical ones. Secondly, the context of this quote
in 1 Cor indicates the OT and not extra-Biblical sources (in 1 Cor 15, there is a
relatively large number, as many as six, quotes taken from the OT). Thirdly, as
has been already mentioned, there are no arguments that would indicate that
Paul had read the work (or its fragments) of a pagan author in ancient Egyptian
language, or in translation into any other languages.

The fragment from Isa 22:13b is part of the prophetic speech against
Jerusalem (Isa 22:1–14), which is referred to be situated in the context of the
speech against the pagan nations (Isa 13-23). There are a number of speeches:
against Babylon (Isa 13:1–14:23), against Assyria (Isa 14:24-27), the Philistines
(Isa 14:28-32), against Moab (Isa 15-16), Damascus and Samaria (Isa 17), Cush
(Isa 18), Egypt (Isa 19), Ashdod (Isa 20), the second time against Babylon (Isa
21:1–10), Edom (Isa 21:11–12) and Saudi (Isa 21:13–17), and against Tyre and
Sidon (Isa 23). Indeed, the inclusion of speech against Jerusalem to the
collection of speeches against the pagan nations raises exegetes' questions. The
second question mark constitutes the issue of such, and not the other location of
the speech in the full collection. The attempts of answering these questions,
connected with the exegetical analysis of the immediate context of Isa 22:13b
will allow us to understand the main content of the text and its contribution to
the theological content of the speech in Isa 22:1–14.

2.1. Ideological Base and the Literary Structure in Isa 22:1–14

Finding an answer to the question of why the speech against Jerusalem was
included in the collection of speeches against the pagan nations require
reflection on the "vision" which was mentioned in Isa 22:1. The vision is full of
sarcasm because it concerns people that certainly abound in it. The inhabitants
of Jerusalem, who are constantly celebrating, are not able to see the approaching
destruction of the city. Their leaders do not see that God is a better defender than
any fortifications and weapons; Shebna does not see that courage, and

responsibility are more important than building the walls.[328] Such a prospect to "see" and perceive the world is no different from the perspective of the pagan. The fact itself justifies the inclusion of a speech against the Holy City to the collection of speeches against the Gentiles. So the location of the speech in the structure of the book conveys the message: the inhabitants of Jerusalem are also the Gentiles.

Why was the oracle against Jerusalem situated in this place of the collection? The titles of oracles included in Chapters 21–22 give some helpful hints to answer this question: "An oracle concerning the Desert by the Sea" (Isa 21:1), "A Prophecy Against Edom" (Isa 21:11), "A Prophecy Against Arabia" (Isa 21:13) and "A Prophecy About Jerusalem" (Isa 22:1). Traditionally, in the exegesis, there was the view that they are the symbolic titles, and that is why all oracles with such titles were grouped by the editor of Isaiah in one place. This hypothesis, however, poses some difficulties because it is not certain whether the titles of Edom and Arabia are only symbolic. Another justification for the proposal, connected with location of the oracle against Jerusalem in the whole collection, is based on the chronological argument. Some exegetes argued that the oracles contained in Chapters 14–23 (except 17 and 18) are arranged in historical order of the events described in them.[329] This proposal is also difficult to match. First, it seems that a chronological sequence of events does not necessarily determine the structure of a literary work. The latter depends largely on the creativity of the author or editor. Second, a deeper analysis of the texts of Isa 21:1–10 and 22:1–14 show that they have two levels of interpretation. The first one refers to the time of Isaiah's activity, while the second indicates the subsequent events: the fall of Babylon in 539 and the fall of Jerusalem in 587 B.C.[330] This is a fact that, the two-level structure of the narrative and interpretation of the portent of the fall of Babylon and the oracle against Jerusalem shows that Babylon and Jerusalem are compared to each other by quite a conscious editorial move of the author or editor.[331]

From a structural point of view, all of Chapter 22 may be divided into two parts: Isaiah 22:1–14 and 22:15–25.[332] The second part is a specific illustration

---

328   J. N. Oswalt, *The Book of Isaiah. Chapters 1–39* (NICOT; Grand Rapids 1986), 405.

329   H. L. Ginsberg, "Reflexes of Sargon in Isaiah after 715 BCE," *JAOS* 88 (1968): 47.

330   R. E. Clements, "The Prophecies of Isaiah and the Fall of Jerusalem in 587 B.C.," *VT* 30 (1980): 421–436.

331   "It is not possible to be dogmatic about the purpose of that association, but surely the realization that Babylon was to be Jerusalem's ultimate enemy must have played a part in this association"; Oswalt, *Book of Isaiah*, 406.

332   G. W. Grogan, "Isaiah," in *The Expositor's Bible Commentary with the New International Version of the Holy Bible*, VI, *Isaiah, Jeremiah, Lamentations, Ezekiel*

of what is generally predicted in the first part. It narrates that Shebna cuts a tomb for himself, while the state's affairs are neglected. Because he rules in an irresponsible manner, God's judgment awaits him. This judgment will be revealed over Jerusalem and all Judea. Shebna was a high king's official, but probably after the criticism from Isaiah, he was unseated and became a writer at the court of King Hezekiah. It was at the time of Sennacherib's campaign against Judah (2 Kgs 18:18–19:2; Isa 36:3–37:2).[333] The episode associated with Shebna is, *inter alia*, the testimony to the use of Aramaic language by the royal officials: "Then Eliakim son of Hilkiah, and Shebna and Joah said to the field commander, 'Please speak to your servants in Aramaic, since we understand it. Don't speak to us in Hebrew in the hearing of the people on the wall'" (2 Kgs 18:26).[334] The first part, however, constitutes the announcement of the Last Judgment. A quote that is of a great interest to us is inscribed in Isa 22:13b, thus in the initial part of Chapter 22. A great number of suggestions regarding the internal structure of Isa 22:1–14 is evidence of the complicated nature of this literary text. It seems that the most appropriate criterion for the division of the text shall be the criterion of content. Starting with the title "An oracle concerning the Valley of Vision" (v. 1) the prophet describes precisely the situation in that valley, up to v. 8a. In v. 8b, the author moves his thoughts to the royal palace, called "the Palace of the Forest," then to the city walls and to the Lower Pool and the Old Pool. The author uses that technique up to v. 11. A picture of preparations before the war is drawn in vv. 8b–11. Then the reader has to deal with chiasm organized around the term "The Lord, the Lord Almighty." It opens v. 12 and ends v. 14. Thematically, vv. 12–14 concern the summoning of the inhabitants of Jerusalem to repentance, the summoning that was ignored, and the result that Jerusalem awaits even more severe punishment than it previously had. In summary, you can determine the structure of Isa 22:1–14 as follows:

1. An oracle against the Valley of Vision (vv. 1–8a);
2. An oracle about the war preparations (vv. 8b–11);
3. The portent of a punishment (vv. 12–14).

(Grand Rapids 1986), 140; G. V. Smith, *Isaiah 1–39. An Exegetical and Theological Exposition of the Holy Scripture* (The New American Commentary 15A. New International Version; Nashville 2007), 380.

333 A. J. Saldarini, "Szebna," in *Encyklopedia biblijna* (ed. P. J. Achtemeier; trans. E. Szymula; Warszawa 1999), 1182.

334 The people of Israel began to use Aramaic language in the Babylonian captivity. When Ezra called people of Israel to listen to the Words Of Law read aloud, he realized that many people do not understand the Hebrew text, so he ordered translation into Aramaic (Neh 8).

Basically, the prophet refers to the past events in Jerusalem which destroyed it partially and caused some damage.[335] This destruction was not, however, total. It did not induce inhabitants to their conversion which entailed a prediction for the next punishment. It seems important therefore, to place Isa 22:1–14 in a historical context. What kinds of events are mentioned in the text? What events do this prophecy foretell? Today no one is likely to advance the thesis that the events refer to the invasion of Nebuchadnezzar in the year 587 or 586 B.C.[336] Usually, scholars propose one of the two solutions. Some of them combine the text with the reign of Sennacherib, the king of Assyria, and his campaign to the west which took place in the year 701[337] while others with Sargon II and his expedition to Ashdod in 711.[338] Sennacherib was the king of Assyria in the years 705–681. His expedition to the west was described in 2 Kgs 18:7–8.13–16, 18:17–19:37. These biblical references should be added to the Assyrian royal inscriptions[339] in order to obtain a more precise picture of the campaign. Hezekiah the king of Judah organized an anti-Syrian coalition, in which were the Phoenician, the Philistines and the southern-Syrian states. In the event of the siege of Jerusalem, Hezekiah built a tunnel supplying the city with water (2 Kgs 20:20; 2 Chr 3:3–4). The coalition built by Hezekiah proved to be too weak. Cities situated on the coast quickly surrendered. A bit more resistance was offered by the Egyptian army under Eltekeh and on Shephela (2 Kgs 18:21, 19:9), but it also had to capitulate. The campaign developed as follows. After defeating Merodach-Baladan, Sennacherib marched west. First, Phoenician cities surrendered without a fight. The King Lula fled to Cyprus (Isa 23:12), and his place in Sidon took Ittobaal (Tuba'lu). Presumably, the rulers of Ammon, Moab and Edom initially supported the anti-Syrian coalition, but they quickly surrendered, in that way isolating Ashkelon, Ekron and Judah. Then the revenge turned against Judah. Sennacherib sent his emissaries to King Hezekiah to persuade him to surrender (2 Kgs 18:17) but he refused on the advice of Isaiah

---

335 B. Wodecki, "Jerusalem – Zion in the Texts of Proto-Isaiah," *PJBR* 1 (2000) 1: 98–99.

336 Historically, this view was shared by E. J. Young (id., *The Book of Isaiah*, I–III [Grand Rapids 1965, 1969, 1972]) and R. E. Clements (*Isaiah 1–39* [Grand Rapids 1980]).

337 M. A. Sweeney, *Isaiah 1–39 with an Introduction to the Prophetic Literature* (The Forms of the Old Testament Literature 16; Grand Rapids 1996), 293.

338 B. S. Childs, *Isaiah* (The Old Testament Library; Louisville 2001), 157.

339 In the Assyrian, royal inscriptions (the Kurkh Monolith, the Black Obelisk, the stele from Tel al-Rimach, tables and columns from Nimrud, annuals) there are mentioned of many kings of Judah and Israel. The mention of Ahaz of Judah, Hezekiah, Manasseh, Ahab of Israel, Jehu, Joash, Manachem, Pekah and Hosea; J. H. Walton et al., *Tablice biblijne. Chrześcijańskie tablice encyklopedyczne,* I (trans. Z. Kościuk; Warszawa 2007), 45.

(2 Kgs 19:5–7). The issue of using Aramaic by the royal officials of Judah is related to this fact. Three of Sennacherib's messengers came to Hezekiah: Tartan arrived there as viceroy, Rabsaris as commander of the eunuchs, and Rabshakeh as the chief cup-bearer. The latter spoke in Hebrew, even though Hezekiah's representatives asked him to speak in Aramaic; he had not given his consent. It was a method of intimidating the inhabitants of Jerusalem, who could only understand a speech delivered in Hebrew. Hezekiah refused to surrender the city because he hoped that the preparations made by him (strengthening of the walls and a cavity of the water-supply tunnel) would help to repel the attack.[340] The King capitulated only when Sennacherib conquered all the cities of Judah, surrounded by fortified walls. Hezekiah had to pay high compensation, draining the royal treasury and tearing off gold ornaments from above the entrance to the temple (2 Kgs 18:14–16).[341] When he sent them to Nineveh, Jerusalem was saved while the remaining lands of Judah were handed over to rulers of Ashdod, Ashkelon, Gaza, and Ekron.[342]

According to another group of exegetes, the text of Isa 22:1–14 reflects the historical situation at the time of Sargon II. He was the king of Assyria in the years 722–705. He took the throne after Shalmaneser, whose death stirred up riots in the country lasting two years. In the year 720, Sargon came against Chaldean Marduk-pail-iodine II (known in the OT as Merodach-Baladan) and against the Syrian-Palestinian coalition, which was supported by Egypt (2 Kgs 17:4). Adding to the rebellion, Merodach-Baladan joined Lula, the king of Sidon, and Sidqia of Ashkelon; after a time Hezekiah joined them as well.[343] The fight against Syro-Palestine consisted in suppressing all resistance and pushing the Egyptian army to the border of Sinai. At that time, there was a deportation of the inhabitants of Samaria, which became the Assyrian province.

---

340 N. Avigad, *Discovering Jerusalem* (Nashville 1980), 46–57.

341 Hezekiah had to pay three hundred talents of silver and thirty talents of gold; C. Schedl, *Historia Starego Testamentu*, IV, *Zew Proroków* (trans. S. Stańczyk; Tuchów 1995), 209.

342 Sennacherib, to celebrate his victory over Judah, put on the walls of the palace at Nineveh some reliefs presenting the conquest of Lachish; M. Cogan, "Sennacheryb," in *Encyklopedia biblijna* (ed. P. J. Achtemeier; trans. E. Szymula; Warszawa 1999), 1098. The sculpture represents a family of Lachish, who goes barefoot into exile. Assyrian annals confirm that Sennacherib conquered forty-six of Hezekiah's fortified cities (*ANET*, 291a, 294a). Lachis was the second most important city that guarded the access to Jerusalem. The conquest of the city describes D. Ussishkin (*The Conquest of Lachish by Sennacherib* [Publications of the Institute of Archeology 6; Tel Aviv 1982]).

343 S. H. Horn and P. Kyle McCarter, "Podzielona monarchia. Królestwa Judy i Izraela," in *Starożytny Izrael. Od Abrahama do zburzenia świątyni jerozolimskiej przez Rzymian* (ed. H. Shanks; trans. W. Chrostowski; Warszawa 2007), 264.

Northern Kingdom fell down (2 Kgs 17), while the South remained on ground that became loyal to Assyria. In order to maintain conquered lands and extend his power, Sargon undertook other expeditions. In the year 717, he wanted to get Carchemish (Isa 10:9). In 716, his aim was to take control over trade routes in the south of Palestine (Isa 19:23) and finally in the years 713–711 to suppress Palestinian riots commanded by Ashdod. At that time Judea was saved only because it did not join the rebellion by the Ashdod (Isa 20).[344] The King of Ashdod was removed and replaced by his brother, but people rebelled against this order of things and acknowledged the power of the usurper. In Judah, however, Isaiah urged people not to put confidence in Egypt. To gain his purpose he symbolically walked about Jerusalem with only a loincloth around his hips. Isaiah's words had to be taken into account, because Judah escaped the disaster, which suggests that it did not join the uprising against Assyria.[345]

What historical background should be accepted for Isa 22:1–14? Is it the matter of Sennacherib's campaign in 701 or rather Sargon's II invasion in 711 B.C.? Several arguments woven from the text of Isa 22 support the first hypothesis.[346] Hezekiah prepared the water system (vv. 9 and 11), the country was destroyed (vv. 5–8a), and after avoiding the conquest by Sennacherib, the king awaited nationwide recovery and an enhancement of the spirit throughout the nation. However, it did not take place in that situation and his bitterness is understandable (vv. 4 and 14).

Nevertheless, in the text, there are elements that may seriously indicate the need for considering the adoption of the second hypothesis. After all, Hezekiah trusted in God for freeing from Sennacherib's invasion. The text does not provide any indications that the siege of Jerusalem took place. There is no mention that the city was surrounded by enemy troops. The mentions of escape and imprisonment in vv. 2b–3 more likely correspond to times of Jeconiah (2 Kgs 24:10–17) and Zedekiah (2 Kgs 25:4–7) then Hezekiah. Eventually, Eliakim, not Shebna, was the Royal writer in 701: "Then Eliakim son of Hilkiah the palace administrator, Shebna the secretary, and Joah son of Asaph the recorder went to Hezekiah with their clothes torn, and told him what the field commander had said" (2 Kgs 18:37). Thus, the hypothesis linking Isa 22:1–14 with the campaign of Sargon against Ashdod in 711 seems to be more likely.

---

344 P. B. Machinist, "Sargon II," in *Encyklopedia biblijna* (ed. P. J. Achtemeier; trans. E. Szymula; Warszawa 1999), 1088–1089.

345 J. Bright concludes that in any event, when the uprising was suppressed, Judah escaped the misfortune. One can suppose that either Judah did not join or engage in it irrevocably; J. Bright, *Historia Izraela* (trans. J. Radożycki; Warszawa 1994), 290.

346 C. R. Seitz, *Isaiah 1–39* (Interpretation. A Bible Commentary for Teaching and Preaching; Louisville 1993), 159.

2.2. Exegetical Analysis of Isa 22:1–14

Vv. 1–8a The prophet begins his speech against Jerusalem, calling it the Valley of Vision (גֵּיא חִזָּיוֹן). It is a formulation analogous to the description of Babylon as the "Desert by the sea." It is theoretically possible but rather unlikely that Isaiah refers to the topographic description of the valley, surrounded by Hinnon, Tyropeon and Kidron. Isaiah usually identifies Jerusalem with Mount Zion. What is more, it is difficult to call "a valley" the city built on hills (Zion, Moriah). Therefore, we should look at this name of the city symbolically. The prophet declares, with a touch of irony or even sarcasm, that although Jerusalem is located at the top, from which you can see far around, it is still a spiritual valley affected by blindness. In the name "the Valley of Vision" you can also see an allusion to the fact that Jerusalem was the place where Isaiah and many other OT prophets had their visions.

The question מַה־לָּךְ אֵפוֹא means "What's the matter with you?" There is a similar use of this phrase in Judg 18:23. It expresses the idea that the prophet does not understand the behavior of the inhabitants of Jerusalem.[347] Instead of relaxing on terraces of their houses and ignoring the spiritual situation throughout the nation, they should repent and pray. Indeed, in hot Judah's climate you can experience a bit of cold, thanks to the wind blowing through the points situated high over the city and unshaded walls of buildings. Like these were precisely the roofs of homes of the inhabitants of Jerusalem. Some exegetes suggest the hypothesis that the inhabitants from the town went out onto the terraces, but not to play or rest. Rather, they were rather on the watch to see if hostile troops or the messengers for the king were approaching. However, this does not give the prophet reasons for their behavior. They should, according to the prophet, devote themselves to penance and prayer and trust in God.

In the next verse, the prophet characterizes the city. Jerusalem is a "town full of commotion … a city of tumult and revelry" (v. 2). Isaiah seems to hear thousands of people talking, laughing loudly and playing, but completely unaware of the seriousness of the situation in which they find themselves. In a prophetic vision, he sees the city differently, however. Its walls are smashed, everywhere in the streets there are corpses of those who died of starvation during the siege, but not those who were "killed by the sword" or "died in battle" (v. 2b). The leaders, instead of activating the nation into a fight, saved themselves by fleeing and leaving the capital (v. 3). Yet, it is not useful for them as they are taken as prisoners; "they have been captured without using the bow" (v. 3a). The phrase מִקֶּשֶׁת literally means "with a bow" or "from a bow," but in this context, the preposition מִן should be treated as having the character of a

---

347   Smith, *Isaiah 1–39*, 384.

privativum.[348] This gives ambivalent meaning to a whole phrase. It may mean that the leaders of Jerusalem were taken prisoners, without shooting a single arrow. This means they did not take up the defense (as we can assume from the context, especially of v. 2) of the city. There is also possibility that the enemies did not even have to use any weapons, as the leaders of the city surrendered without a fight.[349]

This kind of leadership existed in Jerusalem, and Isaiah often condemned it. To support this view, we should cite a few examples: "Your rulers are rebels, companions of thieves; they all love bribes and chase after gifts. They do not defend the cause of the fatherless; the widow's case does not come before them" (1:23); "Therefore my people will go into exile for lack of understanding; their men of rank will die of hunger and their masses will be parched with thirst" (5:13); "And these also stagger from wine and reel from beer: Priests and prophets stagger from beer and are befuddled with wine; they reel from beer, they stagger when seeing visions, they stumble when rendering decisions" (28:7). Such leaders do not care about the welfare of the inhabitants, but about their own convenience. In such circumstances, the inhabitants of Jerusalem look for fun and entertainment only, and they do not predict that they will bring their home to ruins.

Subsequently, the prophet describes the escape of the "leaders" (LXX reads: οἱ ἁλόντες), who were captured. The sequence of the described events can, however, cause some difficulties: "All you who were caught were taken prisoner together, having fled while the enemy was still far away" (v. 3b). A natural question arises: how could those who found themselves in captivity escape? Some suggested an inversion of part of the sentence and recreation of v. 3b as follows: "All your leaders [although] having fled while the enemy was still far away, all ... were caught [and] were taken prisoner together."[350] However, it seems that the author or the editor of this part of Isaiah adopted an earlier lesson to get a fuller chiasmus A–B–B'–A, recorded in a whole v. 3, and based on a scheme of the themes of escape and captivity:

---

348 *BDB*, 583.

349 Such understanding of the phrase מִקֶּשֶׁת can suggest the description of Zedekiah's escape: "By the ninth day of the [fourth] month the famine in the city had become so severe that there was no food for the people to eat. Then the city wall was broken through, and the whole army fled at night through the gate between the two walls near the king's garden, though the Babylonians were surrounding the city. They fled toward the Arabah, but the Babylonian army pursued the king and overtook him in the plains of Jericho. All his soldiers were separated from him and scattered" (2 Kgs 25:3–5).

350 Oswalt, *Book of Isaiah*, 403.

A: *Escape:* "All your leaders have fled together,"
  B: *Captivity:* "they have been captured without using the bow,"
  B': *Captivity:* "All you who were caught were taken prisoner together,"
A': *Escape:* "[although] having fled while the enemy was still far away."

The prophet himself does not want to take part in these feasts and wants to experience more deeply the fate of Jerusalem revealed to him by God. So he asks the undefined recipient: "Turn away from me; let me weep bitterly. Do not try to console me over the destruction of my people" (v. 4). In this verse, Jerusalem is called a "Daughter" (בַּת), which indicates to a very emotional attitude to the city or rather to its inhabitants. The relationship seems to be modeled on family ties. The phrase "O Daughter of Jerusalem (בַּת־עַמִּי)" appears only in Isaiah; it should be read within the context of other statements of the prophets, describing a Jerusalem that has gone astray and is sinful: "Jerusalem has sinned greatly and so has become unclean. All who honored her despise her, for they have seen her nakedness; she herself groans and turns away" (Lam 1:8); "What can I say for you? With what can I compare you, O Daughter of Jerusalem? To what can I liken you, that I may comfort you, O Virgin Daughter of Zion? Your wound is as deep as the sea. Who can heal you?" (Lam 2:13); "Fallen is Virgin Israel, never to rise again, deserted in her own land, with no one to lift her up" (Amos 5:2); "You who live in Lachish, harness the team to the chariot. You were the beginning of sin to the Daughter of Zion, for the transgressions of Israel were found in you!" (Mic 1:13).

Starting from v. 5 the prophet goes directly to the situation within the city, which is in peril and that is the order of "The Lord, the Lord Almighty." Isaiah has already foretold the "Day of Yahweh" in Isa 2:6–22. About the day of the Lord, the prophets usually uses the future tense. Here, however, the day is presented as a past event so that people could draw a lesson for the future from it.[351] The grammatical form *imperfectum* of the verb נַיְהִי in v. 7, subjected to the inversion through the inclusion ו, makes it so the other verbs of this section are read in the past tense. The tragedy that happened in the past can be repeated and resulted in a much more dramatic way because people learned nothing from experience.[352] By way of opposition to the bustle of the city mired in play, the prophet recalls the noise of "tumult and trampling and terror" (וּמְבוּסָה וּמְבוּכָה מְהוּמָה). Meanwhile, after all "In repentance and rest is ... salvation, in quietness and trust is ... strength" (Isa 30:15).

---

351 J. A. Everson, "Days of Yahweh," *JBL* 93 (1974): 329–337.
352 G. W. Grogan notices: "The prophecy was fulfilled when Nebuchadneazar took the city in 586 B.C., though history was destined to repeat itself in A.D. 70—when the Romans overcame Jewish resistance and entered Jerusalem to wreak havoc on its people and its buildings"; id., "Isaiah," 141.

The second part of v. 5, in most translations tells about battering down the walls of Jerusalem (Vulg.: "in valle Visionis scrutans murum"). More often, however, the translation "be in vain" is accepted (LXX: πλανῶνται). This is because the meaning of the verb קֹרֵר is uncertain,[353] and the translators see the parallelism just with the last fragment of v. 5 ("crying out to the mountains"). The verb is phonetically closer to the Ugaritic *qr* and Arabic *qarqara*, and it means "make a noise."[354] This change to the text, however, would be hard to justify because the Hebrew text clearly refers to the walls. In continuation of his writing, the author presents the picture of Jerusalem, which undergoes destruction. Its walls fall, and the cry among the people is growing.

Another verse raises considerable textual difficulties. Most exegetes agree that it mentions Elam and Kira. (Differently Vulg.: „Aelam sumpsit faretram currum hominis equitis et parietem nudavit clypeus"; and LXX: οἱ δὲ Αιλαμῖται ἔλαβον φαρέτρας ἀναβάται ἄνθρωποι ἐφ᾽ ἵπποις καὶ συναγωγὴ παρατάξεως). However, most controversies surround the name of Aram. MT says, "chariots of man" (בְּרֶכֶב אָדָם), but it is very likely that due to the similarity of the ר and ד, the copyists' mistake occurred here.[355] With the adoption of such a correction, the text speaks of Aram and becomes more understandable. Thus you can read its content as: "Elam took up the quiver, Aram harnessed horses, Kir uncoved the shield." Even if it is true that Sennacherib defeated the Elamite during his first campaign against Babylon,[356] it seems unlikely that the Elamite troops presented a significant force in the planned attack on Jerusalem. Hence, there is a need to make one of two possible hypotheses: either Elam, Aram, and Kir posed a significant part of the army in the invasion of Nebuchadnezzar on Jerusalem in 586, or these names are used here in a figurative way, as in Isa 21:2: "A dire vision has been shown to me: The traitor betrays, the looter takes loot. Elam, attack! Media, lay siege! I will bring to an end all the groaning she caused." The second possibility seems more likely, the prophet declares that the same people that have persecuted Jerusalem will destroy Babylon.[357] Isaiah earlier mentioned Elam, which was located to the east of the Tigris. During the invasion of Judah, the region was allied with Assyria: "In that day the Lord will

---

353 *BDB* gives following meanings: "be cold," "make or keep cool," "grow calm"; *BDB*, 903.

354 M. Weippert, "Zum Text von Ps. 195 und Js 22,5," *ZAW* 73 (1961): 97–99; G. R. Driver, "Isaiah 1–39: Textual and Linguistic Problems," *JSS* 13 (1968): 47–48.

355 The adoption of such correction has already proposed G. R. Driver in 1937 ("Linguistic and Textual Problems, Isaiah 1–39," *JTS* [1937]: 40–41). It is probable because the term "chariots of man" appears also in Isa 21:7 (however, in the form of רֶכֶב אִישׁ, but not אָדָם רֶכֶב), where from the copyists could take it.

356 *ARAB*, II, 234.

357 Oswalt, *Book of Isaiah*, 410–411.

reach out his hand a second time to reclaim the remnant that is left of his people from Assyria, from Lower Egypt, from Upper Egypt, from Cush, from Elam, from Babylonia, from Hamath and from the islands of the sea" (Isa 11:11).[358] A more precise location of Kir is unknown.[359] We only know that this is the place to which the Assyrian King Tiglath-Pileser (ca. 745–727 B.C.) abducted prisoners from Damascus (2 Kgs 16:9).[360] Aram, however, has been under the dominion of Assyria since 732, and it completely lost its identity as an independent state.

The picture outlined in vv. 7–8a shows the capital of Judah, which is close to destruction. Valleys surrounding the city are full of enemy troops that pitched camps there. It is a well-armed army, equipped with chariots and equestrians. The latter stand in front of the gate. Jerusalem is defenceless and at the mercy of the enemy, who is aware that: "the defences of Judah are stripped away" (v. 8a).

Vv. 8b–11 The narrative tone changes in v. 8b. In vv. 1–4 the prophet showed the contrast between his inspired vision and blindness of the inhabitants of Jerusalem. In vv. 5–8a he included threats of Yahweh to the city. This part, beginning with v. 8a and extending up to v. 14,[361] shows the response to these threats and the effect of it. This effect is the forthcoming destruction of Jerusalem. The residents of the capital, rather than take care of their relationship with God, are engaged in strengthening the walls, in order to have a good time.[362] Such an attitude towards the Lord must not be unpunished. The city will be subjected to destruction—from a theological point of view—not so much by the enemy, as by the lack of trust in God among the people of Judah.

Seeing the coming danger, the king of Judah, Hezekiah decides to better fortify the city and prepare it for the impending danger. He takes care of armories (v. 8b), cares for and strengthens the walls (vv. 9a and 10) and seeks to provide water (vv. 9b and 11). This type of preparation is reasonable and is not met with criticism from Isaiah. However, instead of taking care, in the first place, of the spiritual health of the people under his authority and keeping the

---

358 L. E. Pearce, "Elam," in *Encyklopedia biblijna* (ed. P. J. Achtemeier; trans. M. Wojciechowski; Warszawa 1999), 250–251.

359 Seitz, *Isaiah 1–39*, 161.

360 R. S. Boraas, "Kir," in *Encyklopedia biblijna* (ed. P. J . Achtemeier; trans. Z. Kościuk; Warszawa 1999), 519.

361 For this reason, C. Westermann sees in vv. 8b–14 a separate theme unit; C. Westermann, *Basic Forms of Prophetic Speech* (trans. H. C. White; Philadelphia 1967), 170–172.

362 Smith, *Isaiah 1–39*, 386.

covenant, the king devotes his time mostly to external activities. Perfectly, the king's priorities reveal the chiastic structure of vv. 8b–11:

A: Armament (vv. 8b–9a);
   B: Water supply (v. 9b);
      C: Mending of defences walls (v. 10);
   B': Water supply (v. 11a);
A': God as a Creator (v. 11b).[363]

Elements corresponding to each other indicate that the issue of armament (A) is in the first place, while concern about the relationship with God is in last one (A'). First, Hezekiah wanted to take care of the armory in the Palace of the Forest. The Palace of the Forest was part of the temple complex, built by Solomon: "It took Solomon thirteen years, however, to complete the construction of his palace. He built the Palace of the Forest of Lebanon a hundred cubits long, fifty wide and thirty high, with four rows of cedar columns supporting trimmed cedar beams. It was roofed with cedar above the beams that rested on the columns—forty-five beams, fifteen to a row" (1 Kgs 7:1–3).

Hezekiah also tried to patch holes and breaches in the walls of the city (v. 9a). Some instead of "breaches" (בְּקִיעֵי) prefer talking about "pools,"[364] to agree v. 9a with v. 9b; however, such a change is not justified, since the text clearly refers to the walls. There are no arguments for the mistake of a scribe. We do not know exactly where these pools mentioned in v. 9b were placed (the Lower Pool), and in v. 11a (the Old Pool). It is usually assumed that the Old Pool was built near the Gihon Spring as the water intake (Isa 7:3, 36:2; 2 Kgs 18:17). The Lower Pool was created in Ahaz's times in the Tyropoeon Valley, and in Hezekiah's times it was joined to the Pool of Siloam.[365] However, there is no doubt that Hezekiah built a canal to bring water into the city. The tunnel connected the Gihon Spring located in the Kidron Valley in the eastern part of the capital with the pool of Siloam placed in its western part. It was discovered in 1880, and an inscription which was on the walls of the tunnel caused the greatest sensation. The inscription confirms information from the Bible. It says about two groups of workers, who drifted from two different ends, and eventually met themselves inside the rock, in the middle of the road. The height

---

363 Chiasmus was quoted after: J. A. Emerton, "Notes on the Text and Translation of Isa. xxii 8–11 and lxv 5," *VT* 30 (1980): 437–446.

364 See: Driver, "Isaiah 1–39," 40–41.

365 A. Mazar, *Archeology of the Land of the Bible. 10,000–586 B.C.E.* (The Anchor Bible Reference Library: New York et al. 1992), 420; L.-H. Vincent and M.-A. Steve, *Jerusalem de L'Ancien Testament* (I; Paris 1954), 295; Oswalt, *Book of Isaiah*, 413; K. Kenyon, *Royal Cities of the Old Testament* (London 1971), 139–140.

of the tunnel varies from a few centimeters to over four meters, whilst its length is 534 meters. The Bible also mentions the construction of the tunnel, recollecting the following: "As for the other events of Hezekiah's reign, all his achievements and how he made the pool and the tunnel by which he brought water into the city, are they not written in the book of the annals of the kings of Judah?" (2 Kgs 20:20).[366] The finds from the era of Hezekiah confirmed the dating of the tunnel. The imprint of a seal in the clay, belonging to the royal official Eliakim, who was the son of Hilkiah, mentioned in 2 Kgs 18:18, says: "Eliakim son of Hilkiah the palace administrator."[367]

The fact that the houses and the destruction of buildings were counted in order to strengthen the city wall (v. 10) is confirmed in 2 Chr 32:5: "Then he worked hard repairing all the broken sections of the wall and building towers on it. He built another wall outside that one and reinforced the supporting terraces of the City of David. He also made large numbers of weapons and shields." In the next statement (v. 11), the prophet reproaches the residents of Jerusalem for caring about the city water system instead of paying more attention to their Creator. The fact that causes some problems is that the suffixes used in the terms: the "Creator" (עֹשֶׂיהָ) and "to shape" (יֹצֵר). These terms are typical for third person singular, but usually feminine. Therefore, we can suppose that the text relates to Jerusalem directly. Interpreters have suggested that God the Creator of all things identifies himself with the city that He has adopted for his dwelling.[368] In other words, Isaiah makes the reproach that the people of Judah's focus on the works of their own hands, not on the One who makes it so these things may exist. After all, the works of human hands do not last (cf. Isa 40:6–7; Pss 56:5; 102:13).

Vv. 12–14 The last section of Isa 22:1–14, which appears in the passage quoted by Paul in 1 Cor 15:32b, is the prophet's reflection on the fact that the inhabitants of Jerusalem offended "the Lord Almighty." They did this by trusting in a self-prepared defense system rather than in God Himself. This insult also manifests itself in the rejection of the call to repentance, and turning

---

366 This information is also confirmed by reference to 2 Chr 32:2–4: "When Hezekiah saw that Sennacherib had come and that he intended to make war on Jerusalem, he consulted with his officials and military staff about blocking off the water from the springs outside the city, and they helped him. A large force of men assembled, and they blocked all the springs and the stream that flowed through the land. 'Why should the kings of Assyria come and find plenty of water?'—they said."

367 A. Millard, *Skarby czasów Biblii. Odkrycia archeologiczne rzucają nowe światło na Biblię* (trans. M. Stopa; Warszawa 2000), 126–127.

368 Oswalt, *Book of Isaiah*, 404.

towards amusements and pastimes. Isaiah says that God has called people living in the capital to repentance, "to weep and to wail, to tear out [their] hair and put on sackcloth" (v. 12). The people, however, rejected this call. This idea is present throughout Isaiah's theology: if exercised worship is not accompanied by the change of heart, such a form of religion is "disgusting" before God (Isa 1; 32:11–13).[369]

The call to repentance and trust in God remained unanswered. Instead, the people have turned to sort of an anti-answer. It has become "joy and revelry, slaughtering of cattle and killing of sheep, eating of meat and drinking of wine" (v. 13a). This contrast between what God expected, and what the inhabitants of Jerusalem committed was accentuated by the prophet with the use of exclamation: וְהִנֵּה ("but see," LXX: δέ of an adversory nature; Vulg.: "ecce"). The prophet describes quite a similar situation in Isa 5:11–13: "Woe to those who rise early in the morning to run after their drinks, who stay up late at night *till* they are inflamed with wine. They have harps and lyres at their banquets, tambourines and flutes and wine, but they have no regard for the deeds of the Lord, no respect for the work of his hands. Therefore my people will go into exile for lack of understanding; their men of rank will die of hunger and their masses will be parched with thirst." The verbs used in v. 13 (הָרֹג, וְשָׁחֹט, אָכֹל, אָכוֹל וְשָׁתוֹ, וְשָׁתוֹת) take the form of *infinitivus absolutus*, by expressing the immediacy and continuity of activities to which they relate. The phrase "slaughtering of cattle and killing of sheep" is double in nature: the first act indicates the intemperance of the people of Jerusalem. The mention of the other is ironic in its character. The customary diet did not contain much meat. The reason was simple. First off, the storing conditions were difficult, and secondly; the oxen were too valuable to easily decide on killing them. In the mention of killing sheep, the irony lies in the fact that in the face of the impending siege, the inhabitants of the capital should be aware that each dose of meat will be needed; meanwhile, they consume large quantities of food in a fun atmosphere.

The phrase "Let us eat and drink … for tomorrow we die!" almost in all translations is marked as a citation, even if there in no formula introducing the quotation.[370] However, the LXX has already introduced the formula citation: λέγοντες, and the whole phrase is read as follows: λέγοντες φάγωμεν καὶ πίωμεν αὔριον γὰρ ἀποθνήσκομεν. The call "let us eat and drink" was written—as mentioned above—in the form of *infinitivus absolutus*, what suggests an immediate and constant action. Nevertheless, the verb "die" (נָמוּת) was written

---

369   Cf. Ps 51:17–21; Joel 2:12–17; Amos 8:10; Mal 1:8–11; Isa 32:11–13.

370   "Although the MT has no verb of saying to introduce the quotation in the verse, the versions are agreed that the one is intended"; Oswalt, *Book of Isaiah*, 405.

with the use of the ordinary *imperfectum* in the form of *qal*. The whole quotation expresses the thought: if it indeed remains nothing but lone death, any sacrifice, repentance and commitment are devoid of sense. Fun and enjoyable use of time are the only things to do. In this quotation resounds the echo of words: "We have entered into a covenant with death, with the grave we have made an agreement. When an overwhelming scourge sweeps by, it cannot touch us, for we have made a lie our refuge and falsehood our hiding place" (Isa 28:15).

What is the source of the quotation in Isaiah? Many authors—as mentioned—refer to Imhotep, a high official, an architect and a doctor at the same time, at the court of Pharaoh Djoser around XXVI century B.C. Tradition says that Imhotep came from the village of Gebelein. He was the high priest of the God Ra at Heliopolis and Chancellor of the Pharaoh. He is also a creator of Step Pyramid and the ancient mortuary complex in Saqqara. His works influenced the later creation of the Hippocratic Oath. During the Middle Kingdom, Imhotep was elevated to the position of a deity, while during the New Kingdom times he was declared the patron of writers. The process of deification and worshiping of Imhotep as the son of Ptah began in 9th century B.C. The Greeks, however, identified him with Asclepias, the god of medicine. While it is true that the phrase "Let us eat and drink, for tomorrow we die" is derived from Imhotep's poem titled *Song of a Harper*, we have to remember that it is also connected with the Egyptian tradition of having feasts. A human skeleton was presented to the guests who used to appear in the banquet hall. The skeleton uttered the words, which were to remind people of the transience and elusiveness of human life.[371] Some claim that it was not a real skeleton, but a skeleton made of wood. It was shown to the guests while someone was playing the harp.[372]

The last verse of this section, v. 14, coincides with the prophecy of Isaiah recorded in Isa 6:9–10: "Go and tell this people: 'Be ever hearing, but never understanding; be ever seeing, but never perceiving.' Make the heart of this people calloused; make their ears dull and close their eyes. Otherwise they might see with their eyes, hear with their ears, understand with their hearts, and turn and be healed." The inhabitants of Jerusalem became blind and deaf to the word of God. Their hearts became hardened, and therefore, they did not understand the things of God. For this reason, the next part of this prophecy must be fulfilled: "the cities lie ruined and without inhabitant, until the houses are left deserted and the fields ruined and ravaged, until the Lord has sent everyone far away and the

---

371   E. Cobham Brewer, *Dictionary of Phrase and Fable* (Philadelphia 1898) [after: http://www.infoplease.com/dictionary/brewers/let-us-eat-drink-for-tomorrow-we-shall-die.html].

372   M. K. Asante, *From Imhotep to Akhenaten: An Introduction to Egyptian Philosophers* (Philadelphia 2004), 87–88.

land is utterly forsaken. And though a tenth remains in the land, it will again be laid waste. But as the terebinth and oak leave stumps when they are cut down, so the holy seed will be the stump in the land" (Isa 6:11b–13). That is why the iniquity of the people will not be forgiven, and sinful people would have to die. The reason is that they did not accept the attitude, which was depicted in 2 Chr 7:14: "if my people, who are called by my name, will humble themselves and pray and seek my face and turn from their wicked ways, then will I hear from heaven and will forgive their sin and will heal their land."

The tone of the statements, "Till your dying day this sin will not be atoned for" (v. 14) becomes very solemn due to the use the title "the Lord Almighty," which is repeated in the closing declaration: "says the Lord, the Lord Almighty." Due to the contents of the statement, the tone is not only solemn and official, but also strict.[373] The Prophet used the standard formula of the oath usually used in the OT here (e.g. Isa 14:24): "The Lord Almighty has sworn, 'Surely, as I have planned, so it will be, and as I have purposed, so it will stand.'"

2.3. The Contribution of v. 13b to Isa 22:1–14

As indicated above, the historical background of Isa 22:1–14 is a campaign of Sargon II in 711 B.C. rather than the invasion of Sennacherib in 701 B.C. In 712, Azuri, the king of Ashdod, was deposed and his place was taken by his brother. A year later, however, Sargon II had to suppress another rebellion in Ashdod, and he just then approached Jerusalem much closer, threatening the city. Ashdod is located in the northern part of Judah, just four kilometres inland, getting further from the Mediterranean Sea. The danger threatening the capital of Judah from the Assyrian army activated the prophet Isaiah; he foretold the failure of the city. The reason lies in the fact that people had lost their trust in God, and began to rely only on the self-defense system and fortifications. The King Hezekiah truly strengthened the city walls, took care of the armory and built a canal supplying Jerusalem with water. After completing the preparations for a possible attack the

---

373 Childs, *Isaiah*, 161. G. W. Grogan remarks: "Verse 14. contains one of the Bible's most terrifying sentences, comparable perhaps to the words of Revelation 22:11. The revelers had probably slaughtered the animals used by them for their feasts at Jerusalem's temple. Let them not think though that sacrifice could be offered to atone for this sin. At the very time when God's promises to protect Jerusalem were being so wonderfully fulfilled, the threat was given that the city would most certainly fall one day before its enemies and that nothing, just nothing, could avert the judgment of God on it"; "Isaiah," 142. It is true that God's declaration of the city's destruction is one of the most severe, which the Bible includes. Nevertheless, it is difficult to justify the idea of killing animals for use during the feasts at Jerusalem temple.

inhabitants of Jerusalem, rather than praying and repenting, began to indulge in amusements and pleasures. It was their behavior that caused the pungent speech of Isaiah, who condemned the attitude of his countrymen.

The fragment, "Let us eat and drink," "for tomorrow we die!" was placed by Isaiah in v. 13b in the last section of Chapter 22. The prophet states that the inhabitants of the capital had the call to conversion for nothing, and that they devoted their time to look for entertainment instead. The very phrase "Let us eat and drink, 'you say,' for tomorrow we die!" is most likely a quote. As its source, some authors give the work written by an Egyptian court official Imhotep, entitled *Song of a Harper*. It is difficult to determine in which way this quote entered into the work of Isaiah. However, the way of thinking of citizens of the city, which was under the threat from an invasion of the Assyrians, was shown here. They relied on the works of their hands—fortifications and other preparations for the battle. They did not trust God, from whom the liberation could come. They indulge in the joy, and fun instead of devoting themselves to the prayer and penance. That is why annihilation was waiting for them. This was confirmed by a solemn and strict prohibition by God and the statement: "Till your dying day this sin will not be atoned for" (v. 14).

3. The Meaning in 1 Cor 15:31–34

Paul, in a personal tone, recorded in the style of diatribe,[374] confesses to the Corinthians: "I die every day—I mean that, brothers—just as surely as I glory over you in Christ Jesus our Lord" (v. 31). From the standpoint of textual criticism, the more probable seems to be the lesson in which the exclamation "brothers" is not used (46, D, F, G, L, Y, 1739, *Byz*, *Lect*). There are also, however, those in which the noun appears (‫א‬, A, B, 33, 81, 104, 330, 1241, it[f, ar], Vulg., syr[pal], goth, arm).[375] Paul appears here in the authority of the Apostle.[376] The confession constitutes a reference to the personal experience of suffering the hardships and adversities for the sake of the gospel. At the same time, by its use, Paul introduces the question placed in v. 32. First, the invocation of "glory"

---

374 T. Schmeller, *Paulus und die 'Diatribe'. Eine vergleichende Stilinterpretation* (NTA 19; Münster 1987), 332–387. Extensive comparative monograph of Pauline and cynic-stoic diatribe was elaborated by R. Bultmann (*Der Stil der paulinischen Predigt und die kynisch-stoische Diatribe* [FRLANT 13; Göttingen 1910]).

375 B. M. Metzger, *A Textual Commentary on the Greek New Testament* (Stuttgart 1994²), 501; Jamieson, Fausset and Brown, *Commentary*, 330.

376 J. R. White, "'Baptized on Account of the Dead': The Meaning of 1 Cor 15:29 in its Context," *JBL* 116 (1997): 494.

(καύχησις), gives to the confession a solemn tone which the Apostle has from the recipients. Second, it is the use of the titular: "in Christ Jesus our Lord" (ἐν Χριστῷ Ἰησοῦ τῷ κυρίῳ ἡμῶν). By using the plural pronoun "our" Paul places himself and his recipients at the same level as Christ. Owing to this, he creates the familiar atmosphere, full of brotherly kindness and mutual openness. The whole formulation "as I glory over you in Christ Jesus our Lord" sounds like an oath.[377] The Apostle seems to say: "just as surely as I glory over you in Christ Jesus our Lord." With this formula, the whole sentence becomes extremely solemn.[378] So Paul makes an oath of that which is the dearest to him: the oath of the lives of the Corinthians in Christ, that of their salvation.

Paul's personal confession sounds: "I die every day" (καθ' ἡμέραν ἀποθνῄσκω). This is a hyperbolic statement, saying that the apostle often puts himself to death.[379] One can recall here such references to Acts as: "After many days had gone by, the Jews conspired to kill him [Paul]" (9:23); "He talked and debated with the Grecian Jews, but they tried to kill him" (9:29); "Then some Jews came from Antioch and Iconium and won the crowd over. They stoned Paul and dragged him outside the city, thinking he was dead" (14:19). The statement "I die every day" also means that Paul spiritually connects himself with the death of Christ.[380] In a metaphorical sense, he uses the phrase in 2 Cor 6:9a as well: "dying, and yet we live on."[381] Establishment of a community at Corinth had to cost Paul a lot of apostolic work. The Corinthians were Paul's "glory," because *inter alia*, he paid with suffering for his preaching among them. In v. 32 the apostle refers to a specific example of his "dying." It is written in the form of a rhetorical question: "If I fought wild beasts in Ephesus for merely human reasons, what have I gained? If the dead are not raised, 'Let us eat and drink, for tomorrow we die'" (v. 32). Exegetes are wondering whether it refers to *damnatio ad bestias*, that is the condemnation on a fight with the animals in the amphitheater. This is unlikely, because after such an experience

---

377 Keener, *1–2 Corinthians*, 128; J. Lightfoot, *A Commentary on the New Testament from Talmud and Hebraica. Matthew – 1 Corinthians, 4, Acts – 1 Corinthians* (Peabody 1997³), 271–272.

378 Parallel wording of the oath can be found with Josephus in *Ap.* 1.255 ("I swear to Zeus"); Fee, *First Epistle to the Corinthians*, 769.

379 Keener, *1–2 Corinthians*, 128; Soards, *First Corinthians*, 1187; Henry, *Commentary*, 2274; Murphy-O'Connor, "The First Letter to the Corinthians," 813.

380 Mare, *1 Corinthians*, 288.

381 This phrase appears in the context of reporting the hazards in connection with the preaching the Gospel; White, "'Baptized on Account of the Dead,'" 496.

almost no one saved his neck.[382] What is more, Paul was a Roman citizen, and such a citizenship most likely excluded him from being devoured by wild beasts.[383] As Paul mentions a specific city, therefore, it seems logical that it refers to a particular event which took place there. It is not a pure metaphor of spiritual struggle, although such metaphors were known in Greco-Roman culture.[384] The fragment 16:8–9 sheds a little more light on this mention. The apostle mentions in it about his desire to stay in Ephesus to devote himself to the missionary work, although he is aware that he has many enemies there.[385] Therefore, those "wild beasts" could have been simply used as images of bad people who openly opposed to Paul, and made things awkward for him and his missionary work. Both the Greek philosophers and biblical authors used the images of a fight with animals to describe adversities and difficult experience. It is enough to mention the following texts: "Dogs have surrounded me; a band of evil men has encircled me" (Ps 22:17); "Many bulls surround me; strong bulls of Bashan encircle me. Roaring lions tearing their prey open, their mouths wide against me" (Ps 22:13–14); "Deliver my life from the sword, my precious life from the power of the dogs. Rescue me from the mouth of the lions; save me from the horns of the wild oxen" (Ps 22:21–22).[386] Regarding adversities in Asia, Paul states also in 2 Cor: "We do not want you to be uninformed, brothers, about the hardships we suffered in the province of Asia. We were under great pressure, far beyond our ability to endure, so that we despaired even of life. Indeed, in our hearts we felt the sentence of death. But this happened that we

---

382 Ignatius of Antioch described such an event. He put the following words into Polycarp's mouth: Ignatius of Antioch described such an event. He put the following words into Polycarp's mouth: "I beseech you that you shew not an unseasonable good will towards me. Suffer me to be food to the wild beasts; by whom I shall attain unto God. For I am the wheat of God; and I shall be ground by the teeth of the wild beasts, that I may be found the pure bread of Christ" (*Rom.* 4.1). Based on this Paul's metaphor showing the struggle with the animals, the author of the apocryphal *Act of the Apostle Paul* presents him as a hero who was not even defeated by wild, hungry beasts; Langkammer, *Komentarz*, 248; Romaniuk, Jankowski and Stachowiak, *Komentarz*, 163; R. E. Osborne, "Paul and the Wild Beasts," *JBL* 85 (1966): 225–230.

383 Fee, *First Epistle to the Corinthians*, 770–771; Keener, *1–2 Corinthians*, 128; Mare, *1 Corinthians*, 288; A. J. Malherbe, "The Beasts at Ephesus," *JBL* 87 (1968): 71–80.

384 Ignatius of Antioch in Rom 5:1 states: "From Syria even unto Rome, I fight with beasts both by sea and land." J. Lambrecht, however, believes that it is a metaphor of the fight; Lambrecht, "Pierwszy List do Koryntian," 1484; Murphy-O'Connor, "The First Letter to the Corinthians," 813.

385 It is also possible that it comes to a fact of imprisonment of the apostle in Ephesus; Romaniuk, Jankowski and Stachowiak, *Komentarz*, 163; Stern, *Komentarz*, 689.

386 Keener, *Komentarz*, 327.

might not rely on ourselves but on God, who raises the dead. He has delivered us from such a deadly peril, and he will deliver us" (2 Cor 1:8–10a). As an Apostle Paul has to endure daily hardships, inconveniences or persecutions. The reference is intended to encourage the Corinthians to ask a question: why does the apostle risk his life, if there is no resurrection?

The formulate κατὰ ἄνθρωπον deserves for a bit more attention. Should it be understood—as some translators want—as "on the people's account" or "for the sake of people"? It seems that in the current context it would be much more appropriate to adopt the meaning, after which the Apostle has already reached himself in 1 Cor 3:3.[387] There, he contrasts purely human behavior to the one under the influence of the Spirit. Similarly, Paul argues that if there is no resurrection, the struggle with the enemies of the gospel takes place on a purely human level, and as a result has no sense. The apostle seems to ask. What is the point in exposing our lives, if there is no hope for resurrection? The question "what have I gained?" seems to imply Paul's conviction that if there is no resurrection, he lives like a fool, and all his efforts go to waste.

After using a rhetorical question to mention events in Ephesus, Paul introduces the quote which was taken from Isa 22:13b. Obviously the quote is the subject of our analysis.[388] In order to advance arguments in an easier way, Paul repeats the *protasis*: "If the dead are not raised." *Apodosis* is the logical conclusion of the previous arguments: "Let us eat and drink, for tomorrow we die."[389] The previous statements have wide repercussions here. If there is no resurrection, it is better to take pleasure instead of fighting with wild animals.[390]

---

387 Soards, *First Corinthians*, 1187; Heil, *Rhetorical Role of Scripture*, 225; Fee, *First Epistle to the Corinthians*, 771; Thiselton, *First Epistle to the Corinthians*, 1251.

388 H. Langkammer says that the prophet could know, "the rakish song, from which he took the most drastic verse out"; *Komentarz*, 24.

389 Since there is not any introduction formula here, some scholars believe that Paul did not want to indicate that the sentence was quoted by him from the OT, but used it rather as a popular saying: "Paul, however, does not necessarily expect his implied Corinthian audience to recognize the quotation in 1 Cor 5:32b as a quotation from Isa 22:13b. Indeed, he does not even introduce it as a quotation from Scripture, much less from Isaiah. Rather, his audience is to recognize it as a popular slogan"; Heil, *Rhetorical Role of Scripture*, 222; vide Cenci, *La nostra risurrezione è una certezza!*, 81; H. Binder, "Zum geschichtlichen Hintergrund von I Kor 15,12," *TZ* 46 (1990): 197.

390 Some exegetes have suggested that some of the Corinthians may have accepted the views of Hymenaeus and Philetus "who have wandered away from the truth. They say that the resurrection has already taken place" (2 Tim 2:18). As for the point of view that was oriented on experiencing spiritual gifts (charismatic) and getting prompting of the Holy Spirit the Corinthians have already now, so in their bodies experience the power of the resurrection; G. Barth, "Zur Frage nach der 1 Kor bekämpfen Auferstehungsleugnung," *ZNW* 83 (1992): 190–

In other words, since some of the Corinthians reject the resurrection of the dead, they show a lack of consistency in their behavior. As they should indulge in pleasures of this world. However, if they believe in the resurrection of Christ, and expect their own resurrection, they should change their behavior.[391] An argument of inconsistency between the theoretical conviction and practical behavior was extremely important in the philosophical tradition of Greece. Mostly, the Stoics devoted serious attention to it.[392]

We should first zero in on the need to find reasons for the rejection of the belief in resurrection by the community of Corinth (or at least among some of its members). Paul does not say the reasons why this situation arose directly. They should be inferred only from his statements, wherewith; he tries to convince his recipients to recognize the resurrection of the dead. In the history of exegesis reasons why the Corinthians rejected the resurrection were rarely adduced. They can be reduced to four:

(1) The Corinthians rejected the belief in the resurrection from the dead because they did not believe in life after death[393] (so-called "materialists")[394];

(2) The Corinthians rejected the belief in the resurrection from the dead. The reason was that they believed that the resurrection had already taken

---

191; H. Langkammer, *Życie człowieka w świetle Biblii. Antropologia biblijna Starego Nowego Testamentu* (Rzeszów 2004), 433.

391 On the relationship between the resurrection of Christ and the expectancy for resurrection of the faithful with their daily conduct see: E. J. Jezierska, "'Życie dla Pana' – zasadą postępowania odkupionych przez Jezusa Chrystusa. Refleksje nad Pawłowym tekstem 2 Kor 5,15," *SS* 1 (1997) 1: 105–110.

392 Vide *Bion* 7,10–11; *Diss.* 1,4,13–17; 2,12; 19.13–22; *Ench.* 49; *Lach.* 188C-E; *Gorg.* 495A; J. M. Rist, "Zeno and Stoic Consistency," in *Essays in Ancient Greek Philosophy* (II; ed. J. P. Anton; New York 1983), 465–477; Asher, *Polarity and Change in 1 Corinthians 15*, 62.

393 R. Bultmann, K. Barth, W. Schmithals were supporters of such an assumption. De Boer specifies this view, adding the assumption that some of the Corinthians may have thought that only those would be able to share eternal life, who would see the parousia. Other deceases do not have any chances for it; de Boer, *Defeat of Death*, 96. Such a hypothesis was put forward by A. Schweitzer, E. Güttgemans, B. Spörlein, H. Conzelmann. See also: Aletti, "L'Argumentation de Paul," 70–71; W. Schmithals reasones: "Die Vorordnung des Pneumatischen vor das Psychische bedeutet ja das Ende der Predigt von Busse und Gnade, während umgekehrt die Nachstellung des Pneumatischen von dem Wissen getragen ist, dass das Geschenk des Pneuma mitgeteilte Leben die freie Gabe Gottes ist, der sich zu dem sündigen und verlorenen Fleisch hinabneigt"; *The Gnosis in Korinth* (FRLANT 48; Göttingen 1956), 137.

394 Aletti, "L'Argumentation de Paul," 78.

place (cf. 2 Tim 2:18). Such a belief was not without influence of Gnostic thought or the mysterious[395] cults (the "spiritualists")[396];

(3) The Corinthians rejected the belief in the resurrection from the dead since they could not understand the physical and material nature of life after death[397];

(4) Paul did not understand the Corinthians, and erroneously attributed them a rejection of faith in the resurrection from the dead.[398]

The opinion that the Corinthians denied any form of life after death (proposition 1) is based on vv. 17–19 and vv. 22–34, where Paul seems to be set against such an opinion. However, v. 29 (the mention about baptism for the dead) suggests that in Corinth, there must have been a conviction about some form of continuation peoples' lives after death. So the first opinion should be rejected. The reason is that there is at least some apparent contradiction between vv. 17–19 and vv. 22–34, where Paul justifies the existence of life after death and in v. 29 where he justifies the practice of baptism for the dead.[399] This verse proves

---

395 H. von Soden, J. Schniewind, W. G. Kümmel, J. M. Robinson, E. Brandenburger, J. H. Wilson, E. Käsemann suggested this view; de Boer, *Defeat of Death*, 97. See also: L. Schottroff, *Der Glaubende und di feindliche Welt. Beobachtungen zum gnostischen Dualismus und seiner Bedeutung für Paulus und das Johannesevangelium* (WMANT 37; Neukirchen 1970); J. Dupont, *Gnosis. La connaissance religieuse dans les épîtres de saint Paul* (Louvain–Paris 1960²).

396 Aletti, "L'Argumentation de Paul," 78.

397 Supporters of this thesis: P. Bachmann, H. Lietzmann, R. J. Sider, J. Murphy-O'Connor, P. Hoffmann, R. A. Horsley; de Boer, *Defeat of Death*, 97. St. Justin berated this view in *Tryph. 80*. C. K. Barrett reports his reference this way: "We may recall Justin's reference (*Trypho* 80) to those false Christians who thought that the future would see the souls of Christians translated at death immediately to heaven, without resurrection"; "Significance of the Adam-Christ Typology," 111.

398 Holleman, *Resurrection and Parousia*, 35–36. These arguments are discussed extensively in several positions: G. Sellin, *Der Streit um die Auferstehung der Toten. Eine religionsgeschichtliche und exegetische Untersuchung von 1 Korinther 15* (FRLANT 138; Göttingen 1986), 17–37; B. Spörlein, *Die Leugnung der Auferstehung. Eine historisch-kritische Untersuchung zu 1 Kor 15* (BU 7; Regensburg 1971), 2–16; Barth, "Zur Frage," 187–191; Hasler, "Credo und Auferstehung in Korinth," 20–21; A. J. M. Wedderburn, "Problem of the Denial of the Resurrection in 1 Corinthians XV," *NovT* 23 (1981): 228–241; A. C. Thiselton, "Realized Eschatology in Corinth," *NTS* 24 (1977–1978): 510–526.

399 More on the practice of baptism for the dead, see: B. M. Forschini, "'Those Who Are Baptized for the Dead': 1 Cor 15:29," *CBQ* 12 (1950): 260–276; J. K. Howard, "Baptism for the Dead: A Study of 1 Cor 15:29," *EvQ* 37 (1965): 137–141; M. F. Hull, *Baptism on Account of the Dead (1 Cor 15:29). An Act of Faith in the Resurrection* (SBL 22; Atlanta 2005); J. Murphy-O'Connor, "Baptized for the Dead" (1 Cor XV:29):

that the Corinthians believe in some form of survival after death. What is more, some exegetes believe that Paul did not understand the Corinthians, or that he had been misinformed as to their belief (proposition 4). If, however, we assume that Paul did not understand the Corinthians or had inadequate knowledge about their beliefs about life after death, then assuming the letter itself, it becomes impossible to understand these convictions. The view that the Corinthians believed that the resurrection has already happened (proposition 2) was under exegetes' discussion for a time but disputes on this issue have been practically prevented. There are too many arguments against the thesis, that it could be maintained.[400] This view was based on the fact that the Corinthians themselves aspired to this so to regard them as "spiritual" men, yielding a peculiar "spiritual triumphalism." They boasted about their maturity (1 Cor 1:29.31, 4:7, 5:6), they claimed that they possessed "wisdom" (1:19–2:7, 3:18–23) and "knowledge" (8:1–3:7), and they also boasted about their spiritual gifts.[401] The Corinthians could not properly understand Paul's teaching that in the baptism, the resurrection with Christ has already taken place, because baptismal immersion is immersion in the death and resurrection of Christ. After the baptism, they are spiritual beings that have already experienced resurrection.

Proposal 3 should be assumed the most likely, because according to it, the Corinthians had trouble in understanding the physical dimension of the resurrection. As the residents of the Greco-Hellenistic world they probably knew the views (in different forms, but containing a common basic idea), articulated in the philosophical tradition about two kinds of people, spiritual and non-spiritual. Souls of the first permeate a transcendent spirit and as a consequence of such an inspiration, physical bodies are only vessels in which the soul is

---

A Corinthian Slogan?, *RB* 88 (1981): 532–543; M. Reader, "Vikariastaufe in 1 Cor 15:29?," *ZNW* 46 (1955): 258–261; J. D. Reaume, "Another Look At 1 Cor 15:29, 'Baptized for the Dead'," *BSac* 152 (1995): 457–475; K. Staab, "I Kor 15,29 in Lichte der Exegese der griechischen Kirche," in *Studiorum Paulinorum Congressus Internationalis Catholicus 1961*, II (AnBib 17–18; Rome 1963), 437–449; M. Rissi, *Die Taufe für die Toten* (Abhandlung zur Theologie des A und NT 42; Zurich 1962); White, "'Baptized on Account of the Dead,'" 489–499; R. E. DeMaris, "Corinthian Religion and Baptism for the Dead (1 Corinthians 15:29): Insights from Archeology and Anthropology," *JBL* 114 (1995) 4: 661–682.

400   Discusses them extensively D. W. Kuck in his study *Judgement and Community Conflict. Paul's Use of Apocalyptic Judgment Language in 1 Cor 3, 5–4, 5* (NovTSup 66; Leiden et al. 1992), 16–25.

401   de Boer, *Defeat of Death*, 103. Referring to this attitude of the Corinthians Paul resorts to sarcasm "Already you have all you want! Already you have become rich! You have become kings—and that without us!" (1 Cor 4:8a).

temporarily trapped.[402] The task of the apostle would be then revealing the idea of resurrection, set firmly in the Jewish tradition (especially promoted by the Pharisaic circles).[403] The resurrection as renewed acceptance of a body would suggest further imprisonment of the soul in the body.

This hypothesis assumes that the Corinthians were, to some extent, under the influence of Greek thought about the resurrection. And the Greek tradition in this respect is very diverse. In some philosophical or literary writings, the Greeks rejected the possibility of resurrection. In others, they treated the resurrection as a single, wonderful event, and eventually they pointed to the possibility of the rising to life (but not the resurrection). An example of the first movement, rejecting the resurrection, may consist in the statement addressed by Achilles to Priam, in which he convinces his interlocutor that it is impossible to return to life after death:

> "War and slaughter have been about your city continually.
> Bear up against it, and let there be some intervals in your sorrow.
> Mourn as you may for your brave son, you will take nothing by it.
> You cannot raise him from the dead, ere you do so
> yet another sorrow shall befall you."[404]

---

402 Burial customs of the ancient Greeks evidence for these views. More about this subject, see: D. Kurtz and J. Boardman, *Greek Burial Customs* (Aspects of Greek and Roman Life; London 1971); R. Garland, *The Greek Way of Death* (London 1985); M. Alexiou, *The Ritual Lament in Greek Tradition* (Cambridge 1974); K. Hopkins, *Death and Renewal* (Sociological Studies in Roman History 2; Cambridge 1983), 212–216; J. M. C. Toynbee, *Death and Burial in the Roman World* (Aspects of Greek and Roman Life; London 1971), 50–64; I. Morris, *Death-Ritual and Social Structure in Classical Antiquity* (Key Themes in Ancient History; Cambridge 1992); K. C. Thompson, "I Corinthians 15,29 and Baptism for the Dead," in *Papers Presented to the Second International Congress on the New Testament Studies held at Christ Church, Oxford 1961* (Studia Evangelica 2; TU 87; Berlin 1964), 651–659; S. C. Humphreys, "Death and Time," in *Mortality and Immortality: The Anthropology and Archeology of Death* (eds. S. C. Humphreys and H. King; New York 1981); M. C. Kearl, *Endings: A Sociology of Death and Dying* (New York 1989), 95–106; A. C. Rush, *Death and Burial in Christian Antiquity* (Catholic University of America Studies in Christian Antiquity 1; Washington 1941), 28–101; J. Lambrecht, *To Meet the Lord: Scripture about Life after Death* (*Pauline Studies*, BETL 125: Leuven 1994), 411–441.

403 J. Holleman puts this idea in terms of the discontinuity between the earthly and the eternal: "Paul explains that there is a discontinuity between these form of life; a discontinuity which can only be bridged by resurrection. Resurrection will therefore be another act of creation, this time resulting in a spiritualized body"; *Resurrection and Parousia*, 38.

404 *Iliad* 24, 554–558.

Similar tenor had the words of Aeschylus, who claimed that for a man who died, there is definitely no return to life:

> "But when the dust has drawn up the blood of a man,
> once he is dead, there is no return to life.
> For this, my father has made no magic spells,
> although he arranges all other things,
> turning them up and down."[405]

In the *Symposium*, its author Plato claimed that the miracle of the resurrection can take place only once (179c). In Greek mythology, there are also known "divine men" who could rise to life. One of them was Apollonius of Tyana. The power of rising to life Greeks attributed also to the Asclepios. This belief was ancient, presumably dating to the 7th century B.C., Hymn *To Demeter*, which uncovers the secret practices that would ensure immortality. The Greek dreams of immortality are also present in the myths about Adonis and Dionysus. According to the first myth, although the lover of Aphrodite was killed; he could return to earth and spend some time with her. According to the second one, although Dionysus Zagreus was torn to pieces, his heart was hidden by one of the goddesses and so Dionysus could be born again. Based on this myth, the feast of the divine resurrection was celebrated in Delphi. Generally, however, in Paul's time the Greeks rejected the possibility of the resurrection of individuals. Among other things, it was the reason why the mission of Paul in Athens ended in failure (Acts 17:18–31).[406]

Food and drink appear in v. 32b as an alternative to the daily dying. If indeed, there is no resurrection, then Pauline lifestyle and exposure to the dangers do not have a reasonable justification. On the other hand, if the recipients of the letter question why Paul chooses a style of life which he leads, subsequently the answer must lead them to the recognition to the truth concerning the resurrection of the dead. In Paul's text, the quotation reads as follows: φάγωμεν καὶ πίωμεν, αὔριον γὰρ ἀποθνῄσκομεν. This quotation, however, is preceded by a conditional sentence: "If the dead are not raised" (εἰ νεκροὶ οὐκ ἐγείρονται). This sentence, which is a kind of *argumentum ad absurdum*, suggests quoting the opinion of some of the Corinthians—those who deny the resurrection of the dead.[407] These people reason like the "godless" about whom the Wisdom of Solomon says: "Time fades away like a shadow,

---

405 *Eumenides* 647–651.

406 M. Rosik, *Ewangelia Łukasza a świat grecko-helleński. Perspektywa literacka i ideologiczna* (Bibliotheca Biblica; Wrocław 2009), 264–266.

407 According to Asher, it is not about *argumentum ad absurdum*, but about the argument built based on the modus Tollens: if A then B, because it is not A therefore, also not B; Asher, *Polarity and Change in 1 Corinthians 15*, 60.

and no one returns from death. So make the most of life especially while you're young. Drink the very best wine, wear expensive perfume, and enjoy the spring flowers. Decorate your head with rosebuds before they wilt. Do your share of celebrating! Party always and everywhere—that is what life is all about" (Wis 2:5–9).[408] This reasoning seems to reflect Stoic thought.[409] It can also be a reflection of the anti-Epicurean polemic, existing in the days of Paul.[410] In writings of Plutarch, for example, the words "eating and drinking" becomes synonymous with life in luxury and pleasures.[411] Ecclesiastes accepts "food and drink," but it can not be an end itself. It is enought to quote such passages: "A man can do nothing better than to eat and drink and find satisfaction in his work. This too, I see, is from the hand of God" (Eccl 2:24); "That everyone may eat and drink, and find satisfaction in all his toil—this is the gift of God" (Eccl 3:13); "Then I realized that it is good and proper for a man to eat and drink, and to find satisfaction in his toilsome labor under the sun during the few days of life God has given him—for this is his lot" (Eccl 5:18).[412]

After the quotation from Isa 22:13b, the Apostle warns the Corinthians about illusive beliefs.[413] He does this by a command and the proverbial formula: "Do not be misled: 'Bad company corrupts good character.'" *Argumentum ad absurdum* changes over to *argumentum ad hominem*, taking the form of encouragement.[414] The proverb "Evil communications corrupt good manners" as mentioned in the first chapter of our research was taken from Menandros, a comedy writer who lived between the fourth and the 3rd centuries B.C. (*Thais* 18).[415] Menandros was close in his views to the Epicureans. Even when he did

---

408 Heil, *Rhetorical Role of Scripture*, 222.

409 Fabris, *Prima Lettera ai Corinzi*, 206; Winter, *After Paul Left Corinth*, 79–80.

410 "In Plutarch's anti-Epicurean writings, for example, the language of 'eating and drinking' was a formula for the dissolute life"; Fee, *First Epistle to the Corinthians*, 772.

411 *Mor.* 1098C, 1100D, 1125D; Grasso, *Prima Lettera ai Corinzi*, 172. The author also cites the saying of Sardanapalus, the last of the legendary king of Assyria (669–626 B.C.). The words are attributed to him: "My feasts and my obscenity remain me"; ibid.

412 Keener, *1–2 Corinthians*, 129; cf. W. Schrage, *Der erste Brief an die Korinther (1 Kor 15,1–16,24)* (EKKNT 7/4; Zürich 2001), 246; S. Park, *Conceptions of Afterlife in Jewish Inscriptions: With Special Reference to Pauline Literature* (WUNT 121; Tübingen 2000), 181–182.

413 J. S. Vos, „Argumentation und Situation in 1 Kor. 15," *NovT* 41 (1999): 313–315.

414 J. R. Asher agrees that we are dealing here with an *argumentum ad hominem*, but denies earlier *argumentum ad absurdum*; *Polarity and Change in 1 Corinthians 15*, 61. Cf. Also: Holleman, *Resurrection and Parousia*, 41.

415 Malina and Pilch, *Social-Science Commentary*, 126; Stern, *Komentarz*, 689; Soards, *First Corinthians*, 1188; Murphy-O'Connor, "The First Letter to the Corinthians," 813; Talbert, *Reading Corinthians*, 125. "Paul cites the slogan not as a literary quotation but

military service, he was a companion of Epicures.[416] In a slightly modified form, Euripides also wrote this sentence (*Fr.* 1013), as well as Diodorus Siculus (*Bib. hist.* 16:54,4) and Philo of Alexandria (*Deter.* 38). Menandros took a lot from Euripides, who was his literary master. Not surprisingly, both writers present the same views in their works.[417]

The phrase ὁμιλίαι κακαί can mean not only "evil communications," but also "bad company."[418] The Apostle encourages in this warning to avoid not only the wrong conversations (which reject the belief in the resurrection), but also to avoid people expressing false convictions. In this case, it is about people who deny the resurrection of the dead. Similar warnings were well known both in Judaism and in early Christian writings. The author of Proverbs warned: "He who walks with the wise grows wise, but a companion of fools suffers harm" (Prov 13:20); "Stay away from a foolish man, for you will not find knowledge on his lips" (Prov 14:7). Not to mention Rom 13:12b–13: "So let us put aside the deeds of darkness and put on the armor of light! Let us behave decently, as in the daytime, not in orgies and drunkenness, not in sexual immorality and debauchery, not in dissension and jealousy."

The whole section ends with yet another call for breaking the evil: "Come back to your senses as you ought, and stop sinning; for there are some who are ignorant of God—I say this to your shame" (v. 34). The call "Come back to your senses!" (ἐκνήψατε δικαίως) has a double meaning: it can point at waking up from a sleep (as in Hab 2:7.19) and it can also point at becoming sober after an abuse of alcohol (Gen 9:24 and 1 Sam 25:37).[419] One cannot be absolutely sure, which meaning the apostle intended although the context ("Let's eat and drink") points to the second meaning. The apostle has already used this exhortation in 1 Cor 6:5. In any case, a call for "awakening" means the abandonment of the illusion ("Come back to your senses") that there is no resurrection. Being in such an illusion causes the wrong (sinful) behavior, so the next call is to stop

---

as a *bon mot* in popular currency"; R. F. Collins, *First Corinthians* (Collegeville 1999), 561. Thiselton points to Menandros as the source of the quotation, but recognizes that in times of Paul's, the words became "*a popular maxim*"; Thiselton, *First Epistle to the Corinthians*, 1254; Winter, *After Paul Left Corinth*, 98–99; S. Longosz, "Czy Paweł Apostoł cytował komediopisarza Menandra (1 Kor 15,33). Opinie Ojców Kościoła," *VoxP* 9 (1989) 17: 907–924; W. T. Wilson, *Pauline parallels. A comprehensive guide* (Louisville 2009), 178.

416 Łanowski, *Menandros*, 312; Mare, *1 Corinthians*, 288; Keener, *Komentarz*, 373.
417 D. Łowicka, "Euripides," in *Słownik pisarzy antycznych* (ed. A. Świderkówna; Warszawa 1982), 195.
418 Thayer, *Thayer's Greek-English Lexicon*, 444.
419 Jamieson, Fausset and Brown, *Commentary*, 330; Soards, *First Corinthians*, 1188; Henry, *Commentary*, 2275.

sinning. Falsification of transmission of the faith is a sin; the Corinthians should be aware of that fact. God gives the mind to a man, in order that he is enlightened to the faith and can decline false teachings. Among the inhabitants of the community, there are, in fact, those who reject God (not knowing him). The rejection or ignorance of God is the same misconception as the one according to which there is no resurrection. Nevertheless, the rejection of belief in the resurrection leads to the fact that the Christian faith becomes "vain."[420]

To conclude, in vv. 31–34 the apostle uses the quote, taken from Isa 22.13b, as the words that could well be attributed to the inhabitants of Corinth, who deny the resurrection of the faithful. This quotation, although derived from Isaiah (and before the work of Menandros), could have been known as the popular saying describing a certain lifestyle. The lifestyle can be attributed to the people who negate resurrection. In a natural way, the negation of the resurrection may lead to the attitude included in a noted earlier call "Let us eat and drink, for tomorrow we die."[421] The apostle relies on his own experience of struggle and all the persecutions he faces. His intention, however, is motivated by the faith in resurrection. If you rebutted the faith, risking your life would be meaningless. A quote from Isa 22:13b can be considered as an example of "evil communications" and the good manners corrupted as a result of them. To reject an attitude, to which the quoted words encourage, you should wake up, and stop sinning. Whoever does not do this is equal to a person who does not recognize God. Whereas, the apostle would like to confuse the Corinthians, who should "sober up" and "wake up." He does this in order to achieve a better understanding of God who brought Christ back to life, certifying that he has the power of resurrecting every dead.

---

420   Hill, "Paul's Understanding of Christ's Kingdom," 320; E. Dąbrowski, *Listy do Koryntian. Wstęp – przekład z oryginału – komentarz* (PŚNT 7; Poznań–Warszawa 1965), 276.

421   "The denial of the resurrection of the dead will result in a libertine life style. This is a deceived and sinning life due to the lack of the knowledge of God"; Saw, *Paul's Rhetoric*, 236.

V. Quotation from Gen 2:7b in 1 Cor 15:45b

1 Cor 14:45b: ἐγένετο ὁ πρῶτος ἄνθρωπος ᾿Αδὰμ εἰς ψυχὴν ζῶσαν

Gen 2:7b (LXX): καὶ ἐγένετο ὁ ἄνθρωπος εἰς ψυχὴν ζῶσαν

Gen 2:7b (HB): נַיְהִי הָאָדָם לְנֶפֶשׁ חַיָּה

1. Source of the Quotation

The text of the LXX generally agrees with the HB. It must be, however, noted that in the term הָאָדָם the translator from Hebrew to Greek is treated as a general term for a man, not for a proper name. This is true because there is an article before the term, which only disappears in the further parts of Genesis. In the text of St. Paul, there are two changes. The apostle introduces the numeral "first" and the proper name Adam into his sentence.[422] It is true that the second change, the introduction of a proper name Adam, is also present in the versions by Theodotion and Symmachus. Albeit, it is known that both translations were written later than 1 Cor. Proselyte Theodotion from Ephesus elaborated his translation at the end of the 2nd century. The Samaritan named Symmachus translated his text a little later.[423] None of these versions could therefore be the source of Paul's interference in the quoted text. Instead, we should recognize that Paul, Symmachus and Teodotion referred to the Jewish tradition, which treated the term הָאָדָם included in the HB in two ways. In other words, the term was understood as a general indication of the whole human race as well as a proper name.[424] If we took these two additional words out of Paul's quotation, its wording would be identical to the wording in the LXX. Changes made by Paul are of the editorial origin, and they can be motivated by the context. The

---

422 Heil, *Rhetorical Role of Scripture*, 231. Stanley claims: "Nothing in either Greek or Hebrew traditions offers any reason to think that Paul might hale found the word in his *Vorlage* of Gen 2.7"; Stanley, *Paul and the Language of Scripture*, 208.

423 M. Rosik, "Literatura żydowska okresu biblijnego i rabinicznego," in M. Rosik and I. Rapoport, *Wprowadzenie do literatury i egzegezy żydowskiej okresu biblijnego i rabinicznego* (Bibliotheca Biblica; Wrocław 2009), 52.

424 Stanley, *Paul and the Language of Scripture*, 208; "Paul has obviously freely adapted language in Genesis [2:7]"; Asher, *Polarity and Change in 1 Corinthians 15*, 114.

Apostle writes about Christ (treating the title as a proper name), so it is quite understandable that carrying out the analogy: Adam–Christ, he also introduces the proper name Adam.[425] The same purpose serves as an introduction of the numeral "first." Since Paul says of Christ as "the last Adam" or "the second Adam," it seems quite natural to introduce the numeral in order to achieve greater consistency of the sentence and inner logic of expression. The Hebrew text of Gen 2:7 can be translated into Greek in a variety of ways without distorting the fundamental thought. Since Paul's translation (besides the two explained incorporations) agrees exactly with the wording of the text of the LXX it must be assumed that the source of Paul's citation is the LXX.[426]

2. The Meaning in the Original Context

In the traditional exegesis, the second description of the creation of a man (Gen 2:4b–7) is assigned to the Yahwist.[427] It is much older than that attributed to the priestly tradition. Many authors see in it more elements than in the first mythological story of the creation of man. According to Yahwist, there was only a desert that God turned into a garden or oasis thanks to the irrigation.[428] When the irrigated land is habitable, God creates a man. He does this by means of the breath, which he passes to a mould from the dust of the ground. Now, Gen 2:4b–7 will be analyzed against a background of this, to obtain properly the thought contained in the passage quoted later by Paul in 1 Cor 15:45b.

2.1. Ideological Base and the Literary Structure in Gen 2:4b–7

This short story, which is by rotation the second description of the creation of man in Genesis, depicts the beginnings of life on earth, which was by the author

---

425 "Editors and copyists seem, to have had some scruples about Paul's treatment of the Old Testament text; in the first clause B and others omit ἄνθρωπος, and in the second P⁴⁶ and Irenaeus omitts Ἀδάμ"; Barrett, "Significance of the Adam-Christ Typology," 112.

426 E. E. Ellis argues that it can be accepted as the source both the text in Hebrew and in Greek. Paul was to change both. He does not justify; however, why not he simply opts for the LXX, where the following quotation in 1 Corinthians 15:45b is the same as in the LXX; id.,"Paul's Use of the Old Testament," 152. R. B. Terry, in contrast, opts for LL interchangeably; id., *Discourse Analysis*, 159.

427 P. E. S. Thompson, "The Yahwist Creation Story," *VT* 21 (1971): 198–208; N. Wyatt, "Interpretation of the Creation and Fall Story in Genesis 2–3," *ZAW* 93 (1981): 10–21.

428 G. von Rad, *Teologia Starego Testamentu* (trans. B. Widła; Warszawa 1986), 119–125.

deliberately contrasted with the earlier state of existence of all creations. The contrast between the first and second description of creation is already noticeable from the initial words. If the priestly author writes of the creation of "the heavens and the earth" (Gen 1:1), the Yahwist reverses the order, telling about God making "the earth and the heavens" (v. 4b). This difference is certainly not accidental. The dichotomy between the two stories is evident also in the terminology ("create"–"make") or in the God's name ("Elohim"– "Yahweh Elohim"). All such differences suggest the beginning of a new section in Gen 2:4b.[429]

There is a supposition among theologians that the Yahwist was the author of his own description of the creation of the earth. The description was much more sophisticated than just the one included in vv. 4b–7, but the final editor of Genesis removed it for the reason that the creation was presented in details in Hexaemeron. If it was possible to confirm this assumption, the story would be probably based on one of the versions of Babylonian myth of creation. The Babylonians believed that the world was created by the demiurge, which defeated a monster personifying the initial chaos. This monster could have been identified with Rahab. Deuteron-Isaiah, the prophet often reaching for the Yahwist work, writes about him (Isa 51:9). The Yahwist of course did not ascribe to this monster any divine attributes as it was in the Babylonian mythology. Monotheism of the Yahwist tradition is firmly drawn throughout the whole work.[430]

Although, as the grammatical analysis presented below will show, all part of Gen 2:4b–7 can be regarded as one sentence, but it is possible to extract some structure-elements from it. Some translations based on these elements break the unity of the Hebrew sentence into several sentences in the languages of translation: "When the Lord God made the earth and the heavens— and no shrub of the field had yet appeared on the earth and no plant of the field had yet sprung up, for the Lord God had not sent rain on the earth and there was no man to work the ground, but streams[431] came up from the earth and watered the whole surface of the ground— the Lord God formed the man from the dust of the ground and breathed into his nostrils the breath of life, and the man became a

---

429 A. Wénin, *D'Adam à Abraham ou les errances de l'humain. Lecture de Genèse 1,1– 12,4* (Paris 2007), 51. Cf.: J. Lemański, *Pięcioksiąg dzisiaj* (SB 4; Kielce 2002), 161; D. M. Carr, *Reading the Fractures of Genesis. Historical and Literary Approaches* (Louisville 1996), 75; P. Weimar, "Die Toledôt – Formel in der priesterschriftlichen Geschichtsdarstellung," *BZ* 18 (1974): 65–93; T. Stordalen, "Genesis 2,4. Restudying a locus classicus," *ZAW* 104 (1992): 163–177.

430 J. S. Synowiec, *Początki świata i ludzkości według Księgi Rodzaju* (Kraków 2001³), 92–93.

431 Ibid., 92.

living being." According to this translation, the grammatical criterion itself shows the structure of this fragment in the following three segments:

1. Lack of vegetation on the ground (vv. 4b–5);
2. Irrigation of arable land (v. 6);
3. The creation of man from the dust of the ground (v. 7).

2.2. Exegetical Analysis of Gen 2:4b–7

Vv. 4b–5 It should be noted once again that from a grammatical point of view the fragment included in vv. 4b–7 consists of only one sentence: "When the Lord God made the earth and heavens, there was no shrub of the field on the earth, nor any grass of the field had yet sprung up—for the Lord God had not caused it to rain upon the earth and there had not been a man yet to till the ground and dig a ditch in the ground to irrigate the whole surface of it—then the Lord God formed the man from the dust of the ground and breathed into his nostrils the breath of life, and the man became a living being" (vv. 4b–7). This long multiple, compound sentence, however, makes a grammatical trouble. It is difficult to say which clause is the main clause: the description of the formation of the first irrigation system (v. 6) or the one illustrating the creation of a man (v. 7)? Syntactically and substantively, the second possibility seems more likely.[432] Verses 4b–6, depicts the creation of the world and constitutes only a specific *terminus a quo*. However, the whole passage describes the creation of a man and God's concern for him. In Gen 1, creation appears to be the ordering of the world "from chaos to the cosmos," whereas here the state of initial ground is seen as the opposite of the arable land. Arable land becomes the human environment, a world of his life, and his surroundings. The main topic of this short story is a relation between "man" and "the land" (אָדָם – אֲדָמָה).[433] Cosmological ideas which inspired the Yahwist are quite different from those presented by the sacerdotal document. In the Yahwist's text, water is a useful element in the creation, while in the priestly tradition and in some psalms it is an obstacle in this work. A position of man is also shown in a different way: in Gen 1 "a man is a summit of a pyramid of the creation" in Gen 2 he is "a center of a wheel."[434]

---

432 G. von Rad, *Genesi. Traduzione e commento* (Antico Testamento 2/4; Brescia 1978⁴), 92.
433 Wénin, *D'Adam à Abraham*, 58–59.
434 von Rad, *Genesi*, 93.

The story begins with a phrase בְיוֹם (v. 4b), meaning "in the day."[435] It is a phrase with temporal meaning.[436] A mention of God whose name is Yahweh Elohim follows the phrase.[437] This name dominates in the entire section 2:4b–3:24.[438] The original version of the text contained only the name of Yahweh, while the name Elohim was added by the priestly editor. The name Yahweh was revealed by God to Moses. It was confirmed by both the Elohist tradition founded in the 8th century (Exod 3:6–15) and the priestly tradition, written in the 6th or 5th century (Exod 6:2–13).[439] The name was originally written using only consonants, was not only in the HB but also in non-biblical documents (Mesha Stele, king of Moab, the seal from the 8th century; ostraca from Tel Arad, the list from Lachish from the 6th century B.C.), and the correct pronunciation of the name is known from Greek transcriptions.[440] The Jews stopped using this name after returning from the Babylonian captivity (538 B.C.). While reading the HB in synagogues, they replaced it with Adonai. Although the etymology of the name Yahweh is still debated by linguists, it is known that the Israelites combined it with the verb "to be" (Exod 3:13–15).[441] Interpretation of the content of the name should concentrate on God's presence in Israel in order to lead and to take care of this nation (Exod 20:2; Deut 5:6).

Although the name Elohim is grammatically plural, the author refers to the only God because in the Bible, the name can be found mostly alongside the singular predicate. Presumably, it was derived from the verb that means "to be

---

435 The phrase corresponds to the Accadian phrase *enūma*; this is also the title of the Babylonian equivalent of Genesis – *Enūma eliš*.

436 Cf. Exod 6:28; Num 3:1; Isa 11:16; Ezra 28:13; C. Westermann, *Genesis* (Biblischer Kommentar. Altes Testament, I; Neukirchen–Vluyn 1974), 270.

437 Yahweh's name appears in Gen 2:4b for the first time in the Bible; T. Brzegowy, *Pięcioksiąg Mojżesza* (Academica 27; Tarnów 2002), 273.

438 E. A. Speiser, *Genesis. Introduction, translations, and notes* (The Anchor Bible; New York 1980³), 15; Westermann, *Genesis*, 270. The most often expressed opinion is that there are two parallel stories, of which the present text was composed; Lemański, *Pięcioksiąg dzisiaj*, 162; G. J. Wenham, *Genesis 1–15* (WBC 1; Waco 1987), 53–54.

439 Attempts to show that the name of Yahweh was known in pre-Mosaic times did not bring any significant results; R. de Vaux, *Histoire ancienne d'Israël. Des origines à l'installation en Canaan* (Paris 1971), 316–325.

440 These transcriptions preserved, among other things in the writings of Clement of Alexandria and Theodoret of Cyrus; G. Fohrer, *Geschichte der israelitischen Religion* (Berlin 1969), 63; Synowiec, *Początki świata*, 93.

441 The origin of the name of Yahweh discussions reports briefly T. Brzegowy; *Pięcioksiąg Mojżesza*, 273–274. The etymology of the name Yahweh is not sure, but usually it is associated with the stem h-j (w)-h, that is to be. According to the etymology of Yahweh is the one WHO IS; ibid., 274.

powerful" or "to be the first." Accordingly, the etymology itself stresses the divine omnipotence. The custom of naming the only God or deities using the plural noun was known in the ancient Near East. Literature and archaeology provide numerous examples of such customs. Cuneiform texts found near Ankara prove that the Hittites called their king using the term "gods." Texts from El-Amarna attribute the name "my gods" to pharaoh. The legend about Danel, discovered in Ras Shamra, relates the title of "gods" to a single deity, called the Lord of Egypt. The Phoenician God Nergal was also described as "gods."[442] The Israelites described the only God with the use of the plural presumably because they wanted to emphasize that He has all the perfect qualities.

God is the One who "made the earth and heavens." In this phrase, the opposition to Gen 1:1 is clear. God is seen as the one who "makes the earth and heavens"; the opposition lies both in a different verb in the semantic field of creative work and in a sequence: the heavens–the earth and the earth–the heavens.[443] Both verses, however, (1:1 and 2:4b) show similarity to Mesopotamian cosmogony where you can find such a record: "When above the heaven had not (yet) been named (and) below the earth had not (yet) been called by name ...".[444] The Jewish believed that the firmament is a plate made of a clear crystal: "Moses and Aaron, Nadab and Abihu, and the seventy elders of Israel went up [on Mount Sinai] and saw the God of Israel. Under his feet was something like a pavement made of sapphire, clear as the sky itself" (Exod 24:9–10; cf. Ezra 1:26). This plate was to be stretched over the earth like a canopy of a tent (Isa 40:22; Job 9:8) and it was based on the mountains forming the edge of the world. The heavens are not available to man (Isa 55:9, Jer 31:37, Bar 3:29, Ps 103:11). Above this firmament, upper waters were placed which by God's will fell to the ground as rain. Just above this water there was chosen home of God (Gen 1:5–7; 21:17; 22:11–15, 1 Kgs 8:30–49; Isa 40:22; Ps 18:11–16). God was surrounded by angels, that constituted his heavenly court. The inhabitants of this court were called variously "the hosts of heaven" (1 Kgs 22:19; Dan 8:10; Ps 103:21), "seraphims" (Isa 6:2), "living creatures" (Ezek 1:5–26), and "cherubims" (Ezek 9:3; 10:1–9). Upper waters were surrounded by reservoirs filled with hail, snow, wind, storms and clouds in which the birds lived. It was thought that the sun, the moon and the stars moved around the firmament of blue light.[445]

---

442 E. Testa, *Genesi. Introduzione – storia primitiva* (Torino 1977²), 251–252; Synowiec, *Początki świata*, 18–19.
443 Cf. Isa 45:12; 48:13; Westermann, *Genesis*, 271.
444 *ANET* 61,I,1.
445 Synowiec, *Początki świata*, 65–67.

God is also the Creator of the earth. The earth was imagined as a circular island surrounded by well-known seas: the Mediterranean, the Dead and the Red Sea.[446] Their waters made up by so-called "subterraneous waters," where the columns were situated in support of the land (1 Sam 2:8; 2 Sam 22:16; Jer 31:37; Ps 118:16). The corners of the world were called "the islands," and were far away from the mainland. The land itself could be fertile ground, as the garden of Eden, but also "a land not sown" (Jer 2:2), the utterly forsaken land (Isa 6:12) or uninhabited one (Jer 2:6). Presumably, the Israelites knew only the countries situated between the Caspian Sea and the Black Sea to the north, the Somali Coast to the south, the Mediterranean Sea to the west and the Iranian Plateau to the east.[447]

The water theme was used by the author of the second description of the creation of a man in a completely different way than in the priestly story. In this second one the ground was surrounded by the waters, over which the Spirit of God was hovering (Gen 1:1). Here there is the lack of water because "the Lord God had not sent rain on the earth and there was no man to work the ground" (v. 5b). The Earth is a desert, where the vegetation is not growing: "no shrub of the field had yet appeared on the earth and no plant of the field had yet sprung up" (v. 5a). It is worth remembering in this context that the harvest in Palestine depended on the rain which falls in the winter time. Only after the introduction of irrigation systems the situation changed. While in Gen 1:11–12 the vegetation occurs on the ground even before the creation of a man, here, however, the vegetation is conditioned by sending rains by God and human agrarian activity. Even if we accept, at the suggestion of some,[448] that the term טֶרֶם does not mean "not yet," but "just," does not fundamentally change the meaning of the verse; thus vegetation appears on the earth after the creation of a man and is dependent on his work. The author mentions two groups of plants: a shrub and the grass. The grass was cited earlier: "Then God said, 'Let the land produce vegetation: seed-bearing plants and trees on the land that bear fruit with seed in it, according to their various kinds'" (Gen 1:11; cf. 1:12). The shrub (שִׂיחַ), however, is only mentioned here and in Gen 21:15 and Job 30:4. It is possible that the linking of both types of plants in v. 5 anticipates the announcement of miserable fruit of

---

446 The first one was called "the Great Sea" (Num 3:46), "the Sea of the Philistines" (Exod 23:31), "the Sea of Jaffa" (Ezra 3:7) or "the West Sea" (Deut 11:24); the second—"the Sea of Arabah" (Deut 4: 49), "The Eastern Sea" (Joel 2:20) and "The Salt Sea" (Gen 14:3); while the third—"The Red Sea" (Exod 13:18); Synowiec, *Początki świata*, 64.

447 Synowiec, *Początki świata*, 65.

448 L. P. Trudinger, "'Not Yet made' or 'Newly Made'. A Note on Genesis 2,5," *EvQ* 47 (1975): 67–68.

the earth, which are food for people (Gen 3:18). The mention of these two types of plants can also suggest a distinction between edible and inedible plants.[449]

V. 6 In v. 6, we encounter the problems of textual criticism. Only here and in Job 36:27, the term אֵד appears: "He [God] draws up the drops of water, which distill as rain to the streams." In Job, the term means "fog" but in v. 6 it is rather about "steam" or "clouds" rising from underground springs. The LXX, the Vulgate and the Syrian versions speak of the spring at this point. It is possible that this term etymologically comes from the Accadian noun *id*, which means "river."[450] Thus the text would read: "but steam spouted from the ground" or "but a cloud rose from the ground."[451] Regardless of which version to accept in principle, its content is clear; it is about the irrigation of the ground.[452] The version of water welling up from the ground is more probable than the version of the man using irrigation. The reason is that the latter makes a man the subject of all the steps described in v. 6. As a result, the adaptation of the thesis of the author saying that it was the man watering the entire surface of the earth seems to be very illogical. The insight of Aquila should therefore be taken as true. He used the verbs in v. 6 in the form of an aorist, so the translation was: "but streams came up from the earth and watered the whole surface of the ground." This translation is acceptable in terms of grammar because the form *jiqtol* is generally used for the description of repeated and ongoing actions. Sometimes, however, it is used similar to *qatal* as well expressing a single action (Deut 32:10; Ps 116:3; Job 15:7).[453]

V. 7 Man's connection with the land is shown by the use of phonetically similar terms: אָדָם i אֲדָמָה: "the Lord God formed the Man from the dust of the ground and breathed into his nostrils the breath of life, and the man became a living being" (v. 7). In the HB, the term אָדָם was used for determining an individual man and all humanity as well (e.g., Jer 51:14).[454] However, the context clearly

---

449 T. Stordalen, "Man, Soil, Garden: Basic Plot in Genesis 2–3 Reconsidered," *JSOT* 53 (1992): 10–11; Lemański, *Pięcioksiąg dzisiaj*, 162.

450 F. I. Anderson, "On Reading Genesis 1–3," in *Background for the Bible* (eds. M. P. O'Connor and D. N. Fredmann; Winona Lake 1987), 137–138.

451 See: *Targum Onkelosa*; Brzegowy, *Pięcioksiąg Mojżesza*, 25.

452 D. Kinder, *Genesis. An Introduction and Commentary* (Tyndale Old Testament Commentaries; Downers Grove 1967), 60; Wénin, *D'Adam à Abraham*, 56; Westermann, *Genesis*, 273.

453 Synowiec, *Początki świata*, 96.

454 F. Maass, "אָדָם 'ādhām," in *TDOT* I: 79–80; J. Roloff, "Adam," in *Das Grosse Lexikon zur Bibel. Altes und Neues Testament* (eds. K. Koch et al.; Wien 2004), 21; C.

determines the meaning of the term used in v. 7. It is about the first man, who from v. 25 of Gen 4, is called by his proper name, Adam (in fact, from that moment in the narrative there is not an article). The Yahwist bases this notion on a simple perception of what happens to the human body after death—because it turns into dust, it must have also arisen from the dust of the earth.

The phrase "dust of the earth" creates a bridge between v. 7 and Gen 3:19: "By the sweat of your brow you will eat your food until you return to the ground, since from it you were taken; for dust you are and to dust you will return!" A man created from the dust of the earth becomes a living being only thanks to God's breath (נְשָׁמָה). Exegetes recognized v. 7 as *locus classicus* of the OT anthropology. In it, there is not any distinction between the soul and the body, but there is a more realistic distinction: the body and the life. This verse is also a kind of supplement to Gen 1:27.[455] The author presents the work of God at the creation of a man by means of two verbs: "mold" and "breathe." The first shows the relationship between a craftsman or a creator and his material which is the subject of his work, as in Ps 94:9 ("Does he who implanted the ear not hear? Does he who formed the eye not see?") or Ps 139:14–15 ("I praise you because I am fearfully and wonderfully made; your works are wonderful, I know that full well. My frame was not hidden from you when I was made in the secret place. When I was woven together in the depths of the earth"). The term יצר is also used to describe the work of a potter (2 Sam 17:28; Isa 29:16; Jer 18:3.3.4.11) or a blacksmith (Isa 44:12). The verb also speaks of the superiority of God over man and his dominion over human life. A man forgetting about it, does it to bring himself to ruin: "You turn things upside down, as if the pottery were thought to be like the clay! Shall what is formed say to him who formed it, 'He did not make me'? Can the pot say of the potter, 'He knows nothing?'" (Isa 29:16).[456] A potter works with clay. The God uses "the dust" in his work. It is a metaphor for human transience.[457] The idea of man coming from the dust is also known in other works of the ancient Near Eastern literature, and even the Greek one.[458]

Westermann, "אָדָם 'ādām person," in E. Jenni, C. Westermann, *Theological Lexicon of the Old Testament* (I; trans. M. E. Biddle; Peabody 1997), 31–33.

455 Kinder, *Genesis*, 60.

456 Jeremiah expresses a similar thought: "But the pot he was shaping from the clay was marred in his hands; so the potter formed it into another pot, shaping it as seemed best to him" (Jer 18:4).

457 Similar in Gen 18:27; Job 10:9; Isa 29:16; Ps 90:3; 104:29; Lemański, *Pięcioksiąg dzisiaj*, 164.

458 It is about the Old Babylonian poem of *Gilgamesh*; Egyptian inscriptions about god named Chnum and the myth of Prometheus; W. van Soden, "Der Mensch bescheidet

The second verb used by the author of Genesis indicating the divine action is the term "to breathe/blow." He points to a strong breath, such as the one which is used in order to light a fire (Isa 54:16; Hagg 1:9). In the same meaning, it appears in the call: "Come from the four winds, O breath, and breathe into these slain, that they may live" (Ezek 37:9b). This breath also means the ability to breathe, and therefore, it is typical of the animals as well (Gen 7:22). Divine breath, which connects to the matter, creates man as a "living being" (חַיָּה לְנֶפֶשׁ),[459] both in his physical and mental dimension. For the Yahwist, both men and animals can be determined by the term, "living beings" (Gen 2:7 and Gen 2:19).[460] God creates life through direct action. The life slinks when God takes his breath: "When you hide your face, they are terrified; when you take away their breath, they die and return to the dust" (Ps 104:29). In a similar way, the confession of Elihu, Job's friend, states: "If it were his intention and he withdrew his spirit and breath, all mankind would perish together and man would return to the dust" (Job 34:14–15). Combining in one sentence (v. 7) the theme of life-giving breath and the motif of dust shows the post-Adam perspective to the reader.

As mentioned above, from the syntactic point of view, a little problematic seems to be the use by the author of God's name as "Yahweh Elohim." Such a "cluster" of names can be found only in the history of paradise and the fall of a man in Genesis. We can also find it in the Pentateuch but only once.[461] It was probably introduced by the editor in order to identify the original name of Yahweh with the name Elohim, which was used in Gen 1.

2.3. Contribution of v. 7b to Gen 2:4b–7

The Yahwist emphasizes the fact that you cannot say that a man "has" a body or "has" a soul, but he is a body and a soul at the same time. In other words, he is a psycho-physical unity. The same thought is also included in 1 Thess 5:23 where the author speaks of spirit, soul and body: "May God himself, the God of peace, sanctify you through and through. May your whole spirit, soul and body be kept

---

sich nicht. Überlegungen zu Schöpfungserzählungen in Babylonien und Israel," in *Bibel und Alter Orient. Altorientalische Beiträge zum Alten Testament* (ed. W. van Soden; BZAW 162; Berlin–New York 1985), 165–173; Lemański, *Pięcioksiąg dzisiaj*, 164.

459   The term נֶפֶשׁ appears in the OT 754 times. It means not only the "soul" or "essence" but also "throat," "neck," "desire," "life"; Lemański, *Pięcioksiąg dzisiaj*, 164.

460   Brzegowy, *Pięcioksiąg Mojżesza*, 275.

461   It is about Exod 9:30, in which the author cites the words of Moses: "But I know that you and your officials still do not fear the Lord God"; Westermann, *Genesis*, 270.

blameless at the coming of our Lord Jesus Christ."[462] It does not matter how many components come into play; it is important to emphasize the man as the unity of these components. By the phrase "the man became a living being" the Yahwist reminds the leader that the human life is a gift from God. As a material being, a man received his body from God and as a spiritual being, received life from Him.[463] God himself is the source of life: "For with you is the fountain of life; in your light we see light" (Ps 36:10). Something of the Creator is in man's nature; the breath of God became his breathing. Such understanding of the phrase "and the man became a living being" is documented by a statement of Elihu: "The Spirit of God has made me; the breath of the Almighty gives me life" (Job 33:4). None of the human beings were equipped with the divine breath. In the light of other biblical texts, it appears that the breath of God was understood as the light that penetrates the inmost being of man (Prov 20:27) and makes him an intelligent being (Job 32:8). With the breath of Yahweh, the man not only lives like an animal, but instead he lives spiritually because God bestowed him on the spiritual sphere as well.[464] Phonetic similarity of "Adam" and "earth" in Hebrew, makes one think about the relationship between humankind and the earth. It also makes us recall for dust man is and to dust he will return (cf. Gen 3:19). The *Palestinian Targum* to Gen 3:19 connects the origin of a man from the ground with his resurrection: ["for dust thou art, and unto dust thou shalt return; for from the dust it is to be that thou art to arise, to render judgment and reckoning for all that thou hast done, in the day of the great judgment"]. So the Jewish Targum tradition has already seen in the image of the creation of a man from the dust of the ground an indirect reference to his resurrection.[465]

3. Meaning in 1 Cor 15:44b–49

In vv. 42–44 Paul uses antitheses as many as four times. His aim is to contrast the two types of bodies: the perishable / inglorious / weak / natural apostle opposed to what is the imperishable / glorious / powerful / spiritual.[466] The last of the

---

462 Kinder, *Genesis*, 60–61.

463 Brzegowy, *Pięcioksiąg Mojżesza*, 275.

464 Synowiec, *Początki świata*, 99.

465 M. McNamara, *I Targum e il Nuovo Testamento. Le parafrasi aramaiche delle bibbia ebraica e il loro apporto per una migliore comprensione del Nuovo Testamento* (Studi biblici; Bologna 1978), 160.

466 Romaniuk, Jankowski and Stachowiak, *Komentarz*, 164; N. Bonneau, "The Logic of Paul's Argument on the Resurrection Body in 1 Cor 15:35–44a," *ScEs* 45 (1993): 79–92; R. H. Gundry, *Sōma in Biblical Theology with Emphasis on Pauline Anthropology* (SNTSMS 29; Cambridge 1976), 176; Hull, *Baptism on Account of the Dead*, 211–212.

antitheses appears in v. 44b: "If there is a natural body, there is also a spiritual body" (Εἰ ἔστιν σῶμα ψυχικόν, ἔστιν καὶ πνευματικόν).[467] This antithesis refers to the earlier opposition of the first and the last Adam, in other words, Adam as the first man and Christ.[468] This sentence was written in a simple conditional mode, which appears in the NT about three hundred times. The structure is the domain of Paul. The logical implication in such a sentence is as follows, "if A, then B."[469] Paul tells about the "natural body" and "spiritual body." First, we must therefore consider the term "body" (σῶμα) within the meaning of it by St. Paul. In 1 Cor, the Apostle uses the term 39 times to determine the physical aspect of human life.[470] This quite basic, literal meaning of the noun prevails throughout his writing.[471] Specific accumulation of the term appears in 1 Cor 6 (a matter of purity), 1 Cor 12 (comparing the Church to the human body) and 1 Cor 15 (ergo chapter analyzed by us). The occurrence of the noun σῶμα in 1 Cor 15 seems to be particularly useful for determining its meaning in v. 44b. At first, it appears in v. 35: "But someone may ask: How are the dead raised? With what kind of body will they come?" Imaginary, rhetorical questions in Paul's argumentation written in the style of diatribe pertains to the nature of the resurrected body. The Apostle

---

467   1 Corinthians 15:35–49 indicates that the apostle is aware of the fact that the earthly body animated by the spirit is not identical to that after the resurrection, the spiritual body; Jezierska, "Chrystologia," 76. Cf.: E. J. Jezierska, "'A jak zmartwychwstają umarli? W jakim ukazują się ciele?' (1 Kor 15,35). Zmartwychwstanie wierzącego i natura jego wskrzeszonego ciała w ujęciu św. Pawła," ŻK 45 (2004) 1: 64–69. A. Paciorek emphasizes both the continuity and differences that exist between the body before and after the resurrection. When it comes to the body after the resurrection, it must be remembered that this is not a simple return to its former state. The body after the resurrection will be different from the present and yet the same; A. Paciorek, Paweł Apostoł – pisma, I (Academica 28; Tarnów 1997), 116; E. Schweizer, "Body," ABD I: 769.

468   L. Kreitzer, "Adam as Analogy: Help or Hindrance?," NB 70 (1989): 278. "His [Paul's] entire purpose in vv. 21–22 is to make the connection between the old and the new, the past and the future, the dead and the living"; Lewis, "So That God May Be All in All", 47; de Boer, Defeat of Death, 98–101; H. C. C. Cavallin, Life after Death. Paul's Argument for the Resurrection of the Dead in 1 Cor 15, I, An Enquiry into the Jewish Background (CBNT 7, 1; Lund 1974), 203–204; Teani, Corporeità e risurrezione, 223.

469   Brodeur, Holy Spirit's Agency, 90.

470   Cf. 1 Cor 5:3; 6:13 (2×).15.16.18 (2×).19.20; 7:4 (2×).34; 9:27; 12:12 (3×).14.15 (2×).16 (2×).17.18.19.20.22.23.24.25; 13:3; 15:35.37.38 (2×).40 (2×).44 (3×). In addition, the term occurs in a metaphorical sense seven times: 1 Cor 10:16–17; 11:24.27.29; 12:13.27. Cf. Thayer, Thayer's Greek-English Lexicon, 611.

471   L. Kreitzer, "Body," in Dictionary of Paul and His Letters. A Compendium of Contemporary Biblical Scholarship (eds. G. F. Hawthorne and R. P Martin; Dovners Grove–Leicester 1993), 71–72.

himself provides the answer, highlighting the fact that God has the power of changing the body of everyone: "When you sow, you do not plant the body that will be, but just a seed, perhaps of wheat or of something else. But God gives it a body as he has determined" (vv. 37–38a). Then he argues that every body has its own "glory/beauty": "There are also heavenly bodies and there are earthly bodies, but the splendor of the heavenly bodies is one kind, and the splendor of the earthly bodies is another" (v. 40). By making a reference to the transformation of different kinds of bodies, the apostle prepares his basic argument. According to him, the human body also experiences changes in the resurrection. Paul assures the Corinthians that the resurrection is not about the revival of natural, mortal body but that after the resurrection the body will have a different nature than the physical, earthly body.

In this context, a quite natural question can be asked about the essence of our "spiritual body" (σῶμα πνευματικόν).[472] Paul's pre-made division of the human division between the natural and spiritual helps to cope with the answer: "The man without the Spirit does not accept the things that come from the Spirit of God, for they are foolishness to him, and he cannot understand them, because they are spiritually discerned. The spiritual man makes judgments about all things, but he himself is not subject to any man's judgment" (2:14–15). The term ψυχικός is used in the NT 6 times; the apostle uses it for opposition to what is spiritual (πνευματικός).[473] The natural man is largely devoid of the light of grace so the light of the Holy Spirit "does not accept the things that come from the Spirit of God." He rejects the "message of the cross" and "is perishing" (1:18). He is not able to understand the revealed truths as he remains closed to the gifts of the Holy Spirit. Such an ability is, however, typical of a spiritual person. The term πνευματικός in the NT, occurs 26 times and Paul uses it 24

---

472   C. Burchard, "1 Kor 15: 39–41," *ZNW* 74 (1983): 233–252; K.-A. Bauer, *Leiblichkeit das Ende aller Werke Gottes. Die Bedeutung der Leiblichkeit des Menschen bei Paulus* (SNTSMS 4; Gütersloh 1971), 94–96; F. Foitzheim, *Christologie und Eschatologie bei Paulus* (FzB 35; Würzburg 1979), 231; G. M. Hensell, *Antitheses and Transformation: A Study of I Corinthians 15:50–54* (St. Luis 1975), 137; H.-H. Schade, *Apokalyptische Christologie bei Paulus. Studien zum Zusammenhang von Christologie und Eschatologie in den Paulusbriefen* (GTA 18; Göttingen 1981), 204; B. M. Ahern, "The Risen Christ in the Light of Pauline Doctrine on the Risen Christian (1 Cor 15:35–37)," in *Resurrexit. Actes du Symposium International sur la Résurrection de Jésus (Rome 1970)* (ed. E. Dhanis; Vatikanstadt 1974), 423–439; J. A. Schep, *The Nature of the Resurrection Body* (Grand Rapids 1964).

473   R. A. Horsley, "Pneumaticos vs. Psychikos. Distinctions of Spiritual Status among the Corinthians," *HTR* 83 (1976): 269–288; B. A. Person, *The pneumatikos – psychikos Terminology in 1 Corinthians. A Study in the Theology of the Corinthian Opponents of Paul and Its Relation to Gnosticism* (SBLDS 12; Missuola 1973).

times.[474] In 1 Cor the term can be found 15 times. Verse 14:37 refers to a person who makes use of the gift of prophecy.[475] It is possible that the anthropological terminology, which Paul uses, was taken from the Hellenistic environment of Diaspora.[476] In terms of the tension between the spirit and the body, Paul says in the 1 Cor 2:10b–16: "The Spirit searches all things, even the deep things of God." In his argumentation, the Apostle seems to apply the philosophically Greek principle that "like can be known by like." This means that the man himself cannot fully know God. This knowledge may result from a revelation from the Holy Spirit. The same principle applies to man—the spirit that is in him knows everything what is human (2:11). As mentioned, Paul contrasts the spiritual man to the natural one. This type of contrast may be surprising. More logical would seem to be the antithesis: the spiritual man–the natural man that is indeed present in Paul. It seems that the apostle adopts the terminology that was used by the Corinthians. Natural people have three characteristics:

(1) they "[do not] accept the things that come from the Spirit of God" (2:14a);
(2) it seems for them foolishness (2:14b);
(3) "[they] cannot understand them, because they are not spiritually discerned" (2:14c).[477]

---

474 Some authors give the number 19, and this number is dependent on which letters of Paul are presumed as his.

475 A. Miranda, "L''uomo spirituale' (pneumatikos anthrôpos) nella prima ai Corinzi," *RivB* 43 (1995): 496–501. The difference between the natural and the spiritual man showed Basil the Great: "The whole of his being is present to each individual; the whole of his being is present everywhere. Though shared in by many, he remains unchanged; his self giving is no loss to himself. Like the sunshine, which permeates all the atmosphere, spreading over land and sea, and yet is enjoyed by each person as though it were for him alone, so the Spirit pours forth his grace in full measure, sufficient for all, and yet is present as though exclusively to everyone who can receive him. To all creatures that share in him he gives a delight limited only by their own nature, not by his ability to give. The Spirit raises our hearts to heaven, guides the steps of the weak, and brings to perfection those who are making progress. He enlightens those who have been cleansed from every stain of sin and makes them spiritual by communion with himself. As clear, transparent substances become very bright when sunlight falls on them and shine with a new radiance, so also souls in whom the Spirit, become spiritual themselves and a source of grace for others" (*Spir.* 9, 22–23).

476 G. E. Sterling, "'Wisdom among the Perfect'. Creation Traditions in Alexandrian Judaism and Corinthian Christianity," *NT* 37 (1955): 367.

477 R. A. Horsley, "'How Can Some of You Say That There Is No Resurrection of the Dead?': Spiritual Elitism in Corinth," *NT* 20 (1978): 205–206.

In this sense, there is some tension between that what is sensual and that what is spiritual. So it becomes clear that the spiritual body, of which Paul says, exists only in relation to the Holy Spirit. The spiritual man is the one who receives knowledge from the Holy Spirit. What is more, the nature of the body after the resurrection must be also associated with the acting of the Holy Spirit. In the context of such an approach to the terms "spiritual" and "natural" in 1 Cor, it is impossible to draw a conclusion about the lack of continuation between the natural and spiritual body after the resurrection. Certainly, merely talking about the change (transformation, v. 51) implies a certain continuity between the two kinds of bodies. At this point, Paul does not focus on the continuation of the body but highlights the otherness of the earthly body after its resurrection.[478]

The apostle continues this thought in the next line, which states that Christ has become "a life-giving spirit" (εἰς πνεῦμα ζῳοποιοῦν).[479] Verse 45 begins with an introductory quotation formula followed by a statement derived from Gen 2:7b: "So it is written: 'The first man Adam became a living being'; the last Adam, a life-giving spirit" (οὕτως καὶ γέγραπται ἐγένετο ὁ πρῶτος ἄνθρωπος Ἀδὰμ εἰς ψυχὴν ζῶσαν, ὁ ἔσχατος Ἀδὰμ εἰς πνεῦμα ζῳοποιοῦν). The formula of the quotation is very clear: οὕτως καὶ γέγραπται. It points clearly at the intention of quoting. Similar formulas are also found in 1 Cor 1:19.31. Indeed, immediately after the first part of the sentence there is a quote that in the original Hebrew text, appears as: נַיְהִי הָאָדָם לְנֶפֶשׁ חַיָּה. The entire sentence from which Paul derived the quotation is: "the Lord God formed the man from the dust of the ground and breathed into his nostrils the breath of life, and the man became a living being" (Gen 2:7). The Apostle acts, however—as shown above—like the LXX text: καὶ ἐγένετο ὁ ἄνθρωπος εἰς ψυχὴν ζῶσαν. He subjects this text to the editorial changes, about what was mentioned while determining the source of the quotation, leaving the initial καὶ, while adding the numeral πρῶτος and the name Ἀδάμ. He completes the quote with the

---

478   An important observation in this regard presents J. A. Schep: "If Paul wanted to teach that the resurrection-body will not be a body of flesh, He would certainly have used another word than *psychikon*"; id., *Nature of the Resurrection Body*, 200. "As regards to whole question of continuity, we may assume that there is a basic correlation in as much as the particular body that dies is the same one that will be raised and transformed. But Paul prefers to remain silent on this point. His central idea is that the natural will cease to exist since it is not suitable to the post resurrection state of the believer. Since it is of the earth, the natural is not suitable for the realm of Spirit. It must be changed, since 'flash and blood cannot inherit the kingdom of God, nor does the perishable inherit the imperishable'"; Brodeur, *Holy Spirit's Agency*, 96.

479   Mare, *1 Corinthians*, 290; Henry, *Commentary*, 2275; Talbert, *Reading Corinthians*, 126; R. Morissette, "La condition de ressucité. 1 Cor 15:35–49: structure littéraire de la péricope," *Bib* 53 (1972): 223.

explanation: "[and] the last Adam, a life-giving spirit." The formula of this quotation may suggest that this explanation was taken from the OT. However, this is a typical editorial supplement. The changes introduced by Paul into the text of Gen 2:7b (adding of a numeral and the name of Adam), quoted on a *midrash pesher* basis have been used to create a more perfect parallelism with the second part of the sentence, where the name of Adam appears. Moreover, the numeral "one" is opposed to the term "last."[480] The effect that Paul reaches introducing the quotation is the result not only of the wording of the quotation and its editorial overwork but also the power of the applied rhetorical procedure. It lies in contrasting the two parts of the sentence included in v. 15:

1 Cor 15:45b: ἐγένετο ὁ πρῶτος ἄνθρωπος ᾿Αδὰμ εἰς ψυχὴν ζῶσαν;
1 Cor 15:45c: ὁ ἔσχατος ᾿Αδὰμ εἰς πνεῦμα ζῳοποιοῦν.[481]

The whole sentence was built in such a way to place an emphasis on its second part. Although the verb ἐγένετο and the noun ἄνθρωπος are not found in this part, however, they constitute the hypothetical parallel of the full implication with the quoted fragment. Their lack eliminates unnecessary repetitions for rhetorical effect intended by the apostle. The term ἐγένετο is a form of a verb "become," which in NT appears as many as 167 times, therein 118 times in Paul and in 1 Cor—41 times.[482] With the aid of it, Paul (after Gen 2:7b) defines a fundamental change: as the dust from the earth "became" a living being, so at the time of the resurrection of Christ it "became" "a life-giving spirit." Such hope applies to a profound transformation of every believer in Christ. When Paul uses the noun ἄνθρωπος in this context, its meaning is largely determined by the previous occurrence of the term in 1 Cor. In principle, the Apostle categorizes all creations according to the Greek philosophical thought. He places people into categories totally different from any other creations: "All flesh is not the same: Men have one kind of flesh, animals have another, birds another and fish another" (v. 39).[483] In the physical life, the man is like an animal, and his body is made of matter. In the other life, however, he will possess a "spiritual body," and this one comes "from heaven" (v. 47). The man not only differs from plants or animals, but he also differs from the angels: "For it seems to me that God has put us apostles on display at the end of the procession, like men condemned to die in the arena. We have been made a spectacle to the whole universe, to angels as well as to men" (1 Cor 4:9). Writing his letter to the people of Corinth, the

---

480   Hull, *Baptism on Account of the Dead*, 214.
481   Heil, *Rhetorical Role of Scripture*, 235; Usami, "How Are the Dead Rised?," 477.
482   Brodeur, *Holy Spirit's Agency*, 107–108.
483   Aristotle says that the man is the only animal which has a certain divine element; *Part.* 656a.

apostle is still aware of the earthly and the heavenly realities. If a man can look, to some extend, into the reality of the heaven, the opposite claim should be also true. As it comes out of this statement, the angels have insight into human affairs as well.

Above all, man differs significantly from God. Human condition is marked by weakness and mortality. This type of essence got into philosophical thought and literature of ancient Greece. The Corinthians and Paul himself were familiar with them. They were convinced that the God's condition is quite different: marked with immortality, power and glory: "For the foolishness of God is wiser than man's wisdom, and the weakness of God is stronger than man's strength" (1 Cor 1:25). By rejecting the cross of Christ, people showed their sinfulness and pride: "But God chose the foolish things of the world to shame the wise; God chose the weak things of the world to shame the strong. He chose the lowly things of this world and the despised things—and the things that are not—to nullify the things that are, so that no one may boast before him. It is because of him that you are in Christ Jesus, who has become for us wisdom from God— that is, our righteousness, holiness and redemption" (1 Cor 1:27–30). These sentences reveal Paul's understanding of who God the Father is. God is the Creator of both the physical and spiritual life, and He is the one who sent Christ down to Earth as the Redeemer. This brief review of Paul's use of the term ἄνθρωπος in 1 Cor reveals the fact that in v. 45 the Apostle reinterprets it in light of Jewish thought. Although he uses philosophical concepts of the Greeks ("spiritual," "natural," "corporal") , the key to this reinterpretation is in Gen 2:7b.

The words that appear in both parts of the sentence in v. 15 correspond with each other, or are based on repetitions ('Αδὰμ εἰς), or on a contrast basis (ὁ πρῶτος - ὁ ἔσχατος; ψυχὴν ζῶσαν - πνεῦμα ζῳοποιοῦν).[484] This is how Paul emphasizes the parallel between the first and last Adam: the first Adam, the first man and representative of all humanity, became a "living soul" in the creation, when God breathed into his nostrils the breath of life. So at the beginning of the new creation Christ—the last Adam, became "a life-giving spirit," when God raised him from the dead.[485] How should we understand the term ψυχή? In

---

484 "The choice of these adjectives, nouns and participles is not accidental; Paul selected them with great care to make his point. Moreover, the syntax of the sentence is quite important. By placing them at the end of each line, Paul puts added emphasis on the nouns and the participles"; Brodeur, *Holy Spirit's Agency*, 106; B. Schneider, "The Corporate Meaning and Background of 1 Cor 15:45b," *CBQ* 29 (1967): 154–155.

485 The role of Christ as the "the second" or "the last" Adam does not point to His preexistence but begins with the Resurrection; J. G. D. Dunn, *Christology in the Making. An Inquiry into the Origins of the Doctrine of the Incarnation* (London 1989²),

Pauline use, it has different meanings. In Paul's letters it occurs just 11 times while in 1 Cor, it constitutes *hapax legomenon*. In most cases, in Paul's writings, the term ψυχή means simply "life" (1 Thess 2:8; Phil 2:30). Paul states that Prisca (Priscilla) and Aquila risked their necks for his "life" (ψυχή; Rom 16:4). To Romans, he quotes the words from Elijah, about those who lie in wait for his "life": "Lord, they have killed your prophets and torn down your altars; I am the only one left, and they are trying to kill me" (Roma 11:3; cf. 1 Kgs 19:10.14). In other places, this term means a "person" or a "human being" (2 Cor 1:23; Rom 2:9, 13:1). Sometimes it can mean "mind" (Phil 1:27). After all, Paul also uses the term ψυχή in the most general sense: "soul" (1 Thess 5:23; 2 Cor 12:15). What meaning (soul, mind, life, a person—a human being) should be preferred in v. 45? Since in this verse there is a deepened clarification of the word "living," it seems that the preferred meaning is "being": "The first man Adam became a living being." Nevertheless, the parallelism of the second part of the sentence, which refers to "a life-giving spirit," would instead require the meaning "soul." It is therefore assumed that the two shades of the meaning (the being and the soul) are present here.

Pauline argumentation assumes that the hope occurs among the Corinthians. Now they are the "living beings," like the first Adam, but after Christ's resurrection, following his example, they may receive spiritual eschatological life.[486] Paul, however, is only interested in two aspects associated with the figure of Adam. The first aspect is that through Adam, death entered the world, and the second one focuses on the cosmic and universal consequences of this fact ("For as in Adam all die"; v. 22a).[487]

107–108. "The Christology of the Last Adam was primarily directed towards illuminating and assuring the Christian's hope of eschatological humanity"; R. Scroggs, *The Last Adam. A Study in Pauline Anthropology* (Philadelphia 1966), 59; cf. R. Scroggs, "Eschatological Existence in Matthew and Paul: *Coincidentia Oppositorum*," in *Apocalyptic and the New Testament* (JSNTSup 24; Sheffield 1989), 125–146; Teani, *Corporeità e risurrezione*, 248–249.

486   S. J. Hultgren develops this idea in his article "The Origin of Paul's Doctrine of the Two Adams in 1 Corinthians 15.45–49," *JSNT* 25 (2003): 343–370. See also: J. G. D. Dunn, "1 Cor 15:45 – Last Adam, Life-Giving Spirit," in *Christ and Spirit in the New Testament: In Honour of C.F.D. Moule* (eds. B. Lindars and S. J. Smalley; Cambridge 1973), 127–141; R. B. Gaffin, "'Life-Giving Spirit': Probing the Center of Paul's Pneumatology," *JETS* 41 (1998): 573–589; A. Johnson, "Turning the World Upside Down in 1 Corinthians 15: Apocalyptic Epistemology, the Resurrected Body, and the New Creation," *EvQ* 75 (2003): 291–309.

487   de Boer, *Defeat of Death*, 111.

Philo identifies the "breath" of God with his "spirit" in the ancient commentary on Genesis (*Leg.* 1,33–42; cf. *Opif.* 6,134–135).[488] Paul, however, attributes to Christ the ability of reviving,[489] because he defines Him with the term πνεῦμα ζῳοποιοῦν. According to the OT and the Jewish tradition, this attribute belongs to God. The immediate context of this verse, however, suggests that our revival come through Christ: "for since death came through a man, the resurrection of the dead comes also through a man. For as in Adam all die, so in Christ all will be made alive" (15:21–22).[490] So in v. 45 Paul continues the analogy: Adam–Christ, outlined earlier in this paper.[491] In vv. 21–22 the Apostle contrasted the two characters. Adam became a cause of the death of all people; Christ, on the contrary, became the pledge of their resurrection. The ascertainment accentuating that Adam is the cause of the death of all people is based on the words of God itself: "Because you listened to your wife and ate from the tree about which I commanded you, 'You must not eat of it,' cursed is the ground because of you; through painful toil you will eat of it all the days of your life. It will produce thorns and thistles for you, and you will eat the plants of the field. By the sweat of your brow you will eat your food until you return to the ground, since from it you were taken; for dust you are and to dust you will return!" (Gen 3:17–19). The Apostle repeatedly uses this text in his letters as the reason of the death which entered the world. There are some statements included in a letter addressed to the inhabitants of Rome worth mentioning: "therefore, just as sin entered the world through one man, and death through sin, and in this way death came to all men, because all sinned ... But the gift is not like the trespass. For if the many died by the trespass of the one man, how much more did God's grace and the gift that came by the grace of the one man, Jesus Christ, overflow to the many! Again, the gift of God is not like the result of the one

---

488 Lewis, *"So That God May Be All in All"*, 49; Barrett, "Significance of the Adam-Christ Typology," 114; "Genesis 2:7 is often used by Philo. He more than once gives a double exegesis, one for the first Adam and another for the 'inner man'. The explanation varies according to the special purpose Philo wanted to express in the different texts"; Usami, "How Are the Dead Rised?," 485.

489 L. Kreitzer, "Adam and Christ," in *Dictionary of Paul and His Letters. A Compendium of Contemporary Biblical Scholarship* (eds. G. F. Hawthorne and R. P. Martin; Dovners Grove–Leicester 1993), 11–12.

490 "In 1 Cor 15:21–22, the emphasis of the typology focuses on Christ as the one through whom resurrection to life comes. This theme is carried through in vv 45–49. In resurrection, one has a spiritual body, like that of the heavenly Christ, in contrast to the physical body which all humanity has in common with the earthly Adam"; M. J. Fretz, "Adam," *ABD* V: 64.

491 Jamieson, Fausset and Brown, *Commentary*, 332; M. Black, "The Pauline Doctrine of the Second Adam," *SJT* 7 (1954): 170–179.

man's sin: The judgment followed one sin and brought condemnation, but the gift followed many trespasses and brought justification. For if, by the trespass of the one man, death reigned through that one man, how much more will those who receive God's abundant provision of grace and of the gift of righteousness reign in life through the one man, Jesus Christ. Consequently, just as the result of one trespass was condemnation for all men, so also the result of one act of righteousness was justification that brings life for all men" (Rom 5:12.15–18).

The belief that through Adam, sin entered the world, is known from the Jewish (non-biblical) tradition and Paul definitely shares it: "That's why all of Adam's descendants sinned and died, just as Adam died in wickedness. The disease of sin struck everyone, so your Law and this wickedness became a part of every person. Soon the bad forced out the good. Years later, you chose your servant David and told him to build a city where you would be worshiped and where sacrifices would be offered to you. The people of Jerusalem did this for a while, but soon they started sinning against you and doing evil, just like their ancestor Adam and his descendants" (*4 Ezra* 3:21–26).[492] The words of the *Syrian Apocalypse of Baruch* have a similar overtone: "For brought untimely death upon all, yet of those who were born from him each one of them has prepared for his own soul torment to come, and again each one of them has chosen for himself glories to come" (54:15). This OT apocryphon admits many times that it was Adam's sin that brought the death to all men. The author of the Fourth Book of Ezra says: "When Adam sinned, he caused misery not only for himself, but for all of us who are his descendants" (*4 Ezra* 7:118).[493] Another apocryphon has a similar overtone: "Because when Adam sinned and death was decreed against those who should be born, then the multitude of those who should be born was numbered, and for that number a place was prepared where the living might dwell and the dead might be guarded" (*2 Bar.* 23:4; cf. 17:2–3).[494] The analogy of Adam–Christ serves Paul as a principle to show solidarity: because of the sin of Adam, all men were subject to the law of death; because of the resurrection of Christ all may find the resurrection.[495]

---

492 E. Brandenburger, *Adam und Christus. Exegetisch-religionsgeschichtliche Untersuchung zu Röm. 5:12–21 (1. Kor. 15)* (WMANT 7; Neukirchen–Vluyn 1962), 15–64; Scroggs, *Last Adam*, 60; J. R. Levinson, *Portraits of Adam in Early Judaism. From Sirach to 2 Baruch* (JSPESup 1; Sheffield 1988).

493 Wilson, *Pauline parallels*, 176.

494 Trans. after Woźniak, *Apokryfy*, 416.

495 Brandenburger, *Adam und Christus*, 16.

The giver of life is the Holy Spirit (2 Cor 3:6.17).[496] God revives and gives life through the Spirit: "But if Christ is in you, your body is dead because of sin, yet your spirit is alive because of righteousness. And if the Spirit of him who raised Jesus from the dead is living in you, he who raised Christ from the dead will also give life to your mortal bodies through his Spirit, who lives in you" (Rom 8:10–11). Since the formulation, חַיָּה נֶפֶשׁ determines a living being, so the analogy between the first and last Adam is clear: the first Adam gives life in the natural order, the last one—in the spiritual order. The verb ἐγένετο points to a specific moment in which both Adam and Christ originate two kinds of people. During the creation, God breathed into Adam the breath of life. At the resurrection, the Father breathed his Spirit into Christ.[497] However, as the verb in the case of first Adam means a change in nature (from the dust of the earth, he became a living being), so in the situation of the last Adam does it mean the change of his state (earthly Jesus "became" the risen Christ; the suffering Servant of Yahweh "became" the exalted Messiah).[498] For this reason, Christ can revive with the Spirit those who believe in him. It is possible because he received this Spirit from his Father at the resurrection.[499] Therefore, when we consider three options proposed by the exegetes to find an answer to the following question: "When did Christ become 'a life-giving spirit'; as pre-

---

496 S. Brodeur in the following way sees the role of the Holy Spirit in the resurrection: "Paul presents the Holy Spirit as the agent of risen life because he is life itself: he is the very life of the Father and the Son now poured out into the world. Thus, while remaining intimately connected to his theology and christology, Paul's pneumatology is nevertheless quite independent from them. According to the apostle, the Spirit too plays a very significant role in the resurrection of the dead"; id., *Holy Spirit's Agency*, 123.

497 Dunn, "1 Cor 15:45 – Last Adam," 129.

498 "For Paul, then, the last Adam became a life-giving Spirit at his resurrection. When God raised him from the dead, the situation of the Son of God was radically altered. The earthly Jesus became the risen Jesus, the suffering servant became the glorious Messiah. Unlike Adam, Christ's nature did not change, but his state most certainly did"; Brodeur, *Holy Spirit's Agency*, 116. Such understanding of the verb "to become" in v. 45 can be confirmed in the light of Phil 2:8–9: "[Christ] humbled himself and became obedient to death—even death on a cross! Therefore God exalted him to the highest place and gave him the name that is above every name." Earthly status of Jesus changed radically when God "exalted" Him above everyone else.

499 According to A. Jankowski as once Yahweh breathed into Adam the breath of life, so in the resurrection of Christ, God the Father breathed into him His Spirit, so that henceforth all life of the New and the Last Adam is revived with the Spirit. Having Taken such implied meaning of Paul's brachylogy from Genesis, we get the following sense: the glorious Christ may give lives to the faithful united with Him as he as the first got the Spirit from the Father at the resurrection; Jankowski, *Eschatologia Nowego Testamentu*, 102; cf. Schneider, "Corporate Meaning and Background," 456.

existent in heaven, during the incarnation or in the resurrection?"—the most likely seems to be the third answer.[500] It should be noted here that the term ζῳοποιέ appears in the NT only 11 times, including 7 times in *Corpus Paulinum*. However, it is always eschatological in its character and occurs in the context of the resurrection.[501]

After *midrash pesher* to Gen 2:7b, in the next verse, Paul returns to the basic question that he raises in this part of 1 Cor 15: "But someone may ask, 'How are the dead raised? With what kind of body will they come?'" (v. 35). The apostle verbalizes the principle of the primacy of what is natural over that what is spiritual: "The spiritual did not come first, but the natural, and after that the spiritual" (v. 46; ἀλλ' οὐ πρῶτον τὸ πνευματικὸν ἀλλὰ τὸ ψυχικόν, ἔπειτα τὸ πνευματικόν).[502] As a result, he emphasizes the sequence of creation; physical body was created first, then the spiritual body was created. Only such a sequence of events is appropriate. Emphasis such as this is not only important from the rhetorical point of view. The apostle admonishes the Corinthians who could say that they had already lived in a spiritual body.[503] Once again, as in v. 44, we can find the two terms "natural" and "spiritual." The principle presented here is based on the reflection of the apostle on the quotation cited from Gen 2:7b. With regard to this reflection, Paul says: "The first man was of the dust of the earth, the second man from heaven" (v. 47; ὁ πρῶτος ἄνθρωπος ἐκ γῆς χοϊκός, ὁ δεύτερος ἄνθρωπος ἐξ οὐρανοῦ). Of course only the first part of the sentence results directly from the reflection on Gen 2:7b. The second has the form of theological ascertainment stemming from the contemplation of Jesus Christ's working. The version containing the term "Man" (ἄνθρωπος) in reference to Christ, has many significant witnesses (ℵ*, B, C, D*, G, 33, 1739*, it[d, g, 61], Vulg., cop[bo]). Other manuscripts do not mention about "a Man" but use the term "the Lord." The latter term clearly indicates who is that man from heaven (see: ℵ[c], A, D[c], K, P, Y, 81, 104, 614, 1739[mg], *Byz*, *Lect*, syr[p, h, pal], goth,

---

500 C. K. Barrett resolves the issue as follows: "None can be ruled out as completely impossible, but the last is the most likely, since for Paul it is with the resurrection that the lifegiving work of Christ begins"; id., "Significance of the Adam-Christ Typology," 113.

501 Brodeur, *Holy Spirit's Agency*, 122.

502 M. Teani points at "two kinds of existence": "Paulo, avendo di mira la particolare situazione di Corinto, parla polemicamente di due successivi e irreversibili modi di essere. Si tratta di due 'ordini di esistenza' profondamente diversi; Adamo e Cristo risorto ne sono i rappresentanti originari"; id., *Corporeità e risurrezione*, 259.

503 "The Apostle teaches them that they still have their natural bodies in this world and that they will only receive their spiritual ones in the world to come. In other words, God made the spiritual body for heaven and not for earth"; Brodeur, *Holy Spirit's Agency*, 125.

arm, *al*).[504] In P[46], there is the term "spiritual man" which is clearly influenced by v. 46. A comparison of Gen 2:7a in the LXX version with the Pauline text is as follows:

Gen 2:7a (LXX): καὶ ἔπλασεν ὁ θεὸς τὸν ἄνθρωπον χοῦν ἀπὸ τῆς γῆς
1 Cor 15:47a: ὁ πρῶτος ἄνθρωπος ἐκ γῆς χοϊκός.

The preposition joined by Paul with *genetivus materiae* (ἐκ γῆς χοϊκός) indicates clearly that the human body is physically made of the same matter as the earth and dust. The noun γῆ appears in the NT about 250 times, usually in the sense of "earth," "land," "soil" or "ground." Paul, however, rarely uses it. In typically Pauline letters, it occurs six times, including three times in 1 Cor. For the first time, it may be found in 1 Cor 8:5–6: "For even if there are so-called gods, whether in heaven or on earth (εἴτε ἐν οὐρανῷ εἴτε ἐπὶ γῆς) (as indeed there are many 'gods' and many 'lords'), yet for us there is but one God, the Father, from whom all things came and for whom we live; and there is but one Lord, Jesus Christ, through whom all things came and through whom we live." So-called gods, according to some, may be somewhere in the universe. Paul's words should therefore be understood "in heaven or on earth." As many as five times (Paul used it six times altogether) the noun γῆ occurs in quotations from the OT, and each time it is understood as a part of creation for: "The earth is the Lord's, and everything in it" (1 Cor 10:26; cf. Ps 24:1); "For the Scripture says to Pharaoh: 'I raised you up for this very purpose, that I might display my power in you and that my name might be proclaimed in all the earth'" (Rom 9:17; cf. Exod 9:16); "For the Lord will carry out his sentence on earth with speed and finality" (Rom 9:28; cf. Isa 10:23); "But I ask: Did they not hear? Of course they did: 'Their voice has gone out into all the earth, their words to the ends of the world'" (Rom 10:18; cf. Ps 18:5); For the fifth time the term "earth" appears only in v. 47. In four cases out of six, it relates to the earth as a work of creation, but only once to the "ground" or "soil." Nevertheless, you cannot draw the conclusion that in v. 47 this term also refers to the earth as the work of God. In v. 47 the meaning of the noun is determined by the preposition "from" and *genetivus materiae* "from the dust of the earth"[505]: so it is about the earth as the material from which the human body was created—about the earth as the dust, land or soil. In any case, this is the way Jews understood Gen 2:7 during Paul's time.

Some readers of the first letter to the Corinthians may be surprised by the fact that according to Paul, what is earthly was in the first place, and what is

---

504 Metzger, *Textual Commentary*, 501–502.

505 The term "dust" (χοϊκός) appears only four times in the NT, and all of these appearances belong to the analyzed fragment; Brodeur, *Holy Spirit's Agency*, 128.

spiritual was after that. However, the Apostle does not express his opinion about definite order but he refers to a "spiritual body" that is, the body after its resurrection.[506] No one can deny that at first there is the earthly body and only later the resurrected one. Thus the Apostle speaks here in eschatological terms. The shift in emphasis between Christ from "the last Adam" (v. 45) to "the second Adam" is a rhetorical measure designed to inspire the hope that in Christ, they can also "go beyond" the state of the first Adam and find Resurrection.[507] Moreover, the term "second" indicates a certain novelty that a resurrected Christ brings. He is no longer just the "last" in line of "earthly men," but he is now the "second" and therefore the one giving a new beginning, different from the "first" state.[508] Going forward, if one understands the "first Adam" as the representative of all mankind, the "second Adam" becomes a representative of the new humanity.

In other terms, Philo of Alexandria spins his considerations. He speaks of the man "from heaven" associated with the eternal Logos (*Conf.* 41:146).[509] According to him, as well as in accordance with the views of the Jews of the Diaspora who were under the influence of Hellenistic thought, the "man from heaven" was the first (Gen 1:26–27). A mention of the man as "a living being" is only later found (Gen 2:7). The first represented the ideal spiritual state of mind that aspired to heavenly things whereas the second one represented the earthly man dedicated to worldly affairs.[510] In the apocryphal literature, the blame was put on Adam for being responsible for sin on earth as well: "et huic [Adam] mandasti diligere viam tuam, et praeterivit eam, et statim instituisti in eo mortem et in nationibus eius ... O tu, quid fecisti, Adam? Si enim tu peccasti, non est factus solius tuus casus, sed et noster qui ex te advenimus" (*4 Ezra* 3:7; 7:48).[511] The similar overtone have the words of *2 Bar.*: "Because when Adam sinned and death was decreed against those who should be born, then the multitude of those who should be born was numbered, and for that number a

---

506 A. Barnes, *I Corinthians to Galatians* (BN; Grand Rapids 1884), 281.

507 Heil, *Rhetorical Role of Scripture*, 242; Brodeur, *Holy Spirit's Agency*, 131. According to the last one the term "the second" "adopts a different nuance by stressing something that is brand new"; ibid.

508 "This human being is not merely the last in the line of earthly people, which is the assumption of v. 45. Rather, by calling him [Christ] 'the second human being,' Paul is suggesting that he exceeds the first due to his glorious resurrection from the dead. Hence he represents a new prototype for humanity, a new possibility for human beings to live in the eschatological age"; Brodeur, *Holy Spirit's Agency*, 131.

509 A. J. M. Wedderburn, "Philo's 'Heavenly Man'," *NovT* 15 (1973): 301–326.

510 Keener, *Komentarz*, 373.

511 Grasso, *Prima Lettera ai Corinzi*, 168.

place was prepared where the living might dwell and the dead might be guarded" (*2 Bar.* 23:4).[512]

To sum up this part of the discussion, in vv. 45–47 the apostle tells the readers to understand that in the first place, there was Adam, who became a "living being" (ψυχὴ ζῶσα). After him, Christ the second Adam came as "the life giving spirit" (πνεῦμα ζῳοποιοῦν). Incorporeal matters, in time order come later than earthly matters. However, the coming of the spiritual matters, is inevitable. Thus, the perspective of the resurrection is sure, but there can be a time lag between the two phenomena. It should be seen on the eschatological horizon that follows the historical order. This reflection is probably directed to the members of the community at Corinth, who are delighted with the use of spiritual gifts, and think that they have already come into the eschatological order/age. Paul states in response: "Already you have all you want! Already you have become rich! You have become kings—and that without us! How I wish that you really had become kings so that we might be kings with you!" (1 Cor 4:8). It should also be noted that the parallel between v. 47a and v. 47b is not accurate, because the formulation ἐκ γῆς χοϊκός corresponds to the phrase ἐξ οὐρανοῦ. There is not a parallel term to the noun χοϊκός. Why? The answer comes to mind when reading vv. 48–49. In these verses, the Apostle contrasts with great emphasis the earthly and heavenly things.

For the opposition of Adam and Christ Paul finds a solution by shifting the content of it to all men: "As was the earthly man, so are those who are of the earth; and as is the man from heaven, so also are those who are of heaven" (v. 48; οἷος ὁ χοϊκός, τοιοῦτοι καὶ οἱ χοϊκοί, καὶ οἷος ὁ ἐπουράνιος, τοιοῦτοι καὶ οἱ ἐπουράνιοι).[513] Every believer in Christ reflects in himself the two situations—the first and last Adam. Paul expresses the truth of the creation of the man from the dust of the earth using a neologism created by himself, "earthly" and "of the earth" (χοϊκός).[514] These terms also indicate man's condition subject to death. Meanwhile "For those God foreknew he also predestined to be conformed to the likeness of his Son, that he might be the firstborn among many brothers" (Rom 8:29). "The phrases, 'from the heaven' and 'heavenly' as before 'spiritual' body, are selected as the opposites of what is from the earth, and they speak of the transcendent sphere of the works of

---

512 Woźniak, *Apokryfy*, 416.

513 C. K. Barrett, *From First Adam to Last* (London 1962), 74.

514 This term does not accrue in the Greek literature before Paul, but in vv. 47–49 it is used four times; Collins, *First Corinthians*, 571; Brodeur, *Holy Spirit's Agency*, 126; W. Brueggemann, "From Dust to Kingship," *ZAW* 84 (1972): 1–18; E. Schweizer, "χοϊκός," *TDNT* IX: 477–478.

God."[515] Ancient Greek cosmology of which Saul of Tarsus was the heir, clearly divided the earthly body from the heavenly body. The apostle expresses this in the immediate context of this passage: "There are also heavenly bodies and there are earthly bodies; but the splendor of the heavenly bodies is one kind, and the splendor of the earthly bodies is another. The sun has one kind of splendor, the moon another and the stars another; and star differs from star in splendor" (vv. 40–41).[516] In Greek classics, the term ἐπουράνιος was used for the gods who lived in the heavens. In this context, it occurs in writings of Plato, Homer, Philo and Josephus.[517] In the light of the faith in risen Christ, the distinction between what is earthly and what is heavenly, takes a new quality. Christ is the beginning of a new humanity and starts its history. While writing about the fact that Christ is "from heaven" (v. 47) and "heavenly" (v. 48), the apostle does not refer to the origin of Christ in terms of his pre-existence. Both the context of statement and its grammar are an indication. Paul describes Christ's existence with the use of these terms after his resurrection, not before incarnation. If the thought of the apostle is about pre-existence and incarnation, it would contradict what he said in v. 46, that is, the spiritual, "was after that."[518] The idea contained herein is clear: "the last Adam" is resurrected at the beginning of the end of time. Existing as a "second man" he is a man "from heaven," and he will transform the human body after the resurrection in the likeness of his glorified body (Phil 3:21).

Philo of Alexandria was educated in ancient philosophy and skillful in allegorical interpretation, and was, like Paul, a Jew from the Diaspora. Philo of Alexandria also speaks of two beings concerning people. He based his knowledge on Gen 1:26 ("Then God said, 'Let us make man in our image, in our likeness, and let them rule over the fish of the sea and the birds of the air, over the livestock, over all the earth, and over all the creatures that move along the ground'"). He speaks about natural man: "Adam lived two hundred and thirty years, and begot offspring in his own image and likeness. Set was like his father and belonged to the same kind of beings. Since then, people have the identical type of bodies, made in the image of the body of Adam. Furthermore, we have also the same type of body, living in a state of destruction until the resurrection. In the future, however, we will wear a different image, the image of the heavenly man; whose body is spiritual"[519] (*Opif.* 6,134–135; cf. *Leg.* 1:31–

515   Jankowski, *Eschatologia Nowego Testamentu*, 103; cf. Morissette, "La condition de ressucité," 215; Lambrecht, "Pierwszy List do Koryntian," 1484.

516   Cenci, *La nostra risurrezione è una certezza!*, 83.

517   Brodeur, *Holy Spirit's Agency*, 35.

518   Fee, *First Epistle to the Corinthians*, 792–793.

519   Grasso, *Prima Lettera ai Corinzi*, 176.

32.53.88.90–95; *Quaest. Gen.* 1:4; 2:56; *Plant.* 44; *Quaest. Ex.* 2,46; *Her.* 7).[520]
For the Alexandrian, as for Paul, the two characters do not indicate individuals
but they are representatives of two groups of people.[521] It should be noted that
the overall vision of Paul's anthropology is very different from the vision of the
Alexandrian.[522] Some exegetes, by means of the difference, explain the denial of
the resurrection by a certain group of the Corinthians.[523]

This statement constitutes a conclusion of Paul's argument: "and just as we
have borne the likeness of the earthly man, so shall we bear the likeness of the
man from heaven" (v. 49; καὶ καθὼς ἐφορέσαμεν τὴν εἰκόνα τοῦ χοϊκοῦ,
φορέσομεν καὶ τὴν εἰκόνα τοῦ ἐπουρανίου). Changing the grammatical third
person singular to the first-person plural is important rhetorically: Paul calls
attention to the situation of the recipients, and his own in relation to them. His
belief should be viewed from the perspective of Christology, and more
precisely, from the paschal perspective and through the prism of the resurrection
of Christ. However, the Judaic tradition (including non-biblical one) knows the
expectation of being close to God after death. Again, it is enough to mention one
text even if apocryphal, in which the visionary reports: "There I saw another
vision; I saw the habitations and resting places of the saints. There my eyes
beheld their habitations with the angels, and their resting places with the holy
ones. They were entreating, supplicating, and praying for the sons of men; while
righteousness like water flowed before them, and mercy like dew *was scattered*

---

520 Murphy-O'Connor, "First Letter to the Corinthians," 813; Barnes, *1 Corinthians to
     Galatians*, 311–319; Horsley, "How Can," 217.
521 "Philo's expositions of the two-'anthropoi' symbolism indicates that he is interested not
     so much in the priority of the individual figure over another individual figure, but in the
     superiority of one type or kind of mankind over another type"; Horsley, "How Can," 219.
522 R. Penna, "Cristologia adamitica e ottimismo antropologico in 1 Cor 15,45–49," in
     L'apostolo Paolo. Studi d'esegesi e teologia (Cinisello Balsamo 1991), 240–268.
     Therefore, E. Dąbrowski states that we do not notice the impact of the speculations on
     Paul since for him the order is just opposite. At first, he mentions about earthly and
     thereafter about heavenly Adam (v. 45). In general, in contemporary to Paul Judaism
     such as understanding was completely unknown; Dąbrowski, *Listy do Koryntian*, 284–
     285. Cf. F. Altermath, *De corps psychique au corps spiritual. Interprétation de 1 Cor
     15: 35–49 par des auteurs des quatre premiers siècles* (BGBE 18; Tübingen 1977), 56.
     In the Pauline doctrine about two kinds of people, there is also not any trace of the myth
     about "original antrophos" (*German Urmensch*), as some researchers suggested; R.
     Reitzenstein, *Die hellenistischen Mysterienreligionen nach ihren Grundgedanken und
     Wirkungen* (Leipzig–Berlin 1927), 341–354; Horsley, "How Can," 216–217; O.
     Cullmann, *The Christology of the New Testament* (Philadelphia 1959), 168; Teani,
     Corporeità e risurrezione, 243.
523 Sterling, "Wisdom among the Perfect," 357–367.

over the earth. And thus *shall it be* with them for ever and for ever" (*1 En.* 39:3–5). The Jews expected the alteration of the body after the resurrection as well: "In what shape will those live who live in Your day? Or how will the splendor of those who (are) after that time continue? Will they then resume this form of the present, and put on these entrammelling members, which are now involved in evils, and in which evils are consummated, or will you perchance change these things which have been in the world as also the world?" (*2 Bar.* 49:2–3; cf. 49:2; 51:3; *1 En.* 108:11).[524]

You have to pay attention to another fact. Paul quotes in v. 45b a fragment from Gen 2:7b but in the immediate context he also makes allusions to other passages out of Genesis. In v. 49 there is a clear allusion to Gen 1:27a: καὶ ἐποίησεν ὁ θεὸς τὸν ἄνθρωπον κατ' εἰκόνα θεοῦ ἐποίησεν αὐτόν. One cannot also exclude the allusion to Gen 5:3a: ἔζησεν δὲ Αδαμ διακόσια καὶ τριάκοντα ἔτη καὶ ἐγέννησεν κατὰ τὴν ἰδέαν αὐτοῦ καὶ κατὰ τὴν εἰκόνα αὐτοῦ. Both fragments derived from Genesis are joined together through the use the term εἰκών. in v. 49. Verse 49 draws our attention to the fact that we are created in the image of the first Adam (Gen 5:3a). Verse 49b plays an important role by indicating the eschatological aspect ("we shall bear") and reminds us of Gen 1:27a. In this context, it should be noticed that Paul depicts the image of the heavenly man, and not God Himself.[525] Paul, making an allusion to Gen 1:27a, interprets this passage Christologically, not theocentrically.

The term "image" (εἰκών) therefore refers to the story of creation: "So God created man in his own image, in the image of God he created him; male and female he created them" (Gen 1:27).[526] In the NT, it is used 23 times, including seven times in the *Corpus Paulinum*, and 3 times in 1 Cor. Most of the uses take the metaphorical meaning: "A man ought not to cover his head, since he is the image and glory of God; but the woman is the glory of man" (1 Cor 11:7); "the light of the gospel of the glory of Christ, who is the image of God" (2 Cor 4:4); "And we, who with unveiled faces all reflect the Lord's glory, are being transformed into his likeness with ever-increasing glory, which comes from the Lord, who is the Spirit" (2 Cor 3:18); "For those God foreknew he also predestined to be conformed to the likeness of his Son, that he might be the firstborn among many brothers" (Rom 8:29). As you can see, every time the term "image" is used, it refers to God or Christ. Through the prism of these occurrences of the term we should have a look at its use in v. 49. "Earthly"

---

524 Woźniak, *Apokryfy*, 425.
525 Lambrecht, "Paul's Christological Use of Scripture," 513.
526 K. Prümm, "Reflexiones theologicae et historicae ad usum Paulinum termini 'eikōn'," *VD* 40 (1962): 232.

people recreate the image of the first Adam in themselves. Every man stood on the side of Adam in his decision to break God's command. This is why we all must die. This is the meaning of Paul's declaration in Rom 5:12: "Therefore, just as sin entered the world through one man, and death through sin, and in this way death came to all men, because all sinned."[527]

Similarly, those who in their faith follow Christ create in themselves his image. The believers are evidently summoned to be like Christ, who in turn is the image of God: "For those God foreknew he also predestined to be conformed to the likeness of his Son, that he might be the firstborn among many brothers" (Rom 8:29). The contemplation of Christ leads to similarity to Him: "And we, who with unveiled faces all reflect the Lord's glory, are being transformed into his likeness with ever-increasing glory, which comes from the Lord, who is the Spirit" (2 Cor 3:18). In another letter to the Corinthians, Paul explains that Christ is the image of God: "And even if our gospel is veiled, it is veiled to those who are perishing. The god of this age has blinded the minds of unbelievers, so that they cannot see the light of the gospel of the glory of Christ, who is the image of God" (2 Cor 4:3–4). Paul explained to the Philippians the same truth concerning the transformation the body after the resurrection. It will take effect by the power of the Christ: "But our citizenship is in heaven. And we eagerly await a Savior from there, the Lord Jesus Christ, who, by the power that enables him to bring everything under his control, will transform our lowly bodies so that they will be like his glorious body" (Phil 3:20–21). Thus, in v. 49 Paul comes to a point in which after the earlier reasoning, it becomes clear that:

(1) The one who accepts the resurrection of Christ cannot claim that "there is no resurrection" (v. 12) since the resurrection of Christ paves the way to all who believe in Him for the resurrection;

(2) Christ's resurrection is actually the first stage of eschatological events; Christ has risen from the dead as the "firstfruits" (v. 20) of all the dead;

(3) There is a parallelism (negative) between the character of Adam and the character of Christ. They are the "representative" characters; Adam's sin brought death to all people but resurrection of Christ leads his believers to the resurrection.[528]

---

527 C. K. Barrett thinks that: "Men has taken Adam's side, they have joined the revolt against God and for that reason die. This is (very nearly if not quite) the meaning of Rom 5,12"; "Significance of the Adam-Christ Typology," 108. Cf. also: B. Byrne, *'Sons of God' – 'Seed of Abraham'. A Study of the Idea of the Sonship of God of All Christians in Paul against the Jewish Background* (AnBib 83; Roma 1979), 117.

528 Barrett, "Significance of the Adam-Christ Typology," 109.

The phrase φορέσομεν καὶ τὴν εἰκόνα τοῦ ἐπουρανίου can be understood in two ways: "we shall bear the likeness of the man from heaven" or "we have borne the likeness of the man from heaven".[529] The first form is included in a few majuscule and minuscule manuscripts and several ancient versions but many codes as well as a significant P[46] contains a second form; an encouragement in the form of the aorist.[530] Eschatological (and didactic) context[531] seems to indicate that the first possibility is the preferable one.[532] But we can not exclude the possibility that even *implicite* this formulation, it contains a moral encouragement to asceticism, and makes an effort to increasingly become more like Christ.[533] Definitively, we have already received the Christian pledge of resurrection during the baptism, but its completion will take place at the end of times.

In summary, Paul used a quote from Gen 2:7b in v. 45b to show the analogy between Adam and Christ (the first Adam–the last Adam, the first Adam–the second Adam, the first man–the second man, earthly man–the man from heaven).[534] As the Apostle contrasts the two characters, the quote points to the fact that Adam gives rise to humanity that fell into sin and therefore, is subject to the law of death. Christ is the origin of this group of people, who through the resurrection will defeat death. Believers in Christ, in fact, become similar to Him in His resurrection. The analogy Adam–Christ can be summarized as follows[535]:

---

529   The verb φορέω occurs only 6 times in the NT, including just 2 times in Paul. It usually takes on a literal meaning ("bear/wear" clothing or weapon). In v. 48a, we deal with a so-called gnomic aorist which is quite common in Greek sayings, proverbs and slogans. Cf.: A. Brunot, *Saint Paul and His Message* (Twentieth Century Encyclopedia of Catholicism 70; trans. R. Matthews; New York 1959), 75–76.

530   Fabris, *Prima Lettera ai Corinzi*, 210.

531   Metzger, *Textual Commentary*, 502.

532   Otherwise Heil who defines v. 49 as "the climactic exhortation." The author argues that this encouragement "urges the audience to conform their lives even now to the confident hope of exceeding their earthbound condition and resembling 'the heavenly one' after their deaths"; id., *Rhetorical Role of Scripture*, 244.

533   The writers who take the second option as more probable emphasize the moral character of Pauline encouragement: "even though the Apostle concentrates on the life to come in 1 Corinthians 15, he never fails to remind his addressees that they are called to follow Christ in the world today. If the life-giving Spirit creates the spiritual body at the parousia, the Holy Spirit sanctifies and empowers Christians so as to help them in their day-to-day moral behavior on earth"; Brodeur, *Holy Spirit's Agency*, 161–162.

534   Barnes, *I Corinthians to Galatians*, 316.

535   B. Witherington III, "Christology," in *Dictionary of Paul and His Letters. A Compendium of Contemporary Biblical Scholarship* (eds. G. F. Hawthorne and R.P. Martin; Dovners Grove–Leicester 1993), 111.

	Adam	Christ
v. 45	the first Adam living being	the last Adam life giving spirit
v. 47	the first man	the second Man
vv. 47–48	of the dust of the earth	from heaven

Paul's argument is based on the *midrash pesher* interpretation of Gen 2:7b, carried in the light of the resurrection of Christ. In vv. 45–46 the term "being" refers to Adam and the term "spirit" to Christ. Using these terms, Paul argues that the spiritual came after the natural. In vv. 47–49 the term "earthly" refers to Adam (as the very etymology of the name indicates) but the term "from heaven" refers to Christ. With the help of the terms, the apostle teaches that believers in Christ bear the likeness of the earthly man; after the resurrection, however, they will bear the likeness of the man from heaven.[536] The use of the quotation from Gen 2:7b gives Paul the possibility to show the reality of the resurrection based on the analogy of Adam and Christ.[537] What is more, using the terms "human being" and "earthly" in relation to the first man and the terms "spirit" and "from heaven" in reference to Christ, the apostle can speak of two types of bodies (natural and spiritual), and using this distinction, he can justify the reality of the resurrection. The shift in meaning from the "living being" for Adam to "life-giving spirit" in reference to Christ served Paul as an argument for the fact that Christ's resurrection has the power to bring life to those who believe in Him.

---

536   Fee, *First Epistle to the Corinthians*, 788; Soards, *First Corinthians*, 1188.
537   Cenci, *La nostra risurrezione è una certezza!*, 84.

VI. Quotation from Isa 25:8a in 1 Cor 15:54b

1 Cor 15:54b: κατεπόθη ὁ θάνατος εἰς νῖκος

Isa 25:8a (LXX): κατέπιεν ὁ θάνατος ἰσχύσας

Isa 25:8a (HB): בִּלַּע הַמָּוֶת לָנֶצַח

1. Source of the Quotation

While comparing the teaching of the HB ("he will swallow up death forever") with the LXX ("Death has been swallowed up in victory/power") the difference between the Hebrew phrase לָנֶצַח (forever), and the verb ἰσχύσας used in the LXX should be noted. The last verb is a present participle of the aorist of the verb "may," "be able to," "to be strong," "to win" or "to help"[538] (Targum reads here לעלמי ("for ever")). Although the LXX translates the Hebrew לָנֶצַח as ἰσχύσας, this translation, however εἰς νῖκος (in later versions of Theodotion and Aquila) is consistent with the Semitic (Aramaic and Hebrew) root (נצח); because this root builds such terms as the "leader" or "success." In addition, the LXX wording εἰς νῖκος also occurs in 2 Sam 2:26; Jer 3:5 and Amos 1:11; 8:7. In 2 Sam 2:26, it is a synonymous parallelism for the phrase "the last times," while in Jer 3:5 the phrase is "forever."[539] Theodotion translates κατεπόθη ὁ θάνατος εἰς νῖκος, while Aquila: καταπόντισει τόν θάνατον εἰς νῖκος.[540] Therefore, Paul in his translation is the closest to the Theodotion teaching and the difference lies in one verb (and more specifically in its form): Paul's wording is κατεπόθη, and Theodotion reads καταπόθη. It is, of course, impossible

---

538   One can also give other meanings to the verb: "to enjoy physical brawn," "to be in a good health," "to be useful," "to be able to," "to tackle," "to have power," "to have an advantage over someone," "to matter"; R. Popowski, *Słownik grecko-polski Nowego Testamentu* (Warszawa 1999²), 156.

539   de Boer, *Defeat of Death*, 127.

540   J. P. Heil explains as follows the divergence in the Pauline text and the translation of Theodotion: "Although the Theodotion version in uncial Q is identical to the Pauline version, it may be a later assimilation to 1 Cor 15:54b, especially since it occurs as a marginal gloss, and the Syrohexapla reading of Theodotion has the active rather than passive form of the verb"; Heil, *Rhetorical Role of Scripture*, 249. A slightly different overtone has the teaching of Symmach: καταπόθηναι τόν θάνατον εἰς τέλος.

that Paul followed Theodotion. Paul made his translation at the end of the second-century A.D. while reviewing the LXX and correcting the text in places where in his opinion, the corrections were necessary. He wanted his text to be in step with the teachings of the rabbis. Some scholars have hypothesized that St. Paul's translation of Isa 25:8 is based on some unknown Aramaic version (*Volksbibel*), but it is difficult to find convincing arguments to support this thesis.[541] It would be better to refer to targums. Babylonian targums were usually close translations of the texts, but Palestinian targums were only their paraphrases. The principle, that *meturgeman* (translator) used to recite the targum from memory after reading the passage, was accepted. Nevertheless, he could not have had the original text in front of his eyes.[542] The original text would then have to go through two stages: it would have to be translated from Hebrew to Aramaic and after that from Aramaic to Greek. Meanwhile, Pauline text is closer to the LXX than the HB when it comes to the degree of verbal compliance. It is safer to assume, therefore, that Paul used the LXX, and because there are deviations from the language of the HB, the apostle could have molded quoted fragments to bring them into line with the Hebrew original.[543]

2. The Meaning in the Original Context

In the sentence "Death has been swallowed up in victory" (κατεπόθη ὁ θάνατος εἰς νῖκος), penned in 1 Cor 15:54b, there is a quote taken from Isa 25:8a. In the original text it reads: בִּלַּע הַמָּוֶת לָנֶצַח. The person who determined the final content of the book placed them in a part called the *Apocalypse of Isaiah*, which includes Chapters 24–27. It seems that this part of the Proto-Isaiah came into being later, possibly during captivity or after Babylonian exile.[544] In this part, there is a talk about God's judgment over the nations. After completing this topic (Isa 24:1–6), the prophet shows the vision of the ruined city (24:7–18a) to continue the topic of general judgment (24:18b–23). Then he presents the worship song of the redeemed (25:1–5), and a vision of the messianic feast (25:6–12). Afterwards, another song was placed, as well as the song of thanksgiving for a victory (26:1–6), an eschatological psalm (26:7–19), eschatological prophecy (26:20–27:1), and the song of Lord's vineyard (27:2–5). *Isaiah Revelation* ends with the announcement of grace in the house of Jacob, penalties for his oppressors (27:6–11) and the final prophecy announcing

---

541 Ellis, "Paul's Use of the Old Testament," 15.
542 A. Mello, *Judaizm* (trans. K. Stopa; Kraków 2003), 59–60.
543 Terry, *Discourse Analysis*, 159.
544 T. Jelonek, *Prorocy Starego Testamentu* (Kraków 2007), 135.

the definitive triumph of God (27:12–13).[545] A literary style of the prophecies recorded here is similar to that of Daniel, Zech 9–14, and the apocryphal *Book of Enoch*. However, Isa 24–27, was also called an "apocalypse," but not for this reason alone. There are several other reasons:

(1) in contrast to the previous chapters of Isaiah, this section contains a prophecy addressed not only to particular nations but also to the whole world;

(2) Isaiah 27:1 promises the destruction of Leviathan, the shy snake which is a legendary creature; in apocalyptic literature, the announcement of a destruction of the mythical creatures occurs time and again;

(3) in apocalypses after the period of destruction a whole new order is usually announced, this element is also present in Isa 24–27, especially in the announcement of a feast;

(4) apocalyptic literature often includes a mention of the resurrection like it is in Isa 26:19.[546]

2.1. Ideological Base and the Literary Structure in Isa 25:1–12

Chapter 25 of Isaiah contains the answer to the promised destruction of the earth and the city (cf. Isa 24). This part of Isaiah's text contains elements of an apocalyptic genre. In Judaism, the apocalyptic literature was in its full bloom starting from the 2nd century B.C., but its beginnings can already be seen in the passages from Isaiah and Daniel. A characteristic of apocalypses is the conviction that they are a record of the revelation concerning the future in which the destruction of evil and the salvation of the righteous are expected.[547] This theme is vividly present in Isa 25 as well as the entire section in Isa 24–27.

---

545 A slightly different division of the *Apocalypse of Isaiah* proposes B. Marconcini: a global catastrophe and saving the Rest (24:1–6), desertion (24:7–12), the faithful scattered throughout the world (24.13–16a), natural disasters (24.16b–20), the destruction of cosmic forces (24:21–23), anthem of survivors (25:1–5), eschatological feast (25:6–8) the end of the anthem of survived (26:9–12), the city of the righteous (26:1–6), the hope for salvation (26:7–13), the announcement of the resurrection (26:14–19); a song of prise (26.20–27.1), the song of the vineyard (27:2–5); eschatological prophecy; B. Marconcini, "L'apocalittica biblica," in *Profeti e Apocalittici* (eds. B. Marconcini et al.; Logos. Corso do Studi Biblici 3; Torino 1994), 218–219.

546 W. J. Doorly, *Isaiah of Jerusalem. An Introduction* (Mahwah 1992), 97–99.

547 *Sensu stricto*, apocalypses include the Jewish apocryphal writings such as: Ethiopian Book of Enoch, the Book of Giants, Slavic Book of Enoch, Hebrew Book of Enoch, the

In terms of literary forms, Isa 25 is made up of songs that directly address the Lord (that is, in the form of prayer) in vv. 1–5, the apocalyptic description of the feast prepared by God in vv. 6–8, and the prophetic announcement of joy that will grasp before God those who escaped the disaster described in vv. 9–12. The very themed integrity, in which various substantive topics occur, determines the structure of Isa 25. The inner structure of this part can be shown in three segments:

A: The thanksgiving song of redeemed (vv. 1–5);

B: The feast prepared by God (vv. 6–8);

C: The joy of survivors (vv. 9–12).[548]

The Apocalypse of Isaiah begins with a description of a universal judgment over the whole world. According to this depiction, God brings those people who have broken the covenant, have not kept the commandments, and have outraged justice and committed unrighteousness, to justice. The reference to the covenant points to the one with Noah which is a universal covenant because the judgment concerns all nations. Since the name of the city is not given, it can pose a symbolic reference to the city whose inhabitants committed a great wrong. Faithfulness of God in punishing evil and rewarding justice is reflected in a thanksgiving song of the survivors (25:1–5). Zion, which God has chosen as his

---

Book of Jubilees, Sibyl Oracles, Fourth Book of Ezra, Syrian Apocalypse of Baruch, Greek Apocalypse of Baruch, Apocalypse of Abraham, Apocalypse of Elijah, the Book of Elijah, Elijah Wisdom, Apocalypse of Zephaniah, Revelation of Ezekiel, the Second Ezekiel, Jacob's Ladder, A Treatise of Shem, Apocalypse of Adam and others; see.: Rosik, "Literatura żydowska," 56–70; Mędala, *Wprowadzenie*, 123–200; M. E. Stone, "Apocalyptic Literature," in *Compendium rerum iudaicarum ad Novum Testamentum*, II, *Jewish Writings of Second Temple Period. Apocrypha, Pseudoepigrapha, Qumran Sectarian Writings, Philo, Josephus* (ed. M. E. Stone; Assen–Philadelphia 1984), 383–442.

548 See: Oswalt, *Book of Isaiah*, 459. D. C. Polaski divides Isa 25 on four parts: vv. 1–5; vv. 6–8; vv. 9–10a; vv. 10b–12; *Authorizing an End. The Isaiah Apocalypse and Intertextuality* (Leiden 2001), 147–149. M. A. Sweeney judges that in Isa 25 there are only two parts: vv. 1–5 and vv. 6–12; *Isaiah 1–39*, 336. Each of them, however, is divided into smaller segments (ibid., 333–336):

I. A common hymn of thanksgiving to the Yahweh (vv. 1–5):
   A: Call to praising (v. 1);
   B: Theme of praise: the destruction of the fortified town (vv. 2–3);
   C: Theme of praise: the defense of the poor (vv. 4–5).
II. Announcing of the blessing and answer to it (vv. 6–12):
   A: Announcing of the blessing (vv. 7–8);
   B: Announcing of the response of Israel and the destruction of Moab (vv. 9–12).

home, will become a center of the renewed world, and God will prepare a feast for all the survivors (25:6–8). Verses 10b–12 of Chapter 25 are losing their universal nature because they include information about the antagonism between Moab and Israel. Therefore, sometimes they are considered to be a gloss. In the next song, again universal in its character, the prophet juxtaposes images of two cities: the city of chaos and the city faithful to God (26:1–6). After the next image, there is a psalm characterized by eschatological motifs indicating the need for seeking God inside the righteous heart. Eschatological prophecy (26:20–27:1) poses a specific response to the words of the psalm; the nation should hide in their rooms, until the wrath of God will pass by. A sign of God's ultimate victory is a victory over Leviathan, the ancient serpent (27:1), which represents hostile powers to Israel (Babylonia, Assyria, Egypt). The next presented image is the image of a vineyard (cf. Isa 5). God is its guardian and takes care of it. The vineyard symbolizes Israel, of course, which will be saved in the Day of Judgment, in contrast to the pagan nations. The announcement of the fall of the fortified town, which may be Jerusalem or Samaria, ends *The Apocalypse of Isaiah.*[549]

2.2. Exegetical Analysis of Isa 25:1–12

Vv. 1–5 The first section of Isa 25 makes up a thanksgiving song of the redeemed. Eschatological literature contains many hymns uttered by people saved by Yahweh (e.g. *1QM* 14:2–18; 18:6b–19:8).[550] The first acclamation of prayer "O Lord, you are my God" has already brought the formula of a covenant to mind (v. 1a). It is often recorded in the pages of the OT: "I will be your God, and you will be my people" (cf. Deut 26:17; 29:12; Hos 2:4; Jer 7:23; 11:4; 24:7; 31:32; Ezek 34:30; 36:28; 37:23). This acclamation sets the tone for the prayer which follows it. This tone is very personal and direct. Although the prophet says (or rather sings) the song in the grammatical form of the first-person singular, he becomes a representative of all saved by the Lord. The victory song is a song of praise: "I will exalt you and praise your name." A theme that is very important in Judaism is the worship and praising of God's name. Rabbinic Judaism has recorded it in the first request of Kaddish: "May His great name be exalted and sanctified in the world which He created

---

549   Jelonek, *Prorocy Starego Testamentu*, 135–138.

550   L. Stachowiak, *Księga Izajasza 1–39. Wstęp – przekład z oryginału – komentarz*, I (PŚST IX/1; Poznań 1996), 368.

according to His will!"[551] In Semitic mentality, a person and her name are inseparable; the name expresses a person and indicates his mission.[552] So we can say that the purpose of praising God's name is to make sure God was known and glorified all over the earth.

The motifs of praising the name of Yahweh are things He intended: "for in perfect faithfulness you have done marvellous things, things planned long ago" (v. 1b). Usually in the Jewish tradition the mention of the great works of God refers to the miracles and signs bound up with the exodus. It is enough to give some examples: "Who among the gods is like you, O Lord? Who is like you— majestic in holiness, awesome in glory, working wonders?" (Exod 15:11); "Many, O Lord my God, are the wonders you have done. The things you planned for us no one can recount to you; were I to speak and tell of them, they would be too many to declare" (Ps 40:6); "I will meditate on all your works and consider all your mighty deeds" (Ps 77:12); "He did miracles in the sight of their fathers in the land of Egypt, in the region of Zoan. He divided the sea and led them through; he made the water stand firm like a wall. He guided them with the cloud by day and with light from the fire all night. He split the rocks in the desert and gave them water as abundant as the seas" (Ps 78:12–15; cf. Ps 88:11– 13; 89:6).

The phrase "[intention] planned long ago" belongs typically to the language of Isaiah; God is the One who consistently leads his plan of salvation of the universe realizing it step by step. The gods of the Gentiles did not have such a plan (cf. 1:26; 3:3; 5:9; 7:5; 8:10; 9:5; 11:2; 14:24.26–27; 16:3; 19:3.11–12.17; 23:8–9; 28:29; 29:15; 30:11; 32:7–8; 36:5; 40:13; 41:28; 44:26; 45:21; 46:10– 11; 47:13). Admittedly, the phrase מֵרָחוֹק can be understood spatially as "away," however, in this case and in this context, the time undertone inscribes better ("long ago," "in days of old"), just as in 2 Kgs 19:25: "'Have you not heard?' Long ago (מֵרָחוֹק) I ordained it. In days of old I planned it; now I have brought it to pass, that you have turned fortified cities into piles of stone."

One of the elements of God's plan was to destroy the city of the wicked. The first part of v. 2 is built according to rule of synonymous parallelism: "You have made the city a heap of rubble, the fortified town a ruin." A great grammatical difficulty creates the expression מֵעִיר as it does not fit perfectly into the context

---

551   M. Rosik, "Judaistyczne tło Modlitwy Pańskiej (Mt 6,9–13)," *Zeszyty Naukowe Centrum Badań im. Edyty Stein* 4 (2008): 41–42. In the same prayer Kaddish, the Jewish prayed so that "His great Name grow exalted and sanctified in the world that He created as He willed." The third blessing "Eighteen Blessings," has already been known in Jesus' days, starts with the words: "You are holy, and Your name is holy."

552   H. Daniel-Rops, *Życie codzienne w Palestynie w czasach Chrystusa* (trans. J. Lasocka; Warszawa 1994), 97.

of the sentence. Many have tried to solve this be all possible means.[553] The most commonly accepted solution is the recognition that the scribe under the influence of the phrase מֵעִיר appearing in the final part of the sentence, changed the definite article into מ. However, the recognition of this מ as an enclitic seems equally likely.[554] In any case, since no specific city is indicated by the prophet, the mention should be understood as a symbolic one; the town or city becomes synonymous with the place over-filled with evil and wickedness. The final part of the verse speaks of "the foreigners' stronghold" (אַרְמוֹן זָרִים), which the LXX translator translates as "city of godless/vainglorious" (τὰ θεμέλια τῶν ἀσεβῶν). This translation shows the way Isaiah's prophecy was understood in the 3rd century B.C. At that time, strangers were considered to be proud or wicked. Pagan nations were treated according to the conviction.

The result of God's action (destruction of the fortified city of strangers which will never be built) is a glory emitted from the mouths of powerful people. The term עַל־כֵּן, introducing v. 3 has a causal undertone. Through its use, the prophet builds the contrast between the cause and the effect. In order that the worship of God become possible, first the foreigners/godless must be annihilated. Why? The possible answer is that a man only recognizes his own strength and is self-confident. It takes the effect that God must resort to destruction, so that a man can be able to recognize evil. Until the man has lost everything he is not able to pay attention to anything except himself. When his situation becomes hopeless, he starts to take pleasure in looking for God, and recognizes in Him his only salvation.[555]

Next in (vv. 4–5), like in the developing poem, the prophet continues to enumerate the reasons why God is glorified. This is so not only because God destroyed the citadel of the wicked but also because He takes the side of the poor and oppressed. The terms "the poor" (דָּל) and "needy in his distress" (אֶבְיוֹן) in v. 4 should be understood—according to the rule *pars pro toto*—as a reference to all the people of Israel.[556] Helping them, God becomes their refuge. God opposes the proud not only because pride is evil in itself but also because it causes evil to others. The motif of God as "refuge" is very common not only in the prophetic writings but also in the entire OT. It is enough to give some examples: "my God is my rock, in whom I take refuge, my shield and the horn

---

553 Fot their list see: J. A. Emerton, "A Textual Problem in Isaiah 25:2," *ZAW* 89 (1977): 64–73.

554 H. D. Hummel, "Enclitic *mem* in Early Northwest Semitic, Especially Hebrew," *JBL* 76 (1957): 104.

555 Oswalt, *Book of Isaiah*, 461.

556 According to L. Stachowiak the poor and the needy were a class of people deprived of their property and without possibility to appeal to their rights. As such people, they became easy victims of exploitation by the rich; Stachowiak, *Księga Izajasza 1–39*, 370.

of my salvation. He is my stronghold, my refuge and my savior—from violent men you save me" (2 Sam 22:3); "You evildoers frustrate the plans of the poor, but the Lord is their refuge" (Ps 14:6); "The Lord is my light and my salvation—whom shall I fear? The Lord is the stronghold of my life—of whom shall I be afraid?" (Ps 27:1); "The Lord is the strength of his people, a fortress of salvation for his anointed one" (Ps 28:8); "The salvation of the righteous comes from the Lord; he is their stronghold in time of trouble" (Ps 37:39); "You are God my stronghold. Why have you rejected me? Why must I go about mourning, oppressed by the enemy?" (Ps 43:2); "God is our refuge and strength, an ever-present help in trouble" (Ps 46:2).[557]

To create a visualization that God is a refuge, the prophet refers to two extreme weather situations in the Middle East; rains and heats. Both long-term storms and drought can cause damage to crops, and as a consequence, lead to depriving people of sustenance. Man is not able to control the climate forces, only divine intervention can be effective.[558] A strange phrase, "for the breath of the ruthless is like a storm driving against a wall (כִּי רוּחַ עָרִיצִים כְּזֶרֶם קִיר)" (v. 4b) should be read as "for the breath of the ruthless is like winter rain"; this change resulted from the similarity of the terms "wall" (קִיר) and "winter" (קֹר), and it perfectly inscribes into the context.[559] Isaiah continues this visual imagery at the ending of v. 5: "As the heat by the shade of a cloud, the song of the dreaded ones will be brought low" (the LXX omits the first part of the phrase). God defeats the proud in a quiet but immediate way as a cloud suddenly appears between dried-up pieces of land, and the sun as the apparition of the Lord itself protects the oppressed. The repercussions of it are clearly depicted in the earlier announcement of Isaiah: "It will be a shelter and shade from the heat of the day, and a refuge and hiding place from the storm and rain" (Isa 4:6).[560]

Vv. 6–8 This passage starts with the announcement of the feast prepared by God.[561] It is a continuation of 24:21–23: "In that day the Lord will punish the powers in the heavens above and the kings on the earth below. They will be herded together like prisoners bound in a dungeon; they will be shut up in prison and be punished after many days. The moon will be abashed, the sun ashamed;

---

557 Cf. also Ps 48:4; 52:9; 57:2; 62:8; 71:7; 91:2; 94:22; 142:5; Isa 4:6; 17:7; 27:5; 16:19.

558 S. Gądecki, *Wstęp do ksiąg prorockich Starego Testamentu* (Gniezno 1993), 105.

559 Targum, however, retains the MT unchanged, while in the LXX the meaning of the verse is completely changed: ἐγένου γὰρ πάσῃ πόλει ταπεινῇ βοηθὸς καὶ τοῖς ἀθυμήσασιν διὰ ἔνδειαν σκέπη ἀπὸ ἀνθρώπων πονηρῶν ῥύσῃ αὐτούς σκέπη διψώντων καὶ πνεῦμα ἀνθρώπων ἀδικουμένων.

560 Cf. Isa 30:2–3; 32:2; 49:2; 51:16; Pss 17:8; 36:8; 57:2; 63:8; 91:1; 121:5–6.

561 Wodecki, "Jerusalem," 105.

for the Lord Almighty will reign on Mount Zion and in Jerusalem, and before its elders, gloriously." All themes and terminology point to the link between 24:21–23 and 25:6–8. The combination of such phrases as "on this mountain" (Zion), and "to all nations" is a specific mixture of Israelite particularism and universalism. Isaiah constitutes a part of the tradition referring to the gathering of nations on Sinai: "In the last days the mountain of the Lord's temple will be established as chief among the mountains; it will be raised above the hills, and all nations will stream to it. Many peoples will come and say, 'Come, let us go up to the mountain of the Lord, to the house of the God of Jacob. He will teach us his ways, so that we may walk in his paths.' The law will go out from Zion, the word of the Lord from Jerusalem. He will judge between the nations and will settle disputes for many peoples. They will beat their swords into plowshares and their spears into pruning hooks. Nation will not take up sword against nation, nor will they train for war anymore" (Isa 2:2–4; cf. Isa 18:7; 45:14; 60:3–4; Ps 96:6–7). Although the expression "all nations" comes from the Deuteronomical tradition (Deut 4:19; 6:14; 7:6–7; 10:15; 14:2), it is not absent from the writings of the prophets (Mic 4:5; Hagg 2:13; Jer 34:1; Ezek 31:12–13; 38:6; Zech 8:20–22). The theme of God who invites to the feast also belongs to the traditional in the theological thought of Israel (Ps 22:27; 23:5; 36:8–9; Jer 31:14).

God is preparing a feast "on the mountain." This formulation occurs in our passage three times (v. 6; v. 7; v. 10). For the Israelites, a mountain was a symbol of the power and glory of God (Ps 18:8; 36:7; 65:7; 104:8) but also His justice (Ps 36:7). Zion is no different.[562] It is associated with the mountain of Moriah where Abraham took his son Isaac as a sacrifice (Gen 22:2; 2 Kgs 3:1), and with the threshing floor of Araunah the Jebusite where the angel of the Lord was to impose a penalty for conducting the census by David (2 Sam 24:16; 2 Chr 3:1).[563] God has chosen it for his home. It will also be the place of the eschatological feast in which God and people will participate.[564]

---

562 The discoveries of Ugaritic texts allowed to identified Zion with mentioned in those texts Mount Zaphon. Zaphon was regarded as a sacred mountain of the Canaanite god Baal. Until recently, the Hebrew word with the same wording as the name of the mountain was translated as "the north." As a result, the words of the Psalmist, "the utmost heights of Zaphon is Mount Zion" (Ps 48:2) can be read as "Mount Zion is Mount Zaphon." S. Richard, "Góra," in *Encyklopedia biblijna* (ed. P. J. Achtemeier; trans. T. Mieszkowski; Warszawa 1999), 357.

563 U. Szwarc, "Świątynia jerozolimska," in *Życie religijne w Biblii* (ed. G. Witaszek; Lublin 1999), 79.

564 L. Alonso Schökel and G. Gutiérrez, *Io pongo le mie parole sulla tua bocca. Meditazioni bibliche* (Bibbia e preghiera 12; Roma 1992), 92.

In the OT, the theme of a feast is associated with the inauguration of the reign of a king (1 Sam 11:15; 1 Kgs 1:9.25) or with the solemn conclusion of a covenant (Gen 31:46.54). In the light of this tradition, one can discern in v. 6 the announcement of the feast starting the reign of Yahweh with the participation of all nations. Some exegetes tried to discern the cultic elements in vv. 6–8, however, the term מִשְׁתֵּה, used to describe the feast, does not have much in common with the banquet/alimentary sacrifice. For in the first place, God will prepare a meal from "fat" and "the best of meats." It is a symbol of abundance and prosperity. The psalmist uses the term "meats" (שְׁמָנִים) in the plural, which—according to the Hebrew grammar—means its highest quality.[565] The psalmist praised meat sacrificed and eaten: "How priceless is your unfailing love! Both high and low among men find refuge in the shadow of your wings. They feast on the abundance of your house; you give them drink from your river of delights" (Ps 36:8–9). He compared the worship of God to the food: "My soul will be satisfied as with the richest of foods; with singing lips my mouth will praise you" (Ps 63:6). God's generosity will be also manifested in offering the finest of wines. The terminology used by the prophet points to the fine wine, free from any sediment.[566] People who will arrive to the feast will have their faces covered with sheets, and the bodies covered with shrouds (v. 7). Two very rare expressions appear in v. 7: הַלּוֹט and מַסֵּכָה. God will tear both off. Almost unanimously the commentators claim that the shroud and sheet on their faces symbolize death.[567] The direct context of the mention of the shroud and sheet indicates such an interpretation as well. In v. 8a, it also speaks about the defeat of death. The covered head is a sign of sorrow and grief: "But David continued up the Mount of Olives, weeping as he went; his head was covered and he was barefoot. All the people with him covered their heads too and were weeping as they went up" (2 Sam 15:30). Similar symbolism is contained in the words of Jeremiah: "Judah mourns, her cities languish; they wail for the land, and a cry goes up from Jerusalem. The nobles send their servants for water; they go to the

---

565   *Gesenius' Hebrew Grammar* (ed. E. Kautzsch; trans. A. E. Cowley; Oxford 1910²), par. 124e.

566   All the adjectives and phrases emphasizing the food served at the banquet are used to show an excess of God's goodness and generosity and the highest quality of products offered by God; Grogan, "Isaiah," 159.

567   Although there are also other interpretations, L. Stachowiak remarks that the closest the author's intention is the symbolic of mourning and grief as an expression of the absence of God's saving care; Stachowiak, *Księga Izajasza 1–39*, 372. G. W. Grogan believes that the cover over the eyes can symbolize the blindness of the heathen nations; however, it is more likely seems to be an interpretation of the cover as the veil of sorrow, and even mourning veil; "Isaiah," 160.

cisterns but find no water. They return with their jars unfilled; dismayed and despairing, they cover their heads. The ground is cracked because there is no rain in the land; the farmers are dismayed and cover their heads" (Jer 14:2–4). Tearing off the cover from their faces and a veil covering the nations, God will defeat death. This victory over death was announced in v. 8a,[568] which Paul cites in 1 Cor 15:54b: בִּלַּע הַמָּוֶת לָנֶצַח. Some exegetes suggest that v. 8 was joined to the original text as a gloss by a later scribe but this hypothesis is not supported sufficiently by strong arguments.[569]

Another oracle from Isa 26:19 continues the announcement death's defeat: "But your dead will live; their bodies will rise. You, who dwell in the dust, wake up and shout for joy. Your dew is like the dew of the morning; the earth will give birth to her dead". Isaiah also uses the term בִּלַּע, to discuss death, which means "swallow." The OT uses the term, when it tells about "swallowing," namely the defeat of the enemies of Israel (Lam 2:2.5.8), or just a righteous man (Ps 52:6). Death and Sheol swallow people too: "Therefore the grave enlarges its appetite and opens its mouth without limit; into it will descend their nobles and masses with all their brawlers and revelers" (Isa 5:14); "Death has climbed in through our windows and has entered our fortresses; it has cut off the children from the streets and the young men from the public squares. Say: This is what the Lord declares: The dead bodies of men will lie like refuse on the open field, like cut grain behind the reaper, with no one to gather them" (Jer 9:21–22).

You cannot say with certainty that death has in v. 8a personal meaning, although such an understanding of the OT can be found in this verse: "Like

---

568 Some exegetes suggest that v. 8a was an interpolation, but this opinion is not universal. On the contrary, others argue, that it is important for the whole structure of vv. 6–8.

569 O. Kaiser thinks that the glossator responsible for the inclusion of v. 8 and 26:19 into the text can be connected with Maccabean times; O. Kaiser, *Das Buch des Propheten Jesaja. Kapitel 13–39* (ATD 18; Göttingen 1976²), 175–178. Of the similar opinion is G. Fohrer, *Das Buch Jesaja*, II, *Kapitel 24–39* (ZBKAT 19,2; Zürich–Stuttgart 1991³), 31–33. U. Barges moves the dating of including the gloss to the time of the destruction of Jerusalem by Ptolemy, I Soter (302–301 B.C.E.); U. Berges, *Das Buch Jesaja Komposition und Endgestalt* (HBS 16; Freiburg 1998), 45. R. Kilian, however, thinks that the whole periscope in Isa 25:6–8 is a commentary later added to the original text and explaining Isa 24:21–23. The same author, however, does not perceive here the idea of the resurrection of the individuals, but he sees it only in Isa 26:19. This latter view undermines all his hypotheses because there is no reason to interpret texts of a similar tone in a different manner; R. Kilian, *Jesaja*, II, *13–39* (NEB; Stuttgart 1980), 149. J. Lemański, however, claims that the current state of research makes possible to recognize the entire periscope in its integral form for the effect of a later editorial work carried out between the fourth and third century before Christ; Lemański, „*Sprawisz, abym ożył!*", 234.

sheep they are destined for the grave, and death will feed on them. The upright will rule over them in the morning; their forms will decay in the grave, far from their princely mansions" (Ps 49:15); "For the grave cannot praise you, death cannot sing your praise; those who go down to the pit cannot hope for your faithfulness" (Isa 38:18); "Death has climbed in through our windows and has entered our fortresses; it has cut off the children from the streets and the young men from the public squares" (Jer 9:21); "I will ransom them from the power of the grave; I will redeem them from death. Where, O death, are your plagues? Where, O grave, is your destruction? 'I will have no compassion'" (Hos 13:14); "Destruction and Death say, 'Only a rumor of it has reached our ears'" (Job 28:22).

The symbol of wiping tears from people's faces by God is extremely vivid.[570] In the ancient Near East tears were not only interpreted as a sign of weakness. Tears more frequently appear over the faces of the inhabitants of those areas than in our western culture, and tears have many meanings.[571] The context indicates that the tears were caused by death, and that it has just been defeated. While the "wiping the tears" refers to "all faces," "taking the shame away" meets only Israel. Nevertheless, is it possible to assign the reference regarding death by referring to the resurrection, to Isaiah? In this case, we should refer to the progress of the biblical idea of the soul lasting after the death, and the idea of immortality tied with the resurrection. This concept in Israeli theological thought underwent a certain evolution.[572] In the period of the patriarchs, this was said to be related to the state of Sheol or abyss, towards which the dead were heading. In the theological thought, a clear distinction between posthumous fate of the righteous and sinners has not been made.[573]

---

570   "The text could say that God will take away the sorrow associated with death, for that is obviously the meaning. But how much more expressive is the picture of the Master of the Universe tenderly wiping the tearstained faces as a mother might her child's"; Oswalt, *Book of Isaiah*, 465.

571   H. M. Wolf, *Interpreting Isaiah. The Suffering and Glory of the Messiah* (Grand Rapids: Academic Press, 1985), 141.

572   S. Pisarek tells about the development of biblical revelation concerning the life after death. According to him the ideas that the Israelites were about life after death at the beginning were very dark and ambiguous. Only later revelation of the resurrection, repaying after death and immortality shed more light on the shadow of the issues of the life and death. The final solution to this problem was to, however, bring the New Testament; S. Pisarek, "Życie i śmierć," in *Vademecum biblijne*, IV (ed. S. Grzybek; Kraków 1991), 74.

573   See the discussion by B. Kulińska, "Pogląd na śmierć jako sen w Starym Testamencie," *SS* 6 (2002): 37–56. In the period before the exile, the ide of life after the death was not associated with the assessment of earthly deeds; ibid., 41.

Human happiness as a sign of God's blessing is seen rather in the temporal perspective. The Psalmist advises for us not to worry about the momentary success of a sinner: "Do not fret because of evil men or be envious of those who do wrong; for like the grass they will soon wither, like green plants they will soon die away" (Ps 37:1–2). During the period of exile and for some time after, it was believed that the dead in the Sheol did not have a separate consciousness (Ps 6:5; Job 3:11). The concept of eternal life in the strict sense introduces only sapiential literature. The author of the Book of Wisdom points out: "The souls of those who have pleased God are safe in his hands and protected from pain. Only in the minds of the foolish are those people dead and their death considered a disaster or destruction. In fact, they are at peace and destined never to die, though others may have thought they were being punished. The Lord will rule them forever and let them rule over nations" (cf. Wis 3:1–4.8). The author makes a clear distinction between the righteous and the sinners' posthumous fate. Those who lived rightfully "will understand truth and live with him in love, because God is kind and merciful to those he chooses to be his holy people. The wicked will be punished, as their evil thoughts deserve. They rebelled against the Lord and abused his people" (Wis 3:9–10). An important segment of science of immortality, namely, the motif of resurrection appears only in Daniel: "Multitudes who sleep in the dust of the earth will awake: some to everlasting life, others to shame and everlasting contempt. Those who are wise will shine like the brightness of the heavens, and those who lead many to righteousness, like the stars for ever and ever" (Dan 12:2–3). In the same manner, offering provided by Judah Maccabee for the dead insurgents should be interpreted: "He also took up a collection, man by man, to the amount of two thousand drachmas of silver, and sent it to Jerusalem to provide for a sin offering. In doing this he acted very well and honorably, taking account of the resurrection. For if he were not expecting that those who had fallen would rise again, it would have been superfluous and foolish to pray for the dead" (2 Macc 12:43–44).

Assuming these relatively late mentions of the resurrection, many exegetes refuse allusions to the resurrection in v. 8a.[574] Nevertheless, it is not so obvious if we read v. 8a in his close context, which has already been cited earlier (Isa 26:19).[575] Interpreting the last verse, especially the fragment "But your dead will

---

574 For example R. E. Clements claims: "The idea of the resurrection of the dead occurs in the Old Testament only as a very late idea (cf. Dan 12:2)"; quotation after: Grogan, "Isaiah," 160.

575 Marconcini, "L'apocalittica biblica," 220–221. Isaiah's passage gives hope that after the time of oppression and bad experience, in which the religious-ethnic community professing Judaism did not bear any fruit of life, God will give its lifeless members a new life; W. Linke, "Zmartwychwstanie Chrystusa i nasze według św. Pawła," in „Dla

live ...," the exegetes often resort to allegory, proving that the phrase refers to a spiritual awakening of the nation or Israel's independence.[576] To what extent, however, this allegorical interpretation is justified; it is not certain. Even those exegetes that accept a literal interpretation of Isa 26:19 believe that it is a text created very late (probably in the 2nd century B.C.) and added to the book during the final wording.[577] Besides some difficulties are raised by the statement: "but your dead will live" (יִחְיוּ מֵתֶיךָ): Does it mean that only those who belong to the Lord by keeping the covenant come to life or maybe all the dead? The v. 8a clearly accentuates the defeat of ("swallowing") death; however, the claim that there is a conscious allusion to the physical resurrection is almost unbelievable. Therefore, the mention of the defeat of death should be always read in a symbolic key. Additionally, it is not about the death in general, but a specific death, of which the presence of an article gives evidence. It is possible that this is a clear allusion to the exile often associated with the death.[578]

Vv. 9–12 The narrative, in the third part of Chapter 25, changes again into a song. It is introduced by וְאָמַר, but in this case, versions under consideration do not harmonize with one another. *1QIs*[a] reads: "you will say"; the Targum reads: "it shall be said"; and the LXX: καὶ ἐροῦσιν. It is a continuation of a song from vv. 1–5, but the image of the feast God had in vv. 6–8 makes it so that this song is sung before the throne of God. Again, there is a mention of the judgment, but this time the equivalent of "all nations" (vv. 1–5) is Moab. Direct context shows that the main motif of the song is a theme of withdrawal of dishonor from the chosen people. God is defined as the One: "we have waited for Him" (זֶה קִוִּינוּ לוֹ). The idea of waiting for God contains the theme of placing trust in Him. In this context, that thought is frequently present in Isaiah: "Yes, Lord, walking in the way of your laws, we wait for you; your name and renown are the desire of our hearts" (Isa 26:8); "O Lord, be gracious to us; we long for you. Be our strength every morning, our salvation in time of distress (literally: 'we wait for you'—קִוִּינוּ לְךָ)!" (Isa 33:2); "Even youths grow tired and weary, and young men stumble and fall; but those who hope in the Lord will renew their strength. They will soar on wings like

---

mnie żyć to Chrystus!". Rok świętego Pawła w parafii św. Jakuba w Skierniewicach (eds. J. Pietrzyk and M. Szmajdziński; Skierniewice 2009), 79.

576 Doorly, *Isaiah of Jerusalem*, 103–105.

577 S. Grzybek, "Zmartwychwstanie w świetle ksiąg St. Testamentu," in *Vademecum biblijne* (IV; ed. S. Grzybek; Kraków 1991), 162.

578 Lemański, *„Sprawisz, abym ożył!"*, 236. "… von Auferstehung spricht der Text nicht, wohl aber davon, dass Yahwehs Heilswillen keine Grenzen mehr gesetzt sind"; H. Wildberger, *Jesaja. Kapitel 13–27* (BK 10,2; Neukirchen–Vluyn 1989[2]), 963.

eagles; they will run and not grow weary, they will walk and not be faint (literally: 'who hope in the Lord'—וְקֹוֵי יְהוָה)" (Isa 40:30–31).

The last part of v. 9 contains a call for the joy of salvation given by God. His salutary help is the basis for the hope of Israel. While the mentions of saving acts of God in the OT often relate to the past, especially the exodus, here the hope is developed into the future. It is about worshiping God for the gifts which will be given to Israel and the whole of humanity. They are announced in vv. 6–8. The motif of salvation is one of the favorite themes of Isaiah (Isa 12:2–3; 33:2–6; 49:6.8; 51:6.8; 52:710; 56:1; 59:11.17; 60:18; 62:1).[579] There are specific similarities between this fragment and Isa 12:2–3. The similarities result from linking the themes of confidence and joy: "Surely God is my salvation; I will trust and not be afraid. The Lord, the Lord, is my strength and my song; he has become my salvation." With joy you will draw water from the wells of salvation."

The image of the Lord's hand resting on Mount Zion means a blessing. What is more, the image of the "hand of Yahweh" can be often found in Isaiah (1:25; 11:11; 19:16; 40:2; 41:20; 59:1; 64:7; 66:2.14). The hand of the Lord will rest on the mountain that is on Zion, because prophets took a liking to this very mountain as the scene of apocalyptic events. According to the prophets, from that place the news of the deliverance will come: "You who bring good tidings to Zion, go up on a high mountain. You who bring good tidings to Jerusalem, lift up your voice with a shout, lift it up, do not be afraid; say to the towns of Judah, 'Here is your God!'" (Isa 40:9); A specified place of gathering of all nations will also be there: "In the last days the mountain of the Lord's temple will be established as chief among the mountains; it will be raised above the hills, and all nations will stream to it" (Isa 2:2; cf. Jer 3:16; Mic 4:1–4). The same Yahweh's hand will, however, crush Moab, which will be trampled: "but Moab will be trampled under him as straw is trampled down in the manure" (v. 10b; כְּהִדּוּשׁ מַתְבֵּן בְּמֹו מַדְמֵנָה). Inconvenient, in this case is the lesson *Ketib*: "in the water" (בְּמֹי); thus the version *Qere* is preferable because it is limited to "in." Besides, בְּמֹו מַדְמֵנָה creates a kind of play on words with the name of the Moabite city, Madmen: "Moab will be praised no more; in Heshbon men will plot her downfall: 'Come, let us put an end to that nation.' You too, O Madmen, will be silenced; the sword will pursue you" (Jer 48:2). We should not forget about geographic nearness of Mount Zion and the mountains of Moab; the latter could be easily visible on a clear day from the hills of Jerusalem, and that is why they could have become "representative" of all the heathen. In any case, Moab is still regarded as a hostile nation to Israel as it was during the Exodus (Num

---

579   J. Salguero, "Concetto biblico di salvezza-liberazione," *Ang* 53 (1976): 11–55.

22:2–7) and later. The motif of trampling the enemy is common in the OT and reflects the well-known tradition, not only in Israel but also throughout the Middle East (Josh 10:24; Isa 51:23; Ps 89:11; 110:1). Changing the grammatical third person to the second one in v. 12 shifts the emphasis from Moab to the more universal perspective. It is difficult to determine what the walls of Moab symbolize. It can be a picture of the entire nation or just only its pride.[580]

2.3. Contribution of v. 8a to Isa 25:1–12

A fragment from Isa 25:8a (בִּלַּע הַמָּוֶת לָנֶצַח), which Paul cites in 1 Cor 15:54b in the form of κατεπόθη ὁ θάνατος εἰς νῖκος, belongs to the main body of Isa 25. This chapter is in turn a part of the *Apocalypse of Isaiah* (Isa 24–27). The main part of Isa 25 describes the eschatological feast on Mount Zion, which God prepared for people ("all nations"). This part was placed between two songs: the thanksgiving song of the saved (vv. 1–5) and the song of joy of survivors (vv. 9–12). The location of v. 8a embeds it into the atmosphere of the eschatological joy and gratitude. The feast which God prepared will be accompanied by tearing off from the human faces all veils which covered them and a shroud which was stretched over-all nations (v. 7). The mentions about covers over peoples' faces and about the shroud, according to the customs prevailing on the ancient Near East, may bring to mind the image of pain and even death. On the other hand, tearing them off can mean overcoming the death. Such is the meaning of v. 8a. This interpretation confirms another mention placed in the context of the next verse. It is the notice of God wiping away tears from all faces (v. 8b). It should be noted that tears appear on faces of residents of the Fertile Crescent more often than in our Western culture, and may indicate feelings associated with different circumstances. It is also associated in a completely natural way with the experience of death. Therefore, wiping away tears symbolizes the elimination of this experience either by consoling oneself to death or—as the context suggests—through the eschatological victory over it.

Basically, the content of v. 8a is based on the assurance that death will be defeated. This victory over the death, its "swallowing," is the dominant motif for celebration of the feast. Contribution of v. 8a to Isa 25:6–8, as well as to a more broad context (Isa 25:1–12), still leaves, however, some unsolved difficulties. At least, two issues are simply uncertain: whether the aforementioned death is personified, and if in v. 8a, there is a direct allusion to the resurrection. Within the immediate context, it is impossible to find an answer to any of these

---

580 Stachowiak, *Księga Izajasza 1–39*, 375.

questions, but reaching for a larger one (but still within the *Apocalypse of Isaiah*), suggests them.

Let us first deal with the issue of personification of the death. One of the most important (although not necessary) aforementioned elements of apocalypses is a message of defeating mythical creatures.[581] For example, in Isa 27:1 there is a reference to the Lord defeating Leviathan: "on that day, the Lord will punish with his sword, his fierce, great and powerful sword, Leviathan the gliding serpent, Leviathan the coiling serpent; he will slay the monster of the sea." Leviathan is known from Ugaritic mythology, in which it was portrayed as an ancient sea monster named Lotan. It fought on the side of underworld god Mot, and was defeated. This tradition was taken over by the biblical authors who have shown God as the conqueror of sea monsters. It not only concerns Isa 27:1 but also other texts: "It was you who split open the sea by your power; you broke the heads of the monster in the waters. It was you who crushed the heads of Leviathan and gave him as food to the creatures of the desert" (Ps 74:13–14).[582] If the *Apocalypse of Isaiah* describes the defeat of the mythical creature, Leviathan, which is shown personally, we may make a conjecture that the death is herein personified. This assumption, however, though highly probable, cannot be taken for granted because the mere mention of the Leviathan is one of the qualifications of Isa 24–27 to the genre of apocalypses. Therefore it is not necessary to enter another character and draw a parallel. Besides, the personified death is not a mythical character but the authors of the Bible tend to see it as a spirit of death.

The second important question about v. 8a is whether it is possible to see in this verse an allusion to the resurrection. The motif of the resurrection is also one of the essential elements of apocalypses (like the theme of defeating of the personal force of evil). In Isaiah, 24–27 this motif is present in the announcement: "But your dead will live; their bodies will rise. You who dwell in the dust, wake up and shout for joy. Your dew is like the dew of the morning; the earth will give birth to her dead" (Isa 26:19). If there is an announcement of the physical resurrection of the dead in this passage, and not the symbolic declaration of independence by Israel, then we should accept the later origin of this verse. In his context, however, we can see in Isa 25:8 an allusion to the resurrection of the dead. Nevertheless, his hypothesis—as shown above—is unlikely.

---

581   Doorly, *Isaiah of Jerusalem*, 97–99.
582   Cf. also: Job 3:8; 26:12–13; 41:1–34; Ps 104:26; J. Unterman, *"Lewiatan,"* in *Encyklopedia biblijna* (ed. P. J. Achtemeier; trans. Z. Kościuk; Warszawa 1999), 668–669.

3. The Meaning in 1 Cor 15:54–56

To determine the interpretation of a quote from Isa 25:8 in v. 54b we should examine the context of these verses. In v. 54 Paul continues the mentioned above oppositions ("perishable"–"imperishable"; "mortal"–"immortality"),[583] but this time in a time sentence: "When the perishable has been clothed with the imperishable, and the mortal with immortality, then the saying that is written will come true: 'Death has been swallowed up in victory'" (v. 54; ὅταν δὲ τὸ φθαρτὸν τοῦτο ἐνδύσηται ἀφθαρσίαν καὶ τὸ θνητὸν τοῦτο ἐνδύσηται ἀθανασίαν, τότε γενήσεται ὁ λόγος ὁ γεγραμμένος· κατεπόθη ὁ θάνατος εἰς νῖκος). The last part of the verse is a quotation from Isa 25:8a. In the version written down by Paul it reads: κατεπόθη ὁ θάνατος εἰς νῖκος. This quote is preceded by an extensive introductory formula: τότε γενήσεται ὁ λόγος ὁ γεγραμμένος. This formula also introduces a quotation from Hos 13:14b put down in v. 55 and joined editorially with a quote from Isa 25:8a.

From the point of view of textual criticism, it should be noted that some manuscripts contain a shorter version of this verse. Probably, it came into being by: *homoioarcton* or *homoioteleuton* (ℵ*, 088, 0121a, 0243, 1739*, it[ar], Vulg., cop[sams, bo], goth, eth, Marcion, Irenaeus[gr, lat], *al*).[584] It should also be accepted that other modifications result from the attempt to correct these omissions. Some scribes made efforts to restore the original version and yet a different sequence of used terms occurs within new settings. There are also proofs bearing witness to the fact that in some cases a verse is omitted entirely (F, G, 614*, 1877*, it[g], cop[boms]), a verse that should be explained by *homoioteleuton* from v. 53. Consequently, the most likely is a lesson quoted above. The antithesis between the perishable and the imperishable or mortal and immortal has already been introduced in vv. 52–53, but herein it begins the anthemic unit. As a result, v. 57 takes a tone of prayer. What is more, the hymn of victory itself is marked by pathos.[585] The transformation of the perishable and the imperishable or the mortal and the immortal will constitute the prophetic fulfillment: הַמָּוֶת לָנֶצַח

---

583 K. Usami explains the nature of the opposition ("perishable"–"imperishable"): "The opposition 'corruptible–incorruptibility' does not simply mean an overcoming of the decay of every human body which is dead, but indicates 'eschatological,' 'everlasting' incorruptibility, related to God's new creation"; "How Are the Dead Rised?," 483.

584 Metzger, *Textual Commentary*, 502.

585 A. S. Jasiński notices that the final hymn (15:54–57) aims to summarize the formal arguments. At the same time, it is a wonderful Christian prayer exalting the victory of life over death; A. S. Jasiński, *Jezus jest Panem. Kyriologia Nowego Testamentu* (Wrocław 1996), 19.

בְּלַע (Isa 25:8a). This transformation will ultimately lead to the resurrection.[586] Since at present, believers live between two resurrections: Christ and their own.[587]

In the resurrection of the faithful, they will realize the prophetic declaration: "Death has been swallowed up in victory." The author of the apocryphal Fourth Book of Maccabees also recalls a similar translation. The book describes the martyrdom of the first of seven brothers (description parallel to 2 Macc 7:4–7). Greek rhetoric recommended flamboyance of description, and this principle had also been applied to describe tortures: "Although the ligaments joining his bones were already severed, the courageous youth, worthy of Abraham, did not groan, but as though transformed by fire into immortality he nobly endured the rackings" (*4 Macc.* 9:21–22).[588] The same book also mentions about "immortality in endless life" (*4 Macc.* 17:12).

It is worth noting Paul's use of the verb "to wear." It is possible that we can find an echo of rabbinical debates herein. One of them was written in the *Sanhedrin* treatise: "Samaritan patriarch asked Rabbi Meir: 'I know that the dead will revive, ... But when they arise, shall they arise nude or in their garments?' — He replied, 'Thou mayest deduce by an *a fortiori* argument [the answer] from a wheat grain: if a grain of wheat, which is buried naked, sprouteth forth in many robes, how much more so the righteous, who are buried in their raiment!'" (*Sanh.* 90b; cf. *midrQoh* 1:10:27b).[589]

The term νῖκος occurs in the NT only four times, including three times in 1 Cor.[590] In Matt 12:20, there is a quotation from Isa 42:3: "A bruised reed he will

---

586 In that way Theophilus of Antioch interpreted the verse in his letter *To Autolycus:* "But before all let faith and the fear of God have rule in thy heart, and then shalt thou understand these things. When thou shalt have put off the mortal, and put on incorruption, then shall thou see God worthily. For God will raise thy flesh immortal with thy soul; and then, having become immortal, thou shalt see the Immortal, if now you believe on Him"; (*Aut.* 1:7).

587 The belivers "live in the midst of an age which is still evil, but which can be endured and overcome by the sure confidence that Christ's resurrection experience and victory over death as the last Adam will be shared by them because they are in Christ (1 Cor 15:42–54)"; S. J. Hafemann, "Corinthians, Letters to," in *Dictionary of Paul and His Letters. A Compendium of Contemporary Biblical Scholarship* (eds. G. F. Hawthorne and R. P. Martin; Dovners Grove–Leicester 1993), 167.

588 M. Wojciechowski, *Apokryfy z Biblii greckiej. 3 i 4 Księga Machabejska, 3 Księga Ezdrasza oraz Psalm 151 i Modlitwa Manassesa* (Rozprawy i Studia Biblijne 8; Warszawa 2001), 168.

589 Stern, *Komentarz*, 689; Morissette, "La condition de ressucité," 212.

590 R. Morgenthaler, *Statistik des Neuestestamentlichen Wortschatzes* (Zürich–Stuttgart 1972), 123.

not break, and a smoldering wick he will not snuff out. In faithfulness he will bring forth justice." Matthew, however, does not follow the text of the HB exactly as it reads: "A bruised reed he will not break, and a smoldering wick he will not snuff out, till he leads justice to victory." He is also not in harmony with the LXX because in this text the verse is as follows: κάλαμον τεθλασμένον οὐ συντρίψει καὶ λίνον καπνιζόμενον οὐ σβέσει ἀλλὰ εἰς ἀλήθειαν ἐξοίσει κρίσιν. Speaking about victory is based on a different part of the text, or it is an editorial adaptation of Matthew. It is important, however, that the evangelist inserted a mention in the quotation that was taken from the first song of The Servant of the Lord (Isa 42:1–9) and which he relates entirely to Jesus. It is Jesus who is proclaimed as the Servant of the Lord, who would win. The context is thus corresponding to what we may find in v. 54: "Death has been swallowed up in victory." It means that death has been defeated by Christ, who is victorious over it, and consequently, he gives part in this triumph to all who believe in him. The other two instances of the term "victory" refers to the current context (v. 55 and v. 57). Thus every time the NT uses the noun "victory," it refers to Christ's victory.[591]

In the next chapter, we are going to deal with the quote from Hos 13:14b, which constitutes the whole v. 55. In this chapter, the quote is as important in the present analysis because it has an influence on the interpretation of Isa 25:8b. It should be mentioned that both citations have the same formula quotation: τότε γενήσεται ὁ λόγος ὁ γεγραμμένος. The apostle editorially combines both quotes adding to the fragment from Isaiah the rhetorical questions: "Where, O death, is your victory? Where, O death, is your sting?" (v. 55; ποῦ σου, θάνατε, τὸ νῖκος; ποῦ σου, θάνατε, τὸ κέντρον;).[592] Paul turns to the death as a personal being; it is emphasized by the use of the second person singular. Changing both HB and the LXX, he asks the death about its victory and its sting. The term "sting" herein should be understood as a tool to stimulate the animals rather than a "poison." Since they are rhetorical questions, it becomes clear to the apostle that the death has been defeated. It has not achieved any victory and no longer can stimulate the human situation, as the sting disciplines animals.

Explaining what the sting of death is, the apostle shows the interrelationship between death, sin, and the Law: "The sting of death is sin, and the power of sin is the law" (v. 56; τὸ δὲ κέντρον τοῦ θανάτου ἡ ἁμαρτία, ἡ δὲ δύναμις τῆς

---

591   Jamieson, Fausset and Brown, *Commentary*, 333.
592   J. Gillmann, "A Thematic Comparison: 1 Cor 15:50–57 and 2 Cor 5:1–5," *JBL* 107 (1988): 445.

ἁμαρτίας ὁ νόμος).[593] Some exegetes were convinced that the whole verse was a marginal gloss incorporated into the body of the text by one of the copyists.[594] Nevertheless, there are no sufficient arguments that would maintain this thesis. Paul affirms herein what he wrote about in Romans: "Did that which is good, then, become death to me? By no means! But in order that sin might be recognized as sin, it produced death in me through what was good, so that through the commandment sin might become utterly sinful" (Rom 7:13). The apostle undoubtedly undermines the saving power of the Law.[595] One can also make a hint of the Greco-Roman world in which the law did not provide justice as well.[596] The explanation that a sin is the sting of death is a part of subject matter often taken up by Paul. He explained to Romans that "For the wages of sin is death" (Rom 6:23). With regard to this case, it is not about particular sins of individuals, but rather about a more general principle. The death is a result of the sin of our first parents, and it has to touch all of us.

The sin of our first parents resulted essentially in three effects: the death, current sins and every form of suffering.[597] The author of Genesis in many different ways represents the effects of the sin of Adam and Eve: "Then the eyes of both of them were opened, and they realized they were naked" (Gen 3:7); "To the woman he said, 'I will greatly increase your pains in childbearing; with pain you will give birth to children. Your desire will be for your husband, and he will rule over you'" (Gen 3:16); "To Adam he said, 'Because you listened to your wife and ate from the tree about which I commanded you, You must not eat of it, Cursed is the ground because of you; through painful toil you will eat of it all the days of your life. It will produce thorns and thistles for you, and you will eat the plants of the field. By the sweat of your brow you will eat your food until you return to the ground, since from it you were taken; for dust you are and to

---

593 Cenci, *La nostra risurrezione è una certezza!*, 86.

594 Alike: F. W. Horn, "1 Korinther 15,56 – ein exegetische Stachel," *ZNW* 82 (1991): 88–105.

595 T. Söding, "'Die Kraft der Sünde ist das Gesetz' (1 Kor 15,56). Anmerkungen zum Hintergrund und zur Pointe einer gesetzeskritischen Sentenz des Apostels Paulus," *ZNW* 83 (1992): 74–84.

596 H. W. Hollander and J. Holleman, "The Relationship of Death, Sin and Law in 1 Cor 15,56," *NT* 35 (1993): 290–291.

597 According to R. Rogowski, as a result of an original sin all descendents of Adam and Eve are born deprived other preternatural gifts (*praeternaturalia*). Tradition used to speak of injuries inflicted on human nature by the original sin. The first one was the body's wound, so the disease, physical suffering and death. The second one—a spiritual wound; *ABC teologii dogmatycznej* (eds. S. J. Stasiak, R. Zawiła and A. Małachowski: Wrocław 1999⁴), 60.

dust you will return'" (Gen 3:17–19).[598] Theologians are still discussing the relationship that exists between the disobedience of the first humans and physical death. Doubtless death is the result of the sin. At least two Genesis texts give evidence that it is true: "And the Lord God commanded the man, 'You are free to eat from any tree in the garden; but you must not eat from the tree of the knowledge of good and evil, for when you eat of it you will surely die'" (Gen 2:16–17) and "The woman said to the serpent, 'We may eat fruit from the trees in the garden, but God did say, You must not eat fruit from the tree that is in the middle of the garden, and you must not touch it, or you will die'" (Gen 3:2–3).

This discussion oscillates between the questions, whether God has planned physical death or not? Would people die physically, if they did not sin or would they be subject to the law of death? The traditional answer to this question is unequivocal: the man in paradise was blessed with the gift of immortality, including his body[599]. In this sense, spiritual death is the separation of human spirit from God, who is also a Spirit. The physical death is the death of the human body. Today, however, the opposite opinions appear, claiming that even in paradise a man was subject to the law of physical death, but God did not intend for people any spiritual death. Dying, which was included in God's plan was to consist in the quiet and slow transition to another state of existence. The transition was to be devoid of pain, suffering and dilemmas associated with separation from the intimates. Otherwise the piling up of difficulties are much greater than the benefits of theological truth about "existence in Paradise," enforcing the concept of the lack of some kind of "transition" towards eternity. By contrast, understanding and presenting the existence of our first parents before their sin, as free from passing and "transition," and therefore not subject to the laws of time, raises the possibility of specific mythologizing of the demythologized biblical message.[600] Such an understanding can be a kind of attempt to reverse the mythical concepts, according to which man has been

---

598   J. H. Sailhamer, "Genesis," in *The Expositor's Bible Commentary with The New International Version* (ed. F. E. Gaebelein II; Grand Rapids 1990), 49–57.

599   *Catechism of the Catholic Church* formulates the truth as follows: "Death is a consequence of sin. The Church's Magisterium, as an authentic interpreter of the affirmations of the Scripture and Tradition, teaches that death entered the world on account of man's sin. Even though man's nature is mortal God destined him not to die. Death was therefore contrary to the plans of God the Creator and entered the world as a consequence of sin. Death of the body, from which man would be independent if he had not sinned, is thus 'the last enemy' of man left to be conquered" (CCC 1008).

600   W. Chrostowski, "Czy Adam i Ewa mieli się nie starzeć i nie umierać? Egzegetyczny przyczynek do nauczania o nieśmiertelności pierwszych ludzi," in *Verbum caro fatum est. Księga Pamiątkowa dla Księdza Profesora Tomasza Jelonka w 70. rocznicę urodzin* (ed. R. Bogacz and W. Chrostowski; Warszawa 2007), 178–179.

seeking immortality for centuries. These concepts were known in the ancient Near East. The Sumerian myth entitled *Enki and Ninhursag* describes Dilmun, a place of pleasure and enjoyment. In this place there are not any diseases, evil or suffering. The Babylonians called Dilmun a "place of life" because according to their beliefs, in that place immortality reigned: "In Dilmun the raven was not yet cawing, the partridge not cackling. The lion did not slay, ... No eye-diseases said there: 'I am the eye disease.' No headache said there: 'I am the headache.' No old woman belonging to it said there: 'I am an old woman.' No old man belonging to it said there: 'I am an old man.'"[601]

Similar are the words of the ancient epic poem of Gilgamesh. It describes the journey of the main character and his friend Enkidu to the place where there is immortality. Immortality is expected to be assured by a mysterious plant, about which Gilgamesh learns from Utnapishtim. There are a lot of similar mythical stories, but we do not need to deal with them in our work. For Christian faith,[602] the physical death is not the biggest problem, but spiritual one, which means eternal separation from God and the state of condemnation.

According to Paul a sin is "sting of death" (κέντρον τοῦ θανάτου).[603] The term "sting" should be understood as a tool for driving animals. Although herein, understanding of the noun as "poison" is acceptable; however, in this context it is less likely.[604] The concept of death existing in some trends of Greek philosophy (Socrates exemplifies it) depicts the death as a gentle and soothing transition to another level of existence, but it does not adhere to the truth about man's sinful nature. The man is subject to death because he is wrongful. Death itself is terrible. Through the paschal events, the death and resurrection of Christ took "sting" of death away. Regardless of whether God planned physical death as a smooth transition to another dimension, or whether it is not intended as a consequence of our first parents' sin; beyond a doubt, after the death of Christ, it took entirely new meaning. The believer in Christ is the one who "die to the Lord" (Rom 14:7; cf. Phil 1:20). Physical resurrection of all bodies is the final

---

601 J. S. Synowiec, *Na początku. Wybrane zagadnienia Pięcioksięgu* (Warszawa 1987), 178.

602 Chrostowski, "Czy Adam i Ewa mieli się nie starzeć i nie umierać?," 179.

603 "According to Paul, there is a clear connection between death and sin, between the power of death and the power of sin, both being active in the life of mankind"; Hollander and Holleman, "Relationship of Death, Sin and Law," 277.

604 If we assume that Paul refers to "poison" (in the sense the term κέντρον is found in Aesop's fables and Rev 9:10), Paul's way of thinking would be as follows: owing to the death of Christ and His resurrection, people's death has lost its poison; Thiselton, *First Epistle to the Corinthians*, 1300; Henry, *Commentary*, 2276.

scenario. The Christians, by the resurrection of their bodies, enter into lives in which "there will be no more death" (Rev 21:4).[605]

Another important explanation of Paul's is: "the power of sin [is] the law" (ἡ δὲ δύναμις τῆς ἁμαρτίας ὁ νόμος). The relationship between sin and the law is a frequent subject of Pauline arguments. The theme also contains faith coverage. This subject is significant not only from a theological point of view; for Paul, it was important on the grounds that he had a personal interest in it. After all, he was educated to be a Pharisee, and they attached crucial importance to the Law. From among the whole impressive number of Jewish political parties present on the religious arena in the first century, it was mostly the Pharisees that stressed the importance of the law. They not only attached importance to the written Torah, but also to the oral Torah, which—as they believed—Moses received on Sinai just as the written Torah. Saul of Tarsus, educated in Jerusalem by Gamaliel, became a Pharisee in the first quarter of the 1st century. It was a time, when the Pharisees began to create "a wall around the Law," which was developed by their successors—the rabbis, after the year 90. Acts of the Law had become to the Pharisees and all the religious Jews a path that leads to God. Particular emphasis was placed on keeping the rules of ritual purity. After meeting with the Risen Christ, Paul's understanding of the relationship between the Law and sin changed. The apostle realized the truth that he penned in Galatians: "know that a man is not justified by observing the law, but by faith in Jesus Christ. So we, too, have put our faith in Christ Jesus that we may be justified by faith in Christ and not by observing the law, because by observing the law no one will be justified" (Gal 2:16). So the Law according to Paul was presented as not having the strength to protect[606] people against sin. Moreover, the Law became just the "power of sin."

Similar ideas can be found in the philosophical thought of ancient Greeks. There is a possibility that the depravity of people indicated by philosophers induced Paul to relate the idea of the law to sin and in consequence, to death.

---

605   P. Grelot, "Śmierć," in *Słownik teologii biblijnej* (ed. X. Léon-Dufour; trans. K. Romaniuk; Poznań–Warszawa 1973), 948–949.

606   Some exegetes claim that because Paul speaks of sin in general hence the phrase "Law" should be treated as general one as well, not just in relation to the Law of the OT. Taking this point of view, the phrase: "the power of sin is the law" in its elucidation refers to the sophistic conception opposing the nature and the law; Hollander and Holleman, "The Relationship of Death, Sin and Law," 279–289. For more on the relationship of sin to the idea of law, see: F. Mickiewicz, "Zagadnienia etyczne," in *Teologia Nowego Testamentu*, III, *Listy Pawłowe, Katolickie i List do Hebrajczyków* (ed. M. Rosik; Bibliotheca Biblica; Wrocław 2008), 323–328; H. Langkammer, *Teologia biblijna Starego i Nowego Testamentu* (BDL 29; Legnica 2007), 390–392.

Similarly to Philo of Alexandria, Paul agrees that the corruption of humanity already has its origin in Adam. However, while the Alexandrian perceives the Jewish Law to be the solution to the problem sin and death to humanity, Paul presents this issue differently. The apostle denies that the law has any power to lead humanity to improvement and salvation. A similar line of thought was represented by cynics who used to speak of the Law in general, not the Jewish Law.[607]

Summing up this part of these considerations, we should note that the quote "death swallowed up in victory" (Isa 25:8 a) in v. 54b recalls the prophecy that will be fulfilled in the future. This will be done during the resurrection of the believers, or at the time when the perishable becomes imperishable, and the mortal turn into immortality. It is expected that in those days, death will not be enjoyed the final triumph, and its sting, which is sin, will lose its power. The strength of sin is the law that gives awareness to the sinner about his inability to overcome sin. Thus, the law makes humanity aware of sin. The sin is in turn a sting of death: in Christ, however, the death has already been defeated, and eventually it will be swallowed by "victory" during the resurrection of the believers.

---

607 Hollander and Holleman, "Relationship of Death, Sin and Law," 289–291.

VII. Quotation from Hos 13:14b in 1 Cor 15:55

1 Cor 15:55: ποῦ σου, θάνατε, τὸ νῖκος; ποῦ σου, θάνατε, τὸ κέντρον;

Hos 13:14b (LXX): ποῦ ἡ δίκη σου θάνατε ποῦ τὸ κέντρον σου ᾅδη;

Hos 13:14b (HB): אֱהִי דְבָרֶיךָ מָוֶת אֱהִי קָטָבְךָ שְׁאוֹל

1. Source of the Quotation

In 1 Cor 15:55 there is the problem of determining the original text. The sequence "victory ... sting" is certified by the P[46], a*, B, C, 1739*[vid], Vulg., cop[sa, bo], al. Other versions instead of the death mention about Hades (a[c], A[c], K, P, Y, 88, 104, 614, Byz, syr[p, h], goth, arm, al). The first version seems to be better authenticated. HB text literally reads as follows: "Death, where is your sting? Hades, where is your destruction?"[608] In the LXX, the first question refers to punishment. The second question, on the other hand, is a rhetorical question, including the word Hades: "Where is your punishment, O death? Where is your sting, O hades?" So the Apostle changes "punishment" from the LXX to "victory" and "Hades" to "death." Changing the order of words within a sentence is motivated by the rhetorical aims.[609]

From the point of view of textual criticism, it should be noted that some versions in which the term "Hades" is used in 1 Cor 15:55, constitute attempts to make Paul's text similar to the LXX; Paul himself never uses the term.[610] Although the quote written by Paul differs both from the LXX and the HB, it seems to be closer to the Greek text. A source of this quote, therefore, must have been taken from the LXX, although to this text, Paul introduced some corrections motivated by rhetorical reasons.[611]

---

608 *Hebrajsko-polski Stary Testament. Prorocy. Przekład interlinearny z kodami gramatycznymi, transliteracją i indeksem słów hebrajskich* (ed. A. Kuśmirek; Warszawa 2008), 1427.

609 Thiselton, *First Epistle to the Corinthians*, 1299.

610 Metzger, *Textual Commentary*, 503.

611 According to R. B. Terry, Paul follows the LXX, that "has a significantly different reading than the Masoretic Text"; id., *Discourse Analysis*, 158. E. E. Ellis, on the other hand believes that in Paul's citation "there is only a slight variation from the LXX"; id., "Paul's Use of the Old Testament," 150.

2. The Meaning in the Original Context

The quotation inserted by Paul into v. 55 was taken from the final fragment of Hosea.[612] In the original context, the questions quoted by Paul are as follows: אֱהִי דְבָרֶיךָ מָוֶת אֱהִי קָטָבְךָ שְׁאוֹל (Hos 13:14b). These questions are part of the section devoted to the theme of destruction of the kingdom of Israel that turned out to be sinful from the very beginning to its existence. Hos 13:12 and 14:1 appoints textual limits of this section.[613] Looking for the meanings of the fragment that Paul quoted in 1 Cor, first we ought to carry out the exegetical analysis of the section of Hos 13:1– 14:1.[614]

2.1. Ideological Base and the Literary Structure in Hos 13:12–14:1

One of the final parts of the Book of Hosea (Hos 13:12–14:1) shows the guilt of Israel and stresses that it cannot remain without punishment. As people do not make atonement for their sins therefore, they will find misfortune. The prophet speaks in his own name and refers both to Israel (Ephraim) and to God himself. The central part of this fragment makes up the words of Yahweh: "I will ransom them from the power of the grave; I will redeem them from death" (13:14). Herein God appears as the Saviour. This statement is to encourage recipients to take an interest in their own destiny. The recipients, however, are absent; they cannot hear God's word (God speaks to them in the third-person plural), and this

---

612 Gądecki, *Wstęp*, 83.

613 The words used in periscope Hos 13: 12–14:1, which cover the analyzed herein utterance included in Hos 13:14, constitute a summary of warnings and threats directed at Israel/Ephraim a lot of times. They predict the destruction of the rumps of the independent state. So the words fit perfectly in the period before the fall of Samaria and the final disappearance of the Northern Kingdom in 722–721 B.C., or simply refer to this as a fact that had already occurred; Lemański, *„Sprawisz, abym ożył!"*, 185.

614 This passage has been the subject of interest from the Fathers of the Church, who often interpreted it metaphorically. Gregory of Nazianzus saw in it showing of insignificance of human life, which is similar to a cloud and vapor. Hilary emphasized the creative power of God. Gregory the Great believed that the blame for people's sins should be put on their bad leaders. He also saw here a reference to Christ's victory over death. Augustine believed that this passage speaks of the defeat of death, although the body makes difficult to lead a clean life; *I dodici profeti* (La Bibbia Commentata dai Padri. Antico Testamento 13; ed. A. Ferreiro; trans. M. Conti; Roma 2005), 79–83.

leads to a bitter conclusion which is the announcement of their punishment.[615] This passage is an integral part of the entire book in the sense that its unity within the text has never been questioned. This is true even if it is sometimes considered as a work of an epigone that was true to the prophet's memory. It fits perfectly into the historical background of Hosea's activity and therefore, a crisis in which the monarchy found itself in the second half of the 8th century B.C. (after many years of economic and political expansion of Jeroboam II, successive rulers change very quickly). Nevertheless, you cannot refer directly to a specific historical event, since it constitutes Yahweh's lamentation because of breaking God's ties with Ephraim. The lamentation is of a general nature. The part of Hos 12–14 provides a synthesis of the history of Israel, which determines the prospects for the future. Ephraim committed the sin of idolatry, and it made sacrifices from people (Hos 13:1–3); it forgot about its God who had chosen it in the desert (Hos 13:4–6), so it should be punished (Hos 13:12–14:1). It is possible that the punishment in its longer term will contribute to the conversion of Ephraim (Hos 14:2–10).

The structure of the analysed fragment determines its elements of content. First, God through the prophet affirms the sin of the chosen people (13:12–13) and then uses a rhetorical question regarding the possibility of deliverance of Ephraim from death (13:14). Subsequently, God portends punishment for Ephraim/Samaria (13:15–14:1). Taking into account the criteria of content, the structure of prophetic oracles can be determined based on three elements:

1. The sin of Ephraim (13:12–13);
2. Question for deliverance from death (13:14);
3. Announcing of the inevitable punishment (13:15–14:1).

2.2. Exegetical Analysis Hos 13:12–14:1

13:12–13 In this section, the author uses a very vivid language with which he presents the dialectic of blame and punishment for committed sin. The prophet reaches for two images of fertility, one derived from the human world and the other one from vegetative life.[616] Both images serve to show the tension between "sins" and "the punishment." Verse 12 speaks about the collective sin of Israel:

---

615 H. Simian-Yofre, "Księga Ozeasza," in *Międzynarodowy komentarz do Pisma Świętego. Komentarz katolicki i ekumeniczny na XXI wiek* (ed. W. R. Farmer; Polish ed. W. Chrostowski; trans. E. Burska; Warszawa 2001²), 1002.

616 J. S. Rogers sees in the figurativeness "more than picturesque speech"; J. S. Rogers, "Hosea," in *Mercer Commentary on the Bible* (eds. W. E. Millo and R. F. Wilson; Macon 1995), 733.

"The guilt of Ephraim is stored up, his sins are kept on record." The content contained herein was opposed to the one comprised in Ps 32:1: "Blessed is he whose transgressions are forgiven, whose sins are covered." If wickedness, and at the same time human sins, are hidden, it means that they cannot be forgiven. To receive God's forgiveness people should first confess their sins.[617] The name of Ephraim replaces here the name of all Israel; semantic shifts in the meaning of the term Ephraim follow gradually. Ephraim was the younger son of Joseph coming from the mother Asenath. Jacob blessed him before his brother Manasseh (Gen 46:1–20)[618]. With time, the tribe of Ephraim began to gain importance. In Joshua 16:4, the author goes from determining the territory of Joseph to its replacement by two territories: Ephraim and Manasseh. The lands of Ephraim were better protected than the lands of Manasseh. In the middle of the 8th century B.C., in Isaiah and Hosea, Ephraim was presented as synonymous with the whole of the Northern Kingdom. On the territory of Ephraim, there were older cult centres: Bethel, Shiloh, and Shechem. In Hosea, Ephraim is also the unfaithful partner of a covenant with God: "I know all about Ephraim; Israel is not hidden from me. Ephraim, you have now turned to prostitution; Israel is corrupt" (Hos 5:3; cf. also the whole fragment from Hos 5:3–14).[619] The prophet compares Israel to the newborn infant, and at the same time to his mother: "Pains as of a woman in childbirth come to him, but he is a child without wisdom; when the time arrives, he does not come to the opening of the womb" (v. 13). The nation could be like a child who is born unconscious. Nevertheless, the day comes in which the child begins his conscious life. Only then, it turns out that his mother's birthing pains were not in vain. Otherwise, the beginning of life is synonymous with victory of death, because human existence is seen as a journey from the womb to the grave. For this reason, Job lamented, "Why then did you bring me out of the womb? I wish I had died before any eye saw me. If only I had never come into being, or had been carried straight from the womb to the grave!" (Job 10:18–19). A comparison of Israel to the nascent child and his mother signed up strongly in the prophetic tradition.[620] Isaiah

---

617   E. B. Pusey, *The Minor Prophets. A Commentary* (BN; Grand Rapids 1885), 132.

618   This is a continuation of the well-known paradigm in the Bible, according to which the younger son becomes the heir, not the older one (Abel, Isaac, Jacob, Joseph, etc.)]; C. S. Ehrlich, "Efraim," in *Słownik wiedzy biblijnej* (eds. B. M. Metzger and M. D. Coogan; Polish ed. W. Chrostowski; trans. T. Kowalska; Warszawa 1996), 140–141.

619   E. F. Campbell, "Efraim," in *Encyklopedia biblijna* (ed. P. J. Achtemeier; trans. M. Wojciechowski; Warszawa 1999), 243.

620   "Osea ci ha lasciato in questi versetti un simbolo magnifico e ricchissimo, che diversi autori dell'AT e NT si sono poi incaricati di sviluppare"; L. Alonso Schökel and J. L.

confessed: "As a woman with child and about to give birth writhes and cries out in her pain, so were we in your presence, O Lord. We were with child, we writhed in pain, but we gave birth to wind. We have not brought salvation to the earth; we have not given birth to people of the world" (Isa 26:17–18). In Hosea's oracle, the obstinacy of a baby who does not want to leave his mother's womb, although the time of delivery has already come, can be a symbolic manifestation of the rejection of the words of the prophet by the people.[621] In this setting, such a mention of the time that came may not be coincidental. It seems that the mention can constitute a bridge between a prophet's work and the image of the time of childbirth—since, in fact, one of the main tasks of prophets was announcing the proper "time" (עֵת). Referring the image of a childbirth which does not take place despite the appointed time, to Ephraim, should be implied in the following way; God gave his people the right time for repentance and confession of their sins that were "hidden" but Israel has not made use of this opportunity. It tends to be like a "stubborn" child. It is the reason of punishment awaiting Israel.[622]

13:14 Of particular interest for our discussion is v. 14: "I will ransom them from the power of the grave; I will redeem them from death. Where, O death, are your plagues? Where, O grave, is your destruction? I will have no compassion." It contains a passage quoted by Paul: אֱהִי דְבָרֶיךָ מָוֶת אֱהִי קָטָבְךָ שְׁאוֹל. Some exegetes wonder if this passage, as well as the sentence preceding it, should be treated as declarative or interrogative sentences. Two arguments advocate for the fact that the sentences are questions:

(1) Similar phrases in Hosea are questions: "What can I do with you, Ephraim? What can I do with you, Judah?" (Hos 6:4a). "How can I give you up, Ephraim? How can I hand you over, Israel? How can I treat you like Admah? How can I make you like Zeboiim?" (Hos 11:8a)[623];
(2) Hosea 14:1 seems to be a clear answer to the questions contained in 13:14: "The people of Samaria must bear their guilt, because they have

Diaz, *I profeti. Traduzione e commento* (ed. G. Ravasi; trans. T. Tosatti and P. Brungoli; Roma 1996³), 1041.

621   Rogers, "Hosea," 734.
622   L. J. Wood, "Hosea," in *The Expositor's Bible Commentary with the New International Version of the Holy Bible*, VII, *Daniel – Minor Prophets* (ed. F. E. Gaebelein; Grand Rapids 1986), 221.
623   Wood, "Hosea," 221.

rebelled against their God. They will fall by the sword; their little ones
will be dashed to the ground, their pregnant women ripped open."[624]

The initial question in v. 14 contains a verb written in the first person singular as
אֶגְאָלֵם which means redemption or ransom. A family member should buy a
person who became a slave out of slavery. Buying a relative out of slavery was
well known institution in Israel. In the days of ancient Israel, the institution also
included a bloody revenge for the murder of a family member. Hosea does not
use this for his theological content. He only asks who should take revenge in
case of somebody's death. How it should be done? Is it possible to save this
person?

The verb גאל meaning,[625] "to buy out," "redeem," "protect," "to bring
back," or "save," comes from the same root as the noun "saviour" (גֹּאֵל).[626] God
appears as a savior in v. 14. In the Holiness Code (Lev 17–26), the term
"saviour" is the one who has the right to pre-emption of ancestral property that
is sold due to poverty. Some examples of such redemption may be found in Ruth
4:13–17 and Jer 32:6–15.[627] In the HB, the Saviour is initially a family advocate.
He is also called the "avenger of blood"; if someone was killed, the closest
family member was obliged to avenge his death. In this context, it is said about
cities of escape (Num 35:12.19–27; Deut 19:6.12; Josh 20:2.5.9). Through this
act of revenge an "avenger of blood" restored the balance in the tribal
community[628] since murder was seen as a stealing of blood belonging to the
whole clan. Death of the murderer was understood as the regaining of spilled
blood. Meanwhile, the author of Exodus sees Yahweh as the one who "will
redeem" (וְגָאַלְתִּי) the Israelites from Egyptian captivity (Exod 6:6). God's action

---

624 For the fact that the sentence should be read as a declarative one speaks at most
     similarity of the ideas contained in Isa 25:8 and 26:19, but they are not strong enough to
     be cogent; W. Michalski, *Ozeasz. Wstęp, nowy przekład, komentarz* to *Pismo Święte
     Starego Zakonu w nowem tłumaczeniu* (Lwów 1922), 130.

625 D. Daube, *Studies in Biblical Law* (New York[2] 1969), 394; A. Jepsen, "Die Begriffe des
     «Erlösens» im Alten Testament," in *Solange es „Heute" heisst. Festgabe für R.
     Hermann* (Berlin 1957), 159; A. Johnson, *The Primary Meaning of גאל* (Supplements to
     Vetus Testamentum 1; Leiden 1953), 71–72; D. A. Leggett, *The Levirate and Goel
     Institutions in the Old Testament. With Special Attention to the Book of Ruth* (Cherry
     Hill 1974), 3–4.

626 The term גאל is present in total 44 times in HB. This term is considered by many
     exegetes as a noun, it is *de facto* an active participle; J. J. Stamm, *Erlösen und Vergeben
     im Alten Testament* (Bern 1940), 45.

627 R. L. Hubbard, "The Go'el in Ancient Israel. Theological reflections on an Israelite
     Institution," *BBR* 1 (1991): 55.

628 J. J. Stamm, "גאל," in *Theological Lexicon of the Old Testament* (eds. E. Jenni and C.
     Westermann; I; Peabody 1997), 291.

is seen analogous to the action of a person who buys his close relative out from captivity (cf. also: Exod 15:13; Ps 77:16; 106:10). The image of God as a liberator has a special intensity in the preaching of Isaiah (Isa 41:14; 43:14; 44:6.24; 47:4; 48:17; 49; 7.26; 54:5.8).[629] In Hosea (13:14) God is seen as the One who has the power of deliverance from death.

In the given line (v. 14) leaving aside the idea of God as a Saviour from death, there is also a theme of Sheol. This term occurs 65 times in the HB. In the NT, it occurs 10 times and is described by the word "Hades." Sheol, in conviction of the Jews, was the place in which souls stayed after death (Gen 37:35; Acts 2:27). Etymologically the term was probably derived from the verb "require" or "ask," and the noun itself expresses the idea that the underworld is insatiable and still demands people's lives.[630] The Bible knows different synonyms of Sheol: "depths" (Num 16:30; Matt 11:23), "the Abyss" (Luke 8:31) "the depths of the earth" (Ps 63:10), and "the lower earthly regions" (Eph 4:9). This last phrase, depicted by Latin *inferiores partes*, started the identification of Sheol with hell (Lat. *infernum*).[631] According to non-biblical Judaism, a special place in hell was appointed for sinners: "These hollow places have been created for this very purpose that the spirits of the souls of the dead should assemble therein, yea that all the souls of the children of men should assemble here. And these places have been made to receive them till the day of their judgement and till their appointed period [till the period appointed], till the great judgement (comes) upon them" (*1 Enoch* 22:10–11).[632] From the point of view of the Jewish cosmology, the position of the Sheol was conditioned by the initial representation of configuration of the sky, earth and the underworld. Because God lives in heaven, and the dead are buried in the ground, so death was seen as a separation from God. However, people imagined some kind of continuation of life after death. Jewish cosmology showed that the distance of the souls of sinners from God was greater than the God's distance to the souls of the righteous. In the underground, the space for sinners was located much deeper than a place for the righteous and pious. However, it seems that the distinction between post-mortem fate of the righteous and sinners can be detected only in

---

629   F. Holmgren, *The Concept of Yahweh as Gō'ēl in Second Isaiah* (New York 1963), 1.

630   Otherwise, the etymology of the name Sheol presents A. E. Bernstain. Namely, he derives it from the verb "to be destroyed," "collapse," "smash," "to ruffle" (about the sea); A. E. Bernstein, *Jak powstało piekło. Śmierć i zadośćuczynienie w świecie starożytnym oraz początkach chrześcijaństwa* (trans. A. Piskozub-Piwosz; Kraków 2006), 172.

631   B. Reicke, "Szeol," in *Słownik wiedzy biblijnej* (ed. B. M. Metzger and M. D. Coogan; Polish ed. W. Chrostowski; trans. T. Mieszkowski; Warszawa 1996), 591.

632   Rubinkiewicz, *Apokryfy*, 151.

the time of Ezekiel (6th century B.C.), so at the time when Oz was created, the distinction could not be clearer.[633] That distance from God does not mean, however, that the dead are not subject to the authority of God. Some passages from the Book of Amos give evidence regarding this conviction: "Though they [the death] dig down to the depths of the grave, from there my hand will take them. Though they climb up to the heavens, from there I will bring them down. Though they hide themselves on the top of Carmel, there I will hunt them down and seize them. Though they hide from me at the bottom of the sea, there I will command the serpent to bite them" (Amos 9:2–3). The words of the similar appeal: "Where can I go from your Spirit? Where can I flee from your presence? If I go up to the heavens, you are there; if I make my bed in the depths, you are there" (Ps 13:7–8). In the moral perspective, Sheol was regarded as a place in which the dead suffer punishment for their sins. Both the prophets and the psalmist, threatened to go to Sheol (Ps 9:18; 31:18; 55:16; Isa 5:14; 28:15.18; 66:24).[634]

The phrase cited by Paul (אֱהִי דְבָרֶיךָ מָוֶת אֱהִי קָטָבְךָ שְׁאוֹל) can be interpreted as a call or a question. Masoretes (as mentioned above) read it as a question, as does the LXX. If you try to refer discussed verse to a specific historical and political situation, you should surely see in the image of the "blooming" of Israel, the times of Jeroboam II.[635] He was the son of Joash and his successor on the throne of Israel in the period around 786–746 B.C. The author of 2 Kings sums up his reign by the words: "He did evil in the eyes of the Lord and did not turn away from any of the sins of Jeroboam son of Nebat, which he had caused Israel to commit" (2 Kgs 14:24). The time of Jeroboam II rulings, however, was successful both economically and politically. He expanded the borders of his country from the Sea of Arabah (the Dead Sea) to the Entrance of Hamath (2 Kgs 14:25). He could also march in from the other side of the Jordan, and take over Damascus, which made enabled him to restore the character of the kingdom from the days of David (2 Kgs 14:28; Amos 6:13). This territorial expansion brought a growth of big cities.[636] For this reason, Hosea recalls times of "thriving among his brothers." However, it is also possible that the fragment announces an event, which took place in 722 or 721

---

633 Some differentiation of the fate of the righteous and the wicked after their death can be found in Ezekiel; Bernstain, *Jak powstało piekło*, 198.

634 Reicke, "Szeol," 591.

635 Wood, "Hosea," 222.

636 R. R. Wilson, "Jeroboam II," in *Encyklopedia biblijna* (ed. P. J. Achtemeier; trans. Z. Kościuk; Warszawa 1999), 440–441.

B.C. that is the downfall of Samaria. Equally important in this case is the suggestion that v. 14 should be interpreted as a question.[637]

The final phrase of v. 14 ("I will have no compassion") may constitute a later gloss. The noun "mercy" in the form used herein exists only once in the whole HB. Assuming a positive connotation of the entire phrase, it should be regarded that God maintains the decision to punish Israel.[638]

13:15–14:1 Only God can save from death, using his power, but the unfaithfulness of Israel stands at the beginning of the events that lead to its destruction; the events caused by the human factor—by Assyria increasing in power. Assyria was the eastern neighbor of the chosen people. God allows these events to take their course so Assyria, "the east wind" can be called the wind from the Lord: "even though [Ephraim] thrives among his brothers. An east wind from the Lord will come, blowing in from the desert; his spring will fail and his well dry up. His storehouse will be plundered of all its treasures" (v. 15). This image is based on two opposites "irrigated land," and "desert" and "fruitfulness" or "infertility." The wind causing destruction is opposed to life-giving water. In Hos 6:3 the prophet talked of the rain expected by people and sent down by God. ("Let us acknowledge the Lord; let us press on to acknowledge him. As surely as the sun rises, he will appear; he will come to us like the winter rains, like the spring rains that water the earth"). He refers here to the sources that He controls himself. The wind of the Lord can reach the depths of the earth to cause the drying up of water, which gives life.

The final punishment for human sin is death. It does not only concern the soldiers who will die on the battlefield, but also children and pregnant mothers: "The people of Samaria must bear their guilt, because they have rebelled against their God. They will fall by the sword; their little ones will be dashed to the ground, their pregnant women ripped open" (13:16). In this context Samaria represents all of Israel. The prophet presumably refers to the fall of Samaria in

---

637 Lemański, „Sprawisz, abym ożył!", 186–187. In favour of positive affirmation are: F. I. Andersen and D.N. Freedman, *Hosea* (AB 24; New York 1980), 639. They base on the LXX text.

638 Andersen and Freedman, *Hosea*, 507; Lemański, „Sprawisz, abym ożył!", 188; R. Martin-Achard, *From Death to Life. A Study of the Doctrine of the Resurrection in the Old Testament* (Edinburgh–London 1960), 86–93; J. Day, "The Development of Belief in Life after Death in Ancient Israel," in *After the Exile* (eds. J. Barton and D. Reimer; Macon 1996), 128–130; A. Chester, „Resurrection and Transformation," in *Auferstehung – Resurrection* (eds. F. Avemaria and H. Lichtenberger; WUNT 135; Tübingen 2001), 58–59; A. Weiser, *Das Buch der zwölf kleinen Propheten* (I; ATD 24; Göttingen ²1956), 99.

722 B.C. Israel incurred the wrath of Assyria during the reign of Pekah (737–732). Pekah along with Rezin, king of Damascus, became the head of a coalition formed against Assyria. He wanted the Southern Kingdom, ruled by Josiah the son of Jotham, and joined the conspiracy (742–735). Since Judah refused to join the conspiracy, Pekah and Rezin decided to oppose to it militarily. At that time, Jotham died and his son Ahaz took over the throne. At the very beginning of his reign, Ahaz asked Tiglath-Pileser for help but the latter breached the coalition. Pekah's policy resulted in reduction of the area of Israel. Consequently, the area included the lands belonging to the tribe of Ephraim and partly to Manasseh. The Last King of Israel, Hoshea (732–724) became a vassal of Assyria. When Shalmaneser V mounted the throne of Assyria, Hosea refused to pay tribute. This step proved to be suicidal and was the main reason behind the fall of Samaria which occurred shortly after when the power was taken over by Sargon II.[639] From the prophetic point of view, the downfall of the capital and Assyrian captivity is seen as a natural consequence of Israel's unfaithfulness to Yahweh.

Terrible images of an infant's death, which Hosea showed to his readers, came back in the prophetic tradition: "Their bows will strike down the young men; they will have no mercy on infants nor will they look with compassion on children" (Isa 13:18). Similar acts of children's murders took place during the military campaign in the ancient Near East. Assyrian reports coming from 9th century B.C. mentioned of the burning of young boys and girls. Furthermore, they referred to the practice of cutting the abdomens of pregnant women, which was witnessed during the reign of King Tiglath-Pileser.[640] The mention of these practices in Hos 14:1 shows the whole horror of God's punishment which Israel will suffer ("Samaria") because of its unfaithfulness.

2.3. Contribution of v. 13b to Hos 13:12–14:1

God poses a rhetorical question in v. 14b ("Where, O death, are your plagues? Where, O grave, is your destruction?") alongside the question before it and put in the same verse ("Will I ransom them from the power of the grave; will I redeem them from death?"; v. 14a). This question constitutes the main fragment of Hos 13:12–14:1. In the opening verses (13:12–13) God, in prophetic oracle expressed through the mouth of Hosea, reveals the guilt of Israel ("Ephraim"). He then poses questions regarding the possibility of deliverance from death (v.

---

639 Bright, *Historia Izraela*, 281–284.

640 J. H. Walton, V. H. Matthews and M. W. Chavalas, *Komentarz historyczno-kulturowy do Biblii Hebrajskiej* (Polish ed. W. Chrostowski; trans. Z. Kościuk; Warszawa 2005), 870.

14) and finally (13:15–14:1) He announces His punishment for Israel ("Ephraim," "Samaria"). From the rhetorical and structural point of view, v. 14 is a "transition" between the theme of unfaithfulness of the chosen people and the announcement of their punishment. As a result, this verse links these thoughts, and it is a reflection of God's intention. People of Israel should be the recipient of God's message but they are "absent" because they are referred to in the third-person plural. In v. 14 God is potentially seen as the one who has the power to save from death and Sheol. The prophet himself does not yet think about the individual resurrection of the dead. This idea was not known at the time of Hosea. Finally, it should be noted that the "analyzed verse expresses the determination of the Lord in punishing Israel. The nation had its chance for repentance, but it did not make use of it. The God of Israel has the power to liberate his people from the misery that they experience. Israel, however, must become worth of this act of grace expressed by the metaphor of being saved from Sheol."[641]

3. The Meaning in 1 Cor 15:54–56

Exegetical and theological analysis of vv. 54–56 has been carried out in the previous chapter; however, that chapter was devoted mostly to the content which allowed for the analysis of the quotation from Isa 25:8a in v. 54. In this part of the study, we will focus on the same passage to express the essential meaning of this quote from Hos 13:14b in v. 55. As mentioned above, the whole section begins with an emphasis on some contradictions: "perishable"–"imperishable," and "mortal"–"immortality." The moment of transformation that would take place was emphasized: "When the perishable has been clothed with the imperishable, and the mortal with immortality, then the saying that is written will come true: 'Death has been swallowed up in victory'" (v. 54). The aorist of the verb ἐνδύσηται temporarily linked with the indefinite term ὅταν leads to the conclusion that the time of this transformation is not clearly indicated, but its effects are irreversible. Once again, Paul returns to the process which consists of three elements in 1 Cor 15: the parousia–the resurrection of the body–the transformation[642]; however, if in vv. 23–28 he used it to show that the resurrection is necessary to overcome the "last enemy"—death, he now describes the process in terms of triumph. Quoting Isa 25:8b, Paul departs from both the HB and the LXX; however, the context of his utterance is similar in both fragments. In Isaiah, it is said that on the day of salvation God will defeat

---

641 Lemański, „Sprawisz, abym ożył!", 188.
642 N. R. Gulley, "Death," ABD II: 110–111.

death; the essence of the quote in 1 Cor is comparable.[643] As mentioned earlier, the two linked quotes constitute a prophecy that still awaits fulfillment. All other quotes coming from the OT and inserted into 1 Cor 15:12–58 form records of the words that have already been fulfilled in Christ. Despite that fact, however, the words in combined quotation from vv. 54b–55 waiting to be fulfilled in the future are not without influence on the present time.[644]

The theme of putting on robes of glory is common in Jewish literature and points to eternal life. It is present in apocryphal literature and apocalyptic in its character. Part of the Ethiopian Book of Enoch can be cited in this context: "And the righteous and elect shall have risen from the earth, and ceased to be of downcast countenance. And they shall have been clothed with garments of glory, and these shall be the garments of life from the Lord of Spirits: And your garments shall not grow old, Nor your glory pass away before the Lord of Spirits" (*1 En.* 62:15).[645] Quite similar idea is contained in *1QS* 4:6–8: "But the reward of all those who walk in it [the way of truth] will be a healing remedy and an abundant well-being in a long life and a fruitfulness of seed, together with all the blessings of eternity and everlasting bliss in life forever, and a crown of glory with a recompense of majesty in light everlasting." Talmud passages also contain donned robes at the resurrection. In the treatise, Sanhedrin cites a conversation between Cleopatra and the Queen of Rabbi Meir: "Queen Cleopatra asked Rabbi Meir: 'I know that the dead will revive, ... But when they arise, shall they arise nude or in their garments?'—He replied, 'Thou mayest deduce by a *fortiori* argument [the answer] from a wheat grain: if a grain of wheat, which is buried naked, sprouteth forth in many robes, how much more so the righteous, who are buried in their raiment'" (*Sanh.* 90b).[646] It is also worth referring to the information contained in Philo in *Quod deterius potiori insidiari soleat*: "The body is mortal, but not the soul. The wise man, therefore, who appears to have departed from this mortal life, lives according to the immortal life" (*Deter.* 49). The Alexandrian philosopher says—like Paul—there are two dimensions, perishable and imperishable. The Apostle refers to the tradition concerning clothing in imperishable and immortality.[647]

Verse 55 is a quotation from Hos 13:14b: "Where, O death, is your victory? Where, O death, is your sting?" (ποῦ σου, θάνατε, τὸ νῖκος; ποῦ σου, θάνατε, τὸ

---

643 Fee, *First Epistle to the Corinthians*, 803.

644 Usami, "How Are the Dead Rised?," 492.

645 Trans. after Rubinkiewicz, *Apokryfy*, 162–263.

646 The same argument adduces Pirke of *Rabbi Eliezer* 33; Grasso, *Prima Lettera ai Corinzi*, 174; Teani, *Corporeità e risurrezione*, 165.

647 Heil, *Rhetorical Role of Scripture*, 256.

κέντρον;).[648] It should be noted that two quotes are introduced by one formula: (τότε γενήσεται ὁ λόγος ὁ γεγραμμένος). Thanks to that, Paul gives the impression that they constitute a wholeness in one of the prophet's books.[649] Once more, it seems that the Jewish apostle used an exegesis method called *gezerah shavah*, attributed to Hillel, and consisting in explanation of one fragment by the other, in which there was the identical word, in this case, the term "victory."[650] The Apostle turns to the death using the immediate expression that appears in this verse as personification. It is obvious that against the death, there will be a battle, and as a result, the death will be defeated as "the last enemy" (v. 26) when all dominion, authority and power are destroyed. Death will be thorn-free since it was swallowed by Christ Himself in His resurrection.

It is possible that Paul already prepared the ground for a quote from Hos 13:14b. In 15:8 the apostle names himself a "stillborn child" (ἔκτρωμα).[651] This term can be found throughout the NT while it was recorded three times in the LXX. It can be found for the first time in the words of Aaron directed to Moses: "Please, my lord, do not hold against us the sin we have so foolishly committed. Do not let her be like a stillborn infant (ἔκτρωμα), coming from its mother's womb with its flesh half eaten away" (Num 12:12); the second time in lamentation of Job: "Or why was I not hidden in the ground like a stillborn child (ἔκτρωμα), like an infant who never saw the light of day" (Job 3:16); Finally, for the third time in the instructions of Qohelet: "A man may have a hundred children and live many years; yet no matter how long he lives, if he cannot enjoy his prosperity and does not receive proper burial, I say that a stillborn child is better off than he (ἔκτρωμα)" (Eccl 6:3). In the comparison to the slink/stillborn child, one can also see an allusion to Hos 13:13: "Pains as of a woman in childbirth come to him, but he is a child without wisdom; when the time arrives, he does not come to the opening of the womb [Ephraim]."[652] This illusion, of course, if it is intended by Paul in 15:8 prepares the present quote from Hos 14:14b.

---

648 Linke, "Zmartwychwstanie Chrystusa," 82.

649 C. D. Stanley suggests that Paul cites the two quotes as they were "anything other than a continuous quotation from a single biblical passage"; id., *Paul and the Language of Scripture*, 209.

650 Keener, *1–2 Corinthians*, 134; id., *Komentarz*, 374.

651 This term can mean not only "stillborn child" but also can indicate the birth after the expected date of farrowing as well as the birth by caesarean section. Cf. Thayer, *Thayer's Greek-English Lexicon*, 200.

652 M. Schaeffer, "Paulus 'Fehlgeburt' oder 'unvernünftiges Kind'?," *ZNW* 85 (1994): 217; Jones, "1 Cor 15:8: Paul the Last Apostle," 7.

To give the quote from Hosea a tone of irony and triumphant mockery of the death that was defeated, the apostle makes the necessary modifications to the text. These modifications have got three directions:

(1) the change of the term "judgement" (δίκη) from the LXX to "victory" (νίκη); by means of it, the apostle settles the quote from Isa 25:8b (in which there is the term) with the present quote. This replacement corresponds with the word games used in the *misdrash* where Jewish exegetes deliberately used to change the traditional vocalization of the text devoid in writing vowels, to carry out their interpretation. There is a quite similar replacement in the LXX once: the translator of the Greek version changes the term "constantly/forever" to "victory" in 2 Sam 2:26. It is possible that this change validated the change introduced by Paul;

(2) by the replacement of the call "O Hades!" used in the LXX by "O Death!"; thanks to that, the exclamation becomes a direct mockery of the defeated death;

(3) by changing the position of the pronoun "your" to emphatic ("Where, O death, is your victory?").

The entire quote retains the present tense, although it describes a future resurrection. Paul realizes, however, that the final process of overcoming the death has already begun with the resurrection of Christ, and nothing will foil God's plans.

Explaining a quote from Hos 14:14b, the apostle says: "The sting of death is sin, and the power of sin is the law" (v. 56). Death as apocalyptic power uses a different revelatory power—the sin as an instrument to initiate the poison "sting" leading to death itself.[653] If the term "sting" is understood as a tool used for driving animals, then the meaning of the sentence "The sting of death is sin" should be interpreted as follows; the sin stimulates death and leads to it. In Rom 3:9, Paul notes that both the Jews and the Gentiles are under the power of sin. He also argues that, "just as sin entered the world through one man, and death through sin, and in this way death came to all men, because all sinned" (Rom 5:12).[654] Paul is convinced that death is a consequence of sin. This truth is anchored in the beliefs of Judaism (Philo, *Quaest. Gen.* 1:51; *2 Bar.* 17:2–3). The opinion is expressed also by apocryphal *4 Ezra*: "And unto him [the man] thou gavest commandment to love thy way: which he transgressed, and

---

653   Horn, "1 Korinther 15,56 – ein exegetische Stachel," 88–105; Söding, "'Die Kraft der Sünde ist das Gesetz' (1 Kor 15,56)," 74–84; J. M. García, "1 Co 15:56: ¿Una polémica contra la ley judía?," *EstBib* 60 (2002); 405–414.

654   Mickiewicz, "Zagadnienia etyczne," 314.

immediately thou appointedst death in him and in his generations" (3:7).[655] The source of sin is life according to "the sinful nature" as the body's desires are hostile to God (Rom 7:18–23; 8:6–8). Asking rhetorically "Where, O death, is your sting?" Paul asks *ipso facto*: "Where, O death is the sin?" This is the sin that was defeated by the death of Jesus Christ on the cross and His resurrection. Sin, which leads to death was defeated and therefore, death cannot already manifest its reign.

The law was still one of the main themes of Paul's theology. This happened both when Paul was an ardent follower of Judaism, as a Pharisee trained by Gamaliel, and when as a Christian he preached the gospels free of the law. This theme recurred constantly in his thoughts and arguments. Paul understands the law in three ways:

(1) as Torah;
(2) as moral directive from which man becomes aware of his sin;
(3) as a general rule determining the causes and consequences of sin.[656]

The law itself is "is holy and good" (Rom 7:12–13), and it should give life. However. in the context of the human tendency to fall the effect is exactly the opposite. According to Rom 1:18–2:29 and 5:12–21, the law makes people realize that they are in the bondage of sin. Thus, the work of Christ can be seen as liberation from the bondage of the Law. It should be noted that in his letters, Paul never criticizes the Greek and Roman law. We should also give weight to the fact that he considers the OT's Law as "spiritual" (Rom 7:14). He uses the Law's texts as a significant argument in his reasoning (1 Cor 9:9; 14:21.34; Gal 3:13). It gives the knowledge of sin: "indeed I would not have known what sin was except through the law. For I would not have known what coveting really was if the law had not said, 'Do not covet.' ... For apart from law, sin is dead" (Rom 7:7–8). Paul adds: "for before the law was given, sin was in the world. But sin is not taken into account when there is no law" (Rom 5:13). The apostle explained to Galatians that it was impossible to get justification through the law, indicating *ipso facto*, the relationship between Christ and the Lain: "if righteousness could be gained through the law, Christ died for nothing" (Gal 2:21). Imposing upon the man many duties in a cultic and moral field, the Law plunged people in the state of sin because no one by himself can fulfill all the commandments (Gal 3:10).[657] The law, therefore, was of great importance in the

---

655 Mędala, *Apokryfy Starego Testamentu*, 375.

656 Thiselton, *First Epistle to the Corinthians*, 1303.

657 P. R. Gryziec, "'Z uczynków Prawa nikt nie może dostąpić usprawiedliwienia' (Rz 3,20)," *RBL* 50 (1997): 16–22; R. Kempiak, "Chrystologiczne podstawy Pawłowej krytyki Prawa," in *Deus meus et omnia. Księga pamiątkowa ku czci o. prof. Hugolina*

economy of salvation as a "tutor." Its role was limited with time (it ended with the coming of Christ) and content (helped in the transition to the stage of the adoption of the Messiah). With the coming of Christ, God's people entered a mature period in their spiritual life and no longer were subject to the supervision of a teacher.[658] Christ himself by his coming and through his teaching interpreted the Law, separated the merely human traditions from the will of God, and radicalized many standards and made their interiorization. He has become not only a teacher of the law but also its executor. Thus, the Law understood in this way, puts emphasis on the commandment of love of God and of the neighbour. What is more, it requires also the love of our enemies.

According to Paul's way of thinking, the way to justification is the faith in Jesus Christ, not performing the deeds of the Law (Gal 2:16; 3:11; Rom 3:20.28).

Christ is the descendent of Abraham; the Law comes from Moses. Abraham received a promise from God; Moses received the Law. The promise is greater than the Law (even by seniority) so Abraham is the father of all believers (both from among the Jews and the Gentiles), Moses is only the protoplast of the chosen people (Gal 3:16).

Pauline principle that the power of a sin is the Law can be explained as follows: the Law manifests its activity when it "acts jointly" with a sin but its consequence is the knowledge of the sin. It does not mean that without the Law people would be in a state of innocence. Without the Law, the sin would remain in a state of death (Rom 7:8). Knowing the Law, the man realizes his hopeless situation—the fact that he will not be able to keep all the commandments of the Law and the fact that he is cannot obtain a justification. Therefore, Paul sees Christ as "the end to the Law" (Rom 10:4). Christ set us from the Law (Rom 7:6), and redeemed from its curse (Gal 3:13).[659]

To sum up, a quote from Hos 13:14b is used in v. 55, which consists of two rhetorical questions: "Where, O death, is your victory? Where, O death, is your sting?" This is a part of the eschatological hymn announcing the ultimate victory of Christ over death, revealed by His resurrection and the promise of the resurrection of the believers.[660] These questions are not without a hint of

---

Langkammera OFM w 50. rocznicę święceń kapłańskich (ed. M. S. Wróbel; Lublin 2005), 167–188.

658 Mickiewicz, "Zagadnienia etyczne," 326.

659 H. Ordon, "Dzieło odkupienia w nauczaniu św. Pawła," in *Biblia o odkupieniu* (ed. R. Rubinkiewicz; Lublin 2000), 177–186.

660 Jasiński, *Jezus jest Panem*, 20.

irony.[661] The apostle weaves them in, showing the following process: parousia of Christ—the resurrection of believers—transformation of the bodies. He thus explains that the cause of death is sin, and the Law shows the sin, and at the same time it makes people realize our human inability to comply with all the regulations of the Law and our powerlessness in gaining forgiveness.

---

661 Romaniuk, Jankowski and Stachowiak, *Komentarz*, 165; Gillmann, „Thematic Comparison," 451.

VIII. The OT Quotations in 1 Cor 15:12–58: Their Role and Redactional Re-Working

Paul's doctrine of the resurrection is based on the revelation contained in the OT and on the interpretation of that revelation in the Pharisee's teaching. After adherence to the Christian faith, the Apostle looked at the doctrine in the light the resurrection of Christ. Extensive research on the OT appointed a group of texts that provide the basis for belief in the physical resurrection of the dead or just speak about it in a direct way.[662] We should mention the texts that speak of the historical experience as a source of hope in the face of death (Gen 5:21–24; 1 Kgs 17:17–24; 2 Kgs 2:2–25; 4:8–37; 13:21; 2 Macc 7:1–42; 12:38–45; 15:12–16), of the covenant in the context of a future life of God's people (Hos 6:1–3; 13:14; Ezek 37:1–14; Isa 52:13; 53:10–11a), and of the images of the resurrection in the last days (Isa 25:8; 26:19; Dan 12:1–3); one should also mention the importance of prayers for those who are just being with God after death (Ps 16:9–11; 17:15; 22:30; 49:15–16; 71:20; 73:23–24). The theory of retribution is also important in the context of the resurrection which became the basis of sapiential search for justice after death (Prov 10:1–22:16; 22:17–24:22; Job 19:25–2; Eccl 3:11b.16–17.21; 9:1b; Sir 1:13a; 7:17; 46:12; 48:11.13; 49:10; Wis 3:8; 4:19; 16:13–14).[663] All these texts shaped Jewish consciousness and beliefs about the future resurrection of the dead.

The Judeo-Christian resurrection terminology rises from the OT references and allusions to the resurrection. The language which the Jews of the Second Temple era used to talk about immortality was very diverse. The Pharisees and those who shared their opinions about posthumous fate of man spoke directly about the resurrection of the body; some of them also used the astral terminology; while others used the parallel phraseology with which the Greeks expressed their conviction about the transmigration of souls.[664] Apocryphal writings from Qumran give a good example of the diversity of this terminology.

---

662 Excellent study on the Old Testament texts that can be treated as a "source of hope" for the resurrection presented J. Lemański in his book that has been already cited many times in this work (id., „Sprawisz, abym ożył!").

663 Ibid., 6–11.

664 Longenecker, *Studies in Paul*, 194.

In *1 Enoch* (91–104) there is a discourse about death, and the author talks about the death. This refers to the symbolism of sleep. Mentioning the dead, he refers to the "soul," or to the "spirit." He also uses astral terminology and points to the resurrection terms. *Jub.* mentions "healing" God's servants who ["will rise in great peace"] (23:30–31). Qumran thanksgiving hymns refer both to human "souls" and the "spirits" existing after the death (*1QH* 1:20–21; 2:20; 5:29–30.34–39; 6:29–35; 11:10–14). In a direct way regarding the resurrection, *1 Enoch* mentions: "These three [places] have been made that the spirits of the dead might be separated. And such a division has been made (for) the spirits of the righteous, in which there is the bright spring of water. And such has been made [a place] for sinners when they die and are buried in the earth and judgment has not been executed on them in their lifetime. Here their spirits shall be set apart in this great pain till the great day of judgment and punishment and torment of those who curse for ever and retribution for their spirits. There He shall bind them for ever" (22:9–11). The resurrection of the dead is also written about directly in *4Q 521, 4Q 385, 1QH* 14;29–30.34; 19:10–12[665] and *4 Ezra* 7:32–38; allusions to the resurrection appear in *2 Bar.* 14:12–13; 30:1–4; 49:1–3, *Sib.* 4:175–191.[666]

The Apostle Paul's conviction about the resurrection from the dead is anchored not only in the OT but also in the teaching of the school of the Pharisee in which he was adept. Flavius Josephus, relating the Pharisaic theories about the resurrection, uses terminology associated with the "immortality of the soul": "[the Pharisees] They also believe that souls have an immortal rigor in them, and that under the earth there will be rewards or punishments, according as they have lived virtuously or viciously in this life; and the latter are to be detained in an everlasting prison, but that the former shall have power to revive and live again" (*Ant.* 18:14).[667] The Pharisaic convictions about the resurrection of the dead are also included in the rabbinical writings so in the writings of the teachers coming from the Pharisees circle: "All Israel has a portion in the World to Come. ... those who deny the resurrection, those who deny that the law is from God, and 'Epicureans,' will have no share in the world to come" (*Sanh.* 10:1).[668] Nevertheless, what sheds most light on the Pauline doctrine regarding the resurrection of the dead is of course the fact of the resurrection of Christ:

---

665 Extensively, the idea of the resurrection in the Scriptures from Qumran discusses Parchem, "Zmartwychwstanie," 115–126.
666 Longenecker, *Studies in Paul*, 198–199.
667 Cf. *Bell.* 2,163.
668 Barth, "Zur Frage," 195; Wilson, *Pauline parallels*, 174.

"But Christ has indeed been raised from the dead, the firstfruits of those who have fallen asleep. ... so in Christ all will be made alive" (1 Cor 15:20.22b).[669]

Giving his reasons for the doctrine of the resurrection of the dead presented in 1 Cor 15:12–58, the Apostle reaches for quotes from the OT six times. These quotes became the subject of analysis throughout this study. These quotes come adequately, one from the Torah, two from the Scriptures, and three from the books of the prophets. This fact itself may already give evidence of Paul's belief that in Jesus Christ the OT prophecies have been fulfilled. For the Jews, among the most authoritative books of the HB were the books of the Torah, in the second-place Prophets and finally in the third-place Scriptures.[670]

After carrying out a detailed analysis upon the meaning of quotes, at first in their original context, and then in the direct context of 1 Cor 15:12–58, one should proceed to the synthetic analysis of their role in Paul's argumentation in favor of the resurrection.

1. Recontextualization of Quotations

The phenomenon of quoting essentially lies in taking a phrase or sentence out from one context and putting it into a different literary context [and in respect to contents]. Such transfer of phrases or sentences from one context to another can make it so that these sentences or phrases lose some shades of their meanings which they had in the first context. Furthermore, they gain new and different meanings. The meaning is modified to a lesser extent when the context, with respect to the content, of the source text and text, including a quote are related—as is the case of citations included in 1 Cor 15:12–58. Our analyses carried out in Chapters II–VII show both the original context of a phrase or sentence that Paul quotes, as well as the context in 1 Cor 15:12–58. In this point, we would like to make a comparison of the original and the new context of the quoted phrases and sentences to see where the direction of their modifications are aimed.

A quotation from Ps 110:1b, written in v. 25b (ἄχρι οὗ θῇ πάντας τοὺς ἐχθροὺς ὑπὸ τοὺς πόδας αὐτοῦ), was taken from the royal Psalm, referring to the

---

669 "... la risurrezione di Gesù è una verità che non riguarda esclusivamente il suo destino, ma la sorte di ogni uomo (v. 13). Ciò che è accaduto a Lui ha una conseguenza eminentemente esistenziale per tutti"; Grasso, *Prima Lettera ai Corinzi*, 165.

670 Sanders, *Il giudaismo*, 64; Chrostowski, "Żydowskie tradycje interpretacyjne," 43; L. Hartman states laconically: "The Scripture was not only Law"; "'Guiding the Knowing Vessel of your Heart'," 19.

ritual of coronation.[671] From the very beginning, Christian interpretation of this Psalm was without a doubt, messianic but in Jewish exegesis it was not always considered to be such.[672] Any mentions of the rule over kings and over enemies make it so the whole text may be incorporated into the theme of kingship. What is important in this context is that the author of the psalm puts an emphasis on the combination of the royal reign and the priesthood. The ruler about whom the author speaks is a theocratic ruler who himself is under the authority of God and participates in his reign. The passage that Paul quotes in v. 25b ("until he has put all his enemies under his feet") constitutes in the psalm the king's promise made by God Himself. The promise concerns the defeat of the king's enemies, as the image of all enemies lying under his feet. In the mentality of the ancient Near East, this metaphor indicates the absolute control and complete dominion over enemies.[673]

Quoting Ps 110:1b, Paul incorporates passage into the context telling of eschatological events. According to him, the events also include overcoming all evil powers which are personified by all dominion, authority and powers (v. 24b) and then the death (v. 26). As it turns out, the Apostle interprets the psalm not only as a royal reign, but also as a messianic reign. He does this by referring the quoted fragment to Christ as the King and Messiah. According to the psalm, God puts enemies under the feet of the king, in Paul's writings; however, the consequence is attributed to Christ. Christ will defeat all his enemies, and then give the kingdom "to God the Father" (v. 24). Paul retains the motifs of reign and the defeat of enemies that are present in the 110th Psalm. He does not, in contrast, refer to the priestly reign, which in Ps 110 appears in the oath of God: "You are a priest forever, in the order of Melchizedek" (v. 4b).

The second quote is also taken from the Psalm (πάντα γὰρ ὑπέταξεν ὑπὸ τοὺς πόδας αὐτοῦ; Ps 8:7b). Recorded in v. 27, it comes from the psalm of a sapiential nature praising the greatness of the Creator and the position of a man in the whole work of creation. The Man though affected by sin knows his dignity, and he knows that God put everything under his feet. In this context, the motif of putting everything under his feet does not appear in the background of fighting with the forces of evil and the victory over them (as in the case of the same motif in Ps 110:1b), but it points to the unique position of a man in the

---

671 Bateman IV, "Psalm 110:1," 438; Westermann, *Praise and Lament*, 245; Rowley, "Melchizedek and Zadok," 461–472.

672 Cf. Matt 22:44; 26:64; Mark 12:36; 14:62; 16:19; Luke 20:42–44; 22:69; Acts 2:34–35; Rom 8:34; 1 Cor 15:25; Eph 1:20; Col 3,1; Heb 1:3.13; 5:6; 7:17.21; 8:1; 10:12–13; 12:2; Rinaudo, *I Salmi*, 599; Callan, "Psalm 110:1," 622–636.

673 Synowiec, *Wprowadzenie do Księgi Psalmów*, 283.

universe created by God.[674] Undoubtedly, the motif of enemies can be obviously found in Ps 8, but it is about the enemies of God: "From the lips of children and infants you have ordained praise because of your enemies, to silence the foe and the avenger" (v. 3). They are also the enemies of a man devoted to God, but it is only God who can curb his enemies. A man in his dignity was endowed by God with "glory and honour" (v. 6b), "You made him ruler over the works of your hands" of God (v. 7a) and was made a little lower than אֱלֹהִים (v. 6a).

The Apostle Paul, reaching for a quote from Ps 8:7b, uses a Christological key. The psalmist writes in such a way that the dignity and exaltation of a man is referred directly to Christ. The motif of putting everything under Christ's feet is not as strongly united with the motif of the fight with forces of evil, defeating all enemies and a victory in the latter, as in v. 25b. Christ—through the use of the quote—is seen as an absolute Lord over all that exists (not only the enemies).[675] Thus Christ is a universal ruler who will hand over the reign of God.

The next quote is from Isa 22:13b and was recorded in v. 32b (φάγωμεν καὶ πίωμεν, αὔριον γὰρ ἀποθνῄσκομεν). In the original context, the words are part of the prophetic speech against Jerusalem (Isa 22:1–14). As indicated in the analysis of Isa 22:1–14 this text should be connected with the campaign of Sargon against Ashdod in 711. The inhabitants of the town were focused on entertainment, neglecting largely the danger coming from the Assyria.[676] At that time, the rule over the town held Shebna, a high royal official, who turned out to be irresponsible ruler.[677] The passage quoted by Paul was inserted through the mouth of Isaiah into the mouths of inhabitants of Jerusalem, who instead of repenting and preparing for the fight, played and were indulged into pleasures. The Apostle Paul, leading his discourse relating to the consequences of the rejection of the resurrection of the dead in a logical manner, reaches the conclusion that the attitude of the Corinthians who denied the resurrection should be as the one outlined in the quotation. They can indulge in carnal pleasures, because any eternal consequence would meet them for that. While the prophet Isaiah describes the real attitude of the inhabitants of the capital of Judah scorning impending danger, Paul hypothetically shows the truth; that such should be the attitude of the Christians who reject the resurrection.

The quote taken from Gen 2:7b and put in v. 45b (ἐγένετο ὁ πρῶτος ἄνθρωπος Ἀδὰμ εἰς ψυχὴν ζῶσαν) in the original context appears in the second story of the creation of man. In the original context of the monotheism, it has

---

674   Ravasi, *Psalmy*, 203.
675   Mare, *1 Corinthians*, 286.
676   Oswalt, *Book of Isaiah*, 405.
677   Saldarini, "Szebna," 1182.

been accented with the human relationship with the earth (indicated by the terminology: אָדָם and אֲדָמָה). The context also depicts the human body as coming from the earth and returning to it after the death. A man becomes a "living being" only through the action of God (לְנֶפֶשׁ חַיָּה).[678] Paul's quotation from Gen 2:7b serves to underline the truth that Christ is the representative of those who rise from the dead. Instead of the relationship with the earth, the eschatological and soteriological aspects are emphasized. Christ not only came back to life but he is also its source because he has become a "life-giving Spirit."

Another quote taken from Isa 25:8a was placed in v. 54b (κατεπόθη ὁ θάνατος εἰς νῖκος). The original context is without a doubt eschatological. In the final related part of the Proto-Isaiah, the prophet announces the judgment over the nations. The announcement of the final defeat of death is connected with the motif of this judgment. In the *Apocalypse of Isaiah* (Isa 24–27) the following statement can be found: "But your dead will live; their bodies will rise. You, who dwell in the dust, wake up and shout for joy. Your dew is like the dew of the morning; the earth will give birth to her dead" (Isa 26:19). If this announcement concerns the resurrection of the dead (not the rebirth of the chosen people); the allusion to the resurrection may also be found in Isa 25:8. Taking a quote from Isaiah, Paul leaves it in its eschatological context. Even so, there are not any direct mentions of the judgment in his epistle; he clearly announces the final defeat of the death by resurrection. It is the only prophecy quoted by Paul in 1 Cor 15:12–58, which still remains to be fulfilled.

Lastly, the final quote from the OT incorporated into the body of 1 Cor 15:12–58 was taken from Hos 13:14b, and placed in v. 55 (ποῦ σου, θάνατε, τὸ νῖκος; ποῦ σου, θάνατε, τὸ κέντρον;). The aim of the two rhetorical questions Hosea posed is to announce that the kingdom of Israel would suffer punishment for the sins of its inhabitants. It is difficult to point to a particular historical situation for which the announcement applies. It is important, however, that any sin cannot be left without punishment but God is seen as the Saviour (וְגֹאֵל),[679] who has the power to save people from the death. Recalling the words of Isaiah, Paul incorporates them into the eschatological context speaking about the defeat of the death and the resurrection of the dead. At the same time, the sin itself Paul describes as a "sting of death."

This brief comparison of the original literary context (with reference to the historical and theological context) of the texts cited by Paul with their new context in 1 Cor 15:12–58 can be displayed as follows:

---

678 Lemański, *Pięcioksiąg dzisiaj*, 164.
679 Stamm, *Erlösen und Vergeben*, 45.

Quotation	Original context	Paul's context
Ps 110:1b in v. 25b	– the theme of victory	– Christ's victory over his enemies (especially the death)
	– the reign of the king-priest and defeating his enemies	– the theme of the reign (omitting the theme of priestly power) and overcoming the power of evil, including the death
Ps 8:7b in v. 27a	– the hymn of praise to the Creator	– eschatological reign of Christ over all creations (not just the enemy)
	– showing the dignity of a man and his dominant position in the work of creation	– showing the dignity of Christ in the perspective of the resurrection
Isa 22:13b in v. 32b	– showing the attitude of the inhabitants of Jerusalem to the coming army of Sargon	– showing the expected attitude of the inhabitants of Corinth, who reject the resurrection
	– the context describes a real situation	– the context describes a hypothetical situation
Gen 2:7b in v. 45b	– the second description of the creation of a man	– description of a "new creation," anchored in the resurrection of Christ
	– human life is a gift from God	– resurrection is a gift from God (the Holy Spirit)
Isa 25:8a in v. 54b	– the eschatological context (the announcement of the judgement over the nations)	– the eschatological context (announcement of defeating the death)
	– the announcement of the final defeat of the death with the possible allusion to the Resurrection	– the announcement of the resurrection of the dead
Hos 13:14b in v. 55	– the announcement of the Israel's punishment for unfaithfulness	– the promise of overcoming the death, whose sting is the sin
	– breach of Law brings punishment	– the Law makes people aware of the sin

The table above shows that Paul sometimes retains some features of the original context but more often, he incorporates the quote into a different body of his text. These deviations are not only caused by the difference of the historical situation of the Israelites to whom the fragments of the cited books relate, but also the situation of the Corinthians to whom Paul addresses his letter. The eschatological perspective is also different. The doctrine of the resurrection had not been sufficiently developed in the OT yet. Some (or all) authors of the books of the OT cited by Paul could have not known it at all or have only may have only had fragmentary knowledge. Paul makes out the OT texts from before paschal perspective, through the prism of truth and resurrection of Christ.

2. Rhetorical Function of Quotations

Paul uses the OT quotes in 1 Cor 15:12–58 for rhetorical purposes. Coming from Tarsus, the apostle could receive rhetorical education in his hometown. Strabo confirms the existence of schools of rhetoric in this important research and development center:

The people at Tarsus have devoted themselves so eagerly, not only to philosophy, but also to the whole round of education in general, that they have surpassed Athens, Alexandria, or any other place that can be named where there have been schools and lectures of philosophers. But it is so different from other cities that there the men who are fond of learning, are all natives, and foreigners are not inclined to sojourn there; neither do these natives stay there, but they complete their education abroad; and when they have completed it they are pleased to live abroad, and but few go back home. But the opposite is the case with the other cities which I have just mentioned except Alexandria; for many resorts to them and pass time there with pleasure, but you would not see many of the natives either resorting to places outside their country through love of learning or eager about pursuing learning at home. With the Alexandrians, however, both things take place, for they admit many foreigners and also send not a few of their own citizens abroad. Further, the city of Tarsus has all kinds of schools of rhetoric; and in general it not only has a flourishing population but also is most powerful, thus keeping up the reputation of the mother-city (*Geogr.* 14.5.13).

Essentially, the rhetorical techniques include defining the semantics of the text by analyzing the context, the way of presenting the ideas that ought to convince of the recipient to the advanced theses, the composition of the speech, the logic of a text and its thematic structure.[680] This part of our analysis will be

---

680 Rosik, *Pierwszy List d Koryntian*, 68. For more on the biblical rhetoric of the NT and Hebrew and Greco-Roman rhetoric from the point of view of their impact on Paul's letters see: E. Güttgemanns, *Fragmenta semiotico-hermeneutica. Eine Texthermeneutik für ein Umgang mit der Hl. Schrift* (FTL 9; Bonn 1983); J. Czerski, *Pierwszy List św. Pawła do Koryntian (1 Kor 1,1–6,20). Wstęp – przekład z oryginału – komentarz, I, Rozdziały 1–6* (OBT 87; Opole 2006), 60–64; R. Meynet, *Wprowadzenie do hebrajskiej retoryki biblijnej* (trans. K. Łukowicz and T. Kot; Myśl Teologiczna; Kraków 2001),

devoted to presentation of these parts of *dispositio* in which quotes from the OT may be found. Then our attention will be focused on the figures, and the rhetorical figures that shape Pauline style of argumentation. *Dispositio* in 1 Cor 15 can be presented as follows:

(1) *praeparatio* (vv. 1–11):
   a. *exordium* (vv. 1–2);
   b. *narratio* (vv. 3–11);
(2) *argumentatio* (vv. 12–34):
   a. *partitio* (v. 12);
   b. *probatio* (vv. 13–34);
(3) *refutatio* (vv. 35–49);
(4) *peroratio* (vv. 50–57);
(5) *exhortatio* (v. 58).[681]

It should be noted that the OT quotations appear sequentially in the following sections of the dispositio: *argumentatio* (three citations), *refutatio* (one quote) and *peroratio* (two citations). As you can see from this arrangement of citations, they do not appear only at the beginning of the structure *(praeparatio)* and at the end *(exhortatio)*.[682] Paul uses the quotes in the essential parts of the *dispositio*, in

20–25; Soggin, *Introduzione all'Antico Testamento*, 112–115; J. Chmiel, *Homilie sakramentalne. Refleksje – szkice – propozycje* (Kraków 1996), 6–7; C. J. Classen, *Rhetorical Criticism of the New Testament* (Tübingen 2000); Aletti, "La dispositio rhétorique dans les épîtres pauliniennes," 385–401; S. Torbus, *Listy św. Pawła z perspektywy retorycznej* (BDL 26; Legnica 2006); id., "Listy św. Pwała w retorycznej kulturze antyku," *TW* 1 (2006): 11–18; P. Lorek, "Podstawowa linearna i chiastyczna, dispositio I Listu do Koryntian," *TW* 1 (2006): 47–60; F. I. Andersen, *Ancient Rhetorical Theory and Paul* (CBET 17; Kamen 1996); J. Classen, "St. Paul's Epistles and Ancient Greek and Roman Rhetoric," in *Rhetoric and the New Testament. Essays from the 1992 Heidelberg Conference* (eds. S. E. Porter and T. H. Olbricht; JSNTSup 90; Sheffield 1993), 265–291; D. Daube, "Rabbinic Methods of Interpretation and Hellenistic Rhetoric," *HUCA* 22 (1949): 239–264; B. Mack, *Rhetoric and the New Testament* (Minneapolis 1990); G. A. Kennedy, *New Testament Interpretation through Rhetorical Criticism* (Chapel Hill 1984); R. Meynet, *L'analyse rhétorique. Une nouvelle méthode pour comprendre la Bible* (Paris 1989); M. M. Mitchell, *Paul and the Rhetoric of Reconciliation: An Exegetical Investigation of the Language and Composition of 1 Corinthian* (Tübingen 1991).

681 Saw, *Paul's Rhetoric*, 223–226.
682 Similarly Saw, *Paul's Rhetoric*. Otherwise, S. M. Lewis, who sees the rhetorical wholeness in vv. 1–34: (1) *exordium* (vv. 1–2); (2) *transitus* (v. 3a); (3) *narratio* (vv. 3b–11); (4) *propositio* (v. 12); (5) *probatio* (vv. 12–28); (6) *peroratio* (vv. 29–34). With such an arrangement, the appropriate *argumentatio* is placed in vv. 12–32; id.,*"So That God May Be All in All"*, 28–37.

which he presents his argument behind the raised thesis. The OT quotations serves the Apostle as arguments.

The style of chapter fifteenth of 1 Cor is a colloquial one which the apostle used every day. In 1 Cor 15 Paul uses 79 nouns, 62 verbs, 34 adjectives and 22 adverbs. There are also words that are not used very often. On 84 *hapax legomena* in 1 Cor, chapter 15 contains 12 of them. Interestingly, none of the *hapax legomena* appear in Pauline quotations from the OT. This means that the apostle chose quotes that can be understood by recipients of his letter, and they did not contain difficult to understand words. This selection of quotations shows Pauline interests of clarity of his argumentation. Indeed, the style of this argumentation can be characterized by correctness, clarity, and conciseness. Rhetorical figures appear in the quotes themselves. What is more, the apostle includes new quotes in context which enabled him to build other rhetorical figures. And so, the use of six quotes from the OT in 1 Cor 15:12–58 relate to the following rhetorical devices:

(1)   asyndeton;
(2)   anaphora;
(3)   antistrophe;
(4)   rhetorical question;
(5)   antithesis;
(6)   apostrophe;
(7)   accumulation;
(8)   personification.

In 1 Cor 15 Paul uses asyndeton (Lat. *dissolutum*). It is a language structure devoid of conjunctions used in order to give condensed and coherent expressions.[683] In an analyzed fragment, an asyndeton occurs several times (v. 14, vv. 1–18, v. 24, v. 35, vv. 42–4, v. 45, v. 4, v. 52, v. 58). As you can see from the above statement, the apostle used the asyndeton in the quote in v. 45: ἐγένετο ὁ πρῶτος, ὁ ἔσχατος. In this way, the argument is more vivid and its strength seems to be enhanced.

The apostle also refers to an anaphora using quotes from the OT in 1 Cor 15:12–58 (Lat. *repetitio*). This consists in starting the neighboring sentences or verses with the same word or group of words. To do this v. 32, he uses a quote from Isa 22:13b: εἰ κατὰ ἄνθρωπον ἐθηριομάχησα ἐν Ἐφέσῳ... εἰ νεκροὶ οὐκ ἐγείρονται. He also uses the arrangement of words in the quotation from Hos 13.14b: ποῦ σου, θάνατε... ποῦ σου, θάνατε. The use of anaphora makes the reasoning more expressive. The repetition of the same word or sequence of words

---

683   Sierotwiński, *Słownik terminów literackich*, 35.

gives a kind of rhythm of speech, so that the style itself can be characterized by considerable vigor. A figure closely related to anaphora is antistrophe (Lat. *conversio*). It consists in repeating the last word or group of words within a sentence. In fragments quoted by Paul from the OT, this figure is used twice, namely in v. 25 and v. 27. For example, the phrase "under his feet" is repeated. In addition to this, at the end of both verses 54b and 55, the term "victory" is used. Yet another rhetorical figure is the frequent repetition of the same words (Lat. *traductio*). These words are called "words-keys" for the given passage. The terms that appear frequently as words (keys) are also included in Pauline quotations from the OT. Among others are: "body," "natural," "spiritual" (vv. 44b–49), "bear" (v. 54), "death," and "victory" (vv. 54–56). The repetition of these words serves not only as the lucidity of the style, but also to make it more elegant.[684]

Paul refers to successive rhetorical figures in 1 Cor 15:12–58. Among other things, the antithesis is built on the basis of quotations from the OT. It lies behind the rule according to which the style of given utterance is based on the juxtaposition of some words or thoughts. The entire piece of 1 Cor 15:44b–49 is built precisely on such antitheses. It should be added herein that one of them constitutes a quote from Gen 2:7b:

> "If there is a natural body
> There is also a spiritual body.
> So it is written:
> The first man Adam became a living being,
> [-------] the last [----------] Adam a life-giving spirit.
> The spiritual did not come first, but the natural,
> and after that the spiritual.
> The first Man was of the dust of the earth,
> The second Man from heaven.
> As was the earthly man, so are those who are of the earth;
> And as is the man from heaven, so also are those who are of heaven.
> And just as we have borne the likeness of the earthly man,
> So shall we bear the likeness of the man from heaven."[685]

There are here the following contrasting statements: "a natural body"–"a spiritual body", "first Adam"–"last Adam", "a soul"–"a spirit", "living"–"life-giving", "first"–"after", "the first man"–"the second man", "earthly"–

---

684 Saw, *Paul's Rhetoric*, 252–253.

685 Brodeur, *Holy Spirit's Agency*, 142. The author adds: "V. 44b offers an excellent example of antithetical parallelism. In this, the thesis statement of the subunit, both clauses of this conditional sentence serve as contrasting statements. Just as Paul had compared the earthly bodies to the heavenly ones in the previous pericope, so here he wants to compare the natural human body to the spiritual one"; ibid.

"heavenly", "from earth"–"from heaven", "we have borne"–"shall we bear", and "the likeness of the earthly man"–"the likeness of the man from heaven."

The selection of quotes and changes that are made within them has a profound impact on the vividness and directness of style of a given pattern of reasoning. In the quotation from v. 32, the recipient expects the future tense of the verb, which characterizes an event that is going to happen "tomorrow" (αὔριον); Paul meanwhile, uses the present tense, although expressing a future action (ἀποθνῄσκομεν). However, a quote from Hos 13:14b creates another figure of speech: questions. Paul inserted some rhetorical questions asked to recipients into the quote in v. 55 (Lat. *interrogatio*). In this way, the apostle uses deliberative rhetorical means by which—through direct reference to the recipient—he makes an impression of straight conversation with the reader of his text. In addition, these questions are addressed to the "death" and thus also create the apostrophe (*metabase*; Lat. *exclamatio*)—a figure consisting in a direct turning to the reality.[686] The quote recorded in v. 32 (from Isaiah 22:13b) was also integrated into the figure called "accumulation" (Lat. *frequentatio*): in vv. 29–34 Paul "accumulates" two real-life examples, and uses them to strengthen his argumentation. Another important rhetorical figure applied by Paul is personification (embodiment, Lat. *conformatio*): the apostle personifies death.[687] There are some arguments where Paul treats the death personally. First, he quotes Isa 25:8a where he asks the death two rhetorical, questions. In a quote included in v. 55, he turns to it twice in a direct way. In the quotations in v. 25b and v. 27a death appears as the enemy of God and is juxtaposed with personal beings, such as Dominion, Authority and Power. The theme of the possibility of defeating death as a personal or even a military opponent in the eschatological battle for dominion over creation,[688] emerges first in Paul's declaration that "flesh and blood cannot inherit the kingdom of God, nor does the perishable inherit the imperishable" (1 Cor 15:50).[689] Verse 50 is recorded in the form of synonymous parallelism. Paul uses the term "Flesh and Blood" to show that the

---

686 I. Saw explains the motivation of such a record: "By this figure Paul seems to instill in the hearer as much indignation as he desires"; Saw, *Paul's Rhetoric*, 262.

687 A similar procedure occurs in Rev 20:14 and *4 Ezra* 8:35; de Boer, *Defeat of Death*, 136.

688 J. P. Heil defines death in Paul's grasp as: "a personified, militaristic enemy (15:26) in the apocalyptic-eschatological battle for control of creation"; Heil, *Rhetorical Role of Scripture*, 254.

689 J. Jeremias, "Flesh and Blood Cannot Inherit the Kingdom of God (1 Cor 15.50)," *NTS* 2 (1955–1956): 151–159; "'Flesh and blood' means man as weak and frail in opposition to God's strength. The sentence emphasizes the incapacity of man to reach by his own means and power the Kingdom of God, i.e., God's salvation and grace"; Usami, "How Are the Dead Rised?," 489.

man with his physical body cannot inherit the kingdom of God. He does this because the term "flesh and blood" is interchangeable with what is perishable. "Flesh and Blood" can be destroyed because of the action of the people's enemy that is personified death.

In addition to the rhetorical figures, the Apostle reaches out for tropes (Greek *tropoi*) or the words and statements in the figurative sense.[690] Synecdoche (metonymy, in which the more general concept is replaced by more detailed, Lat. *comprehensio* or *intellectio*) occurs in the quotation in v. 45: "The first man Adam became a living being" (Gen 2:7b). Adam is here a representative of the entire humanity. The metaphor (Lat. *translatio*) appears, however, in a quote in v. 55: "Where, O death is your sting?" (Hos 13:14b). These two tropes, metaphor and synecdoche, appear in the OT quotations contained in 1 Cor 15:12–58.

All things considered, from the rhetorical point of view, the OT quotes in 1 Cor 15:12–58 perform an educational and deliberative function. They appear in the following parts of the text *dispositio*: *argumentatio* (three citations), *refutatio* (single quote) and *peroratio* (two citations). The Apostle, with the means of the quotes, builds the following rhetorical figures: asyndeton, anaphora, antistrophe, rhetorical questions, antithesis, apostrophe, accumulation and personification. He also uses two rhetorical tropes: metaphor and synecdoche.

3. Messianic/Christological Interpretation of Quotations

Paul interprets texts from the OT from the messianic and Christological perspective. Although the Greek meaning of the name Christ refers to the Messiah it does not mean, however, that the term "Christology" is synonymous with the term "messianic." It may happen that Paul assigned some action to Christ as a man (Jesus), but it is not specifically messianic activity.

The analyses carried out in this work showed that the quotes from Pss 110:1b and 8:7b Paul refers to Christ. The Apostle harmonizes the two quotes so that they can be interpreted with the use of the same key. It is impossible that one of them referred to God (theocentric interpretation) and the other to Christ (Christological interpretation).[691] Since the resurrection of Christ, His reign is

---

690 In rhetoric as the tropes are considered: a metaphor, metonymy, synecdoche, allegory and hyperbole; Sierotwiński, *Słownik terminów literackich*, 271.

691 Pauline effort to get both quotes as close to each other as possible made that some exegetes call them "twin texts" (German *Zwillingstexte*); Lambrecht, "Paul's Christological Use of Scripture," 509.

marked in human history until He comes again and defeats all the forces of evil. Then the end will come, and it will have theocentric character because Christ will hand over the entire kingdom to God the Father. It is worth noting that Ps 110 had messianic nature for the Jews, while Ps 8 was full of praise for the Creator for the dignity He endowed to the man. Meanwhile, Paul interprets both psalms Christologically, and by linking them to Ps 8, he gives to it the characteristics of the messianic psalm.

The quote from Isa 22:13b has not been Christological (or messianic); in an original context, it concerns the inhabitants of Jerusalem, who ignore the danger coming from the Assyrian army. Instead of repenting and preparing for the battle, they are indulged in pleasures. Paul relates it to the people of Corinth who reject the resurrection on the grounds that the attitude of enjoyment and fun should be the logical consequence of their beliefs.

Christologically, however, Paul interprets Gen 2:7b in v. 45b. While the description of the creation of man in Gen 2:7b refers to Adam as the first man, in Paul's grasp, it is referring to Christ. He also states that the earthly was initial and only afterwards did the spiritual appear (v. 46). The first man, Adam, was created from the dust of the earth (v. 47; Gen 2:7) and he has become the "living being" (v. 47; Gen 2:7). So, twice the apostle used Gen 2:7 as a qualifier of the first Adam. This verse, however, also influenced the characteristics of the second/last Adam. It is He who became "a life-giving Spirit" (v. 45b; Gen 2:7b). In Gen 2:7, however, Adam received the "breath of life" and as a result it became a "living being." Paul's interpretation of Gen 2:7 is therefore Christological (similarly as Ps 8:7b in v. 27a). More fully the Christological use of Genesis is seen in v. 49, where there is an allusion to Gen 1:27. Paul claims that we bear the image of the heavenly man within ourselves, so it is Christ not God himself, in Gen 1:27.[692]

Two more quotes from Isa 25:8 and Hos 13:14b were joined by Paul in a way that gave the impression of a single quote. The initial one in the OT could be interpreted by the Jews as indicating the messianic feast; in fact, such an interpretation was common for the first Christians. In Isa 25:8a, seen from the perspective of Isa 26:19, you can see the allusion to the resurrection of the dead and thus to the messianic era. This passage, however, does not refer directly to Christ but announces the final defeat of death. That is certainly the case with the quote taken from Hos 13:14b. Two rhetorical questions do not relate directly to

---

692 "Paul ... not only does he christologize the God-likeness according to which man was created, he also eschatologizes the statement: we shall bear the image of Christ, the heavenly man. Again one is reminded of the same twofold transposition which was at work in Paul's use of Ps. 8.7 in 1 Cor. 15.27a"; Lambrecht, "Paul's Christological Use of Scripture," 514.

the Messiah, but they announce the victory over death and at the same time
indirectly they show the triumph of the Messiah.

Thus, from among the six quotations from the OT cited by Paul in 1 Cor
15:12–58, three *par excellence* refer to Christ (Ps 110:1b; Ps 8:7b; Gen 2:7b).
Two of them are characteristic of the messianic nature (Ps 110:1b; Ps 8:7b),
while one does not apply to the messianic mission of Christ (Isa 22:13b). This is
again contrasted with the other two that talk about the final defeat of death,
which was initiated by the resurrection of Christ (Isa 25:8a; Hos 13:14b).

4. Eschatological Interpretation of Quotations

The resurrection of the dead belongs to the series of eschatological events.[693]
The resurrection of Christ gives the beginning to these events. This disproves
the anthropological dualism of some Corinthians,[694] who may have maintained

---

693   For more on Paul's eschatological thought in 1 Corinthians see.: Barth, "Zur Frage,"
       187–201; G. Barth, "Erwägungen zu 1 Kor 15:20–28," *EvT* 30 (1970): 515–527; J.
       Beker, *Paul's Apocalyptic Gospel: The Coming Triumph of God* (Philadelphia 1982); C.
       Burchard, "1 Kor 15: 39–41," 233–252; B. Byrne, "Eschatologies of Resurrection and
       Destruction. The Ethical Significance of Paul's Dispute with the Corinthians," *DR* 104
       (1986): 288–296; R.B. Hays, "Eschatology and Ethics in 1 Cor," *EA* 10 (1994): 31–43;
       Hill, "Paul's Understanding of Christ's Kingdom," 297–320; Horn, "1 Korinther 15,56
       – ein exegetische Stachel," 88–105; Horsley, "How Can," 203–231; A. Jankowski,
       Eschatologia Nowego Testamentu (Kraków 2007), 97–106; J. Kovacs, "The Archons,
       the Spirit, and the Death of Christ. Do We Really Need the Hypothesis of Gnostic
       Opponents to Explain 1 Cor 2, 2–16," in *Apocalyptic in the NT. Essays in Honor of J.
       Louis Martyn* (ed. J. Marcus and M. L. Soards; JSNTSup 24; Sheffield 1989), 217–236;
       Lindemann, "Parusie Christi und Herrschaft Gottes," 87–107; id., "Paulus und die
       korintische Eschatologie. Zur These von einer 'Entwicklung' im paulinischen Denken,"
       NTS 37 (1991): 373–399; K. Müller, "1 Kor 1,18–25, Die eschatologisch-kritische
       Funktion der Verkündigung des Kreuzes," *BZ* 10 (1966): 246–272; Perriman, "Paul and
       the Parousia," 512–521; K. A. Plank, "Resurrection Theology: The Corinthian
       Controversy Re-examined," *PRSt* 8 (1981): 41–54; J. H. Roberts, "The Eschatological
       Transitions to the Pauline Letter Body," *Neot* 20 (1986): 29–35; K. Romaniuk, *Wiara w
       zmartwychwstanie, pusty grób i pojawienie się zmartwychwstałego Chrystusa* (AL 6;
       Katowice 1981); R. Sider, "The Pauline Conception of Resurrection Body in 1 Cor
       15:35–54," *NTS* 21 (1975): 429–439; Usami, "How Are the Dead Rised?," 468–493;
       Vorster, "Resurrection Faith in 1 Cor 15," 287–307; J. S. Vos, *The Pauline Eschatology*
       (Grand Rapids 1961²); D. J. Dougty, "The Presence and Future of Salvation in Corinth,"
       ZNW 66 (1975): 61–90.

694   de Boer, *Defeat of Death*, 111; C. F. D. Moule, "St. Paul and Dualism. The Pauline
       Conception of Resurrection," *NTS* 12 (1965/1966): 117. In Corinth the denial of the

that after death, the human soul passes to another dimension of existence, and lasts forever. While the Corinthians rejected the resurrection, the Apostle insisted that the resurrection will take place at the end of time and will be combined with the parousia.[695] The series of eschatological events involves some stages:

(1) resurrection of Christ;
(2) parousia;
(3) the resurrection of the faithful;
(4) defeating of the forces of darkness (Dominion, Authority and Power);
(5) defeating the last enemy—the death;
(6) the reign of Christ;
(7) handing over the reign to God and the Father.

In the first place, the Apostle shows the order of the resurrection. Christ was the first who has been raised from the dead, and he became the "firstfruits" of those who will attain the resurrection. According to Paul, there are two categories of people who attain resurrection. The first category represents Christ himself, the second one Christians. Thanks to the resurrection, Christ became "a life-giving Spirit" (v. 45b). There was no change in His nature, but in His state. Christ left the life in earthly existence and began to exist in heavenly one.

The resurrection of Christians is therefore, deep-rooted in the resurrection of Christ. Then after Christ, in the moment of "His coming"—the parousia, all who belong to him will be raised from the dead. The apostle sees a clear connection between the parousia and the resurrection of the faithful. The latter will attain the resurrection after the second coming of Christ and only then the death will be destroyed. On the basis of v. 51 we can make an assumption that Paul expected that the parousia would take place during his life: "Listen, I tell you a mystery: We will not all sleep, but we will all be changed." This interpretation also supports the following phrase: "the dead will be raised imperishable, and we will be changed" (v. 52b). However, taking into account v. 23 and a solemn tone of v. 51, used for rhetorical purposes, it seems more likely that Pauline's "we" refers not only to his generation, but is also fully representative for all others who parousia finds alive. 2 Cor 5:2–4 should be interpreted from the

---

resurrection could result from the dualistic views on man. According to them, the body is a prison for the man and his soul; Langkammer, *Życie człowieka w świetle Biblii*, 433.

695 J. Holleman explains: "Resurrection, Paul's alternative for the Corinthian view on life after death, is not only bodily, it is also eschatological; it will take place at the end of time. Paul counters the Corinthian view that the soul moves into spiritual immortality as soon as a person dies by stressing the fact that the resurrection will only take place at the end of time"; id., *Resurrection and Parousia*, 38.

same point of viein: "Meanwhile we groan, longing to be clothed with our heavenly dwelling, because when we are clothed, we will not be found naked. For while we are in this tent, we groan and are burdened, because we do not wish to be unclothed but to be clothed with our heavenly dwelling, so that what is mortal may be swallowed up by life."[696]

Bodies of resurrected people will be far more different from their natural, mortal bodies. Paul does not deny some form of continuity between the two ones; however, he clearly highlights their difference by means of these antitheses: earthly–heavenly, natural–spiritual, from the dust of the earth–from heaven.[697] The resurrected bodies will be made of "heavenly" matter while the natural bodies were formed "from the dust of the earth," or from the "earth's" matter. Paul believes in the existence of some heavenly substance/matter that will be used to form a glorious body after the resurrection. The apostle views Gen 2:7b (v. 45) from an eschatological perspective where it is said that the first man became a living being. A little further (v. 47) he makes a clear allusion to Gen 1:27: "So God created man in his own image, in the image of God he created him; male and female he created them." Also, the interpretation of this passage is marked by an eschatological feature: Paul claims that "shall we bear the likeness of the man from heaven."[698]

The Apostle does not mention the resurrection of the unbelievers, but this does not mean that he rejects such an idea.[699] Christ's parousia has to lead to the final defeat of evil forces. In this context, the first of the OT quotations occurs in 1 Cor 15:12–58. It is taken from Ps 110:1b. With the help of it, Paul shows Christ's victory over the evil. The last defeated enemy will be death itself. Then

---

696 Intensive study on the subject conducted Perriman; id., "Paul and the Parousia," 512–521.

697 Already at the beginning of the last century, this view was propagated by W. Bousset: "Seiner Herkunft nach ist der erste Mensch von der Erde und daher auch aus irdischem Stoff, der zweite Mensch ist seiner Herkunft nach himmlisch und – dürfen wir im Sinne des Paulus hinzusetzen – deshalb auch von himmlischen Stoff"; *Der erste Brief an die Korinther* (Die Schriften des Neues Testament; Göttingen 1917³), 161. S. Brodeur notices "Paul was contrasting an earthly substance to the heavenly one. For him, the body of the first Adam is composed of a material substance which is earthly, while the body of the last Adam is composed of a material substance which is heavenly"; id., *Holy Spirit's Agency*, 149.

698 Lambrecht, "Paul's Christological Use of Scripture," 514.

699 "With regard to the participation in Adam's death, Paul speaks about all people, both Christians and non-Christians (v. 22a). But with regard to the participation in Jesus' resurrection (v. 22b), Paul speaks about Christians only, since only Christians may consider themselves as being represented by Jesus. Through their unity with Adam, all people share in Adam's death; through their unity with Christ, Christians share in Jesus' resurrection"; Holleman, *Resurrection and Parousia*, 55.

everything—not only the dark powers, but absolutely everything that exists—will be subjected to the lordship of Christ. At this point, Paul uses another quote from the OT, coming from Ps 8:7b: "For he has put everything under his feet" (v. 27a).[700] This time a quote from the psalm serves to underline the universal reign of Christ. In vv. 23–28, the passage is dominated by terminology connected with the reign, for example, "kingdom," "rule," "subject," or "defeat." Psalm 110 was recognized by the Jews and the Christians as the royal one. With the help of it, Paul shows the kingly dignity of Christ. Besides, the apostle is interested in—like early Christian tradition—the use of the picture of a person sitting at the right hand of God in Ps 110:1. The authors of the NT use this picture mostly to show the risen Jesus, who seats at the right hand of the Father (Matt 24:44; 26:64; Mark 12:36; 14:62; 16:19; Luke 20:42; Acts 2:25.34; 7;55.56; Rom 8:34; Eph 1:20; Col 3:1; Heb 1:3.13; 8:1; 10:12; 12:2; 1 Pet 3:22).[701]

Using quotes from Ps 110:1 and Ps 8:7b the apostle speaks of the ultimate defeat of death. The victory over death is the *par excellence* eschatological event. In vv. 23–28 at least, two facts give evidence to it: Paul moves the final victory over death from the resurrection of Christ to parousia (contrary to "pneumatological enthusiasts" in the community of Corinth), and he calls the personified death the "last," and thus the eschatological enemy.[702] The motif of victory over the enemy can be seen not only in quotations from the Psalms, but also in the fragment quoted from Isa 25:8a ("death was swallowed by victory"). What is more, this passage refers indirectly through its context to the image of the downtrodden opponent who was presented in the cited Psalms; and in Isa 25:12 we can read: "He will bring down your high fortified walls and lay them low; he [Lord] will bring them down to the ground, to the very dust."[703]

On the basis of these findings, it would seem that the OT passages quoted by Paul in 1 Cor 15:12–58 have eschatological tones, even though not all of them had the tone in their original context. This is because the apostle inserts the quotations into the scheme of eschatological events. Paul connects the quote from Ps 110:1b with the eschatological defeat of all enemies, including death. The quotation from Ps 8:7b shows the final subjection of everything to Christ.

---

700 U. Heil, "Theo-logische Interpretation von 1 Kor. 15,23–28," *ZNW* 84 (1993): 27–29; Lambrecht, "Paul's Christological Use of Scripture," 502; id., "Structure and Line of Thought in 1 Cor. 15:23–28," *NovT* 32 (1990): 143.

701 Lewis, *"So That God May Be All in All"*, 59; Hay, *Glory At the Right Hand*, 45; J. H. Schütz, *Paul and the Anatomy of Apostolic Authority* (Cambridge 1975), 84–113.

702 de Boer, *Defeat of Death*, 123.

703 Crushing of the enemy as a symbol of defeat occurs also in other parts of the OT: Josh 10:24, Isa 51:23 Ps 89:11 and in Ps 110:1.

He also uses a quote from Gen 2:7b where he refers to the resurrection of Christ, which became the "live-giving Spirit," whereas the quotes from Isa 25:8 and Hos 13:14b refer to the definitive defeat of personified death. Only a quote from Isa 22:13b is not a direct reference to the eschatological events, but shows the attitude the Corinthians should take in the face of these events, if they would like to be in an agreement with their rejection of the resurrection.

5. Application of *Gezerah Shavah* and *Qal Wahomer* Methods in Interpretation of Quotations

In 1 Cor 15:12–58, the apostle uses two methods important for rabbinic exegesis: *gezerah shavah* and *qal wahomer*. The first of these Jewish methods of interpretation of the Bible is called *gezerah shavah*. The method explains one biblical verse using the second one, which contains the same word or phrase. In analyzed quotations, Paul applies this interpretation principle twice and as a result he takes into account four out of six citations, which are the subject of this study. The quotes in v. 25b and v. 27a are connected through the same words "all/everything" and the phrase "under his feet." At the same time, the quotes from v. 54 and v. 55 combine the terms "death" and "victory."

A citation from Ps 8:7b in 15:27a develops the thought underwritten in the quotation from Ps 110:1b in 15:25b. For that reason, there are the same words or phrases in the two quotations. The phrase "all his enemies" from 15:25 is extended in 15:27 to "everything," and the last term includes not only the negative aspect (the enemy), but absolutely everything that exists, including the recipients of the letter itself.[704] The phrase, "until He [God] has put all his enemies under his [Christ] feet" from 15:25b is extended in 15:27a to: "For he [God] has put everything under his feet."[705] The quote included in v. 25b expresses a negative aspect of putting everything under Christ's feet while the citation from v. 27a a positive one.[706]

The sense of such a combination of the two quotations based on *gezerah shavah* is even more apparent when we show it in the chiastic structure of 1 Cor 15:24–28. The statement that death will be finally destroyed results from our

---

704   Heil, *Rhetorical Role of Scripture*, 210; Collins, *First Corinthians*, 554.

705   "V. 27a wiederholt also die Aussage von V. 25b, wobei eine gewisse Änderung natürlich darin liegt, dass ὑποτάσσειν nicht einfach „unterwerfen" meint, sondern die Errichtung einer neuen Weltordnung anzudeuten scheint"; Lindemann, "Parusie Christi und Herrschaft Gottes," 100.

706   Lambrecht, "Structure and Line of Thought," 149.

divagations: The sentence, "The last enemy to be destroyed is death" (v. 26) is a central phrase of a chiasm. It is illustrated in the following scheme[707]:

A 24a Then the end will come,
     24b **when** he hands over the kingdom to **God** the Father,

  B 24c **after** he has destroyed **all** dominion, authority and power.

    C 25a **For** he must reign,
         25b until he has put **all** his enemies *under his feet.*

      D 26 The last enemy to be destroyed is death.

    C' 27a *For he has* put *everything under his feet.*

  B' 27b when it says that *"everything"* has been put under him,
         27c it is clear that this does not include God himself, who put
         everything under Christ.

A' 28 *When* he has done this,
     28b then the Son himself will be made subject to him who put everything
     under him,
     28c so that *God* may be all in all.

Elements, A and A' share the following words: "when" and "God" and (especially the word "God" occurs only once in the whole passage of vv. 24–28) decide on the separation of these elements as parallelled in the chiasm. To support this thesis, the Father in A and the Son in A' are useful because the term "the son" usually can be found in relation to "the Father." In addition, the phrase "all in all" in A' is the equivalent to "the end" in A; for this reason, the parallelism between A and A' is more exact.[708] The parallelism between B and B' is determined by using the terms "after" and "everything."[709] Parallelism between elements C and C' create such terms as, "for," "all/everything" and the phrase "under his feet." In element D, the terms "the last" and "death" form the uniqueness of the whole sentence because in the entire chiasm, they can be found only once.

As the structure of the chiasm shows, it revolves around the ascertainment from v. 26: "The last enemy to be destroyed is death." The quote in v. 25b, derived from Ps 110:1b prepares the ascertainment, but the quote incorporated

---

707 Hill, "Paul's Understanding of Christ's Kingdom," 300; Heil, *Rhetorical Role of Scripture*, 212–213; Lewis, *"So That God May Be All in All"*, 75.

708 Lewis, *"So That God May Be All in All"*, 75. Differently: M. Gielen, "Universale Totenauferweckung und universales Heil? 1 Kor 15,20–28 im Kontext paulinischer Theologie," *BZ* 47 (2003): 92–95.

709 J. P. Heil argues that about the distinction between B and B' also decides the terms: "dominion," "authority" and "power"; id., *Rhetorical Role of Scripture*, 214. However, this argument does not seem convincing, since they appear only in B in contrary to B'.

into v. 27a, taken from Ps 8:7b gives its clarification. The sentence coming before the quote from v. 25b: "For he must reign ...," is based on the understanding of God's command recorded in Ps 110:1b: "Sit at my right hand." Christ as a King from the dynasty of David, he seats at the right hand of God, and he exercises his power authoritatively. Everything will be subjected to him; at first, all the forces hostile to God ("dominion," "authority" and "power") and finally, the death and the whole universe as well.[710] The fact that the main statement of the chiasm is v. 26, not only highlights the definitive defeat of death, as the greatest enemy of God, but also a specific turning point of reasoning. Up to v. 26 Paul presented the *climax* of the destructive power overbearing God's adversaries: Dominion–Authority–Power–death. Starting from v. 27 it indicates the subjection of "everything" to Christ, not only that what is contrary to God. So the tone of the first quote is negative (destruction of evil), the second one—positive (the subjection "everything," including also the good). The phrase "under his feet" in the first quote speaks of defeating evil, however in the second one—it depicts the subjection of everything that exists to Christ, who as the first one rose from the dead. It should be noted that using the quotes from Ps 110:1 and Ps 8:7b, Paul keeps the tone present in the original context. In the first context, the phrase "under his feet" also refers in Ps 110:1b, to the defeat of enemies (negative tone), while in Ps 8:7b, it refers to the subjection of everything under the feet of "the man" (more positive tone). Moreover, the term "everything" used in v. 27bc, repeated herein twice (the first time without the article, the second time with an article), shows a total and universal nature of this submission or subordination. As at the beginning God has put all things under the feet of man (Ps 8:7b) so now is he putting everything under the feet of the Man, who "has indeed been raised from the dead, the firstfruits of those who have fallen asleep" (v. 20). In this way, element B' develops the thought contained in B: if B says that the forces of evil will be subjected to Christ, the element B' says that absolutely everything will be subjected to Him, except of God who put all things under Him.

Similarly, the element A' develops the thought included in the element A. In A there is a mention of "the end" which is to come; in A' Paul gives a logical explanation, which the end will lie in and as a result "God may be all in all." In this way, a lapidary statement enclosed in A finds an additional explanation in A'. Only now it becomes clear why in v. 24b, Paul talks about handing over the reign to "God the Father." This distinction is used to create the more accurate parallel to v. 28, in which it is said that "who (indication to God) put everything under him (indication to the Father)."

---

710 Münderlein, *Die Überwindung der Mächte*, 105–107.

In conclusion, it should be noted that Paul uses the Jewish method of biblical exegesis called *gezerah shavah* for two quotes from the Book of Psalms (Ps 110:1b and Ps 8:7b), which he integrates into a fragment structurally arranged in chiasm; in that way he emphasizes the truth that the death will be finally defeated.[711] Paul used a quote from Ps 110:1b to show the truth that Christ will defeat all the forces of evil. The largest of these forces is death. The quote from Ps 8:7b was used by the apostle to show the truth that absolutely everything will be submitted to Christ, not only the forces of evil. The first quote was used to expose the negative overtone of the message. On the other hand, the second one shows the positive aspect of submitting everything to Christ. By these means, the apostle draws the picture of what he calls "the end," and what will lie in bringing "everything" to the state in which God will be "all in all." This will be done through the destruction of all evil and the subordination of everything to Christ, who is the first resurrected. Paul used both quotes in the broader context to ensure the recipients of the letter that as those who belong to Christ, (v. 23) they will attain the resurrection, "but each in his own turn."[712]

For the second time in 1 Cor 15:12–58, Paul juxtaposes two OT quotations based on a *gezerah shavah* in vv. 54b–55; they are quotations from Isa 25:8a and Hos 13:14b. However, there is a clear difference in this case in the use of Jewish exegetical method by Paul, in comparison with its use concerning citations included in v. 25b and v. 27a. While previously the apostle separated quotes with his explanations, now he compiles them one next to another so closely that they give the impression of a single quote. The reader has to deal with the combined quote. The fact that such a statement, which gives an impression of a single quote, is consciously Paul's intention, shows that he used the introductory formula; it is written in the singular form: "then the saying that is written will come true" (v. 54).[713] It is also worth noting that this is the only quote not only in 15:12–58, but throughout 1 Cor, whose content has not yet come true.[714] The combination of both citations and Paul's editorial interventions (replacing the term "Hades" from the LXX with "death" in the quotation from Hos 13:14b) makes vv. 54b–55 gain as many as three references to death and therefore, the emphasis is put on its definitive overcoming. The fact

---

711 These two quotations from psalms are also arranged with the use of *gezerah shavah* method in Eph 1:20–21; 1 Pet 3:21–22; Heb 1–2; Phil 3:20–21.

712 Heil, *Rhetorical Role of Scripture*, 218–219.

713 C. D. Stanley argues: "Paul gives his reader no indication that vv. 54b–55 might represent anything other than a continuous quotation from a single biblical passage"; Stanley, *Paul and the Language of Scripture*, 209–210.

714 Fee, *First Epistle to the Corinthians*, 803; Thiselton, *First Epistle to the Corinthians*, 1298.

is also highlighted by the use of the verb κατεπόθη, that takes the form *passivum divinum*.[715] Finally, the combination of two citations thanks to the *gezerah shavah* method, given their direct context, should strengthen in the recipients of Paul's letter the hope for the fact that:

(1) The last enemy to be destroyed is death (v. 26);

(2) Death cannot achieve any victory only by the fact that "flesh and blood" are capable of being destroyed, because finally, they will be adorned in the indestructibility (v. 50);

(3) God's "mystery" (v. 51) that the perishable will clothe itself with imperishable, and the mortal will clothe itself with the immortality, "must" (v. 53)[716] be filled;

(4) When there will be the end (v. 24), not only what is perishable and mortal will be transformed (v. 53–54a), but also death itself will be defeated by God. In other words, it will be completely destroyed (v. 54b) and will be devoid of "victory" and "sting" (v. 55).[717]

Two other quotes (Gen 2:7b and Isa 22:13b) do not occur in combination with other quotations from the OT and therefore, we cannot speak here about the application of the *gezerah shavah* method. Paul employed this method in 1 Cor 15:12–58 twice, where the apostle combines Ps 110:1b with Ps 8:7b and Isa 25:8a with Hos 13:14b.

Paul's interpretation of Ps 110:1b and Ps 8:7b reflects the characteristics known to rabbinic pesher. Pesher is a kind of literary genre that includes a clear citation of a quotation from the Bible and then a brief explanation of it. It was mainly widespread in Qumran and in Judaic writings contemporary with qumranic literature; however, it is impossible to find it in the NT.[718] In 1 Cor 15:12–58, on the base of Midrash pesher, Paul explains quotes from Ps 110:1b and Ps 8:7b in vv. 25–28.[719] The whole section comprising vv. 23–28 is

---

715   Heil, *Rhetorical Role of Scripture*, 252.

716   H. Saake, "Die kodikologisch problematische Nachstellung der Negation (Beobachtungen zu 1 Kor 15,51)," *ZNW* 63 (1972): 277–279; A. Romeo, "'Omnes quidem resurgemus' seu 'Omnes quidem nequaquam dormiemus' (1 Cor. 15,51)," *VD* 14 (1934): 142–378.

717   Heil, *Rhetorical Role of Scripture*, 256–257.

718   G. J. Brooke, "Peszer," in *Słownik hermeneutyki biblijnej* (eds. R. J. Coggins, and J. L. Houlden; Polish ed. W. Chrostowski; trans. B. Widła; Warszawa 2005), 664–665. S. Jędrzejowski argues that in the NT we find many texts that bear some traces of pesher or just keep its style; S. Jędrzejewski, "Peszer jako metoda egzegetyczna," *Seminare* 24 (2007): 122.

719   J. Lambrecht of the structure of a section in vv. 23–28 presents in such a way so that to emphasize the importance of midrash: "The order of events (23–28):

composed of a thesis in which Paul shows the order of people rising from the dead and the explanation that contains the aforementioned quotes from the Psalms. These explanations constitute Midrash.

A similar situation occurs in vv. 45–47.[720] Paul quotes Gen 2:7b and then interprets this passage, but not in relation to Adam, the first man, but in relation to Christ—the second/last Man. Paul's interpretation is built precisely around this quote of the resurrection of Christ as a "life-giving spirit." While the first Adam started humanity, which plunged into sin, the second/the last Adam gives rise to the humanity aiming at the resurrection.

Paul included vv. 45–47 in the argument involving vv. 42–49 by applying a different Jewish method of interpretation of the Bible—*qal wahomer*,[721] thus a deduction from a less important case to the more important one, very often used in Midrash.[722] Using this type of reasoning, the apostle shows that at the beginning, there was the perishable / dishonourable / weak / natural, followed by the imperishable / glorious / powerful and spiritual. Similarly, at first there was the earthly man / living being, then came man from heaven / life-giving spirit. The Apostle includes into this reasoning a quote from Gen 2:7b and gives to it a characteristic interpretation in relation to Christ.[723] In this way, he develops the analogy originated in vv. 21–22: Adam–Christ.

6. Application of the Early Christian Tradition in Quoting

Two out of the six quotes from the OT used by Paul in 1 Cor 15:12–58, namely a quote from Ps 110:1b and from Ps 8:7b, probably functioned together in the pre-Pauline tradition. The Apostle joined them in vv. 25–27a: "For he must reign until he has put all his enemies under his feet. The last enemy to be destroyed is death. And put everything under his feet."[724] They are placed together in several places in the NT:

(a) Thesis: Christ, those who belong to Christ, the end (23–24);
(b) Explanation by means of scriptural midrash (25–28)";
id., "Paul's Christological Use of Scripture," 504.

720 Brodeur, *Holy Spirit's Agency*, 143.
721 Morissette, "La condition de ressucité," 210–211.
722 P. S. Alexander, "Midrasz," in *Słownik hermeneutyki biblijnej* (eds. R. J. Coggins and J. L. Houlden; Polish ed. W. Chrostowski; trans. B. Widła; Warszawa 2005), 579. *Qal wahomer* means "light and heavy"; Silva, "Old Testament in Paul," 637.
723 Schneider, "Corporate Meaning and Background," 149.
724 Hasler, "Credo und Auferstehung in Korinth," 29.

"…which he exerted in Christ when he raised him from the dead and seated him at his right hand in the heavenly realm, far above all rule and authority, power and dominion, and every title that can be given, not only in the present age but also in the one to come. And God placed all things under his feet and appointed him to be head over everything for the church, which is his body, the fullness of him who fills everything in every way" (Eph 1:20–23);

"And put everything under his feet. In putting everything under him, God left nothing that is not subject to him. Yet at present we do not see everything subject to him" (Heb 2:8);

"However, our citizenship is in heaven. Moreover, we eagerly await a Saviour from there, the Lord Jesus Christ, who, by the power that enables him to bring everything under his control, will transform our lowly bodies so that they will be like his glorious body" (Phil 3:20–21).[725]

In the first point, there is an allusion to Ps 110:1b, rather than a quote. It should be noted that the quotes from Eph 1:22; 1 Pet 3:21–22[726] and Heb 2:8 serve the inspired authors to emphasize the exaltation of Christ over the forces of evil, when in 1 Pet and Ephesians, they also recollect the resurrection.[727] Thus, these texts have a common reference to the resurrection of Christ; a quote from Ps 110:1b and Ps 8:7b. In the passage from 1 Cor 15:23–28 Paul adapts an early Christological tradition and interprets it in the context of the resurrection.[728] Moreover, this tradition was continued by the early Christians in the non-Bible

---

725   J. Holleman writes: "The use of Psalm 110 (109):1 to describe Jesus' exaltation and enthronement as Lord has a pre-Pauline origin. It is found throughout the scriptures of the New Testament. This shows that it stems from the oldest stratum of the Christian tradition"; id., *Resurrection and Parousia*, 63; Hay, *Glory At the Right Hand*, 73.

726   In this passage, there is an allusion to Ps 110, as it is referred Christ's being at the right hand of God. We should also pay attention to the theme of the resurrection of Christ, baptism and defeat of the forces of evil. All three themes are common to the quoted passage and 1 Cor 15:12–58: "and this water symbolizes baptism that now saves you also—not the removal of dirt from the body but the pledge of a good conscience toward God. It saves you by the resurrection of Jesus Christ, who has gone into heaven and is at God's right hand—with angels, authorities and powers in submission to him" (1 Pet 3:21–22).

727   Lewis, *"So That God May Be All in All"*, 60.

728   in 1 Cor 15.20–28 Paul is adapting and reinterpreting christological traditions known to the Corinthians, traditions in which Psalm 110:1 and Psalm 8:7b had in fact already come to play a fixed role in connection with Christ's resurrection which was understood to entail his exaltation over the principalities and powers"; de Boer, *Defeat of Death*, 118. The Jewish as well as Christian tradition, unalterably made out the psalms as an announcement of the Messiah. Catechesis of the early Church used constantly, especially Pss 110 and 2 to express the enthronement of Christ 'at the right hand of God' after his resurrection and Ascension; Brzegowy, *Psalmy*, 146.

writings, for example, in the works of Polycarp of Smyrna (*Phil.* 2:1), and Justin Martyr (*Tryph.* 121:3, cf. 41:1; 131:5).[729]

Interestingly, in the direct context of the passages from psalms quoted by Paul; there is a mention of baptism (v. 29). The baptism itself was understood by early Christians as a share in the death and resurrection of Christ. Furthermore, 1 Pet 3:21b–22 and Eph 1:20–23 show the close relationship that exists between the Christological tradition of the resurrection of Christ and exalting Him above the powers of darkness (thrones, dominions, principalities, authorities), and the soteriological application of this tradition for baptism. First Peter relates directly to the baptism just before quoting a Christological tradition based on the conjunction of two quotations from the psalms. After Eph 1:20–23, where that Christological tradition is included, there is mention of the resurrection and the life with Christ (2:1–10). Similarities between 1 Cor 15:23–28 and Eph 1:20–23 are striking: in 1 Cor 15:24 and Eph 1:21, there three identical phrases. What is more, they are in the same order, and they determine the powers of evil; in both cases, before the expression for forces of evil, there is the word "all." Psalm 8:7b was modified in the same way: there is a change of the second grammatical person to a third one and in relation to the LXX, the preposition "under" is also changed. Both fragments end with the phrase "all in all." It should also be noted that while in Eph 1:20–23 the first part of verse 1 from Ps 110 is quoted, in 1 Cor 15:25b it is the second part of this verse. In addition, in the Colossians, we also find citations or allusions to Ps 110:1 (2:10.12.15; 3:1) in the context of the resurrection of Christ and his exaltation over the forces of evil. More, there is a motif of baptism understood as burying and resurrection with Christ (2:12).[730]

All these similarities cannot of course be random. There are just too many of them. This brings to mind the conclusion that Ps 110 and Ps 8 had been used in Christological catechesis, which included at least a few elements: a reference to Christ's resurrection and His exaltation above every dominion, authority and power, the mention of Christ's exaltation to the "right hand" of God (Ps 110:1), a reference to subjection everything "under the feet" of Christ (Ps 110:1b, Ps 8:7b) and finally, a reference to the fact that God becomes "all in all."[731]

---

729 Hill, "Paul's Understanding of Christ's Kingdom," 313.

730 On the use of Ps 110 in the entire NT, see: W. R. G. Loader, "Christ at the Right Hand – Ps. CX. 1 in the New Testament," *NTS* 24 (1977): 199–217.

731 de Boer, *Defeat of Death*, 119–120. C. K. Barrett adds: "We should note in passing the use of both Psalm 110:1 and Psalm 8:7. The two Psalms speak in very similar language of the subjection of enemies, or of all things, under the feet of one whom New Testament writers (not only Paul) take to be Christ"; "Significance of the Adam-Christ Typology," 111.

Justifying the resurrection of the dead, Paul goes back to the early Christological tradition, which used Pss 110 and 8 in order to justify the exaltation of Christ over all the forces of evil. Exalted above all dominion, authority and power, Christ finally overcomes death, which is not only evil but also our "last enemy." Paul personified death. It can be placed on the same list as all dominion, authority and power. Consequently, as equal to them, the death is also the man's enemy. It must therefore be destroyed like the other forces of evil. This truth can be expressed by the apostle's words: "until I make your enemies a footstool for your feet" (Ps 110:1b). Defeating the last enemy is equivalent to the quote, "you put everything under his feet" (Ps 8:7b). Just then Christ will reign over everything; he will hand over the kingdom to God who will become "all in all."

Conclusions

In Western Christianity, which does not remain without the philosophical influence of ancient Greece and the legal constructs of ancient Rome, we have become accustomed to identifying the divine and inspired word with the explanations entailed in commentaries. In principle, we agree with the opinion that a divine text is a "fact," whereas the comments thereto constitute the subjective opinion of given authors. It seems, however, that neither the Jewish translators nor the first Christians explaining the Bible performed such a differentiation. For them, the first priority was the significance of the text. Once they found it, they tried to express it as precisely as possible and then, in the second place, they were concerned with the accuracy of given words or their order in the sentence. In other words, in quoting the OT, they were above all concerned with faithfully interpreting the very meaning of the text and not so much the word for word transcription. The same concerns quotations of the OT in *Corpus Paulinum*.

The objects of analyses in this monograph are the OT quotations entailed in a fragment of Paul's correspondence with the Corinthians, where the Apostle of the Nations concentrates the reader's attention on the resurrection of the dead (1 Cor 15:12–58). The image that is formed based on the analyses conducted in this work is that in the Corinthian community there appeared at least a group of followers who rejected the physical resurrection of the dead and accepted an anthropological dualism according to which the human soul becomes freed from the body after death and begins to exist as immortal in another, spiritual dimension of reality. This state—according to those "some" (τινες)—will last forever. The adoption of anthropological dualism leads to the rejection the physical resurrection of the dead. In this perspective, it is neither necessary nor even needed. Since the body is the prison of the soul, it does not seem logical that after the soul's liberation from the body it can become enclosed in another, risen body. This would be a return—according to some Corinthians—to the state of imprisonment. "Some" Corinthians, therefore, committed two mistakes in their thinking about the resurrection, errors that Paul refers to by name:

(1) without negating the resurrection of Christ, they negated the resurrection of the dead;

(2) they erred in asking "How are the dead raised? With what kind of body do they come?" (v. 35), reducing to *ad absurdum* their failure to understand the nature of the risen body.

Faced with such a challenge, the apostle points to an alternative view on life after death: the resurrection of the dead that will take place at the end of time and will be connected with the parousia of the returning Lord. Both the resurrection and the parousia, preceded by the final vanquishing of evil powers, a part of which the Apostle also considers death, belong to the series of eschatological events. The purpose of these events is for Christ to be Lord over everything that exists and to give the Kingdom to God and the Father.

In his didactic (and partly deliberative) disquisition, the Apostle reaches for six quotations from the OT: Ps 110:1b; Ps 8:7b; Isa 22:13b; Gen 2:7b; Isa 25:8a and Hos 13:14b. They were obtained from the text with the aid of detailed analyses conducted in Chapter 1 where the terms "quotation" and "allusion" were specified. After this specification, the fundamental features of the phenomenon of quoting the OT in *Corpus Paulinum* was presented, the structure of 1 Cor 15:12–58 was identified and the context of the said quotations was determined. Their detailed analysis was carried out in the subsequent chapters (II–VII) by firstly specifying the significance of those fragments in their original context and then in the given segments of the structure of 1 Cor 15:12–58. The determination of the significance of the texts quoted by Paul in the original context involved a three-stage process: a presentation of the literary setting and structure of the pericope in which the given text is located, an exegetical analysis of the pericope, and a discussion on the contribution of the quoted fragment to its content. The conclusions to the studies conducted in the above manner have been presented in the last chapter of the monograph. These conclusions can be essentially thus formulated:

(1) three of the quotations come from the Prophetic books, two from the Psalms, and one from the Pentateuch. The fact that Paul most readily reaches to the Prophetic books in his quotations can suggest that the Apostle perceives the fulfilment of the OT prophecies in Christ;

(2) the Apostle fundamentally follows the LXX and changes the quotes mainly for editorial and rhetorical purposes. Regarding the quotation from Isa 25:8a, Paul also tries to make the LXX version as similar as possible to the HB;

(3) five of the above quotations in the original context definitely do not speak about resurrection. Allusions to the resurrection of the dead can be seen only in the quotation from Isa 25:8a. However, Paul the Apostle uses all six in his argumentative disquisition in support of the resurrection;

(4) the Apostle changes the context of the quoted fragments which is essentially natural in using quotations; only sometimes does he retain the main features of the original context. Changes in context usually head towards moving the stress from the historical situation of the addressees of the OT texts to the eschatological perspective in which the inhabitants of Corinth are interested;

(5) the Apostle uses the quotations for rhetorical purposes. The Apostle places them in various parts of the rhetorical *dispositio* of the text. He reaches for rhetorical figures (asyndeton, anaphora, antistrophe, rhetorical questions, antithesis, apostrophe, accumulation and personification) as well as tropes (metaphor and synecdoche);

(6) Paul interprets quotations from Ps 110:1b, Ps 8:7b and Gen 2:7b Christologically, two of which have a specifically messianic character for him (Ps 110:1b; Ps 8:7b). One of the quotations does not concern the messianic mission of Christ (Isa 22:13b), whereas the two remaining speak of the final vanquishing of death which was inaugurated by the resurrection of Christ (Isa 25:8a; Hos 13:14b). The Christological perspective is, therefore, present in all the quotations:

(7) all the quotations were included by Paul in the description of the series of eschatological events in which the Apostle includes the resurrection of Christ, the parousia, the resurrection of the believers, the relinquishment of the powers of darkness (Rule, Authority, Power), relinquishing the last enemy—death (personified), the dominion of Christ, and giving the kingdom to God and the Father;

(8) Paul uses Jewish methods of interpreting biblical texts among which the *gezerah shavah* method is implemented in the quotations from Ps 110:1b and Ps 8:7b, as well as to the quotations from Isa 25:8a and Hos 13:14b, and the *qal wahomer* method used in the quotation from Gen 2:7b;

(9) the Apostle used the early Christian tradition which combined the quotations from Ps 110:1b and Ps 8:7b into one for catechetical purposes. The quotations from these Psalms also jointly appear in other places in the NT.

In Paul's argumentation in support of the resurrection of the dead in 1 Cor 15:12–58, the quotation from Ps 110:1b helped the author to justify his conviction that the parousia will be accompanied by the relinquishment of all evil powers, including death. The quotation from Ps 8:7b shows the truth that Christ has dominion over absolutely everything that exists, not only evil powers. The quotation from Isa 22:13b was used by the Apostle to the Nations to show the logically evident attitude that the Corinthians should adopt. Paul also referred to Gen 2:7b so as to show the typology of Adam–Christ and that the risen Lord is the "life-giving spirit," or the beginning (first fruit) and representative of all who will rise from the dead. Paul seals his conviction on the ultimate relinquishment of death with a quote from Isa 25:8a, which connects with the two rhetorical questions entailed in the quote from Hos 13:14b—this strengthens this statement even more. The author of 1 Cor reaches for quotations from the OT as many as six times in this relatively short (46-verse) disquisition in support of the resurrection. It should be stressed, however, that because the Apostle does not only speak about the resurrection but shows a broader context for the eschatological events, not all the quotations he mentions refer directly to the topic of resurrection but also refer to other eschatological matters.

When exegetes today argue in support of the resurrection of the dead based on the OT, they reach for texts different from those that Paul chose in order to justify to the Corinthians the hope for the rising of the dead. Among the quotations included by Paul in 1 Cor 15:12–58, they mostly refer to Isa 25:8a and Hos 13:14b. However, both fragments constitute arguments in support of the existence of life after death, where "death" in Isa 25:8a can also be understood symbolically. However, these quotes do not refer directly to the idea of resurrection. Paul, justifying his convictions about the resurrection of the dead based on the OT, reveals a broader perspective of eschatological events to the Corinthians without limiting himself to listing the quotes that are the source of direct hope for the rising of the dead. He begins his disquisition by stating the fact of Christ's resurrection, which is unquestionable because Paul himself actually saw the Risen Lord (1 Cor 15:1–11). The same Lord will come back down to earth on the parousia to vanquish all his enemies and begin his kingship. "For he is to be king until he has made his enemies his footstool" (v. 25; cf. Ps 110:1b). The last vanquished enemy will be death, which in Paul's disquisition is characterised by personal traits. This will be when the words of the Psalmist in relation to Christ will come true: God "has put all things under his feet" (v. 27a; cf. Ps 8:7b). Some of the inhabitants of the Corinthian community are inconsistent when they accept the resurrection of Christ while at the same time rejecting the resurrection of the faithful. Since they do not acknowledge rising from the dead, their attitude should rather be characterised by the call: "Let us eat and drink, for tomorrow we shall be dead" (v. 32b; Isa 22:13b). With respect to the nature of bodies after resurrection, Paul argues that it will be different from the nature of earthly bodies because "the first man, Adam, became a living soul; and the last Adam has become a life-giving spirit" (v. 45b; cf. Gen 2:7b). When the followers of Christ will receive new, glorious, incorruptible and imperishable bodies the words of the Prophet will then be fulfilled: "Death is swallowed up in victory" (v. 54b; cf. Isa 25:8a); then one will be able to ask with a hint of irony: "Death, where is your victory? Death, where is your sting?" (v. 55; cf. Hos 13:14b). This scenario of eschatological events depicted by Paul for the inhabitants of Corinth with the use of quotations from the OT may assist in leading them to the conviction that "in Christ all will be made alive" (1 Cor 15:22b).

Abbreviations

AB	Anchor Bible
ABD	*The Anchor Bible Dictionary*, I–VI. Edited by D. N. Freedmann. New York–London–Toronto–Sydney–Auckland 1992.
AL	Attende Lectioni
AnBib	Analecta Biblica
ANET	*Ancient Near Eastern Texts Relating to the Old Testament.* Edited by J. B. Pritchard. Princeton 1969³; *The Ancient Near East Supplementary Texts and Pictures Relating to the Old Testament.* Princeton, New Jersey 1969.
Ang	Angelicum
ARAB	*Ancient Records of Assyria an Babylonia*, I–II. Edited by D. D. Luckenbill. Chicago 1926–1927.
ATD	Das Alte Testament Deutsch
BBR	Bulletin for Biblical Research
BDB	F. Brown, S. Driver and C. Briggs. *The Brown – Driver – Briggs Hebrew and English Lexicon with an appendix containing the Biblical Aramaic. Coded with the numbering system from Strong's Exhaustive Concordance of the Bible.* Peabody 1996².
BDL	Biblioteka Diecezji Legnickiej
BETL	Bibliotheca Ephemeridum Theologicarum Lovaniensium
Bib	Biblica
BGBE	Beiträge zur Geschichte der biblischen Exegese
BN	Barnes' Notes
BSac	Bibliotheca sacra
BT	Biblia Tysiąclecia
BTB	Biblical Theology Bulletin
BU	Biblische Untersuchungen
BZ	Biblische Zeitschrift
BZAW	Beihefte zu Zeitschrift für die alttestamentliche Wissenschaft
CBET	Contributions to Biblical Exegesis and Theology
CBNT	Conienctanea Biblica. New Testament Series
CBQ	Catholic Biblical Quarterly
CCC	Catechism of the Catholic Church
CT	Collectanea Theologica
DR	Downside Review
EA	Ex Auditu
EKKNT	Evangelisch-katholischer Kommentar zum Neuen Testament
EstBib	Estudios Bíblicos
EvQ	The Evangelical Quarterly
FzB	Forschung zum Bibel
FRLANT	Forschungen zur Religion und Literatur des Alten und Neuen Testaments
FTL	Forum Theologiae Linguisticae

GTA	Grace Theological Journal
HBS	Herders Biblische Studien
HTR	The Harvard Theological Review
HUCA	Hebrew Union College Annual
IBS	Irish Biblical Studies
Int	Interpretation
JAOS	Journal of the American Oriental Society
JBL	Journal of Biblical Literature
JETS	Journal of the Evangelical Theological Society
JHC	Journal of Higher Criticism
JSNT	Journal for the Study of the New Testament
JSNTSup	Journal for the Study of the New Testament. Supplement Series
JSOT	Journal for the Study of the Old Testament
JSPESup	Journal for the Study of the Pseudoepigrapha: Supplement Series
JSS	Journal of Semitic Studies
JTS	Journal of Theological Studies
KEK	Kritisch-exegetischer Kommentar über das Neue Testament
LB	Linguistica Biblica
NB	New Blackfriars
NEB	Die Neue Echter Bibel
Neot	Neotestamentica
NICNT	The New International Commentary on the New Testament
NICOT	The New International Commentary on the Old Testament
NKB	Nowy Komentarz Biblijny
NovT	Novum Testamentum
NovTSup	Novum Testamentum. Supplemens
NTA	Neutestamentliche Abhandlungen
NTT	Nederlands Theologisch Tijdschrift
OBT	Opolska Biblioteka Teologiczna
PG	Patrologia Graeca
PJBR	The Polish Journal of Biblical Research
PRSt	Perspectives in Religious Studies
PŚST	Pismo Święte Starego Testamentu
RB	Revue Biblique
RBL	Ruch Biblijny i Liturgiczny
RiS	Rozprawy i Studia
RivB	Rivista Biblica
RTK	Roczniki Teologiczno-Kanoniczne
SB	Studia Biblica
SBB	Stuttgarter biblische Beiträge
SBFLA	Studii Biblici Franciscani iber Annuus
SBL	Society of Biblical Literature
SBLDS	Society of Biblical Literature. Dissertations Series
ScEs	Science et esprit
Sem	Semeia
SiBL	Studies in Biblical Literature
SJT	Scottish Journal of Theology
SMB	Série Monographique de "Benedictina"
SNTSMS	Society for the New Testament Studies. Monograph Series

SR	Scienze delle Religioni
SS	Scriptura Sacra
SSHT	Śląskie Studia Historyczno-Teologiczne
TDNT	*Theological Dictionary of the New Testament*, I–IX. Edited by G. Friedrich. Translated by G. W. Bromiley and D. Litt. Grand Rapids 1999.
TDOT	*Theological Dictionary of the Old Testament*, I–IX. Edited by G. J. Botterweck and H. Ringgren. Grand Rapids 1997; X–XI. Edited by G. J. Botterweck, H. Ringgren and H.-J. Fabry. Translated by D. E. Green. Grand Rapids–Cambridge 2001.
TG	Tesi Gregoriana
THKNT	*Theologisches Handwörterbuch zum Alten Testament.* Edited by E. Jenni and C. Westermann. 1–2, Münche– Zürich 1971–1976.
Theol. Ex. Heute	
	Theologische Existenz Heute
TU	Texte und Untersuchungen zur Geschichte der altchristlicher Literatur
TW	Theologica Wratislaviensia
TynBul	Tyndale Bulletin
TZ	Theologisches Zeitschrift
VD	Verbum Domini
VoxP	Vox Patrum
VT	Vetus Testamentum
VV	Verbum vitae
WBC	Word Biblical Commentary
WW	Word and World
WMANT	Wissenschaftliche Monographien zum Alten und Neuen Testament
WuD	Wort und Dienst
WUNT	Wissenschaftliche Untersuchungen zum Neuen Testament
ZAW	Zeitschrift für die alttestamentliche Wissenschaft
ZBKAT	Zürcher Bibel-Kommentar. Altes Testament
ZHTZ	Zeszyty Historyczno-Teologiczne Zmartwychwstańców
ZNW	Zeitschrift für die neutestamentliche Wissenschaft und die Kunde des Urchristentums (since 1921: Zeitschrift für die neutestamentliche Wissenschaft und die Kunde der älteren Kirche)
ŻK	Życie Konsekrowane

Ancient writers

1 Cor. Hom.	Chrysostom, *Homilies to the First Corinthians*
1 En.	*Book of Enoch (Ethiopian)*
1QH	*Hymns Hodayot*
1QIs^a	First copy of *Isaiah* from Qumran
1QM	*The Rule of the War*
1QpHab	*Commentary to the Book of Habakkuk*
1QS	*The Community Role*
2 Bar.	*Apokalypse of Baruch (Syriac)*
4Q 385	*Pseudo-Ezechiel*
4Q 521	*Messianic Apocalypse*
4 Ezra	*Fourth Book of Ezra*
4 Macc.	*Fourth Maccabees*

Ant.	Flavius Josephus, *Antiquitates judaicae*
Ap.	Flavius Josephus, *Contra Apionem*
Aut.	Theophilus of Antioch, *Ad Autolycum*
Bell.	Flavius Josephus, *De bello judaico*
Bib. hist.	Diodorus Siculus, *Bibliotheca historica*
Bion	Diogenes Laertius, *Philosophon bion kai dogmaton*
CD	*Damascus Document*
Conf.	*Philo* Alexandrinus, *De confusione linguarum*
Deter.	*Philo* Alexandrinus, *Quod deterius insidiari potiori soleat*
Diatr.	Epictetus, *Diatribai*
Diss.	Epictetus, *Dissertationes*
Ench.	Epictetus, *Enchiridion*
Gos. Heb.	*The Gospel of the Hebrews*
Gos. Thom.	*The Gospel of Thomas*
Fr.	Eurypides, *Fragmenta*
Fragm. ad 1Cor	
	Cyril of Alexandria, *Fragmenta in Ep. 1 ad Corinthios*
Geogr.	Strabo, *Geographica*
Gorg.	Plato, *Gorgias*
Her.	*Philo* Alexandrinus, *Quis rerum divinarum heres sit*
Hist. ecc.	Eusebius of Caesarea, *Historia ecclesiastica*
Jub.	*Book of Jubilees*
Lach.	Plato, *Laches*
Leg.	*Philo* Alexandrinus, *Legum alegoriae*
Migr. Abr.	*Philo* Alexandrinus, *De Migratione Abrahami*
midrQoh	*Midrash to Qohelet*
Mor.	Plutarch, *Moralia*
Opif.	*Philo* Alexandrinus, *De opificio mundi*
Part.	Aristotle, *De partibus animalium*
Pes.	*Pesahim*
Phil.	Polycarp, *Epistola ad Philippenses*
Plant.	*Philo* Alexandrinus, *De plantatione*
Princ.	Origen, *De Principiis*
Pss. Sol.	*Psalms of Solomon*
Qidd.	*Qiddushin*
Quaest. Ex.	*Philo* Alexandrinus, *Quaestones et solutiones in Exodum*
Quaest. Gen.	*Philo* Alexandrinus, *Quaestiones et solutiones in Genesin*
Res.	Tertullian, *De resurrectione carnis*
Rom.	Ignatius of Antioch, *Letter to the Romans*
Sabb.	*Shabbat*
Sanh.	*Sanhedrin*
Spir.	Basilius, *De Spiritu Sancto*
Test. Lev.	*Testament of Levi*
Trin.	Augustine, *De Trinitate*
Tryph.	Justin, *Dialogus cum Tryphone*
Vir. ill.	Hieronymus, *De viris illustribus*
Yebam.	*Yebamot*

Bibliography

Commentaries to 1 Corinthians

Allo, E. B. *Saint Paul. Premiere Epître aux Corinthiens.* Paris 1956.

Barnes, A. *1 Corinthians to Galatians*, Barnes' Notes. Grand Rapids 1884.

Barrett, C. K. A *Commentary on the First Epistle to the Corinthians.* London 1971.

Bousset, W. *Der erste Brief an die Korinther.* Die Schriften des Neues Testament. Göttingen 1917[3].

Collins, R. F. *First Corinthians.* Collegeville 1999.

Conzelmann, H.*1 Corinthians: A Commentary.* Hermeneia. Philadelphia 1975.

Czerski, J. *Pierwszy List do Koryntian.* Bibliotheca Biblica. Wrocław 2009.

Czerski, J. *Pierwszy List św. Pawła do Koryntian (1 Kor 1,1–6,20). Wstęp – przekład z oryginału – komentarz, I, Rozdziały 1–6.* OBT 87. Opole 2006.

Dąbrowski, E. *Listy do Koryntian. Wstęp – przekład z oryginału – komentarz.* PŚNT 7. Poznań–Warszawa 1965.

Fabris, R. *Prima Lettera ai Corinzi. Nuova versione, introduzione e commento.* I Libri Biblici. Nuovo Testamento 7. Torino 1999.

Fee, G. D. *The First Epistle to the Corinthians.* NICNT. Grand Rapids 1987.

Grasso, S. *Prima Lettera ai Corinzi.* Nuovo Testamento – Commento esegetico e spirituale. Roma 2002.

Hering, J. *The First Epistle of St Paul to the Corinthians.* London 1962.

Keener, C. S. *1–2 Corinthians.* The New Cambridge Bible Commentary. Cambridge–New York–Melbourne–Madrid–Cape Town–Singapore–São Paulo 2005.

Lambrecht, J. "Pierwszy List do Koryntian." Pages 1456–1486 in *Międzynarodowy komentarz do Pisma Świętego. Komentarz katolicki i ekumeniczny na XXI wiek.* Edited by W. R. Farmer, S. McEvenue, A. J. Levoratt and D. L. Dungan. Polish ed. W. Chrostowski, T. Mieszkowski and P. Pachciarek. Translated by B. Widła. Warszawa 2001.

Lietzmann, H. *An die Korinther I/II.* Tübingen 1949.

Lightfoot, J. A *Commentary on the New Testament from Talmud and Hebraica. Matthew – 1 Corinthians, 4, Acts – 1 Corinthians.* Peabody 1997[3].

Lightfoot, J. B. *Notes on the Epistles of St. Paul*, Peabody 1999[4].

Longenecker, R. N. *Studies in Paul, Exegetical and Theological.* New Testament Monographs. Sheffield 2004.

Malina, B. J. and J. J. Pilch. *Social-Science Commentary on the Letters of Paul.* Minneapolis 2006.

Mare, W. H. *1 Corinthians.* The Expositors Bible Commentary 10. Edited by F. E. Gaebelein. Grand Rapids 1984, 173–297.

Murphy-O'Connor, J. "The First Letter to the Corinthians." Pages 798–815 in *The New Jerome Biblical Commentary*. Edited by R. E. Brown, J. A. Fitzmyer and R. E. Murphy. London 1993.

Orr, W. F. and J. A. Walther. *I Corinthians. A New Translation, Introduction with a Study of the Life of Paul, Notes, and Commentary*. The Anchor Bible 32. New York–London–Toronto–Sydney–Auckland 1976.

Romaniuk, K., A. Jankowski and L. Stachowiak. *Komentarz praktyczny do Nowego Testamentu*, II. Poznań–Kraków 1999, 99–125.

Rosik, M. *Pierwszy List do Koryntian. Wstęp, przekład z oryginału, komentarz*. NKB 7. Częstochowa 2009.

Schmiedel, P. W. *Der Briefe an die Thessalonicher und die Korinther*. Hand-Kommentar zum Neuen Testament II/1. Freiburg 1891.

Schrage, W., *Der erste Brief an die Korinther (1 Kor 15,1 – 16,24)*. EKKNT 7/4. Zürich 2001.

Soards, M. L. "First Corinthians." Pages 1163–1190 in *Mercer Commentary on the Bible*. Edited by W. E. Mills and R. F. Wilson. Macon 1995.

Talbert, C. H. *Reading Corinthians: A Literary-Theological Commentary on 1 and 2 Corinthians*. New York 1992.

Thiselton, A. C. *The First Epistle to the Corinthians. A Commentary to the Greek Text*. The New International Greek Testament Commentary. Grand Rapids–Cambridge 2000.

Weiss, J. *Der erster Korintherbrief*. KEK. Göttingen 1977.

Wette, W.L.M., de. *Kurze Erklärung der Briefe an die Korinther*. Kurgefasstes exegetisches Handbuch zum Neuen Testament II/2. Leipzig 1841.

Witherington III, B. *Conflict and Community in Corinth: A Socio-Rhetorical Commentary on 1 and 2 Corinthians*. Grand Rapids 1995.

Wolff C. *Der erste Brief des Paulus an die Korinther*. THKNT 7. Leipzig 1996.

Other Commentaries

Alonso Schökel, L. *"ContemplateLo e sarete raggianti". Salmi ed Esercizi*. Bibbia e preghiera 27. Roma 1996.

Alonso Schökel, L. and J. L. Diaz. *I profeti. Traduzione e comment*. Edited by G. Ravasi. Translated by T. Tosatti and P. Brungoli. Roma 1996[3].

Alonso Schökel, L. *Trenta salmi: poesia e preghiera*. Translated by A. Ranon. Bologna 1982.

Andersen, F. I. and D. N. Freedman. *Hosea*. AB 24. New York 1980.

Berges, U. *Das Buch Jesaja. Komposition und Endgestalt*. HBS 16. Freiburg 1998.

Childs, B. S. *Isaiah*. The Old Testament Library. Louisville 2001.

Clements, R. E. *Isaiah 1–39*. Grand Rapids 1980.

Doorly, W. J. *Isaiah of Jerusalem. An Introduction*. Mahwah 1992.

Ebeling, G. *Sui Salmi*. Brescia 1973.

Fohrer, G. *Das Buch Jesaja*, II, *Kapitel 24–39*. ZBKAT 19,2. Zürich–Stuttgart 1991[3].

Grogan, G. W. "Isaiah." Pages 3–356 in *The Expositor's Bible Commentary with the New International Version of the Holy Bible*, VI, *Isaiah, Jeremiah, Lamentations, Ezekiel*. Edited by F. E. Gaebelein. Grand Rapids 1986.

Hartley, J. E. *The Book of Job*. NICOT. Grand Rapids 1988.

Henry, M. *Commentary on the whole Bible complete and unabridged in one volume.* Peabody 1997[7].

I dodici profeti. La Bibbia Commentata dai Padli. Antico Testamento 13. Edited by A. Ferreiro. Translated by M. Conti. Roma 2005.

Jamieson, R., A. R. Fausset and D. Brown. *A Commentary on the Old and New Testaments,* III. Peabody 1997.

Kaiser, O. *Das Buch des Propheten Jesaja. Kapitel 13–39.* ATD 18. Göttingen 1976[2].

Keener, C. S. *Komentarz historyczno-kulturowy do Nowego Testamentu.* Edited by K. Bardski and W. Chrostowski. Translated by Z. Kościsk. Warszawa 2000.

Kilian, R. *Jesaja,* II, *13–39.* NEB. Stuttgart 1980.

Kinder, D. *Genesis. An Introduction and Commentary.* Tyndale Old Testament Commentaries. Downers Grove 1967.

Kraus, H.-J. *Psalmen.* Biblischer Kommentar. Altes Testament, II. Neukirchen 1960.

Langkammer, H. *Komentarz teologiczno-pastoralny wszystkich listów św. Pawła Apostoła z okazji Roku świętego Pawła,* I, *Wielkie listy św. Pawła.* BDL 37. Legnica 2009.

Łach, S. *Księga Psalmów. Wstęp – przekład z oryginału – komentarz – ekskursy.* PŚST VII/2. Poznań 1990.

Łach, S. *Księga Rodzaju. Wstęp – przekład z oryginału – komentarz.* PŚST I/1. Poznań 1962.

Manatti, M. and E. de Solms. *Les Psaumes.* Paris 1966.

Michalski, W. *Ozeasz. Wstęp, nowy przekład, komentarz.* Pismo Święte Starego Zakonu w nowem tłumaczeniu. Lwów 1922.

Oswalt, J. N. *The Book of Isaiah. Chapters 1–39.* NICOT. Grand Rapids 1986.

Pusey, E. B. *The Minor Prophets. A Commentary.* BN. Grand Rapids 1885.

Rad, G., von. *Genesi. Traduzione e commento.* Antico Testamento 2/4. Brescia 1978[4].

Ravasi, G. *Psalmy,* I, *Wprowadzenie i Psalmy 1–19 (wybór).* Translated by P. Mikulska. Kraków 2007.

Rinaudo, S. *I Salmi. Preghiera di Cristo e della Chiesa. Quinta edizione completamente rifusa secondo l'uso e l'interpretazione della liturgia rinnovata dal Vaticano II.* Torino 1999.

Rogers, J. S. "Hosea." Pages 721–734 in *Mercer Commentary on the Bible.* Edited by W. E. Millo and R. F. Wilson. Macon 1995.

Romaniuk, K., A. Jankowski and L. Stachowiak. *Komentarz praktyczny do Nowego Testamentu,* I–II. Poznań–Kraków 1999.

Sailhamer, J. H. "Genesis." Pages 1–284 in *The Expositor's Bible Commentary with The New International Version.* Edited by F. E. Gaebelein, II. Grand Rapids 1990.

Seitz, C. R. *Isaiah 1–39,* Interpretation. A Bible Commentary for Teaching and Preaching. Louisville 1993.

Simian-Yofre, H. "Księga Ozeasza." Pages 990–1003 in *Międzynarodowy komentarz do Pisma Świętego. Komentarz katolicki i ekumeniczny na XXI wiek.* Edited by W. R. Farmer. Polish ed. W. Chrostowski. Translated by E. Burska. Warszawa 2001[2].

Smith, G. V. *Isaiah 1–39. An Exegetical and Theological Exposition of the Holy Scripture.* The New American Commentary 15A. New International Version. Nashville 2007.

Speiser, E. A. *Genesis. Introduction, translations, and notes.* The Anchor Bible. New York 1980[3].

Stachowiak, L. *Księga Izajasza 1–39. Wstęp – przekład z oryginału – komentarz*, I. PŚST IX/1. Poznań 1996.

Stern, D. H. *Komentarz żydowski do Nowego Testamentu*. Translated by A. Czwojdrak. Warszawa 2004.

Sweeney, M. A. *Isaiah 1–39 with an Introduction to the Prophetic Literature*. The Forms of the Old Testament Literature 16. Grand Rapids 1996.

Van Gemeren, W. A. "Psalms." Pages 1–882 in *The Expositor's Bible Commentary with the New International Version of the Holy Bible*, V, *Psalms – Song of Songs*. Edited by F. E. Gaebelein. Grand Rapids 1991.

Walton, J. H., V. H. Matthews and M. W. Chavalas. *Komentarz historyczno-kulturowy do Biblii Hebrajskiej*. Polish ed. W. Chrostowski. Translated by Z. Kościuk. Warszawa 2005.

Weiser, A. *Das Buch der zwölf kleinen Propheten*, I. ATD 24. Göttingen² 1956.

Weiser, A. *Die Psalmen*, I–II. Göttingen⁷ 1966.

Wenham, G. J. *Genesis 1–15*. WBC 1. Waco 1987.

Westermann, C. *Genesis*. Biblischer Kommentar. Altes Testament, I. Neukirchen–Vluyn 1974.

Wildberger, H. *Jesaja. Kapitel 13–27*. BK 10,2. Neukirchen–Vluyn 1989².

Wolf, H. M. *Interpreting Isaiah. The Suffering and Glory of the Messiah*. Grand Rapids: Academic Press, 1985.

Wood, L. J. "Hosea." Pages 159–225 in *The Expositor's Bible Commentary with the New International Version of the Holy Bible*, VII, *Daniel – Minor Prophets*. Edited by F. E. Gaebelein. Grand Rapids 1986.

Young, E. J. *The Book of Isaiah*, I–III. Grand Rapids 1965, 1969, 1972.

General Bibliography

Ahern B. M. "The Risen Christ in the Light of Pauline Doctrine on the Risen Christian (1 Cor 15:35–37)." Pages 423–439 in *Resurrexit. Actes du Symposium International sur la Résurrection de Jésus (Rome 1970)*. Edited by E. Dhanis. Vatikanstadt 1974.

Aletti, J.-N. "La dispositio rhétorique dans les épîtres pauliniennes." *NTS* 38 (1992): 385–401.

Aletti, J.-N. "L'Argumentation de Paul et la position des Corinthiens. 1 Co 15,12–34." Pages 63–81 in *Résurrection du Christ et des chrétiens (1 Co 15)*. Edited by L. De Lorenzi. SMB. Section Biblico-Oecuménique 8. Rome 1985.

Aletti, J.-N., M. Gilbert, J.-L. Ska and S. de Vulpillières. *Lessico ragionato dell'esegesi bblica. Le parole, gli approcci, gli autori*. Brescia 2006.

Alexander, P. S., "Midrasz." Pages 572–580 in *Słownik hermeneutyki biblijnej*. Edited by R. J. Coggins and J. L. Houlden. Polish ed. W. Chrostowski. Translated by B. Widła. Warszawa 2005.

Alexiou, M. *The Ritual Lament in Greek Tradition*. Cambridge 1974.

Alonso Schökel, L. and G. Gutiérrez. *Io pongo le mie parole sulla tua bocca. Meditazioni bibliche*. Bibbia e preghiera 12. Roma 1992.

Altermath, F. *De corps psychique au corps spirituel. Interprétation de 1 Cor 15: 35–49 par des auteurs des quatre premiers siècles*. BGBE 18. Tübingen 1977.

The Anchor Bible Dictionary, I–VI. Edited by D. N. Freedmann. New York–London–Toronto– Sydney–Auckland 1992.

Andersen, J. R. D. *Ancient Rhetorical Theory and Paul*. CBET 17. Kamen 1996.

Anderson, F. I. "On Reading Genesis 1–3." Pages 137–150 in *Background for the Bible*. Edited by M. P. O'Connor and D. N. Fredmann, Winona Lake 1987.

Apokryfy Starego Testamentu. Edited by R. Rubinkiewicz. Warszawa 1999.

Armerding, C. E. "Were David's Sons Really Priests?" Pages 75–86 in *Current Issues in Biblical and Patristic Interpretation*. Edited by G. F. Hawthrorne. Grand Rapids 1975.

Arnold, C. E. *Powers of Darkness: Principalities and Powers in Paul's Letters*. Dovers Grove 1992.

Asante, M. K. *From Imhotep to Akhenaten: An Introduction to Egyptian Philosophers*. Philadelphia 2004.

Asher, J. R. *Polarity and Change in 1 Corinthians 15: A Study of Metaphysics, Rhetoric, and Resurrection*. HUT 42. Tübingen 2000.

Auffret, P. "Note sur la structure littéraire du Psaume cx." *Sem* 32 (1982): 83–88.

Austin, J. L. *How to Do Things with Words*. Cambridge 1962².

Avigad, N. *Discovering Jerusalem*. Nashville 1980.

Bachmann, M. "Rezeption von 1. Kor 15 (V.12ff.) unter logischem und unter philologischem Aspekt." *LB* 51 (1982): 79–103.

Bachmann, M. "Zum 'argumentum resurrectionis' von 1 Kor. 15,12ff nach Christoph Zimmer, Augustin und Paulus." *LB* 67 (1992): 2–939.

Bachmann, M. "Zur Gedankenführung in 1. Kor. 15,12ff." *TZ* 34 (1978): 265–276.

Barrett, C. K. *From First Adam to Last*. London 1962.

Barrett, C. K. "The Significance of the Adam-Christ Typology for the Resurrection of the Dead: 1 Co 15,20–22.45–49." Pages 99–122 in *Résurrection du Christ et des chrétiens (1 Co 15)*. Edited by L. De Lorenzi. SMB. Section Biblico-Oecuménique 8. Rome 1985.

Barth, G. "Zur Frage nach der 1 Kor bekämpfen Auferstehungsleugnung." *ZNW* 83 (1992): 187–201.

Barth, G. "Erwägungen zu 1 Kor 15:20 –28." *EvT* 30 (1970): 515–527.

Bartnicki, R. *Ewangelie synoptyczne. Geneza i interpretacja*. Warszawa 2003³.

Bateman IV, H. W. "Psalm 110:1 and the New Testament." *BSac* 149 (1992): 438–353.

Bauer, K.-A. *Leiblichkeit das Ende aller Werke Gottes. Die Bedeutung der Leiblichkeit des Menschen bei Paulus*. SNTSMS 4. Gütersloh 1971.

Becker, J. "Zur Deutung von Ps 110,7." Pages 17–31 in *In Freude an der Weisung des Herrn: Beiträge zur Theologie der Psalmen*. Edited by H. Gross, E. Haag and F.-L. Hossfeld. SBB 13. Stuttgart 1987².

Beker, J. *Paul's Apocalyptic Gospel: The Coming Triumph of God*. Philadelphia 1982.

Belleville, L. L. "Enemy, Enmity, Hatred." Pages 235–238 in *Dictionary of Paul and His Letters. A Compendium of Contemporary Biblical Scholarship*. Edited by G. F. Hawthorne and R. P. Martin. Dovners Grove–Leicester 1993.

Berkhof, H. *Christ and the Powers*. Scottdale 1977.

Bernstain, A. E. *Jak powstało piekło. Śmierć i zadośćuczynienie w świecie starożytnym oraz początkach chrześcijaństwa*. Translated by A. Piskozub-Piwosz, Kraków 2006.

Betz, H. D. and M. M. Mitchell. "Corinthians, First Epistle to the." *ABD* I: 1139–1148.

Binder, H. "Zum geschichtlichen Hintergrund von I Kor 15,12." *TZ* 46 (1990): 193–201.

Bjørndalen, A. J. "Alegoria." Pages 9–11 in *Słownik hermeneutyki biblijnej*. Edited by R. J. Coggins and J. L. Houlden. Polish ed. W. Chrostowski. Translation by B. Widła. Warszawa 2005.

Black, M. "The Pauline Doctrine of the Second Adam." *SJT* 7 (1954): 170–179.

Blank, J. "Erwägungen zum Schriftverständnis des Paulus." Pages 37–56 in *Rechtfertigung. Fs. E. Käsemann*. Edited by J. Friedrich, W. Pöhlmann and P. Stuhlmacher. Tübingen–Göttingen 1976.

Blass, F. and A. Debruner. *Grammatica del greco del Nuovo Testamento*. Edited by G. Pisi. Translated by U. Mattioli and G. Pisi. Brescia 1982.

Boer, M. C., de. "Paul's Use of a Resurrection Tradition in 1 Cor 15,20–28." Pages 641–652 in *The Corinthian Correspondence*. Edited by R. Bieringer. BETL 125. Louvain 1996.

Boer, M.C., de. *The Defeat of Death: Apocalyptic Eschatology in 1 Corinthians 15 and Romans 5*. JSNTSup 22. Sheffield 1988.

Bonneau, N. "The Logic of Paul's Argument on the Resurrection Body in 1 Cor 15:35–44a." *ScEs* 45 (1993): 79–92.

Boraas, R. S. "Kir." Page 519 in *Encyklopedia biblijna*. Edited by P. J. Achtemeier. Translated by Z. Kościuk. Warszawa 1999.

Borowska, M. "Meander i komedia nowa." Pages 901–930 in *Literatura Grecji starożytnej*, I, *Epika – liryka – dramat*. Edited by H. Podbielski. Źródła i Monografie 255. Lublin 2005.

Botha, P. J. J. "The Verbal Art of Pauline Letters: Rhetoric, Performance and Practice." Pages 409–428 in *Rhetoric and the New Testament: Essays from 1992 Heidelberg Conference*. Edited by S. E. Porter and T. H. Olbricht. JSNTSup 90. Sheffield 1993.

Bousset, W. *Die Religion des Judentums im neutestamentlichen Zeitalter*. Berlin 1906.

Borzymińska, Z. "Eliezer ben Hyrkanos." Page 383 in *Polski słownik judaistyczny. Dzieje, kultura, religia, ludzie*. Edited by Z. Borzymińska and R. Żebrowski, I. Warszawa 2003.

Brandenburger, E. *Adam und Christus. Exegetisch-religionsgeschichtliche Untersuchung zu Röm. 5:12–21 (1. Kor. 15)*. WMANT 7. Neukirchen–Vluyn 1962.

Bright, J. *Historia Izraela*. Translated by J. Radożycki. Warszawa 1994.

Briks, P. *Podręczny słownik hebrajsko-polski i aramejsko-polski Starego Testamentu*. Warszawa 1999.

Brodeur, S. *The Holy Spirit's Agency in the Resurrection of the Dead: An Exegetico-Theological Study of 1 Corinthians 15,44b–49 and Romans 8,9–13*. TG 14. Rome 1996.

Brooke, G. J. "Peszer." Pages 664–665 in *Słownik hermeneutyki biblijnej*. Edited by R. J. Coggins and J. L. Houlden. Polish ed. W. Chrostowski. Translated by B. Widła. Warszawa 2005.

Brown, W. P. "A Royal Performance: Critical Notes on Psalm 110:3aγ–b." *JBL* 117 (1998): 93–96.

Brueggemann, W. "From Dust to Kingship." *ZAW* 84 (1972): 1–18.

Brunot, A. *Saint Paul and His Message*. Twentieth Century Encyclopedia of Catholicism 70. Translated by R. Matthews. New York 1959.

Brzegowy, T. *Miasto Boże w Psalmach*. Kraków 1989.

Brzegowy, T. *Pięcioksiąg Mojżesza*. Academica 27. Tarnów 2002.

Brzegowy, T. *Psalmy i inne Pisma*. Academica 10. Tarnów 1997.

Brzegowy, T. *Psałterz i Księga Lamentacji*. Academica 65. Tarnów 2007.

Bucher, T. G. "Die logische Argumentation in 1 Korinther 15,12–20." *Bib* 55 (1974): 465–486.

Bucher, T. G. "Überlegung zur Logik im Zusammenhang mit 1 Kor 15,12–20." *LB* 53 (1983): 70–98.

Bultmann, R. *Der Stil der paulinischen Predigt und die kynisch-stoische Diatribe.* FRLANT 13. Göttingen 1910.

Burchard, C. "1 Kor 15: 39–41." *ZNW* 74 (1983): 233–252.

Bünker, M. *Briefformular und rhetorische Disposition im 1. Korintherbrief.* Göttingen 1984.

Byrne, B. "Eschatologies of Resurrection and Destruction. The Ethical Significance of Paul's Dispute with the Corinthians." *Downside Review* 104 (1986): 288–296.

Byrne, B. *'Sons of God' – 'Seed of Abraham'. A Study of the Idea of the Sonship of God of All Christians in Paul against the Jewish Background.* AnBib 83. Roma 1979.

Caird, G. B. *Principalities and Powers.* Oxford 1956.

Callan, T. "Psalm 110:1 and the Origin of the Expectation That Jesus Will Come Again." *CBQ* 44 (1982): 622–636.

Campbell, E. F. "Efraim." Page 243 in *Encyklopedia biblijna.* Edited by P. J. Achtemeier. Translated by M. Wojciechowski. Warszawa 1999.

Carr, D. M. *Reading the Fractures of Genesis. Historical and Literary Approaches.* Louisville 1996.

Cavallin, H. C. C. *Life after Death. Paul's Argument for the Resurrection of the Dead in 1 Cor 15, I, An Enquiry into the Jewish Background.* CBNT 7,1. Lund 1974.

Cenci, A. M. *La nostra risurrezione è una certezza! Prima e Seconda Lettera di san Paulo ai Corinzi.* Milano 1999.

Chester, A. "Resurrection and Transformation." Pages 47–78 in *Auferstehung – Resurrection.* Edited by F. Avemaria and H. Lichtenberger. WUNT 135. Tübingen 2001.

Chmiel, J. *Homilie sakramentalne. Refleksje – szkice – propozycje.* Kraków 1996.

Chrostowski, W. "Żydowskie tradycje interpretacyjne pomocą w zrozumieniu Biblii." *CT* 66 (1996) 1: 39–54.

Clark, H. and R. Gerrig. "Quotations as Demonstrations." *Language* 66 (1990): 786–788.

Classen, J. "St. Paul's Epistles and Ancient Greek and Roman Rhetoric." Pages 265–291 in *Rhetoric and the New Testament. Essays from the 1992 Heidelberg Conference.* Edited by S. E. Porter and T. H. Olbricht. JSNTSup 90. Sheffield 1993.

Classen, C.J. *Rhetorical Criticism of the New Testament.* Tübingen 2000.

Clements, R. E. "The Prophecies of Isaiah and the Fall of Jerusalem in 587 B.C." *VT* 30 (1980): 421–436.

Cobham Brewer, E. *Dictionary of Phrase and Fable.* Philadelphia 1898.

Cody, A. A *History of the Old Testament Priesthood.* Rome 1969.

Cohn-Sherbok, D. "Paul and Rabbinic Exegesis." *SJT* 35 (1982): 117–132.

Cole, S. G. "Could Greek Women Read and Write?" Pages 219–245 in *Reflections of Women in Antiquity.* Edited by H. P. Foley. New York 1981.

Chrostowski, W. "Czy Adam i Ewa mieli się nie starzeć i nie umierać? Egzegetyczny przyczynek do nauczania o nieśmiertelności pierwszych ludzi." Pages 151–179 in *Verbum caro fatum est. Księga Pamiątkowa dla Księdza Profesora Tomasza Jelonka w 70. rocznicę urodzin.* Edited by R. Bogacz and W. Chrostowski. Warszawa 2007.

Chrostowski, W. "Żydowskie tradycje interpretacyjne pomocą w zrozumieniu Biblii." *CT* 66 (1996) 1: 39–54.

Cogan, M. "Sennacheryb." Page 1098 in *Encyklopedia biblijna*. Edited by P. J. Achtemeier. Translated by E. Szymula. Warszawa 1999.

Conzelmann, H. "On the Analysis of the Confessional Formula in 1 Cor 15,3–5." *Int* 20 (1966): 15–25.

Coppens, J. "La portée messianique du Psaume 110." *Analecta Lovaniensia biblica et orientalia* 3 (1956): 5–23.

Coppens, J. *Le mesianisme royal. Ses origines. Son développement. Son accomplissement.* Paris 1968.

Crockett, W. V. "Ultimate Restoration of all Mankind: 1 Cor. 15:22." Pages 83–87 in *Studia Biblica 1978. Sixth International Congress on Biblical Studies.* Edited by E. A. Livingstone. III, JSNTSup. 3. Sheffield 1980.

Cullmann, O. *The Christology of the New Testament.* Philadelphia 1959.

Daniel-Rops, H. *Życie codzienne w Palestynie w czasach Chrystusa.* Translated by J. Lasocka. Warszawa 1994.

Das Grosse Lexikon zur Bibel. Altes und Neues Testament. Edited by K. Koch, E. Otto, J. Roloff and H. Schmoldt. Wien 2004.

Daube, D. "Rabbinic Methods of Interpretation and Hellenistic Rhetoric." *HUCA* 22 (1949): 239–264.

Daube, D. *Studies in Biblical Law.* New York[2] 1969.

Day, J. "The Development of Belief in Life after Death in Ancient Israel." Pages 125–129 in *After the Exile.* Edited by J. Barton and D. Reimer. Macon 1996.

DeMaris, R. E. "Corinthian Religion and Baptism for the Dead (1 Corinthians 15:29): Insights from Archeology and Anthropology." *JBL* 114 (1995) 4: 661–682.

Deville, R. and P. Grelot. "Królestwo." Pages 403–406 in *Słownik teologii biblijnej.* Edited by X. Léon-Dufour. Translated by K. Romaniuk. Poznań–Warszawa 1973.

Dictionary of Paul and His Letters. A Compendium of Contemporary Biblical Scholarship. Edited by G. F. Hawthorne and R. P. Martin. Dovners Grove–Leicester 1993.

Dietzfelbinger, C. *Die Berufung des Paulus als Ursprung seiner Teologie.* WMANT 58. Neukirchen 1985.

Dietzfelbinger, C. *Paulus und das Alte Testament. Die Hermeneutik des Paulus, untersucht an seiner Bedeutung der Gestalt Abrahams.* Theol. Ex. Heute 95. München 1961.

Dohmen, C. and G. Stemberger. *Hermeneutyka Biblii Żydowskiej i Starego Testamentu.* Myśl Teologiczna. Translated by M. Szczepaniak. Kraków 2008.

Donner, H. "Ugaritismen in der Psalmenforschung." *ZAW* 79 (1967): 322–350.

Dougty, D. J. "The Presence and Future of Salvation in Corinth." *ZNW* 66 (1975): 61–90.

Driver, G. R. "Isaiah 1–39: Textual and Linguistic Problems." *JSS* 13 (1968): 36–57.

Driver, G. R. "Linguistic and Textual Problems, Isaiah 1–39." *JTS* (1937): 36–50.

Driver, G. R. "Psalm 110: Its Form, Meaning and Purpose." Pages 17–31 in *Studies in the Bible Presented to M. H. Segal.* Redited by J. M. Grintz and J. Liver. Publications of the Israel Society for Biblical Research 17. Jerusalem 1964.

Dunn, J. G. D. "1 Cor 15:45 – Last Adam, Life-Giving Spirit." Pages 127–141 in *Christ and Spirit in the New Testament: In Honour of C.F.D. Moule.* Edited by B. Lindars and S. J. Smalley. Cambridge 1973.

Dunn, J. G., *Christianity in Making*, I, *Jesus Remembered*, Grand Rapids–Cambridge 2003.

Dunn, J. G. D., *Christology in the Making. An Inquiry into the Origins of the Doctrine of the Incarnation*, London 1989[2].

Dunn, J. D. G. *The Theology of Paul the Apostle*. London–New York 2005[4].

Dupont, J. *Gnosis. La connaissance religieuse dans les épîtres de saint Paul*. Louvain–Paris 1960[2].

Dziadosz, D. *Gli oracoli divini in 1 Sam 8–2 Re 25. Redazione e teologia nella storia deuteronomistica dei re*. Romae 2002.

Ehrlich, C. S. "Efraim." Pages 140–141 in *Słownik wiedzy biblijnej*. Edited by B. M. Metzger and M. D. Coogan. Polish ed. W. Chrostowski. Translated by T. Kowalska. Warszawa 1996.

Ellis, E. E. "Biblical Interpretation in the New Testament Church." Pages 691–725 in *Mikra. Text, Translation, Reading and Hebrew Bible in Ancient Judaism and Early Christianity*. Philadelphia 1988.

Ellis, E. E. *Paul's Use of the Old Testament*. Grand Rapids 1991.

Emerton, J. A. "A Textual Problem in Isaiah 25:2." *ZAW* 89 (1977): 64–73.

Emerton, J. A. "Notes on the Text and Translation of Isa. xxii 8–11 and lxv 5." *VT* 30 (1980): 437–446.

Encyklopedia biblijna. Edited by P. J. Achtemeier. Translated by Team. Warszawa 1999.

Everson, J. A. "Days of Yahweh." *JBL* 93 (1974): 329–337.

Everts, J. M. "Conversion and Call of Paul." Pages 156–163 in *Dictionary of Paul and His Letters. A Compendium of Contemporary Biblical Scholarship*. Edited byu G. F. Hawthorne and R. P Martin. Dovners Grove–Leicester 1993.

Fisher, L. R. "Abraham and his Priest-King." *JBL* 81 (1962): 264–270.

Fitzmyer, J. A. "Melchizedek in the MT, LXX and the NT." *Bib* 81 (2000): 63–69.

Fitzmyer, J. A. "The Use of Explicit Old Testament Quotations in Qumran Literature and in the New Testament." *NTS* 7 (1960–1961): 297–333.

Fohrer, G. *Geschichte der israelitischen Religion*. Berlin 1969.

Foitzheim, F. *Christologie und Eschatologie bei Paulus*. FzB 35. Würzburg 1979.

Forschini, B. M. "'Those Who Are Baptized for the Dead': 1 Cor 15:29." *CBQ* 12 (1950): 260–276.

Fretz, M. J. "Adam." *ABD* V: 62–64.

Fuller, R. H. "Resurrection." Pages 864–865 in *Harper's Bible Dictionary*. Edited by P. J. Achtemeier. New York 1985.

Gamble, H. Y. *Books and Readers in the Early Church: A History of Early Christian Texts*. New Haven 1995.

Gaffin, R. B. "'Life-Giving Spirit': Probing the Center of Paul's Pneumatology." *JETS* 41 (1998): 573–589.

Gammie, J. G. "Loci of Melchizedek Tradition." *JBL* 90 (1971): 385–396.

García, J. M. "1 Co 15:56: ¿Una polémica contra la ley judía?" *EstBib* 60 (2002): 405–414.

García, J. M. "Acontecimientos después la venida gloriosa (1 Cor 15,23–28)." *EstBib* 58 (2000): 527–559.

Garland, R. *The Greek Way of Death*. London 1985.

Gądecki, S. *Wstęp do ksiąg prorockich Starego Testamentu*. Gniezno 1993.

Gerhardsson, B. *Memory and Manuscript. Oral Tradition and Written Transmission in Rabbinic Judaism and Early Christianity.* Uppsala 1964².

Gerhardsson, B. *The Origins of the Gospel Tradition.* London 1979.

Gerhardsson, B. *Tradition and Transmission in Early Christianity.* Lund 1964.

Gielen, M. "Universale Totenauferweckung und universales Heil? 1 Kor 15,20–28 im Kontext paulinischer Theologie." *BZ* 47 (2003): 92–95.

Gieniusz, A. "Najstarszy przekaz o zmartwychwstaniu: 1 Kor 15,1–11." *ZHTZ* 3 (1997): 73–81.

Gillmann, J. "A Thematic Comparison: 1 Cor 15:50–57 and 2 Cor 5:1–5." *JBL* 107 (1988): 439–454.

Ginsberg, H. L. "Reflexes of Sargon in Isaiah after 715 BCE." *JAOS* 88 (1968): 47–53.

Gnilka, J. *Paweł z Tarsu. Apostoł i świadek.* Translated by W. Szymon. Kraków 2001.

Gnilka, J. *Teologia Nowego Testamentu.* Translated by W. Szymon. Kraków 2002.

Goppelt, L. *Typos. Die typologische Deutung des Alten Testaments im Neuen.* Gütersloh 1939.

Goulder, M. "The Pauline Epistles." Pages 479–502 in *The Literary Guide to the Bible.* Edited by R. Alter and F. Kermode. London 1989.

Grelot, P. "Śmierć." Pages 948–949 in *Słownik teologii biblijnej.* Edited by X. Léon-Dufour. Translated by K. Romaniuk. Poznań–Warszawa 1973.

Gryziec, P. R. "'Z uczynków Prawa nikt nie może dostąpić usprawiedliwienia' (Rz 3,20)." *RBL* 50 (1997): 16–22.

Grzybek, S. "Zmartwychwstanie w świetle ksiąg St. Testamentu." Pages 154–166 in *Vademecum biblijne,* IV. Edited by S. Grzybek. Kraków 1991.

Gulley, N. R. "Death." *ABD* II: 110–111.

Gundry, R. H. *Sōma in Biblical Theology with Emphasis on Pauline Anthropology.* SNTSMS 29. Cambridge 1976.

Güttgemanns, E. *Fragmenta semiotico-hermeneutica. Eine Texthermeneutik für ein Umgang mit der Hl. Schrift.* FTL 9. Bonn 1983.

Hadas-Lebel, M. *Hillel. Maestro della Legge al tempo di Gesù.* Translated by P. Lanfranchi. Casale Monferrato 2002.

Hafemann, S. J. "Corinthians, Letters to the." Pages 164–179 in *Dictionary of Paul and His Letters. A Compendium of Contemporary Biblical Scholarship.* Edited by G. F. Hawthorne and R. P. Martin. Dovners Grove–Leicester 1993.

Harper's Bible Dictionary. Edited by P. J. Achtemeier. New York 1985.

Harris, W. *Ancient Literacy.* Cambridge 1989.

Hartman, L. "'Guiding the Knowing Vessel of your Heart': On Bible Usage and Jewish Identity in Alexandrian Judaism." Pages 19–36 in *The New Testament and Hellenistic Judaism.* Edited by P. Borgen and S. Giversen. Peabody 1997.

Hasler, V. "Credo und Auferstehung in Korinth. Erwägungen zu 1 Kor 15." *TZ* 40 (1984): 12–41.

Hay, D. M. *Glory At the Right Hand. Psalm 110 in Early Christianity.* SBL Monograph 18. Nashville 1973.

Hays, R. B. *Echos of Scripture in the Letters of Paul.* New Haven 1981.

Hays, R. B. "Eschatology and Ethics in 1 Cor." *EA* 10 (1994): 31–43.

Heil, J. P. *The Rhetorical Role of Scripture in 1 Corinthians.* SiBL 15. Leiden–Boston 2005.

Heil, U. "Theo-logische Interpretation von 1 Kor. 15,23–28." *ZNW* 84 (1993): 27–35.

Hengel, M. "'Setze dich zu meinen Rechten!' Die Inthronisation Christi zur Rechten Gottes und Psalm 110,1." Pages 108–112 in *Le Trône de Dieu*. Edited by M. Philonenko. WUNT 69. Tübingen 1993.

Hensell, G. M. *Antitheses and Transformation: A tudy of I Corinthians 15:50–54*, St. Luis 1975.

Heschel A.J., "Mitologia Żydów." Pages 135–148 in *Judaizm*. Edited by M. Dziwisz. Translated by K. Stark. Kraków 1990.

Hiers, R. H. "Parousia." Pages 751–752 in *Harper's Bible Dictionary*. Edited by P. J. Achtemeier. New York 1985.

Hill, C. E. "Paul's Understanding of Christ's Kingdom in I Corinthians 15:20–28." *NovT* 30 (1988) 4: 297–320.

Hollander, H. W. and G. E. van Der Hout. "The Apostle Paul Calling Himself an Abortion: 1 Cor 15,8 within the Context of 1 Cor 15,8–10." *NT* 38 (1996): 224–236.

Hollander, H. W. and J. Holleman. "The Relationship of Death, Sin and Law in 1 Cor 15,56." *NovT* 35 (1993): 270–291.

Holleman, J. *Resurrection and Parousia: A Traditio-Historical Study of Paul's Eschatology in 1 Cor 15*. NovTSup 84. Leiden–New York–Köln 1996.

Holmgren, F. *The Concept of Yahweh as Gōʾēl in Second Isaiah*. New York 1963.

Holtzmann, H. J. *Lehrbuch der neutestamentlichen Theologie*. Edited by A. Jürlicher and W. Bauer. II. Tübingen 1911.

Hooker, M. D. "Beyond the Things That are Written? St Paul's Use of Scripture." *NTS* 27 (1980–1981): 295–309.

Hopkins, K. *Death and Renewal*. Sociological Studies in Roman History 2. Cambridge 1983.

Horn, F. W. "1 Korinther 15,56 – ein exegetische Stachel." *ZNW* 82 (1991): 88–105.

Horn, S. H. and P. Kyle McCarter. "Podzielona monarchia. Królestwa Judy i Izraela." Pages 191–296 in *Starożytny Izrael. Od Abrahama do zburzenia świątyni jerozolimskiej przez Rzymian*. Edited by H. Shanks. Translated by W. Chrostowski. Warszawa 2007.

Horsley, R. A. "'How Can Some of You Say That There Is No Resurrection of the Dead?': Spiritual Elitism in Corinth." *NT* 20 (1978): 203–231.

Horsley, R. A. "Pneumaticos vs. Psychikos. Distinctions of Spiritual Status among the Corinthians." *HTR* 83 (1976): 269–288.

Horst P., van der. "Sortes: Sacred Books as Instant Oracles in Late Antiquity." In *The Use of Sacred Books in the Ancient World*. Edited by L.V. Rutgers et al. Leuven 1998.

Howard, J. K. "Baptism for the Dead: A Study of 1 Cor 15:29." *EvQ* 37 (1965): 137–141.

Hubbard, R. L. "The Go'el in Ancient Israel. Theological reflections on an Israelite Institution." *BBR* 1 (1991): 3–19.

Huhn, E. *Die Messianischen Weissagungen*, II. Tübingen 1900.

Hull, M. F. *Baptism on Account of the Dead (1 Cor 15:29). An Act of Faith in the Resurrection*. SBL 22. Atlanta 2005.

Hultgren, S. J. "The Origin of Paul's Doctrine of the Two Adams in 1 Corinthians 15.45–49." *JSNT* 25 (2003): 343–370.

Hummel, H. D. "Enclitic mem in Early Northwest Semitic, Especially Hebrew." *JBL* 76 (1957): 85–107.

Humphreys, S. C. "Death and Time." In *Mortality and Immortality: The Anthropology and Archeology of Death*. Edited by S. C. Humphreys and H. King. New York 1981.

Hyldahl, N. "Paul and Hellenistic Judaism in Corinth." Pages 204–216 in *The New Testament and Hellenistic Judaism*. Edited by P. Borgen and S. Giversen. Peabody 1997.

Hübner, H. "New Testament, OT Quotation in." *ABD* IV: 1096–1104.

Jankowski, A. *Duch Święty Dokonawcą zbawienia. Nowy Testament o posłannictwie eschatologicznym Ducha Świętego*. Myśl Teologiczna. Kraków 2003.

Jankowski, A. *Eschatologia Nowego Testamentu*. Myśl Teologiczna. Kraków 2007.

Jankowski, A. *Kerygmat w Kościele apostolskim. Nowotestamentowa teologia głoszenia słowa Bożego*. Częstochowa 1989.

Jasiński, A. S. *Jezus jest Panem. Kyriologia Nowego Testamentu*. Wrocław 1996.

Jefferson, H. G. "Is Psalm 110 Canaanite?" *JBL* 73 (1954): 152–156.

Jelonek, T. *Prorocy Starego Testamentu*. Kraków 2007.

Jenni, E. and C. Westermann. *Theological Lexicon of the Old Testament*, I–III. Translated by M. E. Biddle. Peabody 1997.

Jepsen, A. "Die Begriffe des «Erlösens» im Alten Testament." Pages 153–163 in *Solange es „Heute" heisst. Festgabe für R. Hermann*. Berlin 1957.

Jeremias, J. "Flesh and Blood Cannot Inherit the Kingdom of God (1 Cor 15.50)." *NTS* 2 (1955–1956): 151–159.

Jezierska, E. J. "'A jak zmartwychwstają umarli? W jakim ukazują się ciele?' (1 Kor 15,35). Zmartwychwstanie wierzącego i natura jego wskrzeszonego ciała w ujęciu św. Pawła." *ŻK* 45 (2004) 1: 64–69.

Jezierska, E. J. "Chrystologia." Pages 71–130 in *Teologia Nowego Testamentu*, III, *Listy Pawłowe, Katolickie i List do Hebrajczyków*. Edited by M. Rosik. Bibliotheca Biblica. Wrocław 2008.

Jezierska, E. J. "Święty Paweł o zmartwychwstaniu wiernych w Dniu Pańskim." Pages 150–162 in *Miłość wytrwa do końca. Księga Pamiątkowa dla Ks. Profesora Stanisława Pisarka w 50. rocznicę święceń kapłańskich*. Edited by W. Chrostowski. Warszawa 2004.

Jezierska, E. J. "'Życie dla Pana' – zasadą postępowania odkupionych przez Jezusa Chrystusa. Refleksje nad Pawłowym tekstem 2 Kor 5,15." *SS* 1 (1997) 1: 105–110.

Jędrzejewski, S." Peszer jako metoda egzegetyczna." *Seminare* 24 (2007): 111–126.

Johnson, A. "Firstfruits and Death's Defect: Metaphor in Paul's Rhetorical Strategy in 1 Cor 15:20–28." *WW* 16 (1996): 456–464.

Johnson, A. *The Primary Meaning of* גאל. Supplements to Vetus Testamentum 1. Leiden 1953, 67–77.

Johnson, A. "Turning the World Upside Down in 1 Corinthians 15: Apocalyptic Epistemology, the Resurrected Body, and the New Creation." *EvQ* 75 (2003): 291–309.

Jones, P. R. "1 Cor 15:8: Paul the Last Apostle." *TynBul* 36 (1985): 5–34.

Kahle, P. E. *The Cairo Geniza*. London 1947.

Kaznowski, K. "Autor Ps 110." *RTK* 7 (1960): 51–70.

Kearl, M. C. *Endings: A Sociology of Death and Dying*. New York 1989, 95–106.

Kearney, P. J. "He Appeared to 500 Brothers (1 Cor 15:6)." *NT* 22 (1980): 264–284.

Keesmaat, S. C. "Exodus and the intertextual transformation of tradition in Romans 8,14–30." *JSNT* 54 (1994): 29–56.

Keesmaat, S. C. *Paul's use of the Exodus Tradition in Romans and Galatians*. Oxford 1994.

Kempiak, R. "Chrystologiczne podstawy Pawłowej krytyki Prawa." Pages 167–188 in *Deus meus et omnia. Księga pamiątkowa ku czci o. prof. Hugolina Langkammera OFM w 50. rocznicę święceń kapłańskich.* Redited by M. S. Wróbel. Lublin 2005.

Kennedy, G. A. *New Testament Interpretation through Rhetorical Criticism.* Chapel Hill 1984.

Kennedy, H. A. A. *St Paul and the Mystery Religious.* London 1913.

Kenyon, K. *Royal Cities of the Old Testament.* London 1971.

Klinkowski, J. *Zużytkowanie Starego Testamentu w Nowym. Studium egzegetyczne tekstów Ewangelii synoptycznych.* BDL 13. Legnica 2000.

Koch, D.-A. *Die Schrift als Zeuge des Evangeliums. Untersuchungen zur Verwendung und Verständnis der Schrift bei Paulus.* Tübingen 1986.

Koehler, L., W. Baumgartner and J. J. Stamm. *Wielki słownik hebrajsko-polski i aramejsko-polski Starego Testamentu*, I–II. Polish ed. P. Dec. Translated by team. Warszawa 2008.

Kovacs, J. "The Archons, the Spirit, and the Death of Christ. Do We Really Need the Hypothesis of Gnostic Opponents to Explain 1 Cor 2, 2–16." Pages 217–236 in *Apocalyptic in the NT. Essays in Honor of J. Louis Martyn.* Edited by J. Marcus and M. L. Soards. JSNTSup 24. Sheffield 1989.

Kozyra, J. "Aspekty teologiczne paruzji Chrystusa w 1 Kor 15." *SSHT* 10 (1997): 14–44.

Krawczyk, R. *Nadzieje mesjańskie w Psalmach.* Warszawa 2007.

Kreitzer, L. "Adam as Analogy: Help or Hindrance?" *NB* 70 (1989): 278–284.

Kreitzer, L. "Adam and Christ." Pages 9–15 in *Dictionary of Paul and His Letters. A Compendium of Contemporary Biblical Scholarship.* Edited by G. F. Hawthorne and R. P. Martin. Dovners Grove–Leicester 1993.

Kreitzer, L. "Body." Pages 71–76 in *Dictionary of Paul and His Letters. A Compendium of Contemporary Biblical Scholarship.* Edited by G. F. Hawthorne and R. P. Martin. Dovners Grove–Leicester 1993.

Kreitzer, L. *Jesus and God in Paul's Eschatology.* JSNTSup 19. Sheffield 1987.

Kuck, D. W. *Judgement and Community Conflict. Paul's Use of Apocalyptic Judgment Language in 1 Cor 3,5–4.* NovTSup 66. Leiden–New York–Kopenhagen–Köln 1992.

Kulińska, B. "Pogląd na śmierć jako sen w Starym Testamencie." *SS* 6 (2002): 37–56.

Kurtz, D. and J. Boardman. *Greek Burial Customs.* Aspects of Greek and Roman Life. London 1971.

LaCocque, A., "Szczeliny w murze." In *Myśleć biblijnie.* Edited by A. LaCocque and R. Ricoeur. Teologia żywa. Translated by E. Mukoid and M. Tarnowska. Kraków 2003.

Lambrecht, J. "Paul's Christological Use of Scripture in 1 Cor. 15.20–28." *NTS* 28 (1982): 502–527.

Lambrecht, J. "Structure and Line of Thought in 1 Cor. 15:23–28." *NovT* 32 (1990): 143–151.

Lambrecht, J. "To Meet the Lord: Scripture about Life after Death." Pages 411–441 in *Pauline Studies.* BETL 125. Leuven 1994.

Lane-Mercier, G. "Quotation as a Discursive Strategy." *Kodikas* 14 (1991): 199–214.

Langkammer, H. *Obraz Jezusa Chrystusa w świetle Nowego Testamentu. Przyczynek do chrystologii analogicznej Nowego Testamentu.* Rzeszów 2009.

Langkammer, H. *Teologia biblijna Starego i Nowego Testamentu.* BDL 29. Legnica 2007.

Langkammer, H. *Życie człowieka w świetle Biblii. Antropologia biblijna Starego Nowego Testamentu.* Rzeszów 2004.

Lassen, M. "The Use of the Father Image in Imperial Propaganda and 1 Cor 4:14–21." *TynBul* 42 (1991): 127–136.

Lee, J. Y. "Interpreting the Powers in Pauline Thought." *NT* 12 (1970): 54–69.

Leggett, D. A. *The Levirate and Goel Institutions in the Old Testament. With Special Attention to the Book of Ruth.* Cherry Hill 1974.

Leith, D. and G. Myerson. *The Power of Address: Explorations in Rhetoric.* London 1989.

Lemański, J. *Pięcioksiąg dzisiaj.* SB 4. Kielce 2002.

Lemański, J. „Sprawisz, abym ożył!" *(Ps 71,20b). Źródła nadziei na zmartwychwstanie w Starym Testamencie.* RiS 532. Szczecin 2004.

Lewis, S. M. "'So That God May Be All in All': 1 Corinthians 15:12–34." *SBFLA* 49 (1999): 195–210.

Lewis, S. M. *"So That God May Be All in All": The Apocalyptic Message of 1 Corinthians 15,12–34.* TG 42. Rome 1998.

Levinson, J. R. *Portraits of Adam in Early Judaism. From Sirach to 2 Baruch.* JSPESup 1. Sheffield 1988.

Léon-Dufou, X. "Chrystofanie." Pages 125–130 in *Słownik teologii biblijnej.* Edited by X. Léon-Dufour. Translated by K. Romaniuk. Poznań–Warszawa 1973.

Lietzmann, H. *An die Galater.* Tübingen 1923.

Lindars, B. and A. J. Saldarini. "Cytaty ze Starego Testamentu w Nowym Testamencie." Pages 175–179 in *Encyklopedia biblijna.* Edited by P. J. Achtemeier. Translated by T. Mieszkowski. Warszawa 1999.

Lindemann, A. "Parusie Christi und Herrschaft Gottes. Exegese von Kor 15:23–28." *WuD* 19 (1987): 87–107.

Lindemann, A. "Paulus und die korintische Eschatologie. Zur These von einer 'Entwicklung' im paulinischen Denken." *NTS* 37 (1991): 373–399.

Linke, W. "Zmartwychwstanie Chrystusa i nasze według św. Pawła." Page 79 in „Dla mnie żyć to Chrystus!". *Rok świętego Pawła w parafii św. Jakuba w Skierniewicach.* Edited by J. Pietrzyk and M. Szmajdziński. Skierniewice 2009.

Loader, W. R. "Christ at the Right Hand – Ps. CX. 1 in the New Testament." *NTS* 24 (1977): 199–217.

Longenecker, R. N. *Studies in Paul, Exegetical and Theological.* New Testament Monographs. Sheffield 2004.

Longosz, S. "Czy Paweł Apostoł cytował komediopisarza Menandra (1 Kor 15,33). Opinie Ojców Kościoła." *VoxP* 9 (1989) 17: 907–924.

Lorek, P. "Podstawowa linearna i chiastyczna dispositio I Listu do Koryntian." *TW* 1 (2006): 47–60.

Łanowski, J. "Menandros." Pages 312–315 in *Słownik pisarzy antycznych.* Edited by A. Świderkówna. Warszawa 1982.

Łowicka, D. "Euripides." Pages 192–195 in *Słownik pisarzy antycznych.* Edited by A. Świderkówna. Warszawa 1982.

Maass, F. "אָדָם 'ādhām." *TDOT* I: 75–87.

Macgregor, G. H. C. "Principalities and Powers: The Cosmic Background of Paul's Thought." *NTS* 1 (1954–55): 17–28.

Machinist, P. B. "Sargon II." Pages 1088–1089 in *Encyklopedia biblijna.* Edited by P. J. Achtemeier. Translated by E. Szymula. Warszawa 1999.

Mack, B. *Rhetoric and the New Testament*. Minneapolis 1990.

Maier, F. W. "Ps 110,1 (LXX 109,1) im Zusammenhang von 1 Kor 15,24–26." *BZ* 20 (1932): 139–156.

Maile, J. F. "Exaltation and Enthronement." Pages 275–278 in *Dictionary of Paul and His Letters. A Compendium of Contemporary Biblical Scholarship*. Edited by G. F. Hawthorne and R. P Martin. Dovners Grove–Leicester 1993.

Malherbe, A. J. "The Beasts at Ephesus." *JBL* 87 (1968): 71–80.

Marconcini, B. "L'apocalittica biblica." Pages 193–246 in *Profeti e Apocalittici*. Edited by B. Marconcini et al. Logos. Corso do Studi Biblici 3. Torino 1994.

Martin-Achard, R. *From Death to Life. A Study of the Doctrine of the Resurrection in the Old Testament*. Edinburgh–London 1960.

Martin-Achard, R. "Resurrection (OT)." *ABD* V: 680–684.

Mazar, A. *Archeology of the Land of the Bible. 10,000–586 B.C.E.* The Anchor Bible Reference Library. New York–London–Toronto–Sydney–Auckland 1992.

McNamara, M. *I Targum e il Nuovo Testamento. Le parafrasi aramaiche delle bibbia ebraica e il loro apporto per una migliore comprensione del Nuovo Testamento*. Studi biblici. Bologna 1978.

Mello, A. *Judaizm*. Translated by K. Stopa. Kraków 2003.

Metzger, B. M. *A Textual Commentary on the Greek New Testament*. Stuttgart 1994[2].

Meynet, R. *L'analyse rhétorique. Une nouvelle méthode pour comprendre la Bible*. Paris 1989.

Meynet, R. *Wprowadzenie do hebrajskiej retoryki biblijnej*. Translated by K. Łukowicz and T. Kot. Myśl Teologiczna. Kraków 2001.

Mędala, S. *Wprowadzenie do literatury międzytestamentalnej*. Biblioteka Zwojów. Tło Nowego Testamentu 1, Kraków 1994.

Michel, O. *Paulus und seine Bibel*. Darmstadt 1972[2].

Mickiewicz, F. "Zagadnienia etyczne." Pages 307–373 in *Teologia Nowego Testamentu, III, Listy Pawłowe, Katolickie i List do Hebrajczyków*. Edited by M. Rosik. Bibliotheca Biblica. Wrocław 2008.

Millard, A. *Reading and Writing in the Time of Jesus*. Biblical Seminar 69. Sheffield 2000.

Millard, A. *Skarby czasów Biblii. Odkrycia archeologiczne rzucają nowe światło na Biblię*. Translated by M. Stopa. Warszawa 2000.

Miranda, A. "L''uomo spirituale' (pneumatikos anthrôpos) nella prima ai Corinzi." *RivB* 43 (1995): 485–519.

Mitchell, M. M. *Paul and the Rhetoric of Reconciliation: An Exegetical Investigation of the Language and Composition of 1 Corinthians*. Tübingen 1991.

Moeller, H. R. "Biblical Research and O.T. Translation." *Bible Translator* 13 (1962): 16–22.

Morissette, R. "La citation du Psaume VIII, 7b dans I Corinthians XV, 27a." *ScEs* 24 (1972): 314–342.

Morgenthaler, R. *Statistik des Neuestestamentlichen Wortschatzes*. Zürich–Stuttgart 1972.

Morissette, R. "La condition de ressucité. 1 Cor 15:35–49: structure littéraire de la péricope." *Bib* 53 (1972): 208–228.

Morris, I. *Death-Ritual and Social Structure in Classical Antiquity*. Key Themes in Ancient History. Cambridge 1992.

Moule, C. F. D. "St. Paul and Dualism. The Pauline Conception of Resurrection." *NTS* 12 (1965/1966): 10–123.

Moulton, J. H. A *Grammar of New Testament Greek*, II, *Accidence and Word-Formation*. Edited by W. F. Howard. Edinburgh 1929.

Muchowski, P. *Rękopisy znad Morza Martwego. Qumran – Wadi Murabba'at – Masada – Nachal Cheder*. Biblioteka Zwojów. Tło Nowego Testamentu 5. Kraków 2000.

Munck, J. "Paulus tanquam abortivus, 1 Cor 15:8." Pages 180–195 in *NT Essays: Studies in Memory of T.W. Manson*. Edited by A. J. B. Higgins. Manchester 1959.

Murphy-O'Connor, J. "'Baptized for the Dead' (I Cor., XV, 29). A Corinthian Slogan?" *RB* 88 (1981): 532–543.

Murphy-O'Connor, J. "Tradition and Redaction in 1 Cor 15:3–7." *CBQ* 43 (1981): 582–589.

Müller, K. "1 Kor 1,18–25, Die eschatologisch-kritische Funktion der Verkündigung des Kreuzes." *BZ* 10 (1966): 246–272.

Münderlein, G. *Die Überwindung der Mächte. Studien zu theologischen Vorstellung des apokalyptischen Judentums und bei Paulus*. Zürich 1971.

Nickelsburg, G. W. E. "An ektrōma, Though Appointed from the Womb: Paul's Apostolic Self-Description in 1 Cor 15 and Gal 1." *HTR* 79 (1986): 198–205.

Nickelsburg, G. W. E. "Resurrection (Early Judaism and Christianity)." *ABD* V: 684–691.

Nobile, M. "Le citazioni veterotestamentarie di Paulo." Pages 21–27 in *Atti del VII Simposio di Tarso su S. Paulo Apostolo*. Edited by L. Padovese. Turchia: la Chiesa e la sua storia XVI. Roma 2002.

O'Brien, P. T. "Princpalities and Powers: Opponents of the Church." Pages 110–150 in *Biblical Interpretation and the Church*. Edited by D. A. Carson. Nashville 1984.

Ordon, H. "Dzieło odkupienia w nauczaniu św. Pawła." Pages 177–186 in *Biblia o odkupieniu*. Edited by R. Rubinkiewicz. Lublin 2000.

Orłowski, R. *Łukaszowy przekaz o powołaniu Pawła. Studium literacko-teologiczne*. Bibliotheca Biblica. Wrocław 2008.

Osborne, R. E. "Paul and the Wild Beasts." *JBL* 85 (1966): 225–230.

Paciorek, A. *Paweł Apostoł – pisma*, I. Academica 28. Tarnów 1997.

Paciorek, A. "Wydarzenie pod Damaszkiem w świetle nowotestamentowych wypowiedzi." Pages 163–175 in *Mów, Panie, bo sługa Twój słucha. Księga pamiątkowa dla Księdza Profesora Ryszarda Rubinkiewicza SDB w 60. rocznicę urodzin*. Edited by W. Chrostowski. Warszawa 1999.

Pani, G. "Vocazione di Paulo o conversione? La documentazione della lettera ai Galati e ai Romani." Pages 50–64 in *Il simposio di Tarso su S. Paulo Apostolo*. Roma 1993.

Parchem, M. "Zmartwychwstanie, odpłata po śmierci i życie wieczne w literaturze międzytestamentalnej." *VV* 15 (2009): 99–142.

Park, S. *Conceptions of Afterlife in Jewish Inscriptions: With Special Reference to Pauline Literature*. WUNT 121. Tübingen 2000.

Pearce, L. E. "Elam." Pages 250–251 in *Encyklopedia biblijna*. Edited by P. J. Achtemeier. Translated by M. Wojciechowski. Warszawa 1999.

Person, B. A. *The pneumatikos – psychikos Terminology in 1 Corinthians. A Study in the Theology of the Corinthian Opponents of Paul and Its Relation to Gnosticism*. SBLDS 12. Missuola 1973.

Penna, R. "Cristologia adamitica e ottimismo antropologico in 1 Cor 15,45–49." In *L'apostolo Paolo. Studi d'esegesi e teologia*. Cinisello Balsamo 1991.

Perelman, C. and L. Olbrychts-Tyteca. *The New Rhetoric: A Treatise on Argumentation*. Translated by J. Wilkinson and P. Weaver. Notre Dame 1969.

Perri, C. "On Alluding." *Poetics* 7 (1978): 289–307.

Perriman, A. C. "Paul and the Parousia: 1 Corinthians 15.50–57 and 2 Corinthians 5.1–5." *NTS* 35 (1989): 512–521.

Pisarek, S. "Życie i śmierć." Pages 59–70 in *Vademecum biblijne*, IV. Edited by S. Grzybek. Kraków 1991.

Plank, K. A. "Resurrection Theology: The Corinthian Controversy Re-examined." *PRSt* 8 (1981): 41–54.

Polaski, D. C. *Authorizing an End. The Isaiah Apocalypse and Intertextuality*. Leiden 2001.

Polok, B. "Autorytet pism ST w NT na przykładzie starotestamentalnych cytatów w ewangelicznych opisach męki Pańskiej." Pages 45–62 in *Izrael i Biblia Hebrajska w Nowym Testamencie*. Edited by K. Ziaja. Sympozja 53. Opole 2003.

Polski słownik judaistyczny. Dzieje, kultura, religia, ludzie. Edited by Z. Borzymińska and R. Żebrowski. I–II. Warszawa 2003.

Popowski, R. *Słownik grecko-polski Nowego Testamentu*. Warszawa 1999².

Popowski, R. *Wielki słownik grecko-polski Nowego Testamentu. Wydanie z pełną lokalizacją greckich haseł, kluczem polsko-greckim oraz indeksem form czasownikowych*. Warszawa 1955.

Porter, S. E. "Further Comments on the Use of the Old Testament in the New Testament." Pages 98–110 in *The Intertextuality of the Epistles. Explorations of Theory and Practice*. Edited by T. L. Brodie, D. R. MacDonald and S. E. Porter. Sheffield 2006.

Porter, S. E. "The Use of the Old Testament in the New Testament: A Brief Comment on Method and Terminology." Pages 79–96 in *Early Christian Interpretation of the Scriptures in Israel: Investigations and Proposals*. Edited by C. A. Evans and J. A. Sanders. JSNTSup 14. Sheffield 1997.

Price, R. M. "Apocryphal Apparitions: 1 Cor 15:3–11 as a Post-Pauline Interpolation." *JHC* 2 (1995): 69–99.

Prümm, K. "Reflexiones theologicae et historicae ad usum Paulinum termini 'eikōn'." *VD* 40 (1962): 232–257.

Rad, G., von. *Teologia Starego Testamentu*. Translated by B. Widła. Warszawa 1986.

Radi, W. "Der Sinn von gnōrizō in 1 Kor 15:1." *BZ* 28 (1984): 243–245.

Rakocy, W. *Paweł Apostoł. Chronologia życia i pism*. Częstochowa 2003.

Rapoport, I. "Zasady żydowskiej egzegezy tekstu do czasów końcowej redakcji Talmudu." Pages 157–260 in M. Rosik and I. Rapoport, *Wprowadzenie do literatury i egzegezy żydowskiej okresu biblijnego i rabinicznego*. Bibliotheca Biblica. Wrocław 2009.

Reader, M. "Vikariastaufe in 1 Cor 15:29?" *ZNW* 46 (1955): 258–261.

Reaume, J. D. "Another Look At 1 Cor 15:29, 'Baptized for the Dead'." *BSac* 152 (1995): 457–475.

Reicke, B. "Szeol." Pages 591–592 in *Słownik wiedzy biblijnej*. Edited by B. M. Metzger and M. D. Coogan. Polish ed. W. Chrostowski. Translated by T. Mieszkowski. Warszawa 1996.

316 Bibliography

Reid, R. G. "Principalities and Powers." Pages 746–752 in *Dictionary of Paul and His Letters. A Compendium of Contemporary Biblical Scholarship.* Edited by G. F. Hawthorne and R. P. Martin. Dovners Grove–Leicester 1993.

Reitzenstein, R. *Die hellenistischen Mysterienreligionen nach ihren Grundgedanken und Wirkungen.* Leipzig–Berlin 1927.

Richard, S. "Góra." Page 357 in *Encyklopedia biblijna.* Edited by P. J. Achtemeier. Translated by T. Mieszkowski. Warszawa 1999.

Richardson, N. *Paul's Language about God.* JSNTSup 99. Sheffield 1994.

Rienecker, F. and G. Maier. *Leksykon biblijny.* Translated by D. Irmińska. Warszawa 2001.

Riesenfeld, H. *The Gospel Tradition and Its Beginnings. A Study in the Limits of „Formgeschichte".* TU 73. Berlin 1957.

Riesner, R. *Jesus als Lehrer. Eine Untersuchung zum Ursprung der Evangelien-Überlieferung.* WUNT 2,7. Tübingen 1981.

Rissi, M. *Die Taufe für die Toten.* Abhandlung zur Theologie des A und NT 42. Zurich 1962.

Rist, J. M. "Zeno and Stoic Consistency." Pages 465–477 in *Essays in Ancient Greek Philosophy*, II. Edited by J. P. Anton. New York 1983.

Roberts, J. H. "The Eschatological Transitions to the Pauline Letter Body." *Neot* 20 (1986): 29–35.

Rogowski, R. *ABC teologii dogmatycznej.* Edited by S. J. Stasiak, R. Zawiła and A. Małachowski. Wrocław 1999[4].

Roloff, J. "Adam." Page 21 in *Das Grosse Lexikon zur Bibel. Altes und Neues Testament.* Edited by K. Koch, E. Otto, J. Roloff and H. Schmoldt. Wien 2004.

Roloff, J. "Parusie." Page 387 in *Das Grosse Lexikon zur Bibel. Altes und Neues Testament.* Edited by K. Koch, E. Otto, J. Roloff and H. Schmoldt. Wien 2004.

Romaniuk, K. *Uczniowie i współpracownicy Pawła.* Warszawa 1993.

Romaniuk, K. *Wiara w zmartwychwstanie, pusty grób i pojawienie się zmartwychwstałego Chrystusa.* AL 6. Katowice 1981.

Romeo A., 'Omnes quidem resurgemus' seu 'Omnes quidem nequaquam dormiemus' (1 Cor. 15,51), VD 14 (1934) 142–378.

Rosik, M. "Biblijne namaszczenie na króla, kapłana i proroka jako konsekracja. „Namaścił ciebie olejkiem radości" (Ps 45 [44] 8)." *ŻK* 6 (38) 2002: 42–53.

Rosik, M. *Ewangelia Łukasza a świat grecko-helleński. Perspektywa literacka i ideologiczna.* Bibliotheca Biblica. Wrocław 2009.

Rosik, M. "Judaistyczne tło Modlitwy Pańskiej (Mt 6,9–13)." *Zeszyty Naukowe Centrum Badań im. Edyty Stein* 4 (2008): 41–50.

Rosik, M. "Literatura żydowska okresu biblijnego i rabinicznego." Pages 11–155 in M. Rosik and I. Rapoport, *Wprowadzenie do literatury i egzegezy żydowskiej okresu biblijnego i rabinicznego.* Bibliotheca Biblica. Wrocław 2009.

Rowland, C. "Parousia." *ABD* V: 166–170.

Rowley, H. H. "Melchizedek and Zadok." Pages 461–472 in *Festschrift für Alfred Bertholet zum 80. Geburstag.* Edited by W. Baumgartner, O. Eissfeldt, K. Ellinger and L. Rost. Tübingen 1950.

Rush, A. C. *Death and Burial in Christian Antiquity.* Catholic University of America Studies in Christian Antiquity 1. Washington 1941.

Ryken, L., J. C. Wilhoit and T. Longman III. *Słownik symboliki biblijnej. Obrazy, symbole, motywy, metafory, figury stylistyczne i gatunki literackie w Piśmie Świętym.* Translated by Z. Kościuk. Warszawa 2003.

Ryle, H. E. *The Canon of the Old Testament.* London 1892.

Saake, H. "Die kodikologisch problematische Nachstellung der Negation (Beobachtungen zu 1 Kor 15,51)." *ZNW* 63 (1972): 277–279.

Saldarini, A. J. "Szebna." Page 1182 in *Encyklopedia biblijna.* Edited by P. J. Achtemeier. Translated by E. Szymula. Warszawa 1999.

Salguero, J. "Concetto biblico di salvezza-liberazione." *Ang* 53 (1976): 11–55.

Sanders, E. P. *Il giudaismo. Fede e prassi (63 a.C.–66 d.C.).* Translated by P. Capelli and L. Santini. SR. Brescia 1999.

Saw, I. *Paul's Rhetoric in 1 Corinthians 1. An Analysis Utilizing the Theories of Classical Rhetoric.* Lewiston–Queenston–Lampeter 1995.

Schade, H.-H. *Apokalyptische Christologie bei Paulus. Studien zum Zusammenhang von Christologie und Eschatologie in den Paulusbriefen.* GTA 18. Göttingen 1981.

Schaeffer, M. "Paulus 'Fehlgeburt' oder 'unvernünftiges Kind'?" *ZNW* 85 (1994): 207–217.

Schedl, C. *Historia Starego Testamentu,* IV, *Zew Proroków.* Translated by S. Stańczyk. Tuchów 1995.

Schendel, E. *Herrschaft und Unterwerfung Christi: 1. Korinther 15,24–28 in Rxeese und Theologie der Väter bis zum Ausgang des 4 Jahrhunderts.* BGBE 12. Tübingen 1971.

Schenk, W. "Textlinguistische Aspekte der Strukturanalyse, dargestellt am Beispiel von 1 Kor xv. 1–11." *NTS* 23 (1977): 469–477.

Schep, J. A. *The Nature of the Resurrection Body.* Grand Rapids 1964.

Schlier, H. *Principalities and Powers in the New Testament.* Freiburg 1961.

Schmeller, T. *Paulus und die 'Diatribe'. Eine vergleichende Stilinterpretation.* NTA 19. Münster 1987.

Schmid, J. "Die alttestamentlichen Zitate bei Paulus und die Theoria vom sensus plenior." *BZ* 3 (1959): 161–173.

Schmithals, W. *The Gnosis in Korinth.* FRLANT 48. Göttingen 1956.

Schneider, B. "The Corporate Meaning and Background of 1 Cor 15:45b." *CBQ* 29 (1967): 450–467.

Schottroff, L.. *Der Glaubende und di feindliche Welt. Beobachtungen zum gnostischen Dualismus und seiner Bedeutung für Paulus und das Johannesevangelium.* WMANT 37. Neukirchen 1970.

Schreiner, S. "Psalm CX und die Investitur des Hohenpriesters." *VT* 27 (1977): 216–222.

Schütz, J. H. *Paul and the Anatomy of Apostolic Authority.* Cambridge 1975.

Schweitzer, A. *The Mysticism of Paul the Apostle.* London 1956.

Schweizer, E. "1 Korinther 15,20–28 als Zeugnis paulinischer Eschatologie und ihrer Verwandschaft mit der Verkündigung Jesu." Pages 301–314 in *Jesus und Paulus.* Edited by E. E. Ellis and E. Grässer. Göttingen 1975.

Schweizer, E. "Body." *ABD* I: 767–772.

Schweizer, E. "χοϊκός" *TDNT* IX: 472–479.

Scott, J. M. "Paul's use of Deuteronomic Tradition." *JBL* 112 (1993): 645–665.

Scroggs, R. "Eschatological Existence in Matthew and Paul: *Coincidentia Oppositorum.*" Pages 125–146 in *Apocalyptic and the New Testament.* JSNTSup 24. Sheffield 1989.

Scroggs, R. *The Last Adam. A Study in Pauline Anthropology.* Philadelphia 1966.

Sellin. G. *Der Streit um die Auferstehung der Toten. Eine religionsgeschichtliche und exegetische Untersuchung von 1 Korinther 15.* FRLANT 138. Göttingen 1986.

Sevignac, J., de. *Essai d'interprétation du Psaume CX à l'aide de la littérature égyptienne.* Oudtestamentische Studien 9. Leuven 1951.

Sfair, P. "De genuina lectione Ps 8,2." *Bib* 23 (1942): 318–322.

Sider, R. J. "St. Paul's Understanding of the Nature and Significance of the Resurrection in I Corinthians XV:1–19." *NovT* 19 (1977): 132–143.

Sider, R. "The Pauline Conception of Resurrection Body in 1 Cor 15:35–54." *NTS* 21 (1975): 429–439.

Sierotwiński, S. *Słownik terminów literackich. Teoria i nauki pomocnicze literatury.* Wrocław –Warszawa–Kraków–Gdańsk–Łódź 1986⁴.

Silva, D.A., de. "Let the One Who Claims Honor Establish That Claim in the Lord. Honor Discourse in the Corinthian Correspondence." *BTB* 28 (1998): 61–74.

Silva, M. "Old Testament in Paul." Pages 630–642 in *Dictionary of Paul and His Letters. A Compendium of Contemporary Biblical Scholarship.* Edited by G. F. Hawthorne and R. P. Martin. Dovners Grove–Leicester 1993.

Słownik hermeneutyki biblijnej. Edited by R. J. Coggins and J. L. Houlden. Polish ed. W. Chrostowski. Translated by B. Widła. Warszawa 2005.

Słownik pisarzy antycznych. Edited by A. Świderkówna. Warszawa 1982.

Słownik terminów literackich. Edited by J. Sławiński. Wrocław 1998.

Słownik teologii biblijnej. Edited by X. Léon-Dufour. Translated by K. Romaniuk. Poznań–Warszawa 1973.

Słownik wiedzy biblijnej. Edited by B. M. Metzger and M. D. Coogan. Polish ed. W. Chrostowski. Translated by Team. Warszawa 1996.

Soden, W., van. "Der Mensch bescheidet sich nicht. Überlegungen zu Schöpfungserzählungen in Babylonien und Israel." Pages 165–173 in *Bibel und Alter Orient. Altorientalische Beiträge zum Alten Testament.* Edited by W. van Soden. BZAW 162. Berlin–New York 1985.

Soggin, J. A. *Introduzione all'Antico Testamento. Dalle origini alla chiusura del Canone alessandrino. Con appendici sulle iscrizioni palestinesi della prima metà del I millennio a.C. e sui reperti manoscritti dei primi secoli dopo l'esilio.* Brescia 1987⁴.

Soggin, J. A. "Textkritische Untersuchungen von Ps. VIII, vv. 2–3 und 6." *VT* 21 (1971): 565–571.

Söding, T. *Das Wort vom Kreuz. Studien zur paulinischen Theologie.* WUNT 93. Tübingen 1997.

Söding, T. "'Die Kraft der Sünde ist das Gesetz' (1 Kor 15,56). Anmerkungen zum Hintergrundund zur Pointe einer gesetzeskritischen Sentenz des Apostels Paulus." *ZNW* 83 (1992): 74–84.

Spörlein, B. *Die Leugnung der Auferstehung. Eine historisch-kritische Untersuchung zu 1 Kor 15.* BU 7. Regensburg 1971.

Staab, K. "I Kor 15,29 in Lichte der Exegese der griechischen Kirche." Pages 437–449 in *Studiorum Paulinorum Congressus Internationalis Catholicus 1961*, II. AnBib 17–18. Rome 1963.

Stamm, J. J. "Eine Bemerkung zum Anfang des achten Psalms." *TZ* 13 (1957): 470–478.

Stamm, J. J. *Erlösen und Vergeben im Alten Testament*. Bern 1940.

Stamm, J. J. "אגל" Pages 288–296 in *Theological Lexicon of the Old Testament*. Edited by E. Jenni and C. Westermann. I. Peabody 1997.

Stanley, C. D. *Arguing with Scripture: The Rhetoric of Quotation in Letters of Paul*. New York 2004.

Stanley, C. D. "Paul and Homer: Greco-Roman Citation Practice in the First-Century CE." *NT* 32 (1990): 48–56.

Stanley, C. D. *Paul and the Language of Scripture: Citation Technique in the Pauline Epistles and Contemporary Literature*. SNTSMS 74. Cambridge 1992.

Stasiak, S. J. *Eschatologia w Listach Pasterskich. Specyfika terminów rzeczownikowych*. Legnica 1999.

Stendhal, K. *Paul Among News and Gentiles*. Philadelphia 1976.

Stendhal, K. *The School of St. Matthew and its Use of the Old Testament*. Lund 1968.

Sterling, G. E. "'Wisdom among the Perfect'. Creation Traditions in Alexandrian Judaism and Corinthian Christianity." *NT* 37 (1955): 355–384.

Sternberg, M. "Proteus in Quotation – Land: Mimesis and the Forms of Reported Discourse." *Poetics Today* 3 (1982): 107–156.

Stone, M. E. "Apocalyptic Literature." Pages 383–442 in *Compendium rerum iudaicarum ad Novum Testamentum, II, Jewish Writings of Second Temple Period. Apocrypha, Pseudoepigrapha, Qumran Sectarian Writings, Philo, Josephus*. Edited by M. E. Stone. Assen–Philadelphia 1984.

Stone, N. *Names of God*. Chicago 1994.

Stordalen, T. "Genesis 2,4. Restudying a locus classicus." *ZAW* 104 (1992): 163–177.

Stordalen, T. "Man, Soil, Garden: Basic Plot in Genesis 2–3 Reconsidered." *JSOT* 53 (1992): 3–26.

Strack, H. L. and G. Stemberger. *Introduction to the Talmud and Midrash*. Translated by M. Bockmuehl. Edinburgh 1991.

Synowiec, J. S. *Gatunki literackie w Starym Testamencie*. Kraków 2003.

Synowiec, J. S. *Na początku. Wybrane zagadnienia Pięcioksięgu*. Warszawa 1987.

Synowiec, J. S. *Początki świata i ludzkości według Księgi Rodzaju*. Kraków 2001[3].

Synowiec, J. S. *Wprowadzenie do Księgi Psalmów*. Kraków 1996.

Swete, B. H. *An Introduction to the Old Testament in Greek*. Cambridge 1900.

Szwarc, U. "Świątynia jerozolimska." Pages 79–92 in *Życie religijne w Biblii*. Edited by G. Witaszek. Lublin 1999.

Tanger, A. "Psalm 8,1–2. Studies in Texts." *Theology* 69 (1966): 492–496.

Teani, M. *Corporeità e risurrezione. L'interpretazione di 1 Corinti 15,35–49 nel Novecento*. Aloisiana. Pubblicazioni della Pontifcia Facoltà Teologica dell'Italia Meridionale – Sezione "San Luigi" 24. Roma–Brescia 1994.

Teologia Nowego Testamentu, III, Listy Pawłowe, Katolickie, List do Hebrajczyków. Edited by M. Rosik. Bibliotheca Biblica. Wrocław 2008.

Terry, R. B. *A Discourse Analysis of First Corinthians*. Publications in Linguistics 120. Arlington 1955.

Testa, E. *Genesi. Introduzione – storia primitiva*. Torino 1977[2].

Thayer, J. H., *Thayer's Greek-English Lexicon of the New Testament. Coded with Strong's Concordance Numbers*. Peabody 1996[4].

Theological Dictionary of the New Testament, I–IX. Edited by G. Friedrich. Translated by G. W. Bromiley and D. Litt. Grand Rapids 1999.

Theological Dictionary of the Old Testament, I–IX. Edited by G. J. Botterweck and H. Ringgren. Grand Rapids 1997; X–XI. Edited by G. J. Botterweck, H. Ringgren and H.-J. Fabry. Translated by D. E. Green. Grand Rapids–Cambridge 2001.

Theological Lexicon of the Old Testament. Edited by E. Jenni and C. Westermann. I. Peabody 1997.

Thiselton, A. C. "Realized Eschatology in Corinth." *NTS* 24 (1977–1978): 510–526.

Thompson, K. C. "I Corinthians 15,29 and Baptism for the Dead." Pages 651–659 in *Papers Presented to the Second International Congress on the New Testament Studies held at Christ Church, Oxford 1961*. Studia Evangelica 2. TU 87. Berlin 1964.

Thompson, P. E. S. "The Yahwist Creation Story." *VT* 21 (1971): 198–208.

Torbus, S. "Listy św. Pawła w retorycznej kulturze antyku." *TW* 1 (2006): 11–18.

Torbus, S. *Listy św. Pawła z perspektywy retorycznej*. BDL 26. Legnica 2006.

Tournay, R. J. "Les relectures du Psaume 110 (109) et l'allusion à Gédéon." *RB* 105 (1998): 321–331.

Toynbee, J. M. C. *Death and Burial in the Roman World*. Aspects of Greek and Roman Life. London 1971.

Treves, M. "The date of Psalm XXIV." *VT* 10 (1960): 428–434.

Treves, M. "Two Acrostic Psalms." *VT* 15 (1965): 81–90.

Tronina, A. *Teologia Psalmów. Wprowadzenie do lektury Psałterza*. Lublin 1995.

Trudinger, L. P. "'Not Yet made' or 'Newly Made'. A Note on Genesis 2,5." *EvQ* 47 (1975): 67–69.

Tułodziecki, T. "Psalm 110 jako przykład teologii kapłaństwa w Psałterzu." *VV* 12 (2007): 33–56.

Tyrrell Hanson, A. "Cytaty ze Starego Testamentu w Nowym Testamencie." Pages 94–96 in *Słownik wiedzy biblijnej*. Edited by B. M. Metzger and M. D. Coogan. Polish ed. W. Chrostowski. Translated by P. Pachciarek. Warszawa 1996.

Unterman, J. "Lewiatan." Pages 668–669 in *Encyklopedia biblijna*. Edited by P. J. Achtemeier. Translated by Z. Kościuk. Warszawa 1999.

Usami, K. "How Are the Dead Rised? (1 Cor 15:35–38)." *Bib* 57 (1976): 468–493.

Ussishkin, D. *The Conquest of Lachish by Sennacherib*. Publications of the Institute of Archeology 6. Tel Aviv 1982.

Vanhoye, A. *Struttura e teologia nell'Epistola agli Ebrei*. Roma 1996[3].

Vaux, R., de. *Histoire ancienne d'Israël. Des origines à l'installation en Canaan*. Paris 1971.

Vaux, R., de. *Instytucje Starego Testamentu*, I–II. Translated by T. Brzegowy. Poznań 2004.

Vielhauer, P. "Paulus und das Alte Testament." Pages 33–62 in *Studien zur Geschichte und Theologie der Reformation. Fs. E. Bizer*. Edited by L. Abramowski and F. J. G. Goeters. Neukirchen 1969.

Vincent, L.-H. and M.-A. Steve. *Jerusalem de L'Ancien Testament*, I. Paris 1954.

Von der Osten-Sacken, P. "Die Apologie des paulinischen Apostolatu in 1 Kor 15:1–11." *ZNW* 64 (1973): 245–262.

Vos, J. S. "Argumentation und Situation in 1 Kor. 15." *NovT* 41 (1999): 313–333.

Vos, J. S. *The Pauline Eschatology*. Grand Rapids 1961[2].

Vorgrimler, H. *Neues Theologisches Wörterbuch*. Freiburg–Basel–Wien 2000[2].

Vorster, J. N. "Resurrection Faith in 1 Cor 15." *Neot* 3 (1989): 287–307.

Vriezen, T. Z. "Ps 8,2–3." *NTT* 3 (1948–49): 11–15.

Wagner, G. "If Christians Refuse to Act, Then Christ Is Not Risen. Once More, 1 Cor 15." *IBS* 6 (1984): 27–39.

Wagner, R. *Heralds of the Good News: Isaiah and Paul 'in Concert' in the Letter to the Romans.* NovTSup 101. Leiden 2002.

Wagner, S. "אָמַר *'āmar.*" *TDOT* I: 328–344.

Wallis, W. "The Problem of an Intermediate Kingdom in 1 Corinthians 5.20–28." *JETS* 18 (1975): 229–242.

Walton, J. H., H. Wayne Mouse, R. L. Thomas and R. Price. *Tablice biblijne. Chrześcijańskie tablice encyklopedyczne*, I. Translated by Z. Kościuk. Warszawa 2007.

Warzecha, J. *Historia dawnego Izraela.* Warszawa 2005.

Webber, R. C. "A Note on 1 Cor 15:3–5." *JETS* 26 (1983): 265–269.

Wedderburn, A. J. M. "Philo's 'Heavenly Man'." *NovT* 15 (1973): 301–326.

Wedderburn, A. J. M. "The Problem of the Denial of the Resurrection in I Corinthians XV." *NovT* 23 (1981): 228–241.

Weimar, P. "Die Toledôt – Formel in der priesterschriftlichen Geschichtsdarstellung." *BZ* 18 (1974): 65–93.

Weippert, M. "Zum Text von Ps. 105 und Js 22,5." *ZAW* 73 (1961): 97–99.

Wénin, A. *D'Adam à Abraham ou les errances de l'humain. Lecture de Genèse 1,1–12,4.* Paris 2007.

Westermann, C. "אָדָם *'ādām person.*" Pages 31–42 in E. Jenni and C. Westermann, *Theological Lexicon of the Old Testament*, I. Translated by M. E. Biddle. Peabody 1997.

Westermann, C. *Basic Forms of Prophetic Speech.* Translated by H. C. White. Philadelphia 1967.

Westermann, C. *Praise and Lament in the Psalms.* Grand Rapids 1984.

White, E. *The Context of Human Discourse: A Configurational Criticism of Rhetoric.* Columbia 1992.

White, J. R. "'Baptized on Account of the Dead': The Meaning of 1 Cor 15:29 in Its Context." *JBL* 116 (1997): 489–499.

Wickle, H.-A. *Das Problem eines messianischen Zwischenreichs bei Paulus.* Zürich 1967.

Wierzbicka, A. "The Semantics of Direct and Indirect Discourse." *Papers in Linguistics* 7 (1974): 267–307.

Wilson, W. T. *Pauline parallels. A comprehensive guide.* Louisville 2009.

Wilson, R. R. "Jeroboam II." Pages 440–441 in *Encyklopedia biblijna.* Edited by P. J. Achtemeier. Translated by Z. Kościuk. Warszawa 1999.

Windisch, H. "Die Christophanie vor Damascus und ihre religionsgeschichtliche Parallelen." *ZNW* 31 (1932): 1–23.

Wink, W. *Naming the Powers.* Philadelphia 1984.

Winter, B. W. *After Paul Left Corinth. The Influence of Secular Ethics and Social Change.* Grand Rapids 2001.

Witczyk, H. "Narodziny wiary w cielesne zmartwychwstanie Jezusa z Nazaretu." *VV* 15 (2009): 209–227.

Witherington III, B. "Christology." Pages 100–115 in *Dictionary of Paul and His Letters. A Compendium of Contemporary Biblical Scholarship.* Edited by G. F. Hawthorne and R. P. Martin. Dovners Grove–Leicester 1993.

Wodecki, B. "Jerusalem – Zion in the Texts of Proto-Isaiah." *PJBR* 1 (2000) 1: 89–108.

Wojciechowski, M. *Apokryfy z Biblii greckiej. 3 i 4 Księga Machabejska, 3 Księga Ezdrasza oraz Psalm 151 i Modlitwa Manassesa.* Rozprawy i Studia Biblijne 8. Warszawa 2001.

Wróbel, M. "Faryzeusze i saduceusze wobec zmartwychwstania." *VV* 15 (2009): 143–154.

Wyatt, N. "Interpretation of the Creation and Fall Story in Genesis 2–3." *ZAW* 93 (1981): 10–21.

Zimmer, C. "Das argumentum resurrectionis in 1 Kor 15:12–20." *LB* 65 (1991): 25–36.

Żebrowski, R. "Pirke(j) de-Rabi Eliezer." Pages 321–322 in *Polski słownik judaistyczny. Dzieje, kultura, religia, ludzie.* Edited by Z. Borzymińska and R. Żebrowski. II. Warszawa 2003.

European Studies in Theology, Philosophy and History of Religions

Edited by Bartosz Adamczewski

Vol.   1   Bartosz Adamczewski: Retelling the Law. Genesis, Exodus-Numbers, and Samuel-Kings as Sequential Hypertextual Reworkings of Deuteronomy. 2012.

Vol.   2   Jacek Grzybowski (ed.): Philosophical and Religious Sources of Modern Culture. 2012.

Vol.   3   Bartosz Adamczewski: Hypertextuality and Historicity in the Gospels. 2013.

Vol.   4   Edmund Morawiec: Intellectual Intuition in the General Metaphysics of Jacques Maritain. A Study in the History of the Methodology of Classical Metaphysics. 2013.

Vol.   5   Edward Nieznański: Towards a Formalization of Thomistic Theodicy. Formalized Attempts to Set Formal Logical Bases to State First Elements of Relations Considered in the Thomistic Theodicy. 2013.

Vol.   6   Mariusz Rosik: "In Christ All Will Be Made Alive" (1 Cor 15:12-58). The Role of Old Testament Quotations in the Pauline Argumentation for the Resurrection. 2013.

www.peterlang.de